Federal Employees Legal Survival Guide

How to Protect & Enforce Your Job Rights

3rd Edition

By the Attorneys of
the Law Firm

PASSMAN
&KAPLAN

ISBN 978-0-9905152-0-3
Published by Passman & Kaplan, P.C., Washington, D.C.

Disclaimer
This publication is designed to provide accurate and authoritative information in regard to the subject matter covered. It is sold with the understanding that the publisher is not engaged in rendering legal advice or services. If legal advice or assistance is required, the services of a competent professional person should be sought. *From a declaration of Principles jointly adopted by a committee of the American Bar Association and a committee of Publishers.*

18 17 16 15 14 5 4 3 2 1

Library of Congress Cataloging in Publication Data:

Federal employees legal survival guide : how to protect and enforce your job rights / by the attorneys of Passman & Kaplan, P.C..
p. cm.
Includes index.
ISBN 978-0-9905152-0-3 (pbk.)
1. Civil service–United States Popular works. 2. Employee rights–United States popular works.
I. Passman & Kaplan, P.C.
KF5337.Z9F43 2014
Library of Congress PCN pending.

Cover & text designed by Pam Koenig.

Dedication

This book is dedicated to the 2.8 million federal employees who labor daily in the civilian service to serve the American people. More than ever, federal employees are responsible for the well-being of our communities and our way of life as a free people. Federal employees have long been the scapegoats of political leaders looking for someone to blame rather than creating solutions. May this book contribute to the recognition federal employees so richly deserve, but seldom receive.

About the Authors

The authors of this book are attorneys of the law firm of Passman & Kaplan, PC, of Washington, DC. They all specialize in the representation of federal employees. Passman & Kaplan, PC is generally regarded as one of the nation's premier firms specializing in federal sector employment and labor law. As with the first and second editions, Joseph V. Kaplan was the project leader, and, together with Edward H. Passman, reviewed and edited the contributions of the other authors. The following is some further information about the authors:

Joseph V. Kaplan After receiving his law degree from the Gonzaga University School of Law in 1978, and his masters of law in Labor Law from George Washington University Law School in 1979, Mr. Kaplan began his employment with the National Treasury Employees Union as a labor and employment attorney and then as the assistant director for negotiations. In 1986, Mr. Kaplan entered the private practice of law. Mr. Kaplan is the author of several articles about federal employees' rights, and from 1994 to 1998 he was the author of the *Federal Merit Systems Year Book* (Labor Relations Press).

Mr. Kaplan is the co-author of *Litigating Federal Sector Employment and Labor Law Disputes* (Dewey Publications 2002). In addition to being a frequent lecturer and speaker on employment issues, Mr. Kaplan was twice elected President of the Society of Federal Labor and Employee Relations Professionals. Mr. Kaplan serves on the Board of the Metropolitan Washington Employment Lawyers Association. Mr. Kaplan is on the adjunct faculty of the American University School of Public Affairs where, among other things, he teaches legal issues in public administration courses to graduate students. In 2008, Mr. Kaplan was elected as a Fellow to the College of Labor and Employment Lawyers. Mr. Kaplan co-founded Passman & Kaplan, PC, in 1989, and is the firm's managing partner/principal.

Edward H. Passman After receiving his law degree from Harvard University and his master's degree in Business Administration from the University of California, Los Angeles, specializing in labor and industrial relations, Mr. Passman worked for the National Labor Relations Board and then at the Federal Mediation and Conciliation Service. Subsequently, Mr. Passman went on to the American Federation of Government Employees, AFL-CIO where he was in charge of civil service appeals before entering the private practice of law in 1977.

Mr. Passman has authored a number of articles about federal employment and labor law and for many years was a contributing author to *A Guide to Merit Systems Protection Board Law and Practice* (Dewey Publications). He submitted amicus curiae briefs in the U.S. Supreme Court on behalf of the National Employment Lawyers Association (NELA) in the cases of ***West v. Gibson***, 525 U.S. 212 (1999), and ***United States Postal Service v. Gregory***, 534 U.S. 1 (2001). Mr. Passman is a past President of the Society of Federal Labor Relations Professionals and previously served on the Steering Committee of the District of Columbia Bar's Labor and Employment Law Section. He was elected as a fellow of the College of Employment and Labor Lawyers in 2004. Mr. Passman co-founded Passman & Kaplan, PC in 1989.

Amy L. Beckett Senior Associate Amy Beckett joined Passman & Kaplan as an associate in 2009. Ms. Beckett, a 1979 graduate of Mount Holyoke College, received her law degree from New York University in 1982. Ms. Beckett clerked for the Missouri Supreme Court before moving to Chicago, where she practiced law at a large firm, in city government, and with a small firm specializing in labor, pension rights, and union democracy cases. Ms. Beckett took a career break from the full-time practice of law to raise her family, including while living in Melbourne, Australia. After moving to the Washington, DC area, Ms. Beckett worked as a contract attorney for several solo practitioners in plaintiff's employment and discrimination law in Washington, DC and suburban Maryland.

Johnathan P. Lloyd Mr. Lloyd joined Passman & Kaplan, PC as the firm's law clerk in 2008 while earning his law degree at Georgetown University Law Center. Mr. Lloyd's law school experience also included a summer associate position in labor and employment law at the European law firm Capstan Avocats, and an externship with CASA of Maryland, specializing in employee and immigrant advocacy. Following graduation, Mr. Lloyd became an associate of Passman & Kaplan, PC, and currently provides representation to the firm's clients in a wide range of labor and employment matters.

Andrew J. Perlmutter Mr. Perlmutter became an associate with the firm in 2007, and is now a senior associate. Mr. Perlmutter graduated from Cornell University in 2001 with a Bachelor of Arts degree with Distinction in All Subjects, and received his law degree from Georgetown University

Law Center in 2004. Before joining the firm, Mr. Perlmutter worked at another Washington, DC law firm where he also represented federal employees. Mr. Perlmutter is the Federal Employee Rights Liaison to the Amicus Advisory Committee at the National Employment Lawyers Association, and is Co-Chair of the Government Personnel Committee of the American Bar Association's Section of Administrative Law and Regulatory Policy.

Daniel T. Raposa Mr. Raposa became an associate with the firm in 2010. Mr. Raposa earned his law degree from the Washington College of Law at American University, where he graduated cum laude. Before joining the firm, Mr. Raposa worked for another Washington, DC, law firm where he represented federal employees. Mr. Raposa also served as a law clerk at Montgomery County Circuit Court. Mr. Raposa serves on the committee for the District of Columbia Bar Young Litigators section and is also active in the Labor and Employment Law Section.

Adria S. Zeldin After receiving her law degree from Georgetown University Law Center in 1985, Ms. Zeldin was employed with the federal government for 23 years. She was employed at the U.S. Equal Employment Opportunity Commission for 18 years, where she held various positions including that of an EEOC Administrative Judge and Supervisory Administrative Judge from 1995 to 2001. From 2001 to 2009, Ms. Zeldin was employed as agency counsel at three different federal government agencies and represented those agencies in employment and labor actions. Prior to joining Passman & Kaplan in 2010, Ms. Zeldin worked independently as an attorney, mediator, and trainer in the area of federal sector employment law. Ms. Zeldin has presented at professional conferences on various areas of employment discrimination law. Ms. Zeldin is also an experienced mediator and has mediated public and private sector cases of employment, housing, and public accommodation discrimination. Ms. Zeldin is a volunteer arbitrator for the DC Bar Attorney Client Arbitration Board where she arbitrates fee dispute cases.

Samir Yakhou Mr. Yakhou became an associate with the firm in 2012 after serving as the firm's law clerk during law school. Mr. Yakhou earned his Juris Doctor from the George Washington University Law School in 2012, and his bachelor's degree from the University of Illinois at Urbana-Champaign in 2008. Before joining the firm, Mr. Yakhou interned in the general counsel's office of the American Federation of Government employees, the largest union for civilian, non-postal federal employees. Mr. Yakhou's prior experience also includes working as a summer research analyst at the United Nations Development Programme Asia-Pacific Regional Centre in Bangkok, Thailand, where he focused on access to justice.

Passman & Kaplan, PC is also grateful for the contributions to the first and second editions by former Passman & Kaplan attorneys: Kristin D. Alden, Debra A. D'Agostino, James M. Eisenmann, Eric S. Gold, Susan E. Jewell, John P. Mahoney, Sandra Mazliah, Bryan J. Schwartz, and Kenneth C. Wu. Some of their original contributions have been retained in this third edition.

Acknowledgments

Paul H. Tobias, former Chairman of Workplace Fairness served as Executive Producer of the first edition of this book. He is the founder of the National Employment Lawyers Association (NELA) and has practiced employment and labor law for over 53 years.

Carol Cartaino of Seaman, Ohio, was Editorial Director of the first edition. Her more than 30 years experience in book publishing include eight years as Editor-in-Chief at Writer's Digest Books and 10 years as a Trade Book Editor for Prentice-Hall, Inc. She now serves as a freelance editor and consultant to self-publishers.

Pam Koenig, a freelance graphic designer from Cincinnati, Ohio, did the cover and interior design for all three editions. The authors were fortunate that Pam signed on for this third tour!

Workplace Fairness Board of Directors enthusiastically supported the publication of this book. We are happy to partner with Workplace Fairness in the marketing of the e-book edition.

We also thank the following Passman & Kaplan, PC employees who assisted in the production of this book: legal assistant Nicole Davis and former law clerk Ana Olarte del Castillo.

Contents

Preface

The employment rights of federal employees present a mixed blessing. On the one hand, a federal employee is protected from many forms of arbitrary and unfair treatment by supervisors and others in authority. And without a doubt, when it comes to "job security" federal employees are much better off than their counterparts in the private sector. On the other hand, these job security protections stem from a host of laws and regulations that are often confusing, written in "legalese," and subject to varying interpretations by courts, agencies, and other decision-making authorities. There are also a host of "shall nots"—prohibitions of various types of conduct—surpassing those imposed on private-sector employees. These prohibitions further contribute to the "mixed blessing" of federal employee rights.

This book is written for you—the federal employee. While federal personnel officers, union officials, and employment lawyers can (and hopefully will) benefit much from this book, our target audience is the average federal employee. Although this is a "legal guide," we have attempted to minimize the legalese and write in plain English. While not always successful, we tried our best.

We have attempted to explain the most significant aspects of employment rights, benefits, and other conditions of employment that impact large numbers of federal employees. If we have left out a topic, let us know and we will try to include in it the next printing!

This book provides advice on how to protect the many benefits you have. To that end, we provide you with specific "tips" and advice on how to enforce your job rights. In some chapters, this book tells how to enforce your rights, with an explanation of why you would want to select certain options over others. Of course, not every specific situation can be imagined or foreseen. We selected typical situations and options with general applicability to illustrate our points. If your particular situation is unlike those we discuss, consult with an experienced personnel specialist, union official, or employment lawyer.

The basic structure of current civil service law dates to the passage of the Civil Service Reform Act of 1978. But the body of laws, regulations, court decisions, and administrative rulings that govern the employment rights of federal employees is constantly changing. Be mindful that some amendments and changes in interpretations may occur in the future. For example, while we were writing this third edition, employees' rights to appeal removals from sensitive non-critical positions were being curtailed, cases were pending on the issue of whether non-probationary employees, removed for unsuitability, had full appeal rights to the Merit Systems Protection Board, and Senior Executives of the Department of Veterans Affairs had their due process rights all but obliterated. Also, the Equal Employment Opportunity Commission is considering revamping its regulations governing the federal-sector EEO complaint process.

As we said at the outset, this book was written for you. It is your *Legal Survival Guide*. If you believe this book can be improved, we want to hear from you. In the meantime, keep on doing the important work you do every day and do not be afraid to claim the full measure of your rights as a federal employee.

Joseph V. Kaplan
for the attorneys of
Passman & Kaplan, PC
authors
Washington, DC
2014

Guide to Civil Service Acronyms

ADA
Americans with Disabilities Act

ADAAA
ADA Amendments Act of 2008

ADEA
Age Discrimination in Employment Act

ADR
Alternative dispute resolution

AJ
Administrative judge, usually of the MSPB or the EEOC

ALJ
Administrative law judge, usually of the FLRA

AUO
Administratively uncontrollable overtime

AWOL
Absent without leave

CAA
Congressional Accountability Act

CAF
Central Adjudicatory Facility

CBA
Collective Bargaining Agreement (agreement between a union and an employer)

CFR
Code of Federal Regulations

CIA
Central Intelligence Agency

COLA
Cost of living adjustment

CSRA
Civil Service Reform Act of 1978

CSRS
Civil Service Retirement System

CTAP
Career Transition Assistance Plan (hiring priority for certain former employees)

DHS
Department of Homeland Security

DSR
Discontinued service retirement

DoD
Department of Defense

DOHA
Defense Office of Hearings and Adjudications (adjudicates security clearance denial appeals)

DOL
Department of Labor

ECAB
Employee Compensation Appeals Board of the Department of Labor

EEO
Equal Employment Opportunity

EEOC
Equal Employment Opportunity Commission

eOPF
Electronic Official Personnel Folder

EPA
Equal Pay Act of 1963 (also Environmental Protection Agency)

FAD
Final Agency Decision on an employee's discrimination complaint

FBI
Federal Bureau of Investigation

FEGLI
Federal Employees Group Life Insurance

FEHBP
Federal Employees Health Benefits Program

FERS
Federal Employees Retirement System

FECA
Federal Employees Compensation Act (workers' compensation)

FLRA
Federal Labor Relations Authority

FLSA
Fair Labor Standards Act

FMCS
Federal Mediation and Conciliation Service

FMLA
Family and Medical Leave Act

FOIA
Freedom of Information Act

FSIP
Federal Service Impasses Panel

FSLMRS
Federal Service Labor-Management Relations Statute

GAO
Government Accountability Office (formerly General Accounting Office)

GINA
Genetic Information Nondiscrimination Act of 2008

GS
General Schedule pay scale

GSA
General Services Administration

HHS
Department of Health and Human Services

HUD
Department of Housing and Urban Development

ICTAP
Interagency Career Transition Assistance Plan (hiring priority for certain former employees)

IPP
Interagency Placement Program

IRA
Individual Right of Action (appeal of certain PPP claims such as whistleblower reprisal to the MSPB)

LCA
Last Chance Agreement, usually to settle a discipline or adverse action case

LEAP
Law Enforcement Availability Pay

LEO
Law enforcement officer entitled to enhanced retirement annuity

LMRDA
Labor Management Reporting and Disclosure Act

LOD
Letter of Denial (of a security clearance)

LWOP
Leave without pay (approved unpaid leave status)

MAP
Mediation Appeals Program (MSPB ADR program)

MSPB
Merit Systems Protection Board

NAF
Non-appropriated fund

NELA
National Employment Lawyers Association

NLRB
National Labor Relations Board

NTE
Not to exceed (end date for term appointment)

OAA
Otherwise Appealable Action (to the MSPB)

OASI
Old Age or Survivors Insurance

OFO
Office of Federal Operations of the EEOC

OGE
Office of Government Ethics

OLMS
Office of Labor Management Standards

OMB
Office of Management and Budget

OPF
Official Personnel File

OPM
Office of Personnel Management

OSC
Office of Special Counsel

OSHA
The DOL's Office of Safety and Health Administration

OWCP
The DOL's Office of Workers' Compensation Programs

PEOAA
Presidential and Executive Office Accountability Act

PIP
Performance Improvement Period or Performance Improvement Plan

PFR
Petition for Review (usually an appeal to the full MSPB)

PPP
Prohibited Personnel Practice

PSAB
Personnel Security Appeals Board

QSI
Quality Step Increase

RIF
Reduction-in-force

RMO
Responsible Management Official—refers to someone accused of discrimination

ROI
Report of Investigation

RPL
Reemployment Priority List

SCD
Service Computation Date

SES
Senior Executive Service

SF-50
Standard Form 50; Notice of Personnel Action

SF-52
Standard Form 52; Request for Personnel Action

SF-85
Standard Form 85; Questionnaire for Non-Sensitive Positions

SF-86
Standard Form 86; Questionnaire for National Security Positions

SF-171
Standard Form 171; Job Application

TAPER
Temporary Appointment Pending Establishment of a Register

TCC
Temporary Continuation of Coverage (extending health benefits for separated federal employees)

ULP
Unfair Labor Practice

USC
United States Code

USERRA
Uniformed Services Employment and Reemployment Rights Act

USPS
United States Postal Service

VEOA
Veterans Employment Opportunities Act

VERA
Voluntary Early Retirement Authority

VETS
The DOL's Veterans' Employment and Training Service

VSIP
Voluntary Separation Incentive Payment

VTC
Video teleconference

WPA
Whistleblower Protection Act

WPEA
Whistleblower Protection Enhancement Act of 2012

WG
Wage Grade Schedule pay scale

WIGI
Within-grade increase

Glossary of Frequently Used Terms

Accretion of duties
A noncompetitive promotion based on higher-graded duties being added to your position.

Acknowledgment order
An order issued by an administrative judge, usually of the MSPB or the EEOC, noting that your appeal or hearing request has been received, and stating time limits for the processing of aspects of your case, such as discovery.

Administrative judge
A hearing officer of the MSPB or EEOC.

Administrative leave
A period of paid time when an employee is ordered not to report to work, often during an administrative investigation, or the pendency of a proposed adverse action.

Adverse action
A suspension of more than 14 days, demotion, or removal from your position/job.

Affidavit
A written statement signed under oath or under penalty of perjury.

Affirmative defense
An allegation that a management action was not only wrong, but also taken for an illegal reason, such as discrimination or reprisal for whistleblowing.

Agency counsel
The attorney representing agency management in a given case.

Agency file
The agency's administrative record in support of an adverse action.

Alternative dispute resolution
Dispute resolution processes, often mediation, that act as a means for disagreeing parties to come to a settlement agreement.

Annuity
A yearly payment of money for life or a period of time.

Appellant
A person who files an appeal, usually to the MSPB or the EEOC's OFO.

Appointment
The way in which federal employees are hired. The specific type of appointment involved defines your status as a federal employee.

Appropriated fund employee
An employee whose salary is paid from funds appropriated by Congress.

Arbitration
An appeal process, the final step of a union grievance procedure, involving a neutral outside decision-maker.

Basis of discrimination
The form of the discriminatory intent involved in an EEO complaint (for example "discrimination on the basis of race" in a race discrimination case).

Brief
A legal memorandum filed in a legal proceeding.

Board
Usually the Merit Systems Protection Board.

Break in service
A period of nonemployment by the federal government, coming after one period of federal employment.

Burden of proof
The requirement of establishing the truth of an allegation.

Calendar day
A method of measuring time that includes all days, not just workdays.

Career-conditional
A competitive service employee's appointment for the first three years of employment.

Career-ladder Promotion
A non-competitive promotion to a predetermined grade based on increasing complexity of the work and time-in-grade.

Cause of action
Facts sufficient to state an enforceable claim.

Chapter 43
Statute governing PIPs and some post-PIP adverse actions for performance reasons.

Chapter 75
Statute governing most adverse actions, usually for misconduct.

Civil service
Employment with the United States government in a civilian capacity, as distinguished from military or "uniformed" service.

Circumstantial evidence
Evidence of an indirect nature.

Closing argument
The final argument of the parties at the conclusion of a trial or hearing.

Comp time
This is short for "compensatory time," which is time off from work for overtime worked, in lieu of receiving overtime pay.

Comparator
Other individuals who an employee compares themselves against, for example to show that they are being treated differently to show disparate treatment.

Compensatory damages
Monetary compensation for out-of-pocket losses or injuries, including emotional pain and suffering.

Competitive service
Appointment held by employees who must take an examination or "compete" to get hired.

Complainant
An individual who files a complaint (usually of discrimination).

Condition subsequent
A future event that marks the end of an indefinite suspension.

Confidential employees
Employees excluded from union representation because they work in the labor relations or personnel offices or are agency policymakers.

Consequential damages
Monetary compensation for out-of-pocket losses or injuries, which does not include emotional pain and suffering. (Usually applies to pre-WPEA whistle-blower cases).

Constructive adverse action
A resignation, retirement, or absence from work (of more than 14 days) which was voluntary on the surface but was actually coerced by agency officials or obtained by providing inaccurate or misleading information.

Constructive discharge
See constructive adverse action.

Contingency fee
Legal fee based on a percentage of the recovery, or money received.

Creditable service
Periods of employment "service" that count in determining eligibility for programs, such as retirement benefits.

Critical elements
Duties which are critical or essential to the performance of a job or the satisfactory filling of a position.

Debarment
Ineligibility for federal employment.

Default judgment
Judgment in favor of a party in litigation based on some failure by the other party to take some action or to obey some order.

De novo
A new, fresh review of a matter.

Deposition
Testimony under oath that is recorded and subject to cross-examination.

Desk audit
A review of the actual duties performed in a job to determine the correct grade level and series for the person holding that job.

Details
Temporary assignments to other positions, usually within the employee's agency.

Direct evidence
What witnesses saw or heard, proof without the need of drawing inferences.

Disabled veteran
One who suffers a service-connected disability or is receiving benefits through the Department of Veterans Affairs.

Discipline
Punishment/penalty for misconduct, usually a suspension of 14 days or less, including a reprimand. (See "adverse actions" for severe forms of punishment.)

Discontinued service retirement
A form of early retirement for employees involuntarily separated without cause or "fault," including involuntary separations for poor performance, refusal to accept geographical reassignment or ill health.

Discovery
Disclosure to the other party of facts and documents, or taking depositions, in advance of a trial or hearing.

Disparate treatment
Unequal or different treatment.

Document requests
A form of discovery consisting of a list of documents which the recipient is required to provide to the requestor (also called "requests for production of documents").

***Douglas* factors**
The factors used by the MSPB and arbitrators to determine the reasonableness of a penalty in adverse actions. See *Douglas v. VA*, 5 MSPR 280 (1981).

Due diligence
Careful attention to, for example, a search for evidence or to determine appeal/complaint time limits.

EEO counselor
Individual with whom discrimination must first be raised.

EEO investigator
Individual who investigates a complaint of discrimination.

Election of remedies
Choosing between two or more methods for obtaining relief, such as the choice between filing a grievance versus an MSPB appeal in an adverse action case.

Excepted service
Appointment held by employees who do not have to take an examination or "compete" to get hired.

Exempt employee
Employee exempt from overtime coverage of the Fair Labor Standards Act.

Ex parte
Action for/or benefiting one party without notice to or involvement of the other party, such as communicating with an AJ regarding the merits of a pending case.

Federal executive agency
An agency in the executive branch of the government.

Final agency decision
An agency's decision concerning whether discrimination or EEO reprisal occurred in a particular EEO complaint.

Full-time employee
An employee who works at least 32 hours per week.

General schedule employment
White-collar work positions paid on a yearly salary basis.

General release
Giving up all claims of any kind.

Grievance
A challenge to an agency act filed under a union contract or agency procedure.

Grievant
An individual who files a grievance.

Gross-up
An increase to a monetary award (such as back pay) to adjust for tax issues.

GS employees
Employees paid on the General Schedule salary scale.

Hearing
In the EEOC or MSPB, a trial in front of an AJ.

High three
The highest average pay produced by your basic pay during any three consecutive years of federal service, used to determine retirement benefits.

Interim relief
Relief awarded by an MSPB administrative judge to an employee who prevails in his/her appeal, pending appeal to the full MSPB by the agency.

Intermittent employee
A temporary employee who works an irregular schedule determined on a week-by-week basis.

Interrogatories
A form of discovery consisting of written questions to which the recipient is required to respond.

Lateral transfer
Transfer to a position with comparable pay and grade.

Lump-sum settlement
A single amount paid in a settlement covering all injuries suffered. Usually, no taxes are deducted.

Make-whole relief
Relief that puts person back where he was before the agency's action.

Mediation
Intervention of a third party to facilitate the parties' own settlement of a dispute.

Mixed case
An appeal of a personnel action where the employee claims that the action was taken for an illegal reason (for example, discrimination or reprisal for whistleblowing) in addition to just being improper.

Motion
A request (written or oral) to a judge, AJ or ALJ to take some action in connection with a pending case.

Negotiability appeal
Appeal filed by a union with the FLRA, charging an agency with refusal to negotiate concerning a bargainable subject.

Nexus
A connection, usually between incidents or events and an adverse personnel action.

Nonpecuniary compensatory damages
Compensatory damages for non-monetary harm, for example emotional pain and suffering damages.

Notice of right to file
In an EEO complaint, a notice concluding the informal complaint process and giving the complainant 15 days to file a formal complaint (also called a "Notice of Right to File Formal," "Notice of Right to File a Formal Complaint," "Notice of Right to File a Discrimination Complaint," or some variant thereof).

Objection
A formal protest to the decision of a judge in a trial or hearing.

Official Personnel File
The official file maintained on each federal employee, containing records of all personnel actions taken.

Official time
Usually, paid time provided to a union representative to engage in representational duties on behalf of employees, or for employees participating in EEO complaints.

Oral response
An in-person presentation of a response to a proposed adverse action.

Part-time employee
Employee who works less than 32 hours a week.

Pecuniary compensatory damages
Compensatory damages with known dollar amounts associated with them and which can be directly calculated based on concrete evidence (for example, medical expenses).

Permissive subject of bargaining
Those subjects of bargaining which an agency may bargain with a union if the agency so chooses, but cannot be forced to bargain on.

Personal appearance
The "hearing" held to contest the denial or revocation of a security clearance.

Petition for review
An appeal, usually filed to the full MSPB, the EEOC's OFO, or to an appeals court.

Preexisting condition
A condition that existed before the occurrence of some event, such as taking out of an insurance policy.

Preference eligible
Eligible for veterans benefits.

Prehearing conference
A meeting in advance of a hearing in the EEOC or MSPB where the AJ sets the list of witnesses and exhibits for the hearing and fixes the issues to be decided at hearing.

Preponderance of evidence
The amount of evidence that would lead a reasonable person to believe that a fact is more likely to be true than not.

***Prima facie* case**
Evidence that creates a presumption of truth unless disproved.

Priority consideration
The consideration of an employee for promotion or a position before any other applicants for the position are considered.

Probable cause
Reasonable grounds for belief in facts or for instituting action.

Probationary period
The initial period of employment in which an employee can be terminated without adverse action appeal rights.

Pro bono
Representation by a lawyer who charges no fee.

Pro Se
An individual acts as his or her own legal representative, without a lawyer.

Protected conduct
Activity protected by law.

Protected group
Legally protected group defined by a specific trait, for example, race.

Punitive damages
Damages to punish and deter wrongdoers.

Qui tam
A lawsuit by a private individual on behalf of the U.S. government, against someone (for example, a contractor) for defrauding the government.

Quid pro quo
Usually refers to a type of sexual harassment where a sexual favor is requested or demanded in exchange for a favorable personnel action.

Rating of record
Official performance rating given at the end of your appraisal period.

Reasonable accommodation
An agency's obligation to make adjustments to your work situation or environment so that you can perform your job even with your disability or religious restrictions.

Reduction in grade
Lowering of one's grade level.

Release of claims
Written agreement to drop all claims.

Reprisal or retaliation
Actions taken against an employee by an agency in response to that employee's specific earlier protected activity (for example, protected EEO activity or protected whistleblowing).

Requests for admissions
A form of discovery consisting of a list of statements to which the recipient is requested to stipulate.

Retainer
Usually refers to the agreement entered into with a lawyer for legal services, or to the amount paid to a lawyer in advance. (The amount is called a "fee advance" if the agreement is a "fee agreement" rather than a "retainer agreement.")

Retention benefits
Being allowed to retain your pay ("saved pay") or grade ("saved grade") for a specific time period, often after being separated from a particular position and given a lower-graded position in a reduction-in-force.

Retention register
A list ranking employees in a competitive level in order of their standing for retention in a RIF.

Retreat rights
In a RIF, your right to be assigned to a position you previously held.

Saved pay
See retention benefits.

Schedule award
A predetermined amount awarded by the DOL's OWCP for a work-related disability.

Search warrant
Order of a judge to an officer authorizing search.

Seasonal employee
An employee who only works during certain "peak periods," usually returning to the position every year (for example, certain park rangers).

Service computation date
The date calculated to be the "start" of federal employment, mostly used for retirement purposes. Prior military service and prior periods of civil service are usually added to the current period of employment to determine this date.

Setoff
A monetary deduction.

Settlement
An agreement resolving a dispute in exchange for something of value.

Sovereign immunity
The doctrine that government cannot be sued without its consent.

Status quo ante
The state of things before an event, such as a termination or demotion.

Statute
A law passed by a legislative body and set forth in a formal document.

Statute of limitations
The time period in which a complaint or lawsuit can be filed.

Statutory appeals
Appeal rights granted by law, which employees have regardless of whether they are covered by a union contract. Usually refers to MSPB appeals and EEO complaints.

Stay
The suspension or stopping of proceedings.

Subpoena
An order requiring production of evidence or requiring a witness to appear and testify.

SUBSTANTIAL EVIDENCE
The amount of evidence that would lead a reasonable person to accept a fact as true, even though other reasonable persons might disagree. This amount is less than what is needed for "preponderance of evidence."

SUMMARY AFFIRMANCE
A court or administrative tribunal's decision affirming the decision of a lower tribunal, without a written decision or explanation of why.

SUMMARY DISMISSAL
When a court or administrative tribunal dismisses a case without a trial.

SUMMARY JUDGMENT
A court or administrative tribunal's decision based on the law and the undisputed facts, without a trial or hearing.

TERM APPOINTMENT
A position of a fixed or maximum duration.

TIME-IN-GRADE REQUIREMENTS
The requirement that an employee be at a particular grade level for a specified period of time before being eligible for promotion to a higher grade.

TITLE VII
A section of the Civil Rights Act of 1964 prohibiting employment discrimination based on race, sex, religion and national origin.

TORT CLAIM
Claim for wrongful injury to person or property.

VENUE
The place or location of a proceeding.

VETERAN
A person who has served in the U.S. military (uniformed) service.

WAGE GRADE
Blue-collar positions with the federal government, paid at an hourly rate.

WAIVER
Voluntary relinquishment of a known right.

***WEINGARTEN* RIGHTS**
The right to union representation at investigatory interviews.

Introduction

In the 10 years since we wrote the second edition to this book much has changed, yet much as remained the same. The attempts to rescind due process rights of federal employees on a massive scale—those involving the employees of the Department of Homeland Security—were pushed back. Yet, on the heels of that reversal came the recent stunning decision by the U.S. Court of Appeals for the Federal Circuit that employees removed for failing to be suitable for non-classified sensitive positions do not have MSPB appeal rights. In the wake of other political "scandals," such as the one now raging as we go to press—the failure of the Department of Veterans Affairs to timely treat veterans—Congress is considering legislation to make it easier to fire senior level civilian managers. Federal employees continue to be the easy targets of lawmakers incapable of making the tough policy decisions that should be made in the first place.

There are positive developments to report. Baggage screeners of the Transportation Security Agency are now fully protected by the federal sector EEO process. And long awaited changes to the Whistleblower Protection Act came to fruition in the Whistleblower Protection Enhancement Act of 2012. Perhaps we will finally see whistleblowers get the protections they deserve.

As we've seen, federal employees' rights, though seemingly secure, are actually subject to political whim and judicial interpretation. These rights are not stagnant. It is imperative for federal employees to remain knowledgeable of their rights and vigilant in protecting them.

As with the two prior editions, this book is written for you—the federal employee—to empower you to the extent possible so that you do not fall victim to arbitrary or illegal action by agency managers and so you receive the rights and benefits to which you are entitled. There is no doubt that federal employees' rights are a maze of laws and regulations, sometimes incomprehensively drafted. Therefore, when in doubt about your rights or how to protect them, consult an experienced personnelist, union official or employment lawyer. Do remember this though: no agency personnel, human resource or EEO specialist works for you! Make sure you consult with someone who has *your* best interest in mind.

We hope that the *Federal Employees Legal Survival Guide, 3rd Ed.*, will guide you through the confusing journey of understanding your rights and benefits to make your career as a federal employee a little less daunting and more fulfilling.

Introduction to the Second Edition

When we wrote the first edition to the *Federal Employees Legal Survival Guide* in 1999, we noted that times had "changed" and the old belief that a federal employee held a job "for life" had changed in view of government "downsizing" that took place in the 1990's. We noted that federal employees were often "pawns" in a political chess game and the scapegoats for what some people did not like about government. Little could we have known how the tragic events of September 11, 2001, would trigger assaults on federal employees' rights that would dwarf past recent efforts to reduce employees' rights. Under the guise of "national security," those in political power passed through laws to reduce employees' rights to engage in collective bargaining in some agencies and to reduce opportunities to challenge adverse personnel decisions. The Merit Systems Protection Board—the agency created in 1978 to protect employees from unfair agency abuses in disciplining employees—has been stripped of much of its authority over personnel actions involving Department of Defense employees and employees of various agencies who have now been transferred to the Department of Homeland Security.

In this era of attempts to further scale back job rights, it is imperative that federal employees be zealous in the understanding and enforcement of the rights they do have. As with the first edition, this book is written for you—the federal employee—to empower you to the extent possible so that you do not fall victim to arbitrary or illegal action by agency managers and so you receive the rights and benefits to which you are entitled.

As always, when in doubt about your rights or how to protect them, consult an experienced personnelist, union official or employment lawyer. We hope that the roadmap that is this *Federal Employees Legal Survival Guide, 3rd Ed.*, will guide you through the journey of understanding your rights and benefits to make your career as a federal employee a little less daunting.

Introduction to the First Edition

Times have changed. It used to be thought that a job with the federal government was a job "for life." But, the federal government has experienced its own brand of downsizing to match that experienced in the private sector. The federal employee is often a pawn in the political chess game, the scapegoat for what some dislike about government. While many call for a curtailment of government services, or a curb on employees' rights and benefits, they forget that the people affected by these calls are their friends and neighbors—people like you, who are honest and hardworking, and who take pride in serving the American people.

To thrive and survive in the workplace, federal employees must have stamina, creativity, foresight, and a good grasp of their rights. The job rights of federal employees are extremely complicated. Many statutes, government-wide regulations, and agency-issued rules combine to create a complex maze of rights and avenues of redress. Being able to navigate this maze is an important key to job survival and protection of your rights. *Federal Employees Legal Survival Guide* was written to provide federal employees with enough information about their rights so that they are not the hapless victims of agency managers and personnel officials. Management might not have the employee's best interests at heart. Superiors might not have a good grasp of the complicated web of employees' rights. This book will help "level the playing field."

If you are facing some unfair personnel action at work, after you vent your anger and fear to friends and relatives, you must begin to gather your resources to make the best of a bad situation. You must educate yourself in your legal rights, and decide whether you have the justification, and means, to challenge the personnel action. Becoming familiar with the contents of this book is the first step in that process.

You should always feel free to question your supervisors and other agency officials about any action you believe is unfair, not in accordance with agency procedures or guidelines, or that violates laws, rules, or regulations. You and your family depend upon your job. Do not let your superiors intimidate you, and prevent you from getting, or keeping, every right and benefit you are entitled to as a federal employee. If you feel uncomfortable talking to your supervisors, or feel that you can no longer trust them to tell you what is in your best interest, you have the right to seek out others who can advise you and explain the impact a personnel action may have on your employment. Union officials or lawyers with experience in federal employee matters are among those who can provide you with needed guidance, support, and assistance. Remember, you do have the right to take action, and to be protected against reprisal, when you believe that you have been discriminated against, or treated in a way that violates any of your rights under federal laws and regulations or agency regulations.

Federal Employees Legal Survival Guide provides a detailed road map for navigating the complex universe of federal employee rights and appeals. It contains an overview of important laws and regulations that govern the terms and conditions of your employment by the federal government and protect you from mistreatment.[1] It provides guidelines for determining when your rights have been violated, and explains how to enforce these rights or obtain redress for violations. Not all federal employees enjoy the same range of protection and appeal routes. *Federal Employees Legal Survival Guide* explains the differences between the various categories of employees. What you learn in these pages will assure that you follow the appeal routes most applicable to you and your employment situation, and help you comply with all of the critical time deadlines.

---

[1] At various points in this book the authors have provided citations to specific laws and regulations affecting your employment. You can consult these sources directly if you need further information. For example, the book contains many citations to the Code of Federal Regulations (CFR), which can be found in most agency libraries or personnel offices or at public or law school libraries, as well as on the internet.

Whether you decide to negotiate on your own, consult with or hire an attorney, or represent yourself in filing some action against your agency, reading this book will help you understand "the federal employment system" and put you in a stronger position to help yourself. The authors encourage you to contact the National Employee Rights Institute and the other organizations listed in the Appendix for additional guidance and support. We hope that the advice and information contained in *Federal Employees Legal Survival Guide* will ease your way through the maze and enable you to maximize your options.

1

Appointment in the Federal Civil Service and Suitability for Federal Employment

Where Am I and How Did I Get Here?

In This Chapter You Will Learn:

- how federal employees are hired
- types of federal appointments
- rights and benefits for different types of federal employees
- what a "suitability determination" is and how it affects your ability to hold a federal job

Contents Chapter One - Appointment in the Federal Civil Service and suitability for federal employment

Introduction

Let's start at the beginning. How did you first become a federal employee? The federal hiring process usually involves an "appointment." The federal civil service appointment process can be confusing and complex, especially when you are trying to understand what kind of position you occupy and what rights, if any, you have in that position. This chapter describes the different types of federal appointments and explains the rights and benefits associated with each type of employment.

What types of federal service are there?

The federal civil service consists of two broad categories of service. These are the competitive and the non-competitive, or "excepted" service positions. Within each of these services there exist many different classes of positions: temporary, term, career-conditional, and career. The character of the position determines what rights you have to challenge actions such as to reduce your grade or to remove you from employment.

TIP

The federal government has all types of jobs. Knowing the type of position you have will tell you what type of Merit Systems Protection Board rights you have, if any. (See Chapter 4.)

What are the competitive and excepted services?

Competitive service positions usually require some type of preliminary civil service examination and a test (probationary) period which you must successfully complete before gaining competitive service status.

"Competitive examinations" for admission to the competitive service usually involve a review of your qualifications, as stated on your job application (for example, OF-602, SF-171), or your resume. Excepted service positions generally do not require an examination before hiring.

In short, all positions in the federal service are considered competitive unless they are specifically excepted from the competitive service by statute, by the Office of Personnel Management ("OPM"), by the President, or by Congress, in which case they are "excepted service" positions. Ultimately, OPM, Congress, and the President determine whether a position is competitive or excepted. Positions in the Senior Executive Service (SES) are not in the competitive service.

How do I receive an appointment in the competitive service?

As we told you, within the two broad categories of federal employment, there are several variations. Certain classes of employees may acquire competitive status without examination, time limits, or other requirements. Below are explanations of some of these different kinds of appointments in the competitive service.

Can there be competition without an examination?

Although competitive service appointments generally require an examination, there are some positions in the competitive service which do not require an exam. Exception from the examination does not except the position from competition. Thus, the position still falls within the definition of competitive service.

Under certain circumstances, an agency may recommend that a position qualify for "competitive status" without competition. For example, disabled veterans who have completed training in the executive branch prescribed by the Department of Veterans Affairs may be exempted from examination. Other situations which may also result in exceptions include:

- an individual with two years of service at the office of the President or the White House who is transferred to a competitive position at the request of an agency
- an employee who is severely physically or mentally handicapped, who is developmentally disabled, or who has a psychiatric disability who completes two years of service in an excepted position

- OPM excepts the position because it requires specialized qualifications that make examination impractical
- a statute or executive order places a person holding a permanent position into the competitive service

In "rare" cases, OPM may exempt a competitive position from examination due to the unique qualities of the position. OPM may find that, in the interests of good civil service administration, a position cannot be filled through open competitive examination. This finding may result because the position's duties or compensation are unusual or because qualified candidates are so rare. Such positions still require a one-year probationary period.

What is a "career-conditional" appointment?

During your first three years as a career employee, you will have a "career-conditional" appointment. During this period, you will remain in a lower "tenure subgroup" for purposes of a reduction-in-force (see Chapter 9) and therefore have less job security than a "career" status employee.

Federal employees generally seek "career status," which offers greater job security. You reach career status, also known as competitive status, by becoming a career appointment employee and successfully completing three substantially continuous years as a career-conditional employee.

TIP

"Career-conditional" status affects your rights in a reduction-in-force. (See Chapter 9.)

When an employee has "competitive status," the employee has basic eligibility for noncompetitive assignment to a competitive position. An individual with competitive status may be reinstated, transferred, promoted, reassigned or demoted without open competitive examination, as long as the action is consistent with civil service rules and regulations. An employee acquires "competitive status" by completing a probationary period under a career-conditional or career appointment position (or under some other limited means as provided by regulation). In order to be in the competitive service, the employee must have competitive status in a competitive position in a nontemporary appointment.

What happens during the probationary period? Generally speaking, the first year of your appointment is your probationary period. During your probationary period, your agency determines your fitness for your position. If your agency believes that you have failed to demonstrate appropriate qualifications or behavior during your probationary period, it may terminate your employment with only a minimum of procedures. Termination requires only that you be given notice of the reasons for your termination and the effective date. During your probationary period, the agency does not have to demonstrate just cause for your termination. Probationary employees are generally not entitled to appeal their termination to the Merit Systems Protection Board ("MSPB"), except under certain circumstances.

There are two exceptions where a probationer gets MSPB appeal rights. First, if you can demonstrate that you were discriminated against on the basis of your marital status or for partisan political reasons, you may challenge your termination with the MSPB. Second, if you are terminated during your probationary period because of events, activities, or conduct which occurred prior to your appointment, you are entitled to advance notice, an opportunity to respond, and notice of your right to appeal the termination to the MSPB. (See Chapter 4.) After the completion of your probationary period, you are allowed to appeal certain adverse employment decisions, such as suspensions of more than fourteen days, demotions, or removals, to the MSPB. If you do so, the agency must prove that the action "promotes the efficiency of the service" (was taken for good cause).

Disabled veterans who successfully complete certain Department of Veterans Affairs training may be non-competitively appointed and then converted to career or career-conditional appointments. Such veterans can avoid competition and probationary periods, and thus may acquire MSPB rights sooner.

Newly appointed or promoted supervisors must also complete a one-year probationary period to demonstrate successful performance as a supervisor.

During this supervisory probationary year, an agency may demote the newly-promoted supervisor for poor performance to the non-supervisory position he or she previously held. The probationary supervisor does not have MSPB appeal rights if she or he fails the supervisory probation period.

If you are a probationary employee, you do not have the right to protest a termination on the ground that it is unfair or unjust. However, you, as well as temporary employees, do have First Amendment and other Constitutional rights which may afford protection against discharges in violation of those rights—for example, the rights of free speech, freedom of association, freedom of religion, and privacy. Probationary employees also are covered by federal anti-discrimination statutes and may not be terminated because of their race, color, national origin, handicap, age, sex, religion or reprisal for EEO activity.

Probationary employees are also protected from reprisal for protected whistleblowing.

TIP

Sometimes probationary employees can appeal to the MSPB. Employees discriminated against for political reasons or on the basis of marital status are among the probationary employees with MSPB appeal rights.

How do I receive an appointment in the excepted service?

The excepted service includes those positions in the executive branch that are excluded from the competitive service. Positions are excepted from competition when specifically identified as excepted by OPM, by the President, or by Congress. OPM classifies these positions into three categories, called schedules. A job is classified as Schedule A, B, or C, depending on its duties and responsibilities. A significant difference between competitive service and excepted service positions is in appeal rights to the MSPB. (See Chapter 4.)

Schedule A

Schedule A positions cannot involve confidential or policy-determining elements. For a position to fall into Schedule A, OPM must decide that examination is not practical. Schedule A positions may not be in the Senior Executive Service (see page 37 of this chapter). Examples of Schedule A positions are:

- chaplains
- attorneys
- law clerks/trainees
- certain interpreters
- interns and fellows
- certain positions in Federal mental institutions
- positions in remote and isolated locations
- short-term positions
- Presidential appointments without Senate confirmation
- certain part-time or intermittent positions
- temporary and less-than-full-time positions for which examination is impractical
- positions when filled by severely developmentally disabled persons, severely physically handicapped persons or persons with psychiatric disabilities who have demonstrated their ability to perform satisfactorily or who are certified by certain agencies as likely to perform

Schedule B

Like Schedule A positions, Schedule B positions cannot involve confidential and policy-making characteristics. Candidates for Schedule B positions must undergo a non-competitive examination (or review) of their qualifications to ensure that they meet the requirements for the position. Schedule B positions include, for example:

- student appointments
- special positions connected with Senior Executive Service candidate development programs
- Federal career interns
- some reassignments from Senior Executive Service positions to GS-15, or equivalent, positions
- certain veteran assignments

Schedule C

Schedule C positions involve policy-making and are confidential in nature. These are typically referred to as "political" appointments. Schedule C positions cease to exist immediately upon being vacated and are only created by specific request of agency heads. Schedule C positions include transitional appointments that are designed to assist the changes of a new Presidential administration. The number of Schedule C positions is limited. Individual Schedule C appointments may be for 120 days with one 120-day extension.

All Schedule positions (A, B, and C) may be permanent or non-permanent, depending on the need of the agency. Schedule positions may also be temporary (less than one year), intermittent (work that occurs at regular or sporadic intervals), or seasonal. Temporary appointments are generally for less than one year unless extended for an additional year.

The Senior Executive Service

The Senior Executive Service ("SES") is designed to attract senior business executives to the federal service to ensure that the executive management of the federal government meets the nation's goals, policies, and needs. Most high-level career managers in the federal service hold SES appointments. Subject to OPM review, agencies are charged with identifying which positions should be in the SES.

SES positions are divided into two types: those that may be filled with any appointments and those that may be filled only with a career appointee. Career positions are in the competitive service and the incumbent has direct responsibility to the public for management of government operations. A career position is one that must be filled by a career appointee to ensure impartiality or public confidence in the accountability of the position. Overall, career positions are intended to be removed from involvement in the determination of public advocacy of major controversial policies of the Administration or agency.

Are there any special provisions for veterans?

The law has also outlined particular advantages for qualified veterans. Under OPM regulations,[1] the federal government must provide the "maximum of employment and job advancement opportunities" to qualified eligible veterans. If they meet the requirements of the regulations, they are called "preference eligible."

Veterans may be appointed without competition to positions which would otherwise be in the competitive service. After two successful years of continuous employment, the employee is converted to career-conditional or

1 *See* 5 CFR § 307.102.

career status. Veterans readjustment appointees enjoy rights to appeal adverse actions to the MSPB if they have one year of continuous service and are preference eligible. Veterans who are not preference eligible do not have MSPB rights until they are converted to the competitive service. See Chapter 19 for a more detailed discussion of veterans preferences and rights.

TIP

If you are a disabled veteran, you probably get special rights to federal employment.

ARE THERE TYPES OF APPOINTMENTS WHICH ARE NOT PERMANENT OR FULL TIME?

The federal civil service involves several different types of employment which are not permanent and need not be full-time employment.

NONPERMANENT POSITIONS

WHAT IS TEMPORARY "TAPER" EMPLOYMENT? Agencies are allowed to hire individuals by "temporary appointment pending establishment of a register" ("TAPER"). TAPERs are permitted when an insufficient number of applicants are qualified for a position which is expected to last more than one year. TAPER positions are limited to GS-1, WG-1, and WG-2 positions, and those who hold them may only be promoted as high as GS-4 or WG-5.

WHAT IS A "TERM" APPOINTMENT? Term appointments are designed to fill positions when there is no permanent need for the employee's services. Terms may be as short as one year, or as long as four years. An employee serving a term appointment does not acquire competitive status through the term appointment. Term appointments are subject to a one-year trial period and during this year the agency may terminate the employee at any time without proving just cause for termination. The procedures described earlier for probationary employees apply. An agency may ask OPM to extend the term appointment beyond four years.

WHAT ARE "TEMPORARY LIMITED" APPOINTMENTS? Temporary limited appointments are designed to fill positions which will be abolished or which will expire. Temporary limited appointments are also used to temporarily fill permanent positions until an employee who will otherwise be displaced from employment can be permanently assigned. Generally, temporary appointments do not last more than one year but may be extended up to one year. These appointments are usually made competitively, but may be made non-competitively under certain circumstances. Appeal rights to the MSPB depend on the candidate's competitive or non-competitive status. Those who have competitive status have appeal rights.

Less than full-time positions

Most of us tend to think in terms of full-time employment, but many people cannot, or do not wish to, work full time. For them, the federal government offers several alternatives.

Part-time career employment Agencies may establish part-time career employment programs by which vacancies are filled on a part-time basis. Part-time work requires sixteen to thirty-two regularly scheduled work hours per week. Part-time positions may be in either the competitive or excepted service.

Seasonal employment Seasonal employment is "annually recurring periods of work of less than twelve months each year." Seasonal employees are permanent employees and receive full benefits. The employment usually lasts at least six months in a calendar year. If an appointment is expected to last less than six months, it is considered a temporary appointment.

Seasonal employment requires an employment agreement. The agreement must advise that you are subject to release and recall, the reasons for the release and recall, the minimum and maximum periods of work, and your benefits. Release and recall procedures must be established prior to the start of employment and must outline that you will be released to non-duty, non-pay status at the end of the season and recalled at the beginning of the next season. Examples of seasonal employees are some Park Service Rangers whose services are only needed in the summer when the number of visitors to the national parks is very high.

Intermittent employment Intermittent employment lacks regularly scheduled tours of duty. It is allowed only when the work is so sporadic and unpredictable that a tour of duty is impractical. Examples of intermittent employees are those who are hired by the Federal Emergency Management Agency ("FEMA") to help out during emergencies like hurricanes or floods.

WHAT ARE "NON-APPROPRIATED FUND" ("NAF") EMPLOYEES?

Nonappropriated fund employees are those employees of the federal government whose salaries are not paid from funds allocated by Congress, but from funds raised by certain organizations within the agencies. NAF employees are generally found within the Department of Defense agencies working in the Army and Air Force Exchange Service, Army and Air Force Motion Picture Service, Navy Ship's Stores Ashore, Navy Exchanges, Marine Corps Exchanges, Coast Guard exchanges, and other armed forced components.

Generally, NAF employees are not afforded the same rights as other federal employees. Most important, NAF employees are not allowed to appeal adverse actions to the MSPB. NAF employees are, however, afforded equal rights under the Whistleblower Protection Act and other statutes giving protections against discrimination, for example Title VII. (See Chapter 5.)

WHAT IS A "SUITABILITY DETERMINATION?

Just when you thought you had the job in hand, you may need to pass one final hurdle: the suitability determination. Your appointment most likely will be subject to the outcome of a suitability determination if it is one of several covered positions that may be are subject to investigation, even after you have been hired and started work in the new position.

TIP

Removal for suitability reasons is appealable to the MSPB under 5 USC Chapter 75. See Chapter 4 for an explanation of appeal rights if you face removal for misconduct.

A suitability determination concerns your character or conduct that is deemed to have an effect on the integrity or efficiency of the service. Positions covered include those in the competitive service, those in the excepted service where the incumbent can be noncompetitively converted to the competitive service, or a career appointment to the Senior Executive Service. If OPM or agencies with delegated authority make an unfavorable suitability determination after conducting the investigation, they may take the following actions against you: cancel your eligibility for federal employment; propose your removal; removal; and debar you from federal employment.[2]

Final Thoughts

The federal government has many different types of career appointment possibilities. Yours should reflect your own personal considerations and your career goals. Whether you seek a full-time, career-oriented, high-level appointment, or merely temporary or even seasonal employment, each carries its own rules, regulations, and requirements. Knowing these rules is one of the best ways to maximize your options and understand your rights.

2 *See* 5 CFR § 731.

2

Performance Appraisals So How Am I Doing?

In This Chapter You Will Learn:

- how performance standards are established
- how you provide input into your assessment and evaluation
- what rights you have if management says your performance isn't up to standards

Contents Chapter Two - Performance Appraisals

Introduction

As a federal employee, the quality of your job performance is the most important reason for your continued employment as well as for upward mobility in your career. The law (5 USC Chapter 43) requires that your agency make decisions concerning your retention, reassignment, or demotion based upon your work performance in the "critical elements" of your job. A "critical element" is a work responsibility of such importance that unacceptable performance on that one element means that your overall performance is considered unacceptable.

Agencies use the results of performance appraisals to make decisions about training, rewarding, promoting, and removing their employees. In this chapter we will look at what the law requires of you by way of performance, what happens when you don't meet these performance standards, and what recourse you have if you think you have been judged unfairly.

How do they determine what and how well I should do?

In order to periodically measure your job performance, your agency has developed a performance appraisal system. Your agency must make all supervisors and employees (through formal training, for example) aware of all relevant parts of its performance appraisal systems and programs. Under its performance appraisal system, your agency must first establish what are called the "performance standards" of your job. Performance standards are the agency's written descriptions of the performance requirements you must meet in order to be rated at a particular level of performance. Performance standards usually include the quality, quantity, timeliness, and manner of your expected performance within a given time period. An example of a federal employee performance standard is the following from the Coast Guard's Generic Performance Standards:

> PROFICIENT [FULLY SUCCESSFUL]—This is the level of good sound performance. The employee has responded positively to organizational goals. All critical element activities that could be completed are. The employee effectively applies technical skills and organizational knowledge to get the job done.

Because the accuracy of your performance standards is very important to the proper rating of your performance, your agency is supposed to allow you to participate in the drafting of your written performance standards.

TIP

If you are given performance standards that you did not help develop, you should write your supervisor a note or send an email stating whether you think the standards assigned to you are appropriate and indicating that you desire to participate in the development of your performance standards in the future.

To be valid, your performance standards must permit the agency to evaluate your job performance on the basis of clear and objective criteria. These criteria must be related to your job duties and the agency must apply them reasonably. At the beginning of the performance period, your agency must properly communicate the performance standards to you and explain to you the critical elements of your position.

WHAT HAPPENS IF I'M VERY GOOD—OR IF I'M NOT?

Agency performance systems must include a means of recognizing and rewarding you if your performance so deserves. For example, some agencies issue performance awards that may include cash bonuses for outstanding performers. Agency performance systems must also provide means of helping you to improve, if your performance is unacceptable.

Under the law, "unacceptable performance" means performance which fails to meet established standards in one or more critical elements of your position. Your agency's performance system must provide for your reassignment, demotion, or removal if your performance is rated as unacceptable. However, you must also be provided with an opportunity to demonstrate improved performance, and a specific time period in which to do so prior to being disciplined. This is known as a Performance Improvement Period or "PIP." Some agencies have pre-PIP periods to improve performance, usually by collective bargaining agreements. As will be discussed later in this chapter, if your performance remains unacceptable following your PIP, you will likely be removed or demoted. If you are removed or demoted more than two grades because of unacceptable performance, you may be eligible for discontinued service retirement, if you so desire.

Tell me about OPM's regulations and performance plans

The Office of Personnel Management ("OPM") is the federal agency in charge of issuing regulations governing agency performance appraisal systems. Under OPM's regulations, an agency's performance appraisal system must set up an official appraisal or rating period, which is the time period during which an employee's performance will be reviewed. Most agencies have an October 1 to September 30 appraisal cycle; however, agencies can set their own appraisal periods. For example, some agencies have a July-June cycle and others have a calendar year cycle. Additionally, although technically there is no maximum length for performance cycles, the regulations specify that appraisal periods shall generally be designated so that employees are provided a rating of record annually.[1]

TIP

You are supposed to receive a performance plan at the beginning of each appraisal period (normally within 30 days). If you do not receive one timely, contact your supervisor or an Employee Relations official. Additionally, both you and your manager should sign the performance plan, even if it has not changed from the last appraisal cycle.

Once the appraisal period is set up, the agency must draft "performance plans" for the employees covered by the system. Performance plans are the written record of the performance elements that set forth your expected performance, including all critical and non-critical elements and their performance standards.

---

1 *See* 5 CFR § Part 430.

As described earlier, your agency should encourage your participation in establishing your performance plan. You must be covered by an appropriate recorded performance plan based upon the work assignments and responsibilities that you are required to perform during each rating period.

Each performance plan must include performance elements which are used in scoring your performance, including at least one critical element that is essential to satisfactory performance, and any non-critical element(s), which are aspects of individual performance other than critical elements, that may further describe your expected performance. An example of a non-critical element is the following from a Department of Transportation secretary's performance standards:

> LIAISON: Maintains liaison with all levels of management, and with supervisory/secretarial personnel assigned by those organizations to support those tasks.

WHAT ARE THE DIFFERENT PERFORMANCE LEVELS?

Your agency's appraisal system must also set performance standards, i.e., the expression of the performance threshold(s), requirement(s), or expectation(s) that you must meet to be appraised at a particular level of performance. A performance standard may include, but is not limited to quality, quantity, timeliness, and manner of performance. Federal regulations require agencies to establish elements and standards as follows:

- For critical elements:
    1. At least two levels for appraisal must be used with one level being "Fully Successful" or its equivalent and another level being "Unacceptable," and
    2. A performance standard must be established at the "Fully Successful" level and may be established at other levels.
- For non-critical elements, when established:
    1. At least two levels for appraisal shall be used, and
    2. A performance standard(s) shall be established at whatever level(s) is appropriate·

In addition, your agency's appraisal program must include methods of appraising each critical and non-critical element during the appraisal period, such as a mid-year progress review. Your performance on each of your critical and non-critical elements must always be judged against the agency's corresponding performance standard(s). In general, the non-critical elements are less important than the critical elements. Even an "outstanding" rating in every non-critical element of your job will not offset a single "Unacceptable" critical element rating.

Can I get help with meeting the standards if I need it?

Under OPM regulations, agency appraisal programs should provide you assistance whenever your performance is determined to be "marginal," that is, below "Fully Successful" or its equivalent but above "Unacceptable." Moreover, an agency appraisal program must also provide for:

- assisting you in improving unacceptable performance in one or more critical elements, at any time during the appraisal period
- taking adverse action against you based on unacceptable performance

During your official appraisal period, OPM requires that your manager monitor your performance. Monitoring performance includes measuring performance against the performance standards and providing timely feedback. If you are in a telecommuting or other situation where you do not have routine face-to-face contact with your supervisor, you need to keep your supervisor informed about your work progress and make sure your supervisor is giving you feedback.

TIP

Before your performance appraisal is issued, you must be given an opportunity to perform under your position's performance standards for a minimum period of 90 days.

As soon as practicable after the end of your appraisal period, a rating of record must be given to you. A "rating of record" is the official written performance rating prepared at the end of your appraisal period for your performance over the entire period. The rating of record must be "written, or otherwise recorded," e.g., in a newer electronic format such that agencies can produce a paper copy, if needed. Purely oral appraisals do not meet regulatory requirements. Your rating of record must include an overall summary level performance rating score, based on an appraisal of your performance on your critical and non-critical elements. Summary level scores must comply with the following requirements:

For 5 Level Rating Systems:

- Level 1 through Level 5 are the categories, with Level 1 as the lowest and Level 5 as the highest
- Level 1 is "Unacceptable" or its equivalent
- Level 3 is "Fully Successful" or its equivalent
- Level 5 is "Outstanding" or its equivalent.

For 3 Level Rating Systems:

- Level 1 is "Unacceptable" or its equivalent
- Level 2 is "Fully Successful" or its equivalent
- Level 3 is "Outstanding" or its equivalent.

For 2 Level Rating Systems:

Agencies may use a two-level rating score system instead, such as "pass" and "fail." If you receive a rating of record of "Unacceptable" or "Fail," under either rating system, a higher level management official must review and approve the rating.

When a rating of record cannot be prepared at the time specified, your appraisal period must be extended. Once the conditions necessary to complete your rating of record have been met, your rating of record must be prepared as soon as practicable.

TIP

If your agency seeks your input before doing your appraisal, be sure to provide it. Some agencies allow employees to submit self-appraisals or lists of accomplishments. Take advantage of such opportunities.

Your performance rating may be prepared at such other times as an appraisal program may specify for special circumstances including, but not limited to, transfers and for performance on details and other special assignments or for a change in supervisors. Regulations do not require that performance plans be established or performance ratings be provided for employees on detail. Agencies must determine how they will capture information about employee performance while on detail and how they will consider it in producing the rating of record. Agencies must also transfer your most recent ratings of record whenever you transfer to another agency or are assigned to another organization within your agency.

How do I grieve a performance appraisal?

You don't want to get stuck with a performance appraisal that you think does not accurately reflect of your efforts. If you think that the performance appraisal you have been given is unfair or untrue, there are several things you can do, depending upon your circumstances.

What are my appeal alternatives?

If you receive an unfair or incorrect performance appraisal, you have several avenues to challenge it.

- first, at a minimum, you should always submit a written rebuttal to the rating, showing where there are errors in the appraisal
- in addition, you may have the right to file an "administrative grievance" or register other disputes with your employing agency (check out your agency's personnel policies)
- if you are covered by a union contract, you may file a grievance under the procedures set forth in the union's collective bargaining agreement
- if you believe that your appraisal was caused by discrimination on account of your race, color, sex, national origin, religion, disability, age, and/or reprisal for EEO activity, you may file an EEO complaint instead of a grievance, although most union contracts allow employees to file grievances alleging discrimination (see Chapter 6)

TIP

If you receive an unduly critical appraisal, respond by rebutting in writing each inaccurate or negative comment in the appraisal. For example, if the agency appraisal correctly states that you have been late in filing reports, you might point out that there were causes beyond your control such as the breakdown of the computer, the press of other priority assignments, or the untimely reports of coworkers upon whom you relied. You could cite your prior history of timely reporting and that the incidents of untimeliness were isolated and not repeated.

- if you believe that your negative or unfair performance appraisal is in retaliation for your whistleblowing activity, you may file a complaint with the Office of Special Counsel and, ultimately, an Individual Right of Action ("IRA") appeal to the MSPB (see Chapter 7).

Agency administrative grievances are decided by upper-level management and generally do not involve an opportunity for review by an independent authority not employed by your agency. Union grievances that are taken to arbitration, EEO complaints, and whistleblower complaints are subject to review by neutral outsiders and therefore may be more effective avenues for challenging negative or low performance appraisals.

How is my administrative grievance processed?

The purpose of an agency administrative grievance system is to provide you a fair, equitable, and timely forum for internal agency review and resolution of disputes you may have about employment-related matters that arose within your agency. Agency administrative grievance systems generally apply to non-bargaining unit employees. If you are covered by a union's collective bargaining agreement (contract) with your agency, you will generally not be able to use the administrative grievance process. Instead, you will be required to file a grievance under the terms of your union's contract. Employees covered by a union contract, may, however, file administrative grievances where the negotiated grievance procedure in their union contract excludes the matter over which the employee seeks to file a grievance, or where no negotiated grievance procedure is in effect.

TIP

Before filing a union grievance over a performance appraisal, check with the appropriate union officials to confirm that the union will arbitrate your grievance if necessary. Otherwise, the union grievance procedure may be a dead end as compared to other avenues, such as the EEO process.

Generally, administrative grievance procedures apply to any dissatisfaction or "grievance" relating to your employment that is subject to the control of agency management, including complaints alleging any retaliation for filing a prior administrative grievance. This means that, among other complaints, you may file a grievance regarding any performance appraisal over which you are dissatisfied. However, there are a few non-grievable actions you should know about. For instance:

- You may not file an administrative grievance over a performance appraisal that you are entitled to grieve under your union's grievance procedure with the agency. Union grievance procedures are found in the applicable union contract.

- You can never grieve the granting, failure to grant, or the amount of a performance award.

- An SES employee generally cannot grieve a performance appraisal.

- In some agencies, a performance appraisal is not grievable. The appraisal is subject instead to an internal appeal process separate and apart from the agency grievance procedure.

Agency administrative grievance procedures usually contain several steps that are supposed to provide employees with a reasonable opportunity to present a grievance over a performance appraisal to various levels of management decision-makers. It is important that you learn about the procedures and applicable time deadlines for filing and processing grievances in your agency.

Some grievance procedures include a "fact-finding" hearing at some step in the process. However, whether you have a fact-finding hearing is at the agency's discretion. Agency deciding officials at each step in the grievance process must not have been involved in making or influencing the performance appraisal that you are grieving, nor may they be subordinate to any official who issued you the performance appraisal, unless your rating official is the head of the agency.

TIP

Pick up a copy of your agency's grievance procedure from your agency personnel or human resources office. Carefully follow the procedures outlined therein, including any applicable time deadlines.

IS THERE ANYTHING I CAN DO TO BETTER THE ODDS OF WINNING MY GRIEVANCE?

To successfully challenge an appraisal, you need to present to the agency facts that support your reasons for the challenge. You should put them in writing, and in a grievance of this kind, you may challenge your performance appraisal as being:

- factually inaccurate
- unduly critical of your performance
- improper or inaccurate in relation to your performance standards, your position description, or the facts of your actual performance

Document your work during the rating period at issue. If you do not understand a work assignment or your supervisor's feedback about a work assignment, write your supervisor a memo, note, or e-mail asking for clarification of the unclear instructions, or rebutting any untrue negative feedback. Keep records of this correspondence throughout the appraisal period. Submit examples of your work along with your grievance and show which performance standard they exemplify. Produce any written records you have that support your rebuttal.

TIP

E-mail is a convenient way to seek clarification and at the same time create a record for use in your case.

If you need more information to successfully challenge your appraisal, you may request such information from the agency under either the Freedom of Information Act (FOIA), the Privacy Act, or under your union's agreement with management. (See Chapters 8 and 22.) However, as these formal information-requesting procedures are often very time-consuming and potentially costly, you may not have the time or the money to resort to them. The key is for you to keep your own records to support your fully successful performance.

You may also grieve performance appraisals believed to be retaliatory to punish you for your prior grievance activity. More information about challenging performance appraisals and resulting adverse actions can be found in the next chapter.

TIP

Keep a journal, file, or notes on the feedback you receive from your supervisors about your work. Any journal you keep should be written on your own time, not on work time. Keep your journal with you. Do not leave it in public view.

WHAT'S THE DOWN SIDE OF ADMINISTRATIVE GRIEVANCES?

A major problem is that administrative grievance procedures are all "in-house" procedures in which upper level management has the final decision as to whether lower level management's actions should be supported. This is what is often referred to as "the fox guarding the henhouse." As might be imagined, upper level management frequently sides with lower management rather than with the grieving employee. The administrative grievance process does not call for a neutral third party, not employed by the agency, to make an independent and binding decision. Therefore, administrative grievance procedures are limited in their effectiveness for resolving disputes covering performance appraisals.

TIP

Because performance appraisals are used to determine your standing in a reduction-in-force (RIF), an appraisal you believe is unfair should be challenged.

Final Thoughts

Acceptable performance is a crucial factor in your continued employment as a federal employee. Performance standards and performance appraisals should be taken very seriously. Understand your supervisors' expectations for your performance. If you do not understand an assignment or a directive, ask for clarification. Keep records of your work product during a rating period. If your supervisor criticizes your performance, take that criticism very seriously. Work to improve your performance. Good performance, support from coworker witnesses, and strong documentation are the most important protections against adverse performance actions.

3

Performance-Related Discipline

What do they do if they don't like my work?

In This Chapter You Will Learn:

- what happens during your Performance Improvement Period ("PIP")
- what the procedure is for disciplining you for poor performance
- what are your appeal rights

?

Contents Chapter Three - Performance-Related Discipline

Introduction

Federal law provides different procedures for disciplining employees for misconduct and for poor performance. 5 USC Chapter 75 governs misconduct related discipline, while 5 USC Chapter 43 applies exclusively to discipline for poor performers. The discipline we will be discussing in Chapter 4 is generally for misconduct, but some of the information in this chapter about the performance discipline process is similar to what you will learn in Chapter 4. There are distinct differences, however, that you must know to pursue your rights in an effective and timely way if you feel your performance appraisal and any resulting disciplinary action(s) were unjust.

You also need to be aware (just to complicate the picture!) that an agency may choose to use Chapter 75 (misconduct) procedures for poor performers instead of Chapter 43 procedures. There are some advantages as well as disadvantages for a poor performer who is disciplined under Chapter 75.

If the agency uses Chapter 75 to demote or remove a poor performer, it need not first give the employee a Performance Improvement Period (See p. 66 of this chapter) as in a Chapter 43 case. But if the agency uses Chapter 75 procedures, it must meet a higher standard of proof than in a Chapter 43 case. Also, under Chapter 75, the penalty selected by the agency may be reduced by the MSPB to a lesser penalty, unlike in a Chapter 43 case. Thus, it is important for an employee to be aware of whether an agency is proceeding under Chapter 43 or Chapter 75.

What's this I hear about "winner-take-all" appeals?

Under Chapter 43, an agency may only either reduce in grade (demote) or remove you if your performance has been rated as being "Unacceptable." Reassignment is also an option, but it is very rarely used. Agencies have no discretion to impose any other adverse or disciplinary penalties, such as suspensions or reprimands, as alternative means of disciplining you for unacceptable performance. Under Chapter 75, which is discussed in Chapter 4, an agency has broader discretion in choosing a penalty. If you are removed for poor performance under Chapter 43 and appeal to the MSPB or to an arbitrator, your removal cannot be reduced to a lesser disciplinary action by applying the "Douglas standards" for mitigating penalties. If the agency proves that your performance was unacceptable, your demotion or removal will be sustained. Thus, appeals in Chapter 43 performance cases are "winner-take-all" situations.

What's my agency's duty to notify me of unacceptable performance?

If, at any time during the annual performance appraisal cycle, your performance is determined to be unacceptable in one or more critical elements, your agency is required to notify you. The agency must also inform you:

- of the performance requirements or standards that you must attain to demonstrate acceptable performance in your position
- that unless your performance in the critical elements improves to, and is sustained at, an acceptable level, you may either be reduced in grade or removed

Before you can be disciplined, your agency must first afford you a reasonable opportunity to demonstrate acceptable performance on each critical element on which you were rated "unacceptable." The agency must also offer you assistance to help you improve your performance. This period when the agency gives you a reasonable opportunity and assistance to improve is called the Performance Improvement Period or "PIP."

What happens during the Performance Improvement Period?

A Performance Improvement Period is a set period of time given to you to show improvement, if your performance has been rated as unacceptable. During the PIP, the agency is supposed to provide you with a structured program of assignments, instruction, feedback, and performance counseling.

The PIP notice should explain what is required of both you and your agency during the PIP.

If you are placed on a PIP, make sure you understand the PIP notice and the performance standards under which you are expected to perform, especially the standards to meet the "Fully Successful" or equivalent performance level. Ask questions in writing to clarify any standards you do not understand and keep a written record of whether management keeps its promises to meet with you and/or help you during the PIP. Finally, seek advice from a qualified civil service attorney or other experienced representative for more specific guidance.

TIP

If you are ever placed on a PIP:

- *communicate with your supervisor in writing if you have any questions or concerns about the work assignments given to you during the PIP*
- *keep a written journal of what was said during any meetings with your supervisor during the PIP; send confirming emails*
- *unless prohibited by agency rules, keep copies of the written work product you produce during the PIP, as well as the comments received from your supervisor about your work*

What if I improve?

If your performance improves during the PIP, you cannot be reduced in grade or removed. In addition, if your performance continues to be acceptable for one year from the date of the PIP, the agency must remove any entry or other notation of the unacceptable performance from any agency record relating to you. Moreover, if you have performed acceptably for one year from the beginning of the PIP, and then your performance again becomes unacceptable, the agency must afford you an additional PIP before determining whether to propose a reduction in grade or removal.

What if I don't improve?

If your performance during or following the PIP is unacceptable in one or more of the critical elements, then your agency may propose either your reduction in grade (demotion) or your removal. If you receive a proposed reduction in grade or removal, you are entitled to several procedural rights. Specifically, you are entitled to the following:

- *30 days* advance written notice of the proposed action, which identifies the specifics of your alleged unacceptable performance on which the proposed adverse action is based. The notice should also outline the critical elements of your position involved in each instance of unacceptable performance

- representation by an attorney or other representative of your choosing.

- a reasonable time in which to reply to the proposed action orally and/or in writing. An oral reply is recommended because a face-to-face meeting gives you greater flexibility in presenting your position. You can clarify your concerns and explanations, and ask and answer questions. It also gives you the advantage of the human element—an opportunity to establish some rapport with the other side. Take the opportunity to impress the agency's designated deciding official with your sincerity and dedication to your agency, as well as your desire to be a good employee.

If the proposed adverse action is carried out, you are entitled to a written decision that specifies the instances of your unacceptable performance on which the reduction in grade or removal is based. Unless the reduction in grade or removal was originally proposed by the head of the agency, the decision to demote or remove you must be approved by a manager who is in a higher position than the manager who proposed the action. A reduction in grade or removal may be based only on unacceptable performance that occurred during the one-year period ending on the date of the written proposed adverse action notice.

What are my rights to information and accommodation?

If you are facing a proposed demotion or removal, you have the right to review the documentation relied upon by the agency to propose the adverse action. Also request evidence of disparate treatment, such as decisions issued by the proposing and deciding officials to other similarly-situated employees who have been charged with similar allegations of unacceptable job performance. Inform the agency that your request for information is also filed under the Freedom of Information Act and the Privacy Act. (A sample request for information/request for extension of time to reply is provided in Appendix E). Any favorable documentation received from the agency in response to your request(s) for information should be relied upon in your reply to the proposed action.

If your performance problems were caused by a medical condition, you will need to obtain and submit medical documentation from your doctors. If your performance problems are caused by a disability and you are otherwise qualified to perform the basic functions of either your present job or a vacant position, you should ask for reasonable accommodations if you need adjustments to your working conditions.[1]

TIP

If you receive a proposed adverse action, consider requesting an extension of the time given to you to respond. You may need the additional time to request, receive, and review all documents relied upon by the agency in proposing the action.

What happens with the decision?

Barring the granting of a request for an extension of time, the decision to retain, reduce in grade, or remove you for unacceptable performance must normally be made within *30 days* after the date that the advance written notice period expires. An employee who is removed or reduced in grade by two grade levels or more may be eligible for discontinued service retirement. If that situation applies to you, you should consult your agency's personnel or human resource office for more information.

Can an employee be removed from the Senior Executive Service for poor performance?

An employee may be removed from the SES at any time for less than fully successful executive performance. Such an employee is entitled to an informal hearing before the MSPB, however, the removal action will not be delayed if an informal hearing is granted.

---

1 *See* Chapter 5 for a discussion of your rights under the Rehabilitation Act, which prohibits disability discrimination in federal employment.

Do I get to appeal an adverse decision (a demotion or removal) to the MSPB?

The MSPB has jurisdiction over appeals from agency actions involving either reductions in grade or removals for unacceptable performance. MSPB jurisdiction applies broadly to:

- individuals in the competitive service who are not serving a probationary or trial period under an initial appointment and who have completed at least one year of current continuous employment
- veterans-preference eligible employees in an executive agency in the excepted service or Postal Service who have completed one year of current continuous service in the same or similar position
- individuals in the excepted service (other than preference eligibles) who are not serving a probationary or trial period under an initial appointment pending conversion to the competitive service and who have completed at least two years of current continuous service in the same or similar positions in an executive agency

---

TIP

Your notice of personnel action form, or SF-50, should identify your type of appointment and thus whether you are eligible to appeal adverse actions to the MSPB. If in doubt about your appeal rights, consult your personnel office and/or an experienced legal representative.

How do I file an MSPB appeal?

To start your MSPB case, you must file a written appeal with the MSPB. To be timely, you must file your appeal by the *30th calendar day after the effective date* of the removal or reduction in grade. The day after the effective date is considered "day one" of the 30-day filing period. You must file your written appeal with the appropriate MSPB regional or field office by personal delivery, fax, mail, or by the Board's internet filing procedure. (See Chapter 4 for a full discussion of MSPB procedures.)

What do I have to prove on appeal?

If you are removed or reduced in grade for unacceptable performance under Chapter 43, the MSPB will uphold the agency's action against you if the agency proves by substantial evidence that you have failed to meet the performance standards of any of the critical elements at issue in your case. The "substantial evidence" standard of proof is less rigorous than the "preponderance of the evidence" standard that an agency must meet in order to sustain an adverse or disciplinary action against an employee for misconduct charges under 5 USC Chapter 75.

Under Chapter 43, to properly remove you or reduce your grade, an agency must prove by substantial evidence that it did the following:

- set up an OPM-approved performance appraisal system
- communicated objective and reasonable written performance standards and the critical elements of your position to you at the beginning of the appraisal period
- warned you of inadequacies in your performance of critical elements during the appraisal period
- counseled you and afforded you an opportunity for improvement, i.e., a PIP, after proper notice

If the agency is able to show it met the above-listed requirements, the MSPB will sustain the agency's decision to reduce you in grade or remove you for receiving a rating of "Unacceptable" on *even a single critical element* at the conclusion of the PIP.

The key words are "unacceptable performance." Your agency cannot reduce in grade or remove you for "minimally acceptable performance." Actual facts concerning your performance are more important here than legal principles. Employees can win their appeals by proving that their performance was not unsatisfactory under the circumstances. Your appeal should be supported by statements from witnesses, documents, and, if appropriate, expert opinions.

TIP

Former supervisors who have observed your work performance and are able to sing your praise often make good witnesses. Supervisors from another department, or satisfied customers (if your work involves dealing with the public) can make good witnesses too. If your work is very technical, an expert witness from the private sector may be a good idea.

WHAT DEFENSES CAN I USE IN MY APPEAL?

You may defend yourself before the MSPB by alleging that the agency's action constitutes prohibited discrimination or another prohibited personnel practice. (See 5 USC 2302.) You may also raise other defenses to performance-based actions with the MSPB's administrative judge, including the following:

- you were not given your performance standards
- your performance standards were not sufficiently objective or they were unreasonable so as to show an arbitrary abuse of discretion by the agency
- your performance standards could not be reasonably attained and/or were not reasonably applied
- although objective, your performance standards were defined in a manner that defied measurement or quantitative analysis
- the length of the PIP was unreasonably short or long
- your supervisor interfered with your ability to perform during the PIP
- you were overloaded with work during the PIP or were not given promised guidance or assistance
- the action was motivated by bad faith, discriminatory feelings, or reprisal
- the unacceptable performance was caused by a lack of training by the agency
- the agency committed harmful procedural errors in the processing of the adverse action, such as denying you rights as guaranteed by OPM's regulations

Remember, appeals in performance cases are "winner take all." The MSPB or an arbitrator does not have the authority to reduce the penalty to something less than the demotion or removal decided by the agency. Either the adverse action will be sustained or it will be reversed and, in a removal case, you will be returned to your job. As you can see, you cannot take this appeal process lightly. Be prepared with evidence to prove that you performed above the "Unacceptable" level.

WHAT IF I HAVE A "MIXED CASE?"

(NOTE: See also Chapter 6 regarding the discrimination complaint process.)

In the context of a performance-based adverse action, a "mixed case" refers to an MSPB appeal that alleges unlawful discrimination based upon race, color, sex, religion, national origin, age, disability, and/or reprisal for prior EEO activity as an affirmative defense to the agency's demotion or removal action. An MSPB appeal that raises discrimination in connection with an appealable performance-based adverse action must be processed as a mixed case. Nothing requires you, the appellant, to initiate the discrimination allegation through your agency's EEO procedures or through any grievance procedures before alleging it is an affirmative defense to an adverse action under the MSPB's jurisdiction.

To successfully present an affirmative defense of employment discrimination, you must first establish what is called a "*prima facie*" case. To establish a *prima facie* case of unlawful discrimination in a performance case, you are required to prove the following:

- that you are a member of a protected class (because of your race, color, sex, religion, national origin, age, disability, and/or prior EEO activity
- that you were the object of an adverse employment action
- that there was a causal relationship between your race, color, sex, religion, national origin, age, disability, and/or prior EEO activity and the adverse action

Once you establish a *prima facie* case of discrimination by a preponderance of the evidence, which means that there is more evidence to prove your points than there is to disprove them, the burden shifts to the agency to produce a "legitimate, nondiscriminatory reason" for the adverse action.

If the agency produces a legitimate, nondiscriminatory reason, you must then prove the following by a preponderance of the evidence:

- that the agency's proffered reason is untrue, and
- the agency's proffered reason is also a pretext (or cover-up) for unlawful intentional discrimination based on your protected class membership(s)

TIP

- ***Witness support is often crucial to proving discrimination.***
- ***If you raise discrimination as an "affirmative defense," the burden is on you to prove it.***

To win, you must show that the agency's alleged legitimate, non-discriminatory reasons were actually a pretext, cover-up, or farce, and that discrimination was actually the cause of the adverse action. If successful in proving an affirmative defense of discrimination, you will be entitled to have the adverse action reversed. You will be reinstated with back pay, benefits, interest, and, most likely, an award of attorney fees. You might be entitled to an award of compensatory damages for proven emotional and/or physical distress in an amount less than or equal to $300,000. However, you may not prevail if the agency can prove that it would have taken the same adverse action in the absence of discrimination. If that is the case, you may still recoup your attorney fees.

Final Thoughts

If your performance is "unacceptable," you are afforded an opportunity and a time period to improve so as to prevent your removal or reduction in grade. If you are subsequently removed from service or demoted, you have the opportunity to appeal to the MSPB. You can raise defenses in your appeal including affirmative defenses of discrimination or retaliation. You should probably retain a lawyer or other representative with experience in civil service matters to help you defend yourself against the agency's adverse action. Hopefully, you can convince the MSPB that your dismissal was unlawful and that you deserve reinstatement.

While the disciplinary procedures for other matters are similar to performance-related discipline, there are, in fact, differences. Those differences may seem insignificant, but if they come between you winning your appeal and having the discipline removed, they are significant indeed. Make sure you understand the correct procedures for performance-related disciplinary matters. It will put you in a better position to demonstrate that you were not a poor performer.

Misconduct: Adverse Actions and Discipline

4

Oops! What did I do now?

In This Chapter You Will Learn:

- what kinds of agency actions can be taken against you for wrongdoing
- what your rights are within the agency to defend yourself if disciplined
- what your appeal rights are to the MSPB or the EEOC

Note: Discipline for performance-related problems is discussed in Chapter 3.

If you are like most of us, at some point, you make a mistake or do something wrong in the workplace. None of us is perfect. Nonetheless, once hired, one of the most traumatic things that can happen to a federal employee is the imposition of discipline. At its worst, discipline can end your career and make it difficult to obtain future employment. At best, discipline is embarrassing, unsettling, and a blemish on your record. Discipline is a permanent reminder of your mistake which could interfere with the advancement of your career. In short, discipline is not a matter to be taken lightly.

Generally, there are different procedures for disciplining employees for misconduct and for performance.[1] Discipline for performance reasons is covered in Chapter 3.

This chapter focuses on discipline for alleged misconduct such as absenteeism, excessive tardiness, insubordination, sexual harassment, misuse of government equipment, dishonesty, falsification of documents, and other wrongdoing or breach of agency policy.

---

1 The requirements of 5 USC Chapter 75 apply to misconduct, while Chapter 43 applies to poor performers. However, an agency may choose to use Chapter 75 procedures for poor performers instead of Chapter 43. If the agency uses Chapter 75 to demote or remove a poor performer, it need not first give the employee a Performance Improvement Period (PIP) as in a Chapter 43 case. But if the agency uses Chapter 75, it must meet the higher "preponderance of the evidence" standard. Also, the penalty selected by the agency may be mitigated to a lesser penalty, unlike a Chapter 43 case. See Chapter 3 for a full discussion of discipline related to poor performance.

In this chapter we will look at the different types of actions that may be taken against you for alleged misconduct, and what you can do about it.

What's the difference between adverse actions and disciplinary actions?

Even though we may refer in a general way to "discipline" there are really two categories of discipline in the federal sector—"disciplinary actions" and "adverse actions." Knowing the difference is important because they are appealed differently and the appeal can make all the difference in the outcome of your case.

The more severe forms of discipline are called "adverse actions." An adverse action is a removal, a suspension of more than 14 days, a demotion/reduction in grade and pay (not associated with a reclassification), or a furlough of 30 days or less.

A disciplinary action is a suspension of 14 days or less or a reprimand. While an agency can impose other penalties on an employee which may be subject to challenge, such as leave restriction or a reassignment without loss of pay or grade, such actions are not, strictly speaking, disciplinary actions.

Please note that some agencies vary in their terminology for these sorts of personnel actions (for example, referring to some or all disciplinary actions as "corrective actions"). This chapter will use the terms adverse action and disciplinary action as defined above.

Adverse actions may be appealed by eligible employees directly to the MSPB. Lesser disciplinary actions generally may be appealed through agency grievance procedures or negotiated grievance procedures if you are covered by a union contract.[2]

Whether you receive a disciplinary action or an adverse action, the standard for imposing this action is the same: it must promote the "efficiency of the service." What does this standard mean? When an agency imposes discipline, it is the agency that has the burden of proving that the discipline was warranted.

---

2 Cases involving EEO discrimination will be discussed below in the "mixed case" section. Cases involving whistleblower reprisal are discussed in Chapter 7. Cases involving discrimination for uniformed service under USERRA are discussed in Chapter 19.

To do that, the agency will have to prove three things:

1. you committed the misconduct charged
2. the penalty selected is not overly harsh in the circumstances of your case
3. there is a "nexus," or connection, between the misconduct and the ability of the agency to carry out its mission

The good news is that in most situations, your supervisor may not discipline you without advance notice and an opportunity for you to present your side of the story. While many of the procedures described in this chapter are applicable to both adverse actions and disciplines, we will focus on adverse actions because they are more severe and career-threatening.

AM I COVERED BY ADVERSE ACTION APPEAL RIGHTS TO THE MSPB?

Adverse action appeal procedures generally apply to:

- employees in the competitive service who have passed a one-year probationary period
- employees in the excepted service who have completed two years of current continuous service in the same or a similar position
- "preference-eligible" veterans in the excepted service or the U.S. Postal Service who have completed one year of current continuous service in the same or a similar position

---

TIP

For a full listing of employees covered by adverse action procedures, see 5 CFR 752.401(c). For a full listing of employees covered by disciplinary procedures, see 5 CFR 752.201 (b). To determine your status, look at one of your recent SF-50 "Notice of Personnel Action" forms. Whether you are in the competitive or excepted service, the length of your probationary period should be indicated. If you are unsure, ask your personnel officer, union official, or a civil service lawyer.

Beware. Sometimes personnel officials take a restrictive view of who is entitled to MSPB appeal rights and are mistaken about whether you qualify for them.

What's the agency's procedure for taking action against me?

In order to correctly proceed against you for an adverse action or disciplinary action, your manager must follow certain procedures and rules. In order to initiate an adverse action against you, management must first issue a "proposal."

The proposal

A proposal is a written notice of proposed action informing you of:

- the charges against you
- the facts supporting the charges against you
- the fact that you have the right to review the material or evidence the agency is relying upon in proposing this action against you[3]

Once the agency issues this proposal, it may only take an action against you based on what was in the proposal. The agency cannot impose a penalty more severe than the one it proposed, or based on conduct not contained in the proposal notice. If the agency believes that your penalty should be severe due to some aggravating factor, such as a prior disciplinary record, then that aggravating factor must be contained in the proposal or the agency cannot use it to enhance your penalty. The decision to impose the adverse action cannot be put into effect sooner than *30 days* from the date of the proposal notice.[4]

Although the proposal notice tells you that you have the right to review the materials the agency is relying upon in proposing the action, there is usually other information which you should request and review in order to present a proper reply. Examples of this information are:

- the regulations you have allegedly violated
- the agency's adverse action procedures or instructions to supervisors
- the agency's "table of penalties" for offenses
- your complete Official Personnel File ("OPF")
- copies of disciplinary and adverse actions issued to other employees charged with similar offenses

The agency usually will not give you this information unless you ask for it. While the agency might not be obligated to provide you this information at the reply stage under the statutes governing disciplinary and ad-

---

3 *See* 5 USC § 7513.

4 This 30 day deadline does not apply in disciplinary action cases.

verse actions, it may be required to provide you this information under the Freedom of Information Act or the Privacy Act. (See Chapter 22.)

TIP

Always ask the agency for copies of the material or evidence it is relying on in proposing the action against you.

If you are covered by a union contract, the union can request this information under a separate statute giving unions the right to information necessary to represent employees.[5] Cite these relevant statutes as the bases for your request to cover the situation where the agency will not give you this information as part of your right to present a reply to the proposed action. A sample "information request" is found in Appendix E-5.

TIP

Because it might take the agency time to gather all this material for you, make sure you also ask the agency to extend the deadline for your reply in order to give you enough time to receive and review the information.

THE REPLY

A reply is your response to the agency's proposal for discipline against you. As a federal employee, you are entitled to a reasonable amount of work time to review the material relied on by the agency and to prepare a reply to the proposal. You are also entitled to a reasonable amount of time to present the reply from the date the proposal is issued, but generally not less than *7 days* from that date.[6]

---

5 *See* 5 USC § 7114(b)(4)(B).

6 *See* 5 USC § 7513(b)(2). For disciplinary action cases, the minimum response deadline is only *24 hours*. 5 CFR § 752.203(c).

TIP

The initial response deadlines for adverse and disciplinary actions are extremely short. If you need more time to answer than the agency has provided you, ask for it. Agencies usually give extensions of time to present replies to proposals, as long as requests for extensions are not unreasonable or abusive.

The reply is extremely important. Don't pass up this opportunity to tell your side of the story. There are several important purposes of the reply. Most important, it is your chance to set the record straight and try to convince management that you are not guilty of the misconduct charged, or that the facts are not as alleged. If there is misconduct, you want to convince the agency that the penalty selected is too harsh, given your past work record, mitigating factors, discipline given to other employees for similar offenses, etc. You also want to establish the fact that you understand your mistake and can be counted on to comply with agency rules in the future.

Your reply can be in writing or it can be done in person (an "oral" reply), or both. In most situations, it is preferable to give an oral reply, supported by written documents. The oral reply gives you an opportunity to clear up any questions that management officials may have, and allows your sincerity to come through in a way that it may not in a written reply. You need not go through this process alone. You have the right to be represented by an attorney or other personal representative during the reply.

TIP

Begin discussing the issue of scheduling the oral response early—ideally, in the same initial letter asking for an extension of the response deadline and for copies of the documents relied upon in proposing the adverse action and other relevant evidence. See Appendix E-2 for a sample of this initial letter.

Before we discuss what you should do at the reply, you should know what a reply is not. A reply is not a hearing. A reply should not be management's opportunity to cross-examine you about the charges. Rather, the reply is your right to present your response to the charges and to the proposed penalty. Do not feel compelled to answer all of management's questions, especially where you believe they are designed to get you to admit to something you are not prepared to admit to.

WHAT SHOULD I DO AT THE REPLY? All of the arguments that you have against the proposal should be made at the reply stage. While you are not prevented from adding new arguments or facts at a later appeal, it is best to present all of your arguments and facts at the reply. The goal is not to win on appeal, but to get the proposal rescinded.

It is usually a good idea to start out by giving a detailed, but succinct, history of your employment including awards, promotions, relevant education, or military service, etc. This lets the deciding official know, right off the bat, that you have been an asset to the agency.

Next, address the charges against you. Be as specific as possible. While you are not permitted to have witnesses present testimony at the reply, you are permitted to present affidavits or other statements from employees or other witnesses to the events at issue.

TIP

Since you cannot bring live witnesses with you to the oral response, your preparation should include seeking favorable witness testimony relevant to your defense. For best effect, this testimony should be in affidavit form. See Appendix E-3 for a boilerplate format for use in preparing these affidavits.

Do not bypass the opportunity to obtain and submit witness support for your position. If you obtained other documents that are helpful to your argument, make sure you present them to the deciding official. Make sure to retain a copy of any information you provide.

After discussing the facts of the charges against you, you must then address the penalty proposed in case the deciding official chooses not to believe your version of the facts. In 1981, the MSPB issued a now-famous decision listing the factors to be considered in determining the appropriate penalty.

In *Douglas v. Veterans Administration*,[7] the MSPB identified the following possible mitigation factors:

- the seriousness of the offense
- the employee's position, including whether it is a fiduciary or supervisory role
- the employee's past disciplinary record
- the effect of the offense on the employee's ability to perform satisfactorily or upon management's confidence in the employee's ability to perform
- the employee's past work record: length of service, job performance, dependability
- the consistency of the penalty with those imposed on similarly situated employees
- the consistency of the penalty with the agency's table of penalties
- the notoriety of the offense
- the clarity with which the employee was on notice of rules allegedly violated
- the employee's potential for rehabilitation
- mitigating circumstances, such as unusual job tensions, personality problems, bad faith, or malice on the part of the supervisor
- the adequacy of alternative sanctions to deter future misconduct

Not all *Douglas* factors apply to every case. In your reply, discuss the factors which apply to your case and will help show why the penalty proposed is too harsh. Ignore those factors which do not help you make your argument.

If the misconduct alleged has no relationship to your ability to perform on the job, then say so. This argument may be appropriate when you are charged with conduct that occurred away from the workplace.

Lastly, in your reply, you will want to raise "affirmative defenses," if possible, i.e., allegations that the action proposed against you is based on some illegal or improper motivation by the agency. The most common affirmative defenses employees raise are that:

- the action is based on illegal discrimination
- the agency failed to reasonably accommodate an employee's disability
- the action was in reprisal for protected whistleblowing

---

7 *See* 5 MSPR 280, 305-06 (1981).

If there is any truth to all, or part, of the allegations against you, consider making a settlement offer in the reply. For example, if the agency has proposed your removal, you could offer to accept a 30-day suspension without further appeal.

What is an "LCA" and why should I beware of it? Be careful, however, when entering into settlements with the agency.[8] Sometimes, the agency will propose a "last chance agreement" ("LCA"). The LCA generally provides that, in exchange for not firing you, you make a promise not to engage in further misconduct. The typical LCA further provides that if the agency discovers that you have engaged in further misconduct, you can be removed without appeal rights. These agreements usually give the agency wide discretion. Before entering into a LCA, consult with a union officer or a lawyer with expertise in these matters.

The decision letter

After your reply, the agency will issue a "decision letter" notifying you of its decision. The decision should indicate which charges the agency has found sustained and those found not sustained. Often, the decision letters are shorter than the proposal letters and merely refer back to the proposal notice. In reaching its decision, the agency cannot reply on any actions or factors not contained within the earlier proposal notice. Similarly, the penalty imposed cannot be more severe than the one proposed. The decision letter must also notify you of your appeal rights.

For most employees, you will be notified of

- your right to appeal to the MSPB
- the time limit for filing that appeal (*30 days* from the effective date of the action)
- the address of the MSPB's regional or field office to which your appeal should be sent
- if you raised an affirmative defense of discrimination, your right to initiate the EEO process by seeing an EEO counselor within *45 days* of your notice of the decision
- if you are in a unionized work unit and the adverse action is covered within the scope of the negotiated grievance procedure, your right to file a grievance over the action within the time frames permitted under the collective bargaining agreement

---

[8] *See* Chapter 32 concerning settlements.

The appeal

If you do not like the decision made by management in the decision letter, all is not lost. In appropriate situations, you may have another bite at the apple. You may have the right to appeal. Appeals are your second chance at getting the decision you want in your action. Depending on the circumstances, appeals may be within your agency or to another agency outside your own, such as the MSPB or the EEOC, or to an arbitrator. The external appeal rights may be the most important, since decisions on agency appeals often side with their own managers' proposals. An external appeal gives you the chance to have someone outside of your agency review the agency's decision. Whatever your circumstances dictate, if you did not receive a satisfactory decision after the proposal and reply, take the next step and appeal.

TIP

The appeal routes in the federal sector are complex and usually have very short time deadlines. If you file your appeal in the wrong forum or miss the filing deadline, you may lose the right to ever challenge the agency's action. Pay careful attention to the appeal rights as explained to you by the agency. Sometimes, the agency misinforms employees about appeal rights. If this happens to you, when you file your appeal it may still be considered timely as long as you acted with "due diligence" in filing your appeal correctly after you learned of the agency's misinformation.

Disciplinary actions Disciplinary actions, which are suspensions of less than 15 days, are generally not appealable to the MSPB, except as discussed below where certain affirmative defenses are present. For the most part, you will have to challenge a disciplinary action through the EEO process, through the "agency grievance procedure," or if you are represented by a union, through the negotiated grievance/arbitration procedure in the collective bargaining agreement.

There are two exceptions which will permit you to appeal a disciplinary action to the MSPB:

- If you believe that the suspension was reprisal for protected whistleblowing (see Chapter 7), you must file a complaint with the Office of Special Counsel ("OSC"). You may file an appeal to the MSPB after *120 days* have passed with no action by the OSC, or within *65 days* of the OSC closing its investigation, whichever occurs first.

- If you believe that the suspension is discriminatory on the basis of your past or present uniformed service, you may file an appeal with the MSPB alleging a violation of the Uniformed Services Employment and Reemployment Rights Act ("USERRA") (see Chapter 19).

Of these various alternatives, the agency grievance process is the least effective because it merely involves one level of agency management considering what another level of management did. This is like the proverbial fox guarding the chicken coop. You will have a better chance of getting a satisfactory result if you can make a plausible claim in one of the other forums discussed.

ADVERSE ACTIONS Adverse actions are generally appealable directly to the MSPB. However, different situations can call for different procedures.

- If you believe that *discrimination* played a part in the agency's decision you can either file directly with the MSPB *or* first go through the EEO complaint and investigatory process (see Chapter 6). This is called a "mixed case" and will be discussed in greater detail below.

- If you believe that reprisal for protected whistleblowing played a part in the agency's decision you can either file directly with the MSPB, *or* first file a complaint with the Office of Special Counsel in the hopes that OSC will investigate your complaint. After the OSC completes its review of your case, you will then be given notice of your right to file with the MSPB.

- If you are covered by a *union* contract, you will have the right to pursue your appeal through the collective bargaining agreement's grievance provisions. You will need the union's consent to have your case submitted to arbitration, however.

- If you believe that reprisal for uniformed service played a part in the agency's decision, you can either file directly with the MSPB, *or* first file a complaint under USERRA with the Department of Labor, Veterans Employment and Training Service (VETS) in the hopes that DOL will investigate your complaint. After the DOL completes its review of your case, you will then be given notice of your right to file with the MSPB.

You cannot, however, file a union grievance and an MSPB appeal over the same action. You can only challenge your adverse action through one process or the other—but not both. This choice is referred to as an "election of remedies." Your election is made at the time you either file a written grievance or file your appeal with the MSPB. Once filed, you cannot switch out of one forum and into the other. Therefore, before filing a union grievance it is best to first get the union to commit to going to arbitration. Please note that this election of remedies only applies to union grievances, and not to non-union agency grievances.

TIP

Is it better to challenge an adverse action to the MSPB or to an arbitrator? Although the MSPB and arbitrators apply the same law, the record shows that when it comes to determining the appropriateness of a penalty imposed for misconduct, arbitrators tend to overturn harsher penalties, in favor of less strict ones, more often than the MSPB.

WHAT ABOUT MSPB PROCEDURES?

The MSPB has regulations for filing appeals.[9] Know well what they are so that you do not miss any of the deadlines and you do whatever is required to successfully pursue your appeal.

TIP

The MSPB has a pretty good website explaining its procedures. So visit: www.mspb.gov.

WHEN DO I FILE?

An appeal to the MSPB must be filed within *30 calendar days* after the effective date of the adverse action. The first day *after* the adverse action is "day one" in the counting. For example, if your decision letter is issued

---

9 *See* 5 CFR Part 1201.

on March 2nd with an effective date of March 5th, day one in counting is March 6th, and your appeal to the MSPB must be filed no later than April 4th.

TIP

If the 30th day falls on a Saturday, Sunday, or Federal holiday, the deadline for filing an MSPB appeal is extended until the next federal business day.

The MSPB does not excuse late filings unless there is "good cause." This is a strict standard. The most common cases where the MSPB finds good cause is when the agency supplied the employee with wrong information about filing requirements or the employee had a proven medical condition which prevented timely filing. The best advice is not to let the filing deadline pass!

Where do I file?

Your initial MSPB appeal should be filed with the Board's regional office that has geographical jurisdiction over your employing office. (See Appendix L for a listing of the MSPB's regional offices.)

Appeals may also be filed electronically, on-line. To do so, go to the Board's website at "www.mspb.gov" and follow the links to "How to File an Appeal." Then select "MSPB e-Appeal Online." To get there faster, the direct site for the "e-Appeal" is: https://e-appeal.mspb.gov, and then select the option for "New Appeal."

What do I file?

If you receive an adverse action, your agency is supposed to include a copy of the MSPB appeal form. Just follow the instructions on the form. They are not complicated. It is not necessary to use the MSPB's appeal form, however. An "appeal letter" to the MSPB is just as effective as the Board's own form.

Whichever way you choose to present it, your appeal should contain the following information:

1. your name, address, and telephone number
2. the name and address of the agency that took the adverse action against you

3. the nature of the adverse action (for example, 30-day suspension) and the effective date of the adverse action
4. a request for a hearing
5. a description of why the adverse action was improper, such as your denial of the misconduct charged and a claim that the penalty chosen is too harsh and does not promote the efficiency of the service
6. identification of any affirmative defenses (for example, the action taken was discriminatory in violation of Title VII of the Civil Rights Act of 1964, as amended; the action was reprisal for protected whistleblowing in violation of the Whistleblower Protection Act; the action was taken on account of service in the uniformed services in violation of the Uniformed Services Employment and Reemployment Rights Act)
7. a statement that you have not filed a grievance or EEO complaint over the same matter which is the subject of your appeal
8. the name, address, and telephone number of your attorney or other representative
9. the remedy requested (for example, reinstatement, back pay and benefits, reimbursement of reasonable attorney fees and costs). If you claimed discrimination or whistleblower reprisal as an affirmative defense, you may be entitled to "compensatory damages" for certain out-of-pocket expenses and emotional distress. See Chapter 5 and Chapter 7.
10. your signature and the date of your appeal

How do I file?

The MSPB requires that you file two copies of your appeal. How you do it depends on the circumstances. Look at the chart below for what best suits your needs.

Method	When Considered filed by the MSPB
Mail. Certified mail is best, but not required	When postmarked
Overnight delivery. (for example, Federal Express)	When deposited with the delivery service
Hand delivered	When received by the MSPB
Facsimile transmission (fax)	The date of the fax transmission
Online	The date the appeal is submitted

WHAT HAPPENS AFTER THE APPEAL IS FILED?

You only have a slight breather after you file your appeal. No sooner do you get it all taken care of and filed, when a new process begins. This one starts with an Acknowledgment Order and moves along from there. The MSPB appeal process is relatively fast, often taking not more than *120 days* from the date you file your appeal until an administrative judge issues a decision.

WHAT'S THIS "ACKNOWLEDGMENT ORDER" I RECEIVED? After your appeal is filed, the MSPB will issue you an "Acknowledgment Order." This order is very important for several reasons.

- the administrative judge assigned to your appeal will be noted in the Order
- if there are problems with timeliness or the MSPB having jurisdiction over your appeal, the Order should put you on notice of that fact
- the Order will tell you what kind of evidence or argument you must present to the judge to demonstrate that the MSPB has jurisdiction over your appeal. Note: If the judge notes a problem with the MSPB jurisdiction, for example through an Order to Show Cause, this would be a good time to seek out the assistance of an attorney or other representative with MSPB experience, if you have not already done so
- the Order marks the time limit for beginning "discovery" (see following). You must initiate discovery within *30 calendar days from the date of the Order* (*not* from the date you receive the Order)
- the Order instructs your agency to submit various information to the MSPB, known as the "agency file." A copy will be sent to you
- the Order typically instructs the agency to contact you or your representative, if you have one, to discuss settlement

WHAT IS "DISCOVERY?" Discovery is the process by which you learn information from the other side which may be helpful in presenting your case. Discovery is important to you as appellant (someone who bring an appeal) because you can learn of witnesses who will be helpful to your view of your case or who can support your claim that the penalty is unreasonable. Discovery is also used to obtain documents relevant to your case. For example, if the personnel officer wrote a memorandum to the deciding official stating that no employee has ever received more than a reprimand for doing the same thing you did, you could get that kind of information in discovery. ***See Appendix P for a sample MSPB discovery request.***

TIP

If you need more time to complete discovery or to engage in settlement discussions, you and the agency can ask the administrative judge to "suspend" the proceedings for 30 days. You can ask for up to two case suspensions of 30 days apiece.

There are generally four discovery methods or devices:

- **Interrogatories:** Questions that you send to the other side to answer. Require that these questions be answered under oath. Absent prior approval from the judge, you are limited to 25 interrogatories.

- **Requests for documents:** Requests for specific types of documents which the agency might have in its possession which you believe are relevant to your case. The agency will only be required to turn over documents already in existence. It is not required to compile information for you.

- **Requests for admissions:** If there are certain facts that are easily provable, you might ask the agency to "admit" them. These "admissions" can be introduced as evidence and save you time (and risk) of having to prove them at the hearing. For example, you might ask an agency to admit that its table of penalties allows for only a five-day suspension for an employee's first instance of AWOL.

- **Depositions:** Oral questioning of potential witnesses, usually done under oath in the presence of a court reporter. If you cannot afford a court reporter, you can tape record the deposition. In that event, have the witness declare under penalty of perjury that the answers he or she gives will be truthful. Absent prior approval from the judge, you are limited to 10 depositions.

If the agency fails to comply with your requests for documents or fails to answer interrogatories within *20 days,* you can file a "motion to compel" discovery with the administrative judge. The judge will then rule on the appropriateness of your requests and can order the agency to produce the requested information.

Depositions are the most expensive form of discovery. The average cost of a day-long deposition just for court reporting costs are $1000 in the Washington, D.C. area as of when this Guide when to press, which includes the court reporter's fee for attendance and typing up the deposition. Where numerous witnesses are involved, the expense can run into thousands of dollars.

What is a "prehearing submission?" Shortly after you receive the Acknowledgment Order, you will receive a Scheduling Order. This Order will tell you when the hearing will take place,[10] when your prehearing submission is due, and when the prehearing telephone conference will take place.

TIP

One common problem with the schedule for the prehearing submission is that some administrative judges set the date for the submission before discovery is even completed. If that occurs, you can request the deadline be extended. If the administrative judge fails to move the deadline for the prehearing submission, include a statement that you reserve the right to amend your witness and/or exhibit list pending the completion of discovery.

In the prehearing submission, you are required to

- outline the facts you think are in dispute
- list each witness you want to call at the hearing with a summary of each witness' testimony
- attach each document you want to introduce as evidence at the hearing

---

TIP

If you want to make sure that an agency witness is present at the hearing to be questioned by you, make sure you place him/her on your own witness list. If you fail to list a witness or include an exhibit, you will likely be precluded from introducing that witness or document at the hearing. Also be sure to list yourself on the witness list, as well as any relevant friendly witnesses supporting your case.

---

[10] If you need to reschedule the hearing, it must be done as soon as possible. The request to reschedule has to be in the form of a motion, accompanied by an affidavit explaining the good cause for rescheduling the hearing.

During the prehearing telephone conference, the administrative judge will rule on whether you can call the witnesses you listed or introduce the exhibits you attached. If a potential witness is no longer employed by the federal government, you will have to ask the administrative judge to issue a subpoena to require the witness' appearance at the hearing. If the administrative judge denies any of your requests and you believe the exhibit or witness is important, you must "object" to the judge's ruling. Ask that your objections be noted in the summary of the conference. When the hearing starts, it is good practice to renew your requests to present the witnesses and/or exhibits, and to renew your objections if the judge again denies your requests.

TIP

Important advice for your telephone conference with the judge and the agency's attorney, if you will be speaking to these people directly because you are not represented by counsel:

- *Be prepared!*
- *Be courteous!*
- *Don't be distracted. Don't have the TV going or kids trying to get your attention in the background.*
- *Try not to be intimidated.*
- *If you don't understand something, ask the administrative judge to explain it. The MSPB has specifically instructed administrative judges to be mindful of the possible needs of unrepresented employees for explanations of legal matters.*

WHAT HAPPENS AT THE HEARING? The hearing is an administrative trial. Usually, there are no opening statements. In adverse actions, the agency presents its case first. During the agency's case, you can cross-examine the agency's witnesses. When the agency completes its case, you present your witnesses. The agency gets to cross-examine your witnesses.

Occasionally, the side who goes first will get to call rebuttal witnesses after the opposing side's case. A rebuttal witness is there for the express purpose of giving testimony at odds with something presented before. Where witnesses' versions of events differ, the judge will have to assess the witnesses' credibility, and decide whose version is more believable, just as a jury does in a regular court case.

In most cases, the judge will permit each side to make a closing argument to summarize the testimony and reference the applicable law. In complex cases, the judge may request or permit the parties to file written closing arguments or briefs.

In adverse actions alleging misconduct, the agency must prove the alleged misconduct by a "preponderance of the evidence." This means that the agency must prove that it is more likely than not that the misconduct occurred. If you raise an affirmative defense such as discrimination, you must prove your affirmative defenses by the same preponderance of the evidence standard.

What is an "initial decision?" How is it appealed? Shortly after the hearing, the administrative judge will issue a written decision. This is called the "initial decision." The initial decision will become a "final" decision unless it is appealed. An appeal to the full Board is called a "petition for review" ("PFR"). An initial decision can be appealed to the full MSPB by filing a petition for review within *35 calendar days* of the date of the initial decision (not the date you receive it). If you do not file your PFR from the initial decision to the MSPB within this time period, the initial decision will become the final decision of the MSPB.

TIP

Late filing of a PFR is subject to the same "good cause" excuse discussed above regarding filing the appeal.

Final MSPB decisions, either by the full MSPB after a review of your PFR, or if you let your initial decision become final by not appealing to the full Board, are appealable to the U.S. Court of Appeals for the Federal Circuit located in Washington, DC. An appeal to the Federal Circuit is due *60 days* after the MSPB decision becomes final. An MSPB decision will only be reversed by the Federal Circuit if it was arbitrary and capricious, an erroneous interpretation of law, or not supported by the evidence.

TIP

The Federal Circuit almost always sustains the MSPB's decisions!

What if I claimed discrimination as an affirmative defense? If you claimed discrimination as an affirmative defense you can have the MSPB's decision reviewed by the EEOC. (See the discussion of "mixed cases" following.) If you want court review, you may not file with the Federal Circuit. Instead, you must file a complaint in the U.S. district court having jurisdiction over your employing office.[11] You may be entitled to a jury trial on your discrimination claim.

The district court will review your discrimination claim *de novo*, i.e., as if your MSPB hearing never occurred. However, the civil service issues raised in your MSPB appeal will only be reviewed "on the record" by the district court judge like the Federal Circuit would. You are not entitled to a jury trial on these civil service issues.

What are "mixed cases?"

A "mixed case" is any case in which an employee alleges that an adverse action was based, in whole or in part, on prohibited discrimination. The MSPB appeal you file must contain all of the items required in a routine MSPB appeal, as discussed above, plus the following:

- an allegation that discrimination occurred, describing the type of discrimination, for example, race, sex, national origin, religion, age, disability, genetic information, or retaliation for your earlier EEO activity
- a description of how the discrimination occurred
- if you have filed a grievance or EEO complaint, any action taken by the agency in response

Do I have to choose between the MSPB and EEO? If you have received a personnel action which is directly appealable to the MSPB and you are

[11] *See Kloeckner v. Solis*, 133 S.Ct. 596 (2012).

raising an allegation of discrimination, you have a choice to make as to how and where to appeal the action. This choice is referred to as an "election of remedies." You have the following choices:

- file your appeal with the MSPB, just as you would any other appeal described above. Your appeal to the MSPB is due *30 calendar days* from the effective date of the personnel action

- pursue your appeal through the administrative process for investigating complaints of discrimination under regulations issued by the EEOC. (See Chapter 6.) Remember that to start the EEO process you must first contact the EEO counselor within *45 days* of when you learned of the discriminatory event

Regardless of which procedure you select, the hearing of the personnel action will be conducted by the MSPB, and does not go to the EEOC for a hearing. What's the difference between the two? If you elect the EEOC route, your agency is supposed to conduct an investigation of your allegations of discrimination. If it does, then by the time you get to the hearing, you might have received affidavits and other evidence from the agency that you would have had to obtain on your own if you filed your appeal directly with the MSPB.

If you elect the EEO route, you will still have to file an appeal with the MSPB at some point. If the agency has issued a final decision on your discrimination complaint (remember, there is no EEOC hearing before

---

TIP

When do you file an EEO complaint rather than file with the MSPB first? In most cases, it makes sense to file your complaint directly with the MSPB. You will generally get a faster decision. However, if your appeal needs discovery that you cannot afford, pursuing the EEO route may, through the investigation done by the agency, provide you with information that will better enable you to pursue your claim. However, because it is well recognized that many investigations are incomplete, do not overestimate this advantage. Also, if you missed the short 30-day time limit to appeal to the MSPB, your "mixed case" appeal may still be timely if you contact an EEO counselor within 45 days.

---

this decision is issued), you must file your MSPB appeal within *30 days* of receiving the agency's final decision. Or, if more than *120 days* have passed since you filed your formal EEO complaint and your agency has not yet issued a decision, you may file your MSPB appeal at any time until the agency finally issues the decision, at which time you would then have *30 days* to file the MSPB appeal.[12]

Can the EEOC review my MSPB decision?

You may ask the EEOC to review a final decision of the MSPB in a mixed case where the MSPB does not find discrimination. The EEOC's review primarily focuses on the MSPB's analysis of discrimination issues. This is done by filing a "petition for review" with the EEOC. The rules about filing a petition for review with the EEOC are rather strict and are as follows:

- the petition must be filed within *30 days* of receipt of the final MSPB decision or within *30 days* after an MSPB initial decision becomes final
- it must be sent to the Office of Federal Operations, Equal Employment Opportunity Commission, P.O. Box 77960, Washington, DC 20013
- it must be sent by certified mail, return receipt requested
- copies of the petition must be served on all parties and on the Clerk of the Board, MSPB, 1615 M Street, NW, Washington, DC 20419
- it must contain a signed statement showing the date you served a copy on all parties and the manner of service (for example, hand delivered, first-class mail)

If the EEOC disagrees with the MSPB and finds discrimination, the EEOC will send the decision back to the MSPB, and the MSPB will adopt the EEOC's finding of discrimination.

What are "constructive adverse actions?"

Constructive adverse actions primarily consist of constructive removals and constructive suspensions. For example, a constructive removal, usually a resignation or a retirement, occurs when you initiate a personnel action

[12] If you have separate EEO claims pending at the time you file a "mixed case" at the EEO office, the two cases shouldn't mix. Mixed cases and non-mixed cases have different deadlines and should be processed separately, and you retain the ability, when the time comes, to take the non-"mixed case" claims to the EEOC for a hearing rather than the MSPB. If your agency's EEO office attempts to mix the claims together or to insist that all claims should go to the MSPB for hearing, be sure to object in writing.

seemingly voluntarily, but later claim that the action was, in reality, involuntary. A "voluntary" action may be deemed involuntary if it was based on agency duress or coercion, or when the decision was based on erroneous or incomplete information supplied by an agency.

EXAMPLE 1. You are considering retiring and ask your agency to compute the day you will first be eligible for an immediate annuity. The agency computes the day, and you retire on that date. Several months after not receiving an annuity, you learn from OPM that you were six months short of retirement eligibility. Because you retired in reliance on erroneous information supplied by the agency, your seemingly voluntary retirement is, in reality, involuntary, as you would not have retired had you known you were not eligible for an immediate annuity.

EXAMPLE 2. An agency wants to get rid of you as an alleged problem employee. At 5:00 p.m. on a Friday, you are called into your supervisor's office and told that if you do not resign immediately you will be fired and your career ruined, with no likelihood of being hired by the federal government again. The agency has not issued a proposal of removal and refuses your requests to see the evidence against you and to have the weekend to think the matter over. In fear, you tender your resignation. Because your resignation was coerced, it will likely be deemed involuntary.

EXAMPLE 3. An employee is the victim of recurring severe and pervasive sexual harassment, which continues even after she has complained to management. As a result she suffers severe emotional distress. Working conditions become so intolerable she is forced to resign.

Suspensions can also be the subject of adverse action appeals when the agency has put you on leave status against your will. The theory is that if the agency mandates that you not work when you desire to, and are able to, you have been constructively suspended. An example would be if the agency determines you are unable to perform your job because of a physical disability.

If the enforced leave is for a period of more than fourteen days, then you may have a suspension that is appealable to the MSPB. The MSPB will usually examine the circumstances that led to your absence to determine whether it was self or agency initiated and whether there was work you could perform within the particular medical restrictions you have presented to the agency. For example, your doctor said you could go back to work but couldn't lift more than twenty-five pounds. The agency then said it had no work that fit this requirement and mandated that you take sick leave. Such a case is ripe for appeal to the Board as soon as the enforced leave goes beyond fourteen days.

In the case of constructive adverse actions, the MSPB appeal should be filed within *30 days* of when you first had reason to believe that the action was involuntary. Almost every constructive adverse action involves the issue of whether the appeal was timely filed (prior to the *30-day* deadline for filing an appeal). This is so because most of these appeals tend to be filed more than 30 days after a resignation or retirement. Be prepared to submit an affidavit to the MSPB judge indicating when you became aware that your resignation/retirement was involuntary and when you became aware that you had 30 days to file an MSPB appeal.

It is generally very difficult to prove that your resignation was involuntary. The MSPB rarely finds the situation so intolerable or coercive as to be considered a constructive discharge.

TIP

If you have any doubts at all about whether your retirement or resignation was involuntary, you must exercise "due diligence" to find out what your rights are by contacting a personnel official, union representative, attorney, or other person knowledgeable about federal personnel issues, and then, act promptly. If you fail to act to protect your rights, your MSPB appeal may be dismissed for untimeliness, no matter how good a case you have.

What about shortened notice periods and indefinite suspensions?

The normal requirement that you be given *30 days* advance notice before the agency takes an adverse action does not always apply. Under a section of the statute[13] referred to as "the crime provision," if an agency has a reasonable cause to believe that you committed a crime for which a prison sentence may be imposed, the agency need only give you *7 days* notice before taking an adverse action.

---

13 *See* 5 USC § 7513 (b)(1).

The crime provision also provides for an indefinite suspension. This allows an agency to suspend you without pay for an indefinite or indeterminate period of time. Again, the agency need only give you *7 days* notice of its proposal to indefinitely suspend and the reasons for the proposal when the crime provision is invoked.

You must be given the opportunity to respond. In order to propose an indefinite suspension, the agency must have reasonable cause to believe that a crime has been committed for which a sentence of imprisonment may be imposed. Your agency can also suspend you indefinitely if your security clearance has been revoked.

The decision to indefinitely suspend you must be subject to some specific act (a "condition subsequent") which will end the suspension, such as the results of a criminal trial. If at the time of that condition subsequent you are restored to duty, you do not receive back pay for the time of the suspension. If the agency delays in returning you to duty, then you may be entitled to some measure of back pay.

The indefinite suspension procedures also apply if your required security clearance has been provisionally revoked until a final decision on your clearance is made.

What about adverse actions based on loss of security clearance and "Non-Critical Sensitive" eligibility?

Perhaps the most common circumstance where agencies use interim suspensions is cases where an employee's security clearance has been suspended pending further investigation by the agency's security office. Proposed indefinite suspensions in security clearance cases must give the normal 30 days advance notice and an opportunity to respond, unless the crime provision would independently apply. Generally, employees have no due process to present their response to the proposed suspension to someone with authority to reverse the security clearance determination.[14] However, if an agency's regulations provide greater procedural protection to employees, then the agency must follow the terms of its own regulations.[15] Also, if the agency's policies give the deciding official the option of placing the employee on paid leave while the security clearance suspension is on appeal, or the option of reassigning the employee to a non-security clearance

[14] *Cf. Gargiulo v. Dept. of Homeland Security*, 727 F.3d 1181 (Fed.Cir. 2013).

[15] *See, e.g., Jones v. Dept. of the Navy*, 2014 MSPB 10 (2014); *Ulep v. Dept. of the Army*, 2014 MSPB 9 (2014).

position, then the employee has a due process right to ask to be kept in paid status (whether paid administrative leave or reassignment) in his or her response to the proposed indefinite suspension.[16] Unfortunately, even if the security clearance is later reinstated, the employee is unable to receive back pay during the period of indefinite suspension.[17] If your agency puts you on administrative leave pending a security clearance determination, you cannot appeal that determination.

All adverse actions in the security clearance context (including removals, demotions and indefinite suspensions) are difficult to challenge, as under current Supreme Court caselaw, the MSPB cannot look at the legitimacy of the security clearance revocation, only whether or not the proper procedures have been followed.[18] This exception was recently expanded by the courts to apply not only to adverse actions based on loss of security clearances in the most formal sense, but also to adverse actions due to an agency's decision to rescind qualification for 'non-critical sensitive' and similar non-security clearance eligibilities.[19] If the Agency fails to provide advance notice and a chance to respond, or otherwise fails to follow its own procedures in issuing the adverse action or in processing the denial of security or other qualification, then the adverse action may be legally defective and subject to reversal on appeal.[20] Absent such technical procedural violations, under current caselaw, the MSPB and the courts are likely to rubber-stamp the agency's adverse actions. Employees facing such adverse actions are thus advised to focus their efforts to appealing decisions concerning their security clearance revocation, or loss of eligibility for 'non-critical sensitive' positions through whatever appeal mechanism may be available.[21] See Chapter 10 for a discussion of security clearance issues and 'non-critical sensitive' positions.

---

16 *See Buelna v. Dept. of Homeland Security,* 2014 MSPB 45 (2014).

17 *See Biggers v. Dept. of the Navy,* ___ F.3d ___, Case No. 2013-3059 (Fed.Cir. March 21, 2014); *Jones v. Dept. of the Navy*, 978 F.2d 1223 (Fed. Cir. 1992).

18 *See Dept. of the Navy v. Egan,* 484 U.S. 518 (1988); *Gargiulo v. Dept. of Homeland Security,* 727 F.3d 1181 (Fed.Cir. 2013).

19 *See Kaplan v. Conyers et. al.*, 733 F.3d 1148 (Fed. Cir. 2013), *cert. denied sub nom. Northover v. Archuleta,* 572 U.S. ____, Case No. 13-607 (March 31, 2014).

20 *See Romero v. Dept. of Defense,* 527 F.3d 1324 (Fed. Cir. 2008); *Ulep v. Dept. of the Army,* 2014 MSPB 9 (2014).

21 Individuals who believe that their security clearance revocation is in retaliation for whistleblowing may have an appeal avenue under Presidential Policy Directive 19 (PPD-19). See Chapter 7 for further details.

What about adverse actions based on "Suitability" issues?

Under Office of Personnel Management (OPM) Regulations, persons joining federal service can be subjected to adverse actions for issues unrelated to work misconduct (issues deemed to render the individual 'unsuitable' for federal employment), including:

- misconduct or negligence in employment (current or prior);
- criminal or dishonest conduct (current or prior);
- material, intentional false statement, or deception or fraud in examination or appointment;
- refusal to furnish testimony in certain administrative proceedings;
- alcohol abuse, without evidence of substantial rehabilitation;
- illegal use of narcotics, drugs, or other controlled substances without evidence of substantial rehabilitation;
- knowing and willful engagement in acts or activities designed to overthrow the U.S. Government by force; and
- any statutory or regulatory bar which prevents the lawful employment of the person involved in the position in question.[22]

Although these 'suitability' rules are generally associated with the process of appointing an individual into federal service, the suitability action can take place long after the employee starts work.[23] Individuals found not to meet these 'suitability' criteria are not only subject to removal, but also possible debarment from federal service for up to three years.[24] Depending on which agency the individual works at or is applying to work for, the 'suitability' –based adverse actions are either proposed and decided on by OPM, or by the employing agency in question.[25] From the employee's or applicant's perspective, the procedure is similar to that for other adverse action as discussed earlier in this chapter: *30 days* advance notice of the charges, opportunity to review the evidence in support of the charge and to respond to the charge (although if OPM is proposing the adverse action, the employing agency also has a chance to file a response to OPM).[26]

Suitability actions are appealable to the Merit Systems Protection Board.[27] If the affected employee has sufficient time in service to otherwise qualify for MSPB appeal rights (that is, they have 1 year of continuous ser-

---

22 *See* 5 CFR § 731.202(b).
23 *See Aguzie and Barnes v. OPM,* 116 MSPR 64 (2011).
24 *See* 5 CFR §§ 731.203, 731.204, 731.205.
25 *See, e.g.,* 5 CFR § 731.103.
26 *See* 5 CFR §§ 731.301 *et seq.*, 731.401 *et seq.*
27 *See* 5 CFR § 731.501.

vice in the competitive service or in the excepted service if they are preference eligible veterans, or if they have 2 years of continuous service in the excepted service otherwise), then the adverse action is deemed to occur under Chapter 75 procedures, and will only be upheld if the removing agency proves that removal meets the "efficiency of the service" standard and is consistent with *Douglas* mitigation factors.[28] If the affected individual does not otherwise qualify for MSPB appeal rights, then their appeal to the MSPB is limited: the removing agency is not required to prove that removal promotes "efficiency of the service", the individual cannot argue for mitigation of the penalty under *Douglas*, and a remanded suitability decision is then subject to a final decision by the removing agency or OPM without further ability to re-appeal to the MSPB.[29]

What are my remedies in MSPB appeals?

If you win your MSPB appeal, you are entitled to a *status quo ante* remedy, that is, you are entitled to be placed in a situation as close as possible to the situation you would have been in had the agency not taken the action against you. For example, in a removal case, you would be entitled to be returned to your position and to receive all the back pay (with interest) and benefits (such as annual and sick leave, health insurance benefits, retirement credit) that you would have received had you not been terminated.

Any income you earned to make up for your lost federal pay while you were terminated must be offset, or deducted, from the amount of back pay to which you are entitled. The remedy of back pay is not supposed to provide you with a "windfall," such as would occur if you were entitled to keep all pay earned elsewhere as well as receiving all of your federal back pay. The calculation of back pay is governed by the Back Pay Act[30] and OPM's implementing regulations. The MSPB does not normally award punitive or compensatory damages. However, in mixed cases where discrimination (other than age discrimination) is proven or cases involving whistleblower reprisal, the MSPB does have authority to award compensatory or consequential damages.

Can I get attorney fees?

If you prevail in your MSPB appeal by obtaining some relief, even if it is not all relief you sought, you may be entitled to reimbursement of reasonable

[28] *See Aguzie and Barnes v. OPM*, 116 MSPR 64 (2011).
[29] *See* 5 CFR § 731.501.
[30] *See* 5 USC § 5596.

attorney fees and costs you incurred in bringing your MSPB appeal. If you had an attorney represent you in the reply to the proposed action before the agency, attorney fees and costs for the reply are also reimbursable.

Attorney fees are not automatic, but are reimbursed under the Back Pay Act if warranted "in the interest of justice." Under well-established MSPB case law, reimbursement of attorney fees is generally warranted in the interest of justice where the agency knew or should have known that it would not prevail in the case, the action taken by the agency was clearly without merit, where the agency committed gross procedural error in taking the action, or where the agency committed a prohibited personnel practice.

Attorney fees are only awarded if you actually had an attorney represent you in the MSPB appeal. If you were successful in a "mixed case" appeal, USERRA or whistleblower reprisal claim, you may be entitled to reimbursement for attorney fees under the discrimination statute you raised, USERRA, or the Whistleblower Protection Act, which might entitle you to higher fees in some circumstances, or reimbursement of costs that the Back Pay Act does not cover.

TIP

Under present MSPB caselaw, attorneys' fees and costs are not awarded unless the MSPB administrative judge issues a decision on the case. Some agencies, in cases they expect to lose, will unilaterally reverse the personnel action—especially at the last minute—to avoid paying attorneys' fees by having the case dismissed as "moot." This "mooting" cannot occur if you are asserting an affirmative defense with compensatory damages (discrimination or whistleblower reprisal). If you have such a claim in your case, you should include it in your original MSPB appeal to prevent this "mooting" tactic.

What about "interim relief?"

If you win your MSPB appeal in the initial decision issued by the administrative judge, keep in mind that the agency can appeal to the full Board by filing a petition for review. However, in that event, the agency must still afford you "interim relief," that is, you must be returned to your former position and to the agency's rolls unless the agency claims to the Board that returning you to your position would create an undue hardship. In that event, the agency must still return you to the payroll, although you may still be kept off the job.

Compliance with MSPB decisions

Agencies are obligated to comply with MSPB orders. If you prevail in your MSPB appeal, the order attached to the MSPB decision will specify the deadlines by which the agency must complete certain actions (such as cancelling a demotion, or reinstating a terminated employee). The agency is supposed to send you a notice telling you exactly what actions it has taken to comply with the MSPB's order. If the agency does not take all the action it was supposed to, you must file a petition for enforcement with the MSPB regional office within *30 days* of the date the agency sent its notice of alleged compliance with the order. Or, if the agency does not send a notice of compliance at all, you must file a petition for enforcement within *30 days* of the date you "knew or should have known" that the agency did not comply with the order. You must include a statement of why you believe the agency has not complied with the order. The agency may respond to your petition for enforcement within *15 days* of your filing it, and you may reply to the agency's response within *10 days* of the date of the agency's response. The MSPB administrative judge may simply issue a decision finding the agency in compliance or not, or may hold a hearing to decide the issue.

Compliance with settlement agreements

If the agency fails to comply with a settlement agreement, you can seek enforcement of the agreement with the MSPB. If the MSPB has jurisdiction over your appeal, you should ask the judge to enter the settlement agreement into the MSPB record of the case for enforcement in the event of a later compliance issue. The best practice is to put a provision right into the settlement that you and the agency both agree that the settlement should be made part of the MSPB's record for enforcement purposes. Usually, settlement agreements will require you to notify the agency that you believe it has not complied with the settlement agreement within *30 days* of the date you "knew or should have known" that the agency had failed to comply before you file a petition for enforcement with the MSPB. Then, if the agency fails to correct the issue, you can file a petition for enforcement of the settlement agreement within *30 days* of the agency's refusal to correct the issue, or, if the agency does not respond at all, within *30 days* of the date you sent your notice to the agency alleging non-compliance. You must include a statement of why you believe the agency has not complied with the settlement agreement. The agency may respond to your petition for enforcement within *15 days* of your filing it, and you may reply to the agency's response within *10 days* of the date of the agency's response. The MSPB administrative judge may simply issue a decision finding the agency in compliance or not, or may hold a hearing to decide the issue. If the judge finds that the agency did not comply with the agreement, you can request either that

1. the agency be required to comply with all terms of the agreement; or
2. that your case be reinstated at the same stage of the process it was in when the parties reached settlement.[31]

Can I enforce my settlement agreement in court?

If your settlement agreement provides that you will receive monetary relief which the agency has failed to pay to you, or if the breach of the settlement agreement has resulted in monetary harm, you may seek enforcement of those provisions that relate to monetary relief in the U.S. Court of Federal Claims. You cannot seek enforcement in court of any provisions of the agreement that relate to equitable (non-monetary) relief (such as changes to a performance rating, restoration of leave, etc.).[32]

TIP

If you feel the Agency has not complied with an MSPB order, or has not met the terms of a settlement agreement DO NOT WAIT – immediately seek advice on initiating a petition for enforcement, and make sure the petition is submitted by the deadline.

---

[31] *See Lutz v. USPS*, 108 MSPR 695, 699-700 (2/28/08).

[32] *See Cunningham v. United States,* C.A.F.C. No. 2013-5055 (4/9/14).

What happens with other categories of employees?

Probationary Employees

Employees who are in their probationary period do not receive the same advance notice and chance-to-respond procedures as do employees who have completed their probationary period. Instead, probationers can be subjected to immediate termination or other adverse actions. The agency is required to provide a notice specifically describing the reasons for the termination.[33]

Once terminated, probationary employees can only appeal directly to the MSPB if they allege that they were discriminated against on the basis of marital status or partisan political affiliation.[34] However, probationary employees can challenge discrimination and EEO reprisal in their removal through the normal federal sector EEO complaints process described in Chapter 6, and are not covered by the "mixed case" procedure discussed above. Probationers can also challenge whistleblower reprisal through the Independent Right of Action process described in Chapter 7, or under USERRA as described in Chapter 19.

TIP

Agencies seeking to remove probationers often implement the removal near the end of the probationary period. Sometimes, agencies will miscalculate the end of the probationary period, removing an employee who just completed his/her probationary period. If you are removed as a probationer near the end of your probationary period, be sure to discuss the effective dates for your appointment and removal with a union representative or attorney. Be sure to tell your attorney or representative of any immediately preceding federal positions you held as that time may count toward satisfying your probationary period.

---

[33] *See* 5 CFR § 315.804(a).

[34] *See* 5 CFR § 315.806(c).

Postal Service employees

Two categories of employees of the U.S. Postal Service have adverse action appeal rights to the MSPB:

- preference-eligible veterans with at least one year of current, continuous service in the same or a similar position
- supervisory/managerial employees with at least one year of current, continuous service in the same or a similar position

Many other Postal Service employees who do not have MSPB appeal rights are nonetheless covered by union contracts and may grieve and arbitrate such disciplinary actions. For a more complete discussion of Postal Service employees see Chapter 25.

Other categories of employees

There are various other categories of federal employees who do not have MSPB rights, because Congress has not granted them or has taken them away.

For discussion of several of these other special categories, see Chapter 26 (for Congressional employees and employees of the Executive Office of the President) and Chapter 29 (for other employees covered by special rules). If you are in doubt about whether you have MSPB appeal rights or other appeal rights, consult with a knowledgeable personnel official, union representative, or attorney.

Final Thoughts

Every disciplinary action must be taken very seriously because of the consequences to your career. This chapter has provided you with guidance on how to handle such a situation and informed you of the appeal process. It is generally best that you consult with someone who is knowledgeable about federal personnel rules and the disciplinary procedures before you make any irrevocable decisions. Above all do not panic! You can prevail over an unjust discipline.

5

Discrimination: What It Is and How To Prove It

Can't We All Just Get Along?

In This Chapter You Will Learn:

- what laws protect federal employees from discrimination
- what kind of employment discrimination is illegal
- whether accommodation of your disability may be required
- the legal definition of sexual harassment
- how to determine if actions toward you have been discriminatory
- what kind of evidence can be used to show discrimination

Contents Chapter Five - Discrimination: What it is and How to Prove it

INTRODUCTION

As an employee, you are protected by federal anti-discrimination laws.[1] The laws prohibit agencies from taking action against any employee on the basis of the following: race, religion, color, national origin, sex, age, disability, genetic information, and reprisal. Such improper acts are referred to as "discrimination."[2]

In this chapter we will discuss the legal bases of employment discrimination and see who is and is not covered by the federal statutes that prohibit employment discrimination.

In general, you are protected by these laws only if you fall into the category or "protected class" of persons that the law protects. For instance, the Age Discrimination in Employment Act ("ADEA") only covers employees age 40 or older. Of course it takes more than a mere claim of discrimination to prevail. You must prove that you were the victim of discrimination. In this chapter you will also learn how you can tell if you come within the law and how to prove discrimination.

---

1 This chapter contains some material adopted from Chapters 9 and 11 of Workplace Fairness' book *Job Rights and Survival Strategies, A Handbook for Terminated Employees* by Paul H. Tobias and Susan Sauter. Some of the material was also reprinted July 27, 1997 in a *National Business Employment Weekly* article written by Tobias and Sauter and is used here with permission of the publishers and authors.

2 Actions taken against employees based on other factors, such as union membership or whistleblowing, are dealt with in the specific chapters concerning these subjects.

What is Title VII of the Civil Rights Act of 1964?

Title VII of the Civil Rights Act of 1964 protects employees from discrimination in employment on the bases of sex, race, color, religion, national origin, or reprisal. Sexual harassment, pregnancy discrimination, and gender stereotyping are forms of prohibited sex discrimination. Federal employees are covered by Title VII of the Act.

Discrimination on the basis of race, color, national origin, or gender

Illegal discrimination occurs when an employer treats one employee differently from another employee when the two are similarly situated except for one of the categories or bases above. Illegal discrimination also occurs when an employer takes some adverse action, such as discipline or a reduction-in-force, based on a bias or prejudice that the employer has against a trait or characteristic of the employee that is identified in Title VII. Finally, illegal discrimination occurs when an employer's employment decisions or policies, although seemingly neutral, adversely impact one class of persons more harshly than another and the reason for the harsher impact is related to one of the protected categories above.

Discrimination is illegal under Title VII only when the difference in treatment, or bias, is intentional and based on one or more factors that the law prohibits an agency from considering. If an employment policy or decision adversely impacts a class of employees, the policy is illegal only if the class affected is a class protected by law. These classes are often referred to in the law as "protected categories" or "protected groups."

Example: Several people apply for a promotion. One of the applicants, Applicant A, is an Iraqi by birth. The agency decides to hire Applicant B because Applicant B has two more years of experience, but also because the agency fears the Iraqi-American employee would not be accepted by other employees. By taking the employee's national origin into account in making its decision, the agency has violated Title VII.

Example: A supervisor makes demeaning remarks to an employee of Asian heritage, repeatedly, over a long period of time, because the supervisor does not like Asians. That supervisor is acting against an employee because of the employee's national origin. Such conduct is prohibited. Even if the Asian employee is not terminated, the harassment based on national origin violates the law.

TIP

Not all discrimination is forbidden by the Civil Rights Act. For example a victim of discrimination because of a "personality" dispute with a supervisor will have no claim unless the mistreatment motive is race, color, religion, sex, age, disability, national origin, genetic information, or reprisal.

Discrimination is not always based on disparate (different) treatment of an individual employee. Discrimination can also occur when an employer makes an employment decision which seems to be free from discrimination and based on neutral factors, but the effect adversely impacts a protected group more severely than a non-protected group.

Example: An agency adopts a policy not to renew the term appointments of employees without a four-year college degree although the positions do not require a college degree. In this agency, 15% of the 100 African-American employees have four-year degrees, while 80% of the 100 white employees do. The agency's policy results in a disproportionately large percentage of African Americans being terminated from employment (85% of the African Americans and 20% of the whites). Unless the agency can show a legitimate business necessity for the policy, the policy is unlawful because of its "disparate impact" on African Americans, race being a protected category under Title VII.

Sex discrimination

Sex discrimination involves treating someone (an applicant or employee) unfavorably because of that person's sex. Sex discrimination also can involve treating someone less favorably because of his or her connection with an organization or group that is generally associated with people of a certain sex.

Discrimination against an individual because that person is transgender is discrimination because of sex in violation of Title VII. This is also known as gender identity discrimination. In addition, lesbian, gay, and bisexual individuals may bring sex discrimination claims. These may include, for example, allegations of sexual harassment or other kinds of sex discrimination, such as adverse actions taken because of the person's non-conformance with sex-stereotypes.

Religious discrimination

Title VII prohibits discrimination against an employee because of that employee's religion or lack of religion. Religion should have no bearing on hiring, firing, other disciplinary action, or any other decisions affecting career advancement. Harassment of an employee based on the employee's religious affiliation also violates Title VII.

Am I entitled to reasonable accommodation for my religion? Religion is different from the other Title VII categories which only prohibit employment discrimination. When it comes to religion, agencies are also required to provide reasonable accommodations to employees with a conflict between their religion and their job unless doing so would impose an undue hardship on the employer. Incurring more than minimal direct or indirect expense can be considered an "undue hardship" in this case.

Similarly, an agency need not change an established seniority system or violate a collective bargaining agreement in order to accommodate an employee who, for example, cannot work on Saturday. If a requested accommodation for religion requires more than minimal change, expense, or effort, the agency may successfully argue that accommodation of the request would constitute an undue hardship.

TIP

If you need an accommodation for religion, it is your responsibility to ask for it. Your request should be in writing. If your requested accommodation is denied, ask why it was denied. If the explanation does not appear to be reasonable or accurate, or the agency has not shown undue hardship, you may be the victim of religious discrimination.

Is it illegal to discriminate against me because of my age?

The Age Discrimination in Employment Act (ADEA) prohibits discrimination based on age against federal employees aged 40 years or older. Similar to the anti-discrimination provisions of Title VII, the ADEA prohibits an employer from treating an employee who is 40 or older differently than an employee under 40 because of the older employee's age. The ADEA was designed to eliminate the termination of older employees, and the refusal to hire older employees, based on stigmatizing and false stereotypes about older workers, for instance, that they are less adaptable to change, are out of touch with modern technology, or slower than younger employees in doing their jobs.

Evidence of age discrimination includes age-biased remarks, statistical evidence showing an agency or department pattern of older workers being disproportionately terminated, retention of less qualified, younger employees doing the same job, other older workers victimized by the same decision-maker, or replacement by younger employees.

Is it illegal to discriminate against me on the basis of my pay and compensation?

The Equal Pay Act requires that men and women in the same workplace be given equal pay for equal work. The jobs need not be identical, but they must be substantially equal. Job content, not job titles, determines whether jobs are substantially equal. All forms of pay are covered by this law, including salary, overtime pay, bonuses, stock options, profit sharing and bonus plans, life insurance, vacation and holiday pay, cleaning or gasoline allowances, hotel accommodations, reimbursement for travel expenses, and benefits. If there is an inequality in wages between men and women, employers may not reduce the wages of either sex to equalize their pay.

If you allege a violation of the EPA, you may go directly to court. You are not required to file an EEO complaint if you are a federal sector employee, or an EEOC charge if you are a private sector employee, before going to court.

The time limit for filing an EPA charge with the EEOC and the time limit for going to court are the same: within two years of the alleged unlawful compensation practice or, in the case of a willful violation, within three years. The filing of an EEOC charge under the EPA does not extend the time frame for going to court.

Equal Pay/Compensation and Sex Discrimination

Title VII also makes it illegal to discriminate based on sex in pay and benefits. Therefore, someone who has an Equal Pay Act claim may also have a claim under Title VII.

Other types of discrimination

Title VII, the ADEA, and the ADA prohibit compensation discrimination on the basis of race, color, religion, sex, national origin, age, or disability.

Unlike the EPA, there is no requirement under Title VII, the ADEA, or the ADA that the jobs must be substantially equal.

The burdens of proof under the EPA are different than under the other anti-discrimination statutes; Title VII, ADEA, ADA. Under the EPA, the employee only needs to demonstrate a sex-based wage disparity in substantially equal jobs. If the employer cannot rebut that, the employer must show that the disparity is based on an affirmative defense such as a seniority, merit, or incentive system, or on any other factor other than sex.

Is it illegal for an employer to discriminate against me if I am disabled?

The Rehabilitation Act of 1973 prohibits employment discrimination against federal employees with a disability who can otherwise perform the job. The American with Disabilities Act of 1990 and the ADA Amendments Act of 2008 apply the same standards as the Rehabilitation Act to federal and private sector employees. Job applicants as well as current employees are protected by these Acts. For purposes of the Act, a "disability" is defined as a physical or mental condition that substantially limits you in a major life activity. Only those with permanent, chronic, or long-term conditions are considered disabled. The physical or mental condition must be more than temporary, but it does not have to be incurable. Short-term disability that results from an accident such as a broken arm or illness such as the flu does not qualify as a disability.

The law protects you if you

- currently have a disability
- have a record of having a disability, or
- are perceived as having a disability, even if you do not. There is a perceived disability when the agency sees or regards an employee as disabled regardless of the employee's actual condition or qualifications.

To be considered substantially limited in a major life activity, your limitation must be more than marginal, but less than debilitating. Whether a disability is substantially limiting is determined on a case-by-case basis. There are no rigid rules that will tell you whether or not a particular disability is substantially limiting or not. If you think that your disability fits into the law, ask your agency to accommodate your disability. If the agency does not do so, and you think you have a good case, pursue your rights under the law.

Major life activities include caring for oneself, performing manual tasks, seeing, hearing, eating, sleeping, walking, standing, lifting, bending, speaking, breathing, learning, reading, concentrating, thinking, and communicating. Major life activities also include the operation of a major bodily function, including but not limited to, functions of the immune system, normal cell growth, digestive, bowel, bladder, neurological, brain, respiratory, circulatory, endocrine, and reproductive functions. Working is also a major life function in a broad sense. If your physical or mental condition prevents you from working in a class or broad range of jobs in various classes, your disability could affect the major life activity of working. If the disability prevents you from performing only a limited class of jobs, your disability may not be considered to limit you in the major life activity of working. In other words, if your illness prevents you only from working for a particular supervisor or in a particular building, you most likely will *not* qualify as a disabled person under the law.

The law may also protect those with mental impairments that affect major life functions, for example, someone with a learning disorder, clinical depression, or schizophrenia. A physical or mental impairment can be a disability even if it is episodic or in remission such as epilepsy, MS, diabetes or schizophrenia. Also, the effect of corrective measures, such as medication or prosthetics, is not considered when determining if an impairment is a disability. The law covers persons with an alcohol or drug addiction so long as they are not currently using drugs or alcohol. You cannot be fired because you are a recovering alcoholic. However, you can be fired for being under the influence of alcohol on your job.

Of course, like the other discrimination laws, the Rehabilitation Act requires that you be qualified for your job in order to be protected from discrimination. This means that you are able to perform the essential functions or elements of your job (or the one you are applying for) either with or without some form of accommodation. If you cannot perform the essential functions of the job no matter what accommodations the employer makes for you, you are not a "qualified" individual with a disability with respect to that position. The agency may be required, however, to restructure your position or take away less essential duties as part of its obligation to reasonably accommodate you. This is discussed in more detail below.

Do I have a right to reasonable accommodation for my disability?

The Rehabilitation Act requires that agencies provide "reasonable accommodation" for the known disabilities of their employees to enable an employee to perform the essential functions of a job, unless to do so would be an undue hardship for the employer. Unlike Title VII, which has a low standard for determining undue hardship for religious accommodation, the law requires the employer to do more to try to accommodate the disabled employee. "Reasonable accommodation" refers to an agency's obligation to make adjustments to your work situation or environment so that you can perform your job even with your disability. Reasonable accommodations could take the form of restructuring your job duties, providing you with special equipment to enable you to perform your job, modifying your work schedule, altering the physical workplace, providing an assistant (such as an interpreter for a deaf employee), eliminating nonessential functions of the position, or placing you in a vacant position for which you are qualified. Just what accommodations are "reasonable" depends on the circumstances of each case. Generally, the employee has the obligation to first request reasonable accommodation and to suggest possible accommodations to management.

Do I have to provide medical information to the agency?

You should engage in an informal interactive process with the agency to identify the appropriate reasonable accommodation. The agency can ask you relevant questions that will enable it to make an informed decision regarding an accommodation. The agency may need to ask questions concerning the nature of your disability and your functional limitations in order to identify an effective accommodation. While you do not have to be able to specify a precise accommodation, you do need to describe the problems posed by the workplace barrier. If the disability and the need for an accommodation is not obvious, the agency may ask you for information about your disability and your functional limitations in order to identify an effective accommodation.

The agency can ask for documentation in order to establish that you have a disability and that the disability necessitates a reasonable accommodation. Thus, an agency, in response to a request for reasonable accommodation, cannot ask for documentation that is unrelated to determining the existence of a disability and the necessity for an accommodation. This means that in most situations the agency cannot request your complete medical records because they are likely to contain information unrelated to the disability at issue and the need for accommodation. If you have more than one disability, the agency can request information pertaining only to the disability that requires a reasonable accommodation.

TIP

Requests for reasonable accommodation for disability should be put in writing to the appropriate agency official so that you have a record of the request for any possible EEO complaint over the agency's failure to grant your request.

When is reassignment required?

Reassignment is a form of reasonable accommodation that must be provided, absent undue hardship, to an employee who, because of a disability, can no longer perform the essential functions of the position s/he holds, with or without reasonable accommodation. Reassignment is a "last resort" accommodation that must be considered if there are no effective accommodations that would enable the employee to perform the essential functions of his/her current job, or if all other possible accommodations would impose undue hardship.

Reassignment is available only to current employees, not to applicants for employment. In addition, reassignment may be made only to a vacant position. The law does not require that agencies create new positions or move employees from their jobs in order to create a vacancy.

If your agency terminated you because it claimed it could not accommodate your disability or otherwise fails to accommodate your disability, you may have been the victim of prohibited discrimination. Be familiar with the EEOC's procedures, discussed in Chapter 6, and MSPB appeals of "mixed cases," discussed in Chapter 4.

Is it illegal to discriminate against me based on my genetic information?

The Genetic Information Nondiscrimination Act of 2008 (GINA) prohibits the use of an employee's genetic information in any aspect of employment including hiring, firing, pay, assignments, promotions, etc. Genetic information is information about an individual's genetic tests, genetic tests of family members, and family medical history. GINA prohibits an employer from intentionally acquiring genetic information about applicants and employees. GINA strictly limits the disclosure of an employee's genetic information. Therefore, employees are protected against discrimination because of impairments they might develop, such as carpal tunnel syndrome or types of cancer, because of their family medical history or genetic information. Under GINA, genetic information may never be used to make an employment decision because it does not tell an employer anything about an employee's current ability to work. GINA also prohibits harassment of an employee because his/her genetic information. Harassment can include making offensive or derogatory remarks about an employee's genetic information.

What is sexual harassment?

Employees have the right to be free of unwelcome, pervasive, or severe sexual misconduct.

Unwelcome sexual advances, requests for sexual favors, and other verbal or physical conduct of a sexual nature constitute sexual harassment when (1) submission to such conduct is made either explicitly or implicitly a term or condition of your employment, (2) submission to or rejection of such conduct is used as the basis for employment decisions affecting you, or (3) such conduct has the purpose or effect of unreasonably interfering with your work performance or creating an intimidating, hostile, or offensive working environment. Both the victim and the harasser can be either a woman or a man, and the victim and the harasser can be the same sex. In 1998, the U.S. Supreme Court determined that same-gender sexual harassment is also prohibited under Title VII.

Sex/gender stereotyping is illegal

Sex stereotyping based on sexual orientation is illegal under Title VII. Sexual harassment which involves offensive and derogatory comments based on an individual's actual or perceived sexual orientation is illegal.

For example, a gay man who was harassed because he intended to marry a man and not a woman was found to state a claim of hostile work environment sexual harassment. A female who was harassed on the job and called derogatory names based on her perceived sexual orientation was found to state a claim of hostile work environment sexual harassment. A man who was harassed because he did not conform with traditional male stereotypes also was found to state a claim of hostile work environment sexual harassment.

Similarly, courts have held that discrimination and harassment on the basis of sex can include individuals who are gay, lesbian, bisexual, heterosexual, or transgender.

When is the agency responsible for sexual harassment?

An agency is strictly liable for sexual harassment by its supervisors, where the employee suffers some tangible employment action, such as termination, demotion, or an adverse change in working conditions due to the harassment. If harassment does not result in tangible job detriment, the agency is still liable unless it can show:

- the agency used reasonable care to prevent and correct any harassment
- the employee "unreasonably" failed to complain to management

Merely because engagement in some sexual activity by the victim was "voluntary," is not a defense when sexual advances by a supervisor are not "welcome." The courts have held that sporadic use of abusive language, gender-related jokes, occasional teasing, and isolated incidents (unless extremely serious) do not constitute harassment. The frequency of the misconduct, and its severity (whether it is humiliating or merely offensive), are important factors to be considered. The agency may be liable for the sexual harassment committed not only by supervisors but also coworkers in the event the agency had knowledge of the harassment and did not take adequate steps to correct the situation, for example, by appropriate discipline. Sexual harassment claims often lead to retaliation by the supervisor, which is also a violation of Title VII.

Sexual harassment cases are often hotly contested. If the victim has witnesses or other powerful evidence such as documents, or there is a pattern of misbehavior, the employee can frequently obtain some form of justice through the EEO complaint process as described in the next chapter.

Other protections for sexual orientation and transgender discrimination

The Civil Service Reform Act protects federal government employees and applicants from discrimination in personnel actions (See Chapter 7 PPP). Sexual orientation and transgender (gender identity) discrimination are included under the prohibitions against discrimination in the CSRA. The Office of Special Counsel and the Merit Systems Protection Board enforce the prohibitions against federal employment discrimination in the CSRA. (See Chapter 7: How Do I File an OSC Complaint.)

Executive Order 13087 prohibits discrimination in employment on the basis of sexual orientation. Your agency should have procedures for making a complaint of discrimination under the Executive Order. These procedures are separate from your agency's EEO process and you cannot appeal claims of discrimination under the EO to the EEOC.

If you are a member of a union, your collective bargaining agreement might also contain procedures for filing a grievance on the basis of sexual orientation and transgender discrimination.

Evidence of discrimination

In order to determine if you have been discriminated against, you must first evaluate the evidence. Evidence is the facts, such as actions, statements, or documents. Your personal opinions do not constitute evidence. Make sure you are dealing with objective facts, that is, what can be seen, heard, or determined by someone other than yourself.

For instance, suppose you think that because you are a male you did not get a performance award you deserved. It may be true, but you must be able to show discrimination based on some fact that all can see. For example, show that everyone with your qualifications, longevity, and ratings received an award except you, and all of the others are female and you are male. When we feel that we have been victims of discrimination, it is an emotional situation. We may have "gut feelings," but an outside objective observer may have another explanation. Keep things in their proper prospective. Your subjective feelings and speculations about discrimination are not evidence. What happened to create those feelings and beliefs may be. Analyze the actual hard facts before determining whether to go forward. After all, those who review the matter will not be in your head and have your feelings. They will only be able to rely on observable evidence.

Evidence can be direct or circumstantial. It is always best to have direct evidence. However, circumstantial evidence may work well, too. For example, when you wake up in the morning and there is snow on the ground, you can infer from "circumstantial evidence" that it snowed the night before. Similarly, you can also infer intentional discrimination from hard evidence such as differing treatment of similarly situated employees.

Direct evidence

"Direct evidence" is the best way to show discrimination. It includes statements by managers or supervisors that directly relate the action against you to your protected class status. For example, if an agency manager tells you that "you are being RIFd because you are near retirement age and the agency wants to project a younger image," you have direct evidence that your protected class status (age) was the cause of your termination. This evidence can be in the form of verbal comments or statements written in letters, memos, or notes. Evidence of the use of racial or ethnic epithets would constitute "direct evidence." Also, negative comments about your having filed an EEO complaint are direct evidence of reprisal.

Circumstantial evidence

The likelihood of obtaining direct evidence of discrimination is pretty slim. Most agency managers and supervisors are too sophisticated and too well-trained to openly express their biases and prejudices. In almost every case, an employee must rely on circumstantial evidence.

There is a famous U.S. Supreme Court case, *McDonnell Douglas v. Green,*[3] which sets forth the requirements for determining whether there is sufficient circumstantial evidence to support a finding of discrimination in a non-direct evidence case. The "McDonnell Douglas Test" establishes a presumption (or likelihood) of discrimination (also called a "*prima facie* case") if you can answer "yes" to the following four questions:

1. Are you a member of a protected class? For example, if you are claiming age discrimination, are you over forty? If you are claiming disability discrimination, are you disabled?

2. Were you qualified for the position? For example, if your job required certain past job experience, do you have that experience?

3. Did your agency take, or fail to take, some action against you? For instance, were you demoted or terminated? Were you passed over for promotion?

4. Were you replaced by a person who is not in your protected class (or in the case of age discrimination, someone substantially younger than you)?

If you can answer these questions with "yes," then because you were qualified for the job and then disadvantaged in favor of someone not in your protected class, the law will presume that your protected class status was the reason for the agency's action.

The law recognizes that you can be discriminated against even if you are not replaced by someone outside the protected class, for example, during a reduction-in-force, where the job disappears altogether.

---

[3] *See McDonnell Douglas Corp. v. Green,* 411 U.S. 792 (1973).

Positive responses to the following questions will also help you gather sufficient circumstantial evidence to raise a presumption of discrimination:

1. Were you treated differently than a similarly situated person who is not in your protected class?

2. Did managers regularly make rude or derogatory comments directed at your protected class status or at all members of your class and related to work? For example, "Women don't belong on a military base" or "Women are too emotional to make good managers."

3. Are the circumstances of your treatment so unusual, egregious, unjust, or severe as to suggest discrimination?

4. Does your agency have a history of showing bias toward persons in your protected class?

5. Are there noticeably few employees of your protected class at your workplace?

6. Have you noticed that other employees in your protected class complain about discrimination, particularly by the supervisor or manager who took the action against you?

7. Are there statistics in your department or agency that show favoritism towards or bias against any group?

8. Did your agency violate well-established agency policy or rules in the way it treated you?

9. Did your agency favor less qualified, non-protected employees in the same job selection, layoff, or retention decisions?

When evaluating circumstantial evidence, no single piece of evidence is usually enough to prove discrimination. On the other hand, there is no "magic" amount or type of evidence that you must have to prove discrimination.

Countering your agency's denials

When an agency is accused of discrimination, it has the opportunity to offer a legitimate non-discriminatory reason for its conduct. This is not difficult for the agency to do. All that the law requires is that the employer "articulate" or state a reason for its decision. The agency does not have to prove the stated reason is the true reason. Once the agency articulates this reason, your presumption of discrimination is gone and you will have to offer additional evidence, as discussed below.

Assuming that your agency does offer an alternate explanation for terminating your employment, you must next consider whether you can prove that this stated reason is just a pretext, or cover-up, for discrimination. There are several ways to do this. You can show that the stated reason is:

- factually untrue
- insufficient to have actually motivated the decision, or
- so implausible that your agency could not have legitimately relied upon it

You can show that your protected status is more likely to have motivated your agency than the stated reason. You can show other powerful direct or circumstantial evidence of discrimination.

If you can demonstrate any of the above, you may be able to prove that the agency's stated reason is just a cover-up or pretext for discrimination. The law requires that you show not only that the stated reason is false, but that the unlawful factor was the real reason, or that the employer's stated reason and your protected status both played a role in the agency's decision or treatment of you.

TIP

If you have a claim of discrimination, you should be sure to consult an EEO counselor within 45 days (see Chapter 6). For assistance, contact your union, a private lawyer, or an outside organization such as Blacks in Government ("BIG") or Federally Employed Women ("FEW").

Retaliation (reprisal) claims

Employees often believe that after they file a discrimination claim, the agency will bring even more negative actions against them. In fact, sometimes this is the case. Fortunately most of the federal laws that protect employees' rights contain provisions that make it unlawful for an agency to retaliate against someone who engages in conduct which the law protects. The following are key questions you should ask yourself in considering a claim for retaliation.

Is my conduct protected conduct?

"Protected conduct" includes all aspects of trying to oppose or remedy discrimination, such as:

- filing a charge of discrimination
- threatening to file a charge
- complaining about, opposing, or protesting perceived discrimination against you or another employee
- assisting someone else in opposing discrimination, or giving evidence or testimony to an investigator
- refusing to engage in conduct that you believe to be discriminatory[4]
- refusing to assist an agency (by testimony or otherwise) in discriminating, and
- requesting reasonable accommodation

Did my agency take adverse action?

Your agency must have retaliated against you in some way that affects the terms and conditions of your employment before the conduct is deemed to be unlawful. Usually, unlawful retaliation takes the form of harassment, discipline, or termination. You must show that your job was adversely affected by your agency before you can proceed with a retaliation claim.

Did my agency know about my protected conduct?

You must show that your agency knew that you engaged in protected conduct. This requires showing that the person who made the actual decision about your job knew about the protected conduct.

Sometimes the decision-maker directly observes your conduct—for example, reads your written complaint of discrimination. Sometimes you can show the decision-maker learned about your protest from others. If you cannot prove that your agency knew about your protected conduct, you will not be able to prove a case of retaliation.

Do I have evidence that my protected conduct led to adverse action?

The most difficult part of a retaliation claim is showing a causal connection between your protected conduct and the adverse action taken against you.

---

[4] Be very careful about refusing to follow a supervisor's instruction because you believe it to be discriminatory. If you are wrong, you can be disciplined, including terminated, for insubordination. The best thing to do is note your objection in writing and ask the supervisor to reconsider the matter.

Timing can be evidence of a causal connection. For example, if your agency disciplines you shortly after you file a charge of discrimination, one can infer that your protected conduct was the real reason for the discipline. Other ways to establish causal connection include showing that employees who engaged in protected activity were disciplined, while other employees who engaged in the same alleged misconduct but did not engage in protected activity were not disciplined. There may be other circumstances which justify an inference that your discipline was motivated by your protected activity.

TIP

You may have a valid claim of retaliation for making a complaint even if your complaint is not proven. Government officials have no right to punish you as long as your complaint is made in good faith.

How can I counter my agency's denials?

You can disprove your agency's stated reasons for your termination or discipline in retaliation cases using the same kind of evidence used to show "pretext" in a discrimination case. For example, you can show that the employer's excuse is factually untrue, that it was insufficient to have actually caused the adverse decision, that it is simply unworthy of credence, or so riddled with errors that your agency could not realistically have relied on its stated reason. Remember, it is always going to be up to you, as an employee alleging retaliation, to prove unlawful motivation.

Final Thoughts

Federal employees generally are protected by the same discrimination laws as private employees. The method of enforcement of the law is different, as other chapters in this book will explain. Remedies are also different. Unlike employees in the private sector, federal employees cannot recover punitive damages against their employer, the U.S. government, even if the discrimination is malicious. Become familiar with the EEO complaint process described in the next chapter and remember to contact an EEO counselor within *45 days* of the alleged act of discrimination or when you first had a "reasonable suspicion" that you were subjected to discrimination.

Going through the exercise of asking yourself the questions in this chapter before you decide to go forward with a claim of discrimination can be extremely helpful. It will help you get a clearer idea of your allegations and whether you want to pursue them. Many times we have thoughts in our heads about something, but once we put it all out on the table and examine it, it may not be quite what we thought it was. Bringing a claim for discrimination will not be an easy thing to do, even if it is absolutely true that it occurred. It costs time, energy, and maybe even money. It will disrupt your workplace relationships and your working environment. This doesn't mean you shouldn't bring a legitimate claim of discrimination. It just means that you want to be sure that when you do, it has some factual basis, and that you are prepared for the stress that will likely follow.

6

Discrimination: The Complaint Process

Now that I know I'm being treated unfairly, what do I do about it?

In This Chapter You Will Learn:

- what to do if you think you have been discriminated against
- whether you must have your claim heard within your agency
- whether you can seek relief in court if you don't like your outcome

Contents Chapter Six - Discrimination: The Complaint Process

Introduction

As a federal government employee, you have greater protections against discrimination than private sector employees. Private sector employees are generally governed by the same statutes which protect against discrimination due to race, sex, national origin, color, religion, age, physical or mental disability, unequal pay, or retaliation. However, as a federal employee, you have special administrative processes for handling your complaints of discrimination, which include hearings before the Equal Employment Opportunity Commission ("EEOC").

If you prevail in your case, you are entitled to receive "make-whole" relief, including back pay with interest, benefits, and correction of personnel records where applicable. Compensatory damages up to a cap of $300,000 are available for demonstrated pain and suffering caused by discrimination as well as pecuniary damages for expenses incurred and reinstatement of leave used. This same cap applies also to consolidated cases involving separate claims. In other words, no matter how many separate claims you have, if they are joined in one case, compensatory damages are capped at $300,000. Reasonable attorney fees are also available where you are represented by counsel, except in administrative cases under the Age Discrimination in Employment Act (ADEA), for which no attorney fees are available. Compensatory damages are also not available for age discrimination.

If unsuccessful before the EEOC or after *180 days* from filing a formal complaint, you may also take your case to federal district court and be entitled to a jury trial.

Federal agencies play a major role in the use of alternative dispute resolution (ADR) administrative process. The EEOC regulations now include more emphasis on ADR, as part of the informal EEO process, without eliminating the investigative and hearing procedures.

What is Equal Employment Opportunity ("EEO") counseling?

If you believe that you have been discriminated against and want to file a discrimination complaint, you must first contact an EEO counselor within *45 days* after becoming aware of the discriminatory action. The time limits may be extended when:

- there is a "continuing violation," involving many incidents extending over a period of time
- you did not have a "reasonable suspicion" of discrimination until a later date
- you were misinformed of the applicable requirements

In any event, you must first contact an EEO counselor who is an agency employee to begin the process. If you do not know of an available counselor, contact the agency EEO office and request one. This initial contact should be in writing, setting forth:

- a summary of the claim of adverse discriminatory treatment (denial of promotion, disciplinary action, or whatever)

- the applicable basis of discrimination (for example, race, sex, etc.) or bases if there is more than one, and
- the relief requested

Keep in mind that the EEO counseling process and the filing of the formal complaint may often be obstructed by agency personnel who try to discourage complainants or who provide erroneous advice.

The EEOC counselor has *30 days* to complete counseling and will normally use that time to meet with your supervisors and other employees to learn more information and to attempt an informal resolution. The counselor may ask for additional time to complete counseling. You are not required to agree to more time. You may also request ADR which may last up to 90 days. Most cases are not settled at the informal stage.

TIP

Beware of counselors who discourage you or other employees from filing formal complaints. Seek other advice in that situation. Attorney fees may not be available during the informal EEO process.

How do I file a formal complaint?

When the EEO counselor has completed his or her efforts, or ADR is unsuccessful, you should receive a notice of your right to file a formal complaint of discrimination. At that point, you have only *15 days* to reduce your complaint to writing—use the form provided. Keep the information provided to a minimum, including the dates involved and only summarizing the issues complained of. Still, carefully draft the issues in the formal complaint because it may be difficult to change or amend the claim at a later date. The basis of your complaint (race, sex, etc.) can be supplemented prior to the EEO investigation and usually before the EEOC hearing. Send the completed formal complaint to the agency's EEO office by certified mail, return receipt requested, request a copy of the EEO counselor's report, and keep copies of all relevant documents. If you file your complaint by email, you can request a delivery and read receipt.

What happens to my complaint?

After receiving your formal complaint, the agency should issue an acknowledgement letter and provide you with a copy of the EEO counselor's report. The agency then issues an acceptance/rejection letter setting forth the issues accepted and indicating if it has rejected any issues. Read this letter very carefully, as it should explain your appeal rights to the Office of Federal Operations ("OFO") of the EEOC if the complaint is totally rejected. If your complaint is partially rejected, your recourse is to wait until your request for an EEOC hearing is assigned to an administrative judge (AJ) who will decide whether to reinstate the rejected issue(s).

It is not unusual for agencies to try to redefine or reject complaints for a number of procedural reasons, and these should be appealed when invalid. These reasons include alleged untimeliness, failure to state a legal claim, mootness, and a variety of other reasons, including the failure to accept an agency offer of full relief. However, the latter should not be a major problem. If you have requested emotional distress damages and attorney fees, any agency offer of job restoration and back pay would not in fact provide full relief.

Agencies have often engaged in the frivolous rejection of formal complaints as a tactic to discourage complainants. When this occurs, you have to file a notice of appeal with OFO using the form provided (EEOC Form 573, Notice of Appeal/Petition). This is a simple form, which only provides procedural information and must be accompanied by a copy of the agency's rejection letter. You then have *30 days* to file a supporting statement on behalf of your appeal. You may request an official extension for good cause from OFO.

Will there be an investigation?

Assuming that your complaint is accepted, the next step is preparing for the agency EEO investigation. At one time these were performed in house by agency investigators. Now, with only a few exceptions, for example, the Departments of Defense, Transportation, and Veterans Affairs, the overwhelming number of investigations are performed by independent contractors.

The typical EEO investigation is usually conducted by affidavit, beginning with the affidavit of the complainant and then continuing with the responsible management officials ("RMOs") and any other witnesses. Unless provided by the investigator, you should request written questions for which you can prepare your responses. The Department of Defense will sometimes conduct investigative hearings, which require you to be present throughout most of the day.

TIP

Prepare your own detailed affidavit with supporting documents, including a proposed witness list, in advance of the EEO investigation to ensure completeness and to avoid the last-minute crunch. Agency EEO investigators often contact complainants directly, without adequate notice, and extensions may be difficult to obtain if you are not prepared in advance.

The EEO investigations vary in quality, depending upon the bias and competency of the investigators, who are often former agency employees. Quality control is often nonexistent as agencies frequently downsize their EEO staff. All agencies are now required to offer alternative dispute resolution (ADR) procedures, primarily mediation, during the informal EEO process, prior to the EEO investigation. This should be a good time for you to obtain an informal resolution if the agency is serious about engaging in meaningful negotiations.[1]

TIP

If the agency does not complete its investigation within the 180-day time limit, you can request an EEOC hearing and move to have the EEOC issue sanctions against the agency for the failure to complete the investigation within the 180-day time limit. However, at times it might be advantageous to await the results of the EEO investigation, if you are not sure of the merits of your case and need more information.

It is important to cooperate in all phases of the processing of the case. Prepare an up-to-date list of proposed witnesses and a summary of their expected testimony to try to convince the EEO investigator to interview your witnesses. Request the opportunity to provide a rebuttal affidavit after receiving copies of the RMOs' affidavits, as you will ultimately have to prove that the agency's reasons for taking action were a pretext for discrimination.

---

1 *See* Chapter 32 concerning settlement negotiations.

TIP

One of the worst mistakes you can make in the EEO process is not to request an EEOC hearing. Even if you are planning to file your case in U.S. district court, there are still advantages in requesting an EEOC hearing, including fewer restrictions on covered issues, discovery, and the possibility of settlement.

How do I request an Equal Employment Opportunity Commission hearing?

Following the receipt of the agency EEO Report of Investigation ("ROI"), you have *30 days* to review the file and request an EEOC hearing. Carefully review the ROI to make sure that it is complete and impartial. If a hearing is not requested, the agency will automatically begin to process a Final Agency Decision ("FAD"). You must file your request for an EEOC hearing with the applicable EEOC district or field office and serve a copy on your agency's EEO office. Send the completed request by certified mail, return receipt requested, and keep copies of all relevant documents. It is strongly recommended that you request an EEOC hearing where you will be able to do discovery, have witnesses testify on your behalf, and introduce exhibits.

Is settlement a possibility?

ADR is now part of the informal EEO counseling process. Some agencies also attempt mediation prior to a case being referred to the EEOC for adjudication. In other cases, settlement efforts may not begin until after the case is sent to the EEOC and the agency assigns a representative, usually an attorney. If settlement is reached, the terms of the agreement should be reduced to writing as soon as possible to avoid further disputes.

If the agency violates the settlement agreement, you can proceed to force the agency to obey the agreement. Settlement agreements are enforceable in compliance actions, which have to be filed first with the agency. If you are not successful in obtaining compliance, you can file with the OFO of the EEOC, for enforcement. In the event of a breach of a settlement agreement, you can either request that the agreement be carried out or that your case be reinstated from where processing left off. However, OFO almost always orders specific performance of the breached provision(s).

What happens if I don't settle?

After an EEOC hearing has been requested, the agency assembles the entire file and sends it to the EEOC for assignment of an EEOC administrative judge ("AJ"). Since Title VII operates mainly by conciliation, a non-litigation alternative is always preferred. Some EEOC offices may attempt settlement efforts early on while others will wait until assignment of an AJ. If mediation assistance is required, do not hesitate to contact the AJ for help. Almost all AJs will prefer to have the matter settled before a hearing.

After a case has been assigned a docket (case) number, you will normally be given a period of time to complete discovery, usually *70-90 days, which can be extended*. Cases that also involve an adverse action, for example, suspension of more than fourteen days, demotion, or removal, are called "mixed cases." These cases are normally filed with the MSPB. See Chapter 4. While the EEOC is supposed to complete case processing within 180 days, delays of one or more years are not uncommon.

In some cases the complainant may allege that he/she has been forced to resign or retire due to intolerable working conditions. This is called a "constructive discharge," and you should try to convince the EEOC to retain jurisdiction if your major claim is discrimination. Otherwise, the constructive discharge allegation will be referred to the MSPB, but may subsequently be heard by the EEOC if the MSPB finds no jurisdiction.

Discovery

Discovery is the process by which you attempt to:

- obtain documents the other side has in its possession that may be helpful to your case
- ask written questions, and
- request admissions of undisputed facts by the other side

In addition to written discovery, each side has the opportunity to take depositions where questions are asked under oath, typically before a court reporter who prepares a transcript, although tape recording may suffice in less complex cases. While agencies may use discovery as well, sometimes they do not take advantage of the opportunity. However, there is a possibility that the agency may request an independent medical examination ("IME") by a doctor of its choosing, where your mental or physical health is an issue.

Discovery is more limited in EEOC procedures than provided by the MSPB or the U.S. district court rules. This is primarily because of the lack of subpoena power and the inability to compel non-governmental witnesses to participate in discovery. Also, some AJs unduly limit discovery in practice (this varies from office to office). It is a good approach to start off with a round of written discovery, including interrogatories, document requests, and requests for admissions, before moving on to depositions. ***See Appendix Q for a sample discovery request.***

You are typically limited to one set of 30 interrogatories, 30 document requests, and 30 requests for admissions, although you may want to request an exception in complex consolidated cases. Document requests are important to fill the gaps in the agency EEO investigation. Requests for admissions may be useful in obtaining concessions where agency witnesses or documents have admitted key facts.

Often you will need the information provided by discovery to prevent dismissal of your case. There is a provision for summary affirmance of the agency action without a hearing similar to summary judgment in court, where there are no disputed facts. Often an agency will file a motion for summary judgment, or occasionally the AJ may request that either party file such a motion.

This is an important motion which requires your best efforts to avoid a summary dismissal depriving you of the opportunity to present evidence in person and by live witnesses. When a motion for summary judgment is filed by the other side, you must carefully set forth your entire case with supporting documents, including any necessary affidavits or depositions and legal argument, to avoid being dismissed without a hearing.

It is generally recommended that you exhaust all efforts at settlement before taking any depositions. Depositions require much preparation and are expensive, especially if a court reporter transcribes the proceedings.

But depositions do help to clarify written discovery responses, which are usually prepared by agency counsel, and to pin down the agency witnesses for the hearing. Depositions are also a way to test the strength of your case prior to hearing. Equally as important, depositions may also serve to discourage agency management and make your employer more open to settlement.

If depositions are taken, you should depose the main agency witnesses prior to the agency filing a motion for summary judgment, if possible. Also depose any agency witnesses who have not given affidavits in the EEO investigation.

The prehearing conference

After discovery is over, the AJ will hold a prehearing conference. Prior to this conference, which is often held by telephone, the parties will have submitted their proposed witness lists with a summary of their expected testimony and their proposed exhibits. Be sure to describe in detail the expected testimony of proposed witnesses, including expert witnesses, who are usually necessary in disability cases and in substantiating compensatory damages where you have incurred medical treatment.

While it is obviously advisable to interview proposed witnesses in advance of the prehearing conference, sometimes it is not possible. Under these circumstances, you must inform the AJ that your list is only tentative and may be revised after completing witness interviews.

The AJ will normally continue with settlement negotiations at the prehearing conference as well as rule on the parties' witnesses and exhibits. AJs will often try to narrow the witness list. Contest any attempt to unreasonably limit your witnesses. Some AJs may limit you to a certain number of witnesses but may also give you the opportunity to select the ones you want. This is more desirable than the AJ making the final choices.

The EEOC hearing

The purpose of the EEOC hearing is to convince the AJ that your version of the facts should be accepted and you should be provided with your requested remedy. The EEOC hearing may be divided into two parts, one concerning the proof of discrimination and the other compensatory damages, especially if there will be expert witnesses to such damages. Compensatory damages are generally for pain and suffering, commonly due to emotional distress. When there are no expert witnesses, the AJ may hold only one hearing.

Regardless of the availability of expert mental health and/or other professional witnesses, it is a good idea to have family members and coworkers testify as to the change in your emotional and/or physical condition as a result of the discrimination that you have suffered. Family members can graphically describe the effects of the job-related discrimination on your obligations and relations with your spouse and children.

You will usually be given the opportunity for an opening statement setting forth your theory of the case and why you believe you were discriminated against, a brief summary of the testimony and evidence to be produced, and the requested remedy. The remedy requested should include all out-of-pocket expenses you have incurred, including lost sick and annual leave, medical expenses, back pay, benefits, and interest where applicable, compensatory damages, and attorney fees, if you have been represented by an attorney. As the complainant, you have the burden of proof and will put forth your case first, followed by the agency. After completion of the agency's case, you may request rebuttal testimony on new issues or facts raised by the agency witnesses.

Sometimes it is advantageous to call agency witnesses during your case if you expect to receive favorable testimony from them. In any event, you should generally testify last to give you the opportunity to hear the other witnesses and to fill in any gaps in the testimony. Be sure to oppose agency objections to your evidence when not warranted, explain your objections to agency evidence for the record, and make detailed offers (descriptions) of what you are trying to prove when relevant evidence is improperly excluded. It is always important to state your arguments concerning disputes about objections to evidence so that the court reporter will transcribe them for the record. This will help any appeal tribunal that reviews the record to understand and hopefully adopt your position.

The closing argument

After the conclusion of the hearing, the parties may present closing arguments either orally or in post-hearing written memoranda. In closing arguments, the parties summarize the facts and the applicable law and regulations and present reasons why the AJ should rule in their favor. The form of argument depends upon the desires of the representatives as well as the AJ. In rare cases the AJ may discourage closing arguments. Agency lawyers generally prefer written closing arguments. Except in factually or legally complex cases, oral closing arguments are much easier for the complainant and should not adversely affect the outcome.

Some experienced AJs may suggest legal issues to be addressed in memoranda which are often called briefs. Briefs are written arguments submitted by the parties. If briefs are to be filed and there is conflicting testimony which will result in the AJ having to make credibility resolutions as to who is telling the truth, it is generally a good idea to request that the parties be given copies of the transcript prior to preparing their post-hearing briefs.

The AJ's decision and filing an appeal

Except for "bench" decisions, which are short-form decisions usually rendered orally shortly after the close of the hearing (and generally more supportive of the agencies), the AJ will render a decision in writing sometime after the close of the hearing. The written decision with findings and conclusions will be sent to both parties along with copies of the transcript and the time limits for the final agency action, which is *40 days* after receipt. When the AJ finds discrimination, however, it is not unusual to have a second hearing limited to damages where you can offer proof of compensatory damages for pain and suffering. Often the AJ will attempt settlement negotiations to avoid a second hearing. In any event, the AJ will also have to determine the amount of attorney fees you are entitled to.

If you prevail and you are represented by counsel, your attorney will have to submit his/her request for reasonable attorney fees and costs. Attorney fees are generally payable only for service performed after the filing of a formal written complaint and after the agency has been notified of representation, except for services performed in reaching a determination to represent the complainant. The computation of attorney fees is generally based on market rates in your geographic area.

There is then usually a lull, although sometimes settlement negotiations will occur, until the agency issues its final action. As you might expect, agencies almost always accept decisions favorable to them and have a tendency to reject decisions unfavorable to them. If the final agency action does not fully implement the AJ's decision, it must notify you of the right to appeal to the OFO of the EEOC, or to go directly to court. In addition, the agency must simultaneously file an appeal with OFO and has 20 days to file its brief. Where you have waived your right to an EEOC hearing, the agency is supposed to issue its Final Agency Decision (FAD) within 60 days of receiving notification that you have requested an immediate decision or within 60 days of the end of the 30-day period for requesting a hearing. The FAD must also notify you of your appeal rights to OFO and Federal district court.

Defeating motions for summary judgment (decisions without a hearing)

In most EEO cases, both sides spend a lot of time and energy arguing about what really happened—what the facts are. The administrative judge's job is to consider the evidence and arguments and then decide the facts necessary to rule on your claims. This is called "fact finding." The judge is the finder of fact, or, in other words, the person who decides what the facts are. After the judge has decided what the facts are, s/he will also decide what legal conclusions flow from those facts. The main reason for holding a hearing is so that the judge can see the witnesses testify in person and make determinations about whether the witnesses are credible or not, which helps the judge decide what the facts are. In most cases, figuring out who is lying and who is telling the truth makes a big difference in the outcome of the case. In these cases, a hearing is crucial to help the judge make credibility determinations by seeing the witnesses testify with his or her own eyes. In some cases, both sides essentially agree about what the facts are, but disagree about what those facts mean (what legal conclusion should be reached). In these situations, a judge does not need to hold a hearing to make credibility determinations, and can simply make her legal conclusions based on the facts the parties agree to; this is called a summary judgment—issuing a decision without a hearing.

In most situations, you will want a hearing to convince the judge that you and your witnesses are telling the truth about what really happened and what the facts are. Even though you may see major disputes on important facts, the agency may nevertheless ask the judge to grant it summary judgment—issue a decision in its favor without a hearing. How can you overcome a motion for summary judgment and avoid losing your chance to argue your case at a hearing?

Judges are not supposed to grant summary judgment for either side if there are disputes of "material facts." Material facts are facts that will affect the legal outcome of the case. In order to avoid summary judgment, you must convince the judge that there are material facts in dispute. Some ways to highlight disputes of material fact include:

- Point out to the judge specific portions of your affidavit or deposition testimony that directly contradict specific portions of the wrongdoer's or other witnesses' testimony.
- Point out to the judge specific contradictions in the wrongdoer's or other witnesses' own testimony.
- Point out to the judge specific portions of the wrongdoer's or other witnesses' testimony that are not credible.
- Point out to the judge other reasons that the wrongdoer or other witnesses are not credible (if they had been disciplined for lack of candor or falsification in the past, for example, or if they had admitted to lying about something).
- Explain why your version of events is more likely true and how that is important to the case.
- Point out to the judge specific testimony/facts/documents that support specific points you have made.

- Point out key admissions either in testimony or in the other side's discovery responses.
- Point out "direct evidence" of wrongdoing, or evidence that clearly points to an unlawful motive, such as a statement by the wrongdoer that, "people who file EEO complaints deserve what they get," (in a retaliation case) or "we need a young buck in this position," (in an age discrimination case).
- Prepare a supplemental affidavit to rebut the agency's version of the facts.

Often when you respond to a motion for summary judgment, you will have to do more than just point out disputes of material fact. You will also have to make your arguments showing that you meet the legal threshold for making an EEO claim and that you can overcome the agency's stated legitimate reasons for its actions by proving that the real reason for the actions was discrimination or retaliation. EEOC's Management Directive-110, Appendix L, provides a good guide showing what you must prove to meet the legal threshold for the various kinds of discrimination and retaliation claims, how the agency can rebut your claim, and what you must show to overcome that rebuttal and prevail.

TIP

Responding to a Motion for Summary Judgment is extremely important. Don't hold back, trying to save key evidence or arguments for the hearing—after all, if you don't make it past summary judgment, there won't be a hearing!

SANCTIONS

Once you have requested a hearing with the EEOC, an administrative judge will be assigned to your case. The AJ assigned to your case has authority to sanction (discipline) you or the agency for bad conduct in the EEO complaint process. While sanctions against complainants (like you) are not very common, you can be subject to sanctions if, for example, you fail to respond to or meet the deadlines in the AJ's orders, fail to reasonably cooperate with the agency in discovery, or fail to respond to the agency's motions. This kind of conduct can even result in the AJ issuing a decision in the agency's favor as a sanction against you.

Agencies can also be subject to sanctions for improper conduct in the EEO process. In certain circumstances, sanctions can be a very powerful tool for correcting harm done by an agency's bad actions. Some situations in which AJs may sanction agencies include:

- When an agency fails to meets its deadline for completing an EEO investigation (including providing you with the Report of Investigation (ROI)). The agency is supposed to complete its EEO investigation and provide you with the ROI within 180 days of the date you filed your formal complaint (provided you never amended your complaint by adding new issues after you filed your formal complaint, and never granted the agency an extension for the investigation). If you amended your complaint by adding new issues after you originally filed your formal complaint, the agency's deadline for completing the investigation is 180 days after the date of the amendment, or 360 days after you filed your formal complaint, whichever is less. It is possible that an AJ could issue a default decision in your favor simply because the agency did not complete its investigation of your EEO claim on time. If the agency's deadline for completing the investigation has passed—DO NOT WAIT—immediately contact an attorney about requesting a hearing and filing a motion for sanctions against the agency.

- When the agency's investigation is incomplete. If the agency failed to include critical information in the ROI, you can request the AJ sanction the agency for its inadequate investigation. Sanctions for incomplete investigations are not very common since many judges take the position that you will have a chance to correct an incomplete investigation through the discovery process. Still, if an investigation is particularly poor, the AJ may require the Agency to pay for the discovery you need to do to fill in the gaps, including attorney fees and court reporter costs.

- When an agency fails to initiate discovery on time. The deadline for initiating discovery will be noted in the Acknowledgement and Order you receive after you make your hearing request; that deadline is often as short as 20 days after you receive the order. This means that within 20 days of the date the agency received the Acknowledgment and Order, it must send you some kind of discovery request.

If the agency fails to send you any discovery request by the deadline, the AJ may deem the agency's right to engage in discovery waived, and you will not have to answer any of its discovery requests or be subject to a deposition. Be careful though; the same deadline for initiating discovery applies to you, and you can be subject to the same penalties for missing it.

- When an agency fails to comply with an AJ's order. When either party fails to respond to or comply with an order, an AJ may sanction the party to discourage it from disobeying orders in the future, and to correct any harm done by the party's disobedience.

- When an agency fails to produce evidence. If the agency did not cooperate in an EEO investigation by providing the information the investigator requests, or if the agency did not fully respond to your discovery requests, even after the AJ ordered them to, or if the agency says it destroyed evidence relevant to your case, you can request that the AJ sanction the agency. Sanctions for this kind of conduct can include issuing an adverse inference against the agency that the information it failed to produce would have been beneficial to you and/or a ban on introducing any evidence on a particular issue into the record of the case.

- When an agency witness or attorney fails to show up at a scheduled deposition or interferes with a deposition. An AJ could require that the agency pay the costs incurred in the missed or botched deposition (such as court reporter fees, or fees incurred by your attorney for a deposition that did not take place or that took much longer than expected because of undue interference), ban the witness from offering testimony at the hearing, and/or issuing an adverse inference against the agency that the witness' would have been beneficial to you.

TIP

Carefully review all documents you receive from the agency or the EEOC relating to your EEO complaint, and record all deadlines that apply to you AND to the agency. This will help ensure you are not vulnerable to sanctions, and make you aware of the possibility of seeking sanctions against the agency if it is not meeting its deadlines.

Sanctions can sometimes make all the difference in the outcome of a case, but they are a complicated issue, which is another reason why it is helpful to have an attorney familiar with federal employment law guiding you through EEO litigation.

Appeals to the EEOC and U.S. District Courts

Where you have received a favorable written decision from the AJ and the agency appeals the AJ's decision, you have a good chance of winning an appeal. Appeals to the EEOC are time-consuming, and can take up to two years for an appeal, although decisions finding discrimination are given a higher priority. Requests for reconsideration by the EEOC can take another year. A final Commission decision is not appealable by the agency.

Even if you are planning to go to court, it is generally a good idea to request an OFO decision and reconsideration, if necessary, in order to relieve you of any immediate time limits for filing in the U.S. district court. During this period you should be searching for competent counsel to represent you in court.

After receiving a final negative EEOC decision, you now have *90 days* to file a complaint in federal court and request a jury trial. Unless you have already lined up counsel, you will find that the time moves very quickly. It is very important that you select the appropriate U.S. district court in which to file suit. This is called venue, and it is normally the judicial district where the discrimination took place. For overseas cases, venue is usually the location of the agency headquarters.

If you have been unsuccessful in obtaining counsel, after filing suit in U.S. district court *pro se*, i.e., representing yourself, you can request court-appointed counsel. The availability of *pro bono* (without charge) counsel will depend upon the court and your financial situation (specifically, whether you are indigent). In some cases, it may also be possible to obtain a lawyer on your own, who will represent you for a contingency fee (a percentage of recovery).

After the government answers the complaint, in most district courts there is now a provision for meeting and conferring to plan discovery and to exchange the names and reports of expert witnesses. Following the completion of discovery, if not sooner, you can almost always expect the government to file a motion for summary judgment to prevent the case from going to trial.

TIP

Your local bar association may maintain a list of attorneys who practice employment discrimination law. The National Employment Lawyers Association (NELA) is a good source of referrals of employment law specialists. NELA can be contacted at:

> *2201 Broadway, Suite 402*
> *Oakland, CA 94612*
> *415/296-7629*
> *fax: 415/667-9445*
> *website: nela.org*

See Chapter 30, How to Find a Lawyer.

As a last resort you can consult the Yellow Pages of your telephone directory under "lawyers." Employment lawyers who advertise frequently list their area of expertise.

A motion for summary judgment requests that the court makes a determination on the case based on the documents already submitted to the court by the parties. The government alleges that based on the documents submitted, there are no disputed issues of fact necessitating a trial. You counter that there are. If the motion for summary judgment is granted, your claim is dismissed and the case is over, with you having lost.

Assuming that the case continues, your case will be set for trial following a pretrial conference. The pretrial proceedings are more formal in federal court. You will have to make a detailed written submission with all supporting exhibits to the judge or magistrate. The courts encourage ADR. Your case may be sent to a mediator for attempted resolution. If you are successful at settlement or trial, you may be awarded compensatory damages and attorney fees, in addition to the specific relief requested. After trial and any final motions, the losing party may file an appeal with the appropriate U.S. court of appeals.

Compliance with EEOC decisions

If you prevail in your EEOC case, the order attached to the AJ's decision will specify the deadlines by which the agency must complete certain actions (such as cancelling a suspension, or paying compensatory damages). The agency will then issue a Final Agency Decision (FAD) implementing the AJ's decision in full, or, if it decides to do anything but fully implement the AJ's decision, the agency must appeal the decision to the EEOC's Office of Federal Operations (OFO). Until the OFO has issued a decision on the agency's appeal, the agency does not have to comply with any parts of the AJ's decision that it has appealed. However, once the OFO issues a decision, the agency is obligated to abide by whatever that decision is.

If the agency has failed to comply with the order in the AJ's or OFO's decision, you must file a petition for enforcement with the OFO raising the compliance issue within 30 days of the date you "knew or should have known" that the agency did not comply with the order. The petition for enforcement must describe how the agency has failed to comply with the order and provide relevant evidence of the noncompliance. The OFO will take steps to determine if the agency has complied with the order or not; if not, the OFO will take action to achieve compliance. If the agency still fails to comply with the order, further action may be necessary, and the EEOC may request that the head of the agency provide justification for why the agency has failed to comply with the order, or may refer the matter to the Office of Special Counsel. If the OFO finds the agency has not complied with the AJ's order, it will issue you written notice of your right to file an enforcement action in federal court. If the OFO finds the agency was not in compliance with the order, you can recover any additional attorney fees and costs you incurred bringing the enforcement action.

Compliance with settlement agreements at the EEOC

If the agency fails to comply with a settlement agreement, you may seek enforcement of the agreement with the EEOC, regardless of what stage your EEO complaint was in when you reached settlement. You can request either that 1) the agency be required to comply with all terms of the agreement; or 2) that your complaint be reinstated at the same stage of the EEO process it was in when the parties reached settlement. However, before you can ask the EEOC to enforce the agreement or reinstate your complaint, you must notify the agency's EEO office in writing that you believe the agency has not complied with the settlement agreement and you must send this "notice of noncompliance" to the agency within 30 days of the date you "knew or should have known" that the agency had failed to comply. Then, the agency has 35 days to send you a written determination that it has either corrected the issue or that it believes it is in compliance with the agreement. If the agency does not resolve the issue to your satisfaction, you may file a petition for enforcement with the OFO within 30 days of the date of the agency's written response to your allegation of breach of the agreement. Or, if the agency does not respond, you may file a petition for enforcement after 35 days have passed from the date you sent the agency your written notice that it failed to comply with the agreement. Your petition for enforcement must state the reasons you think the agency is not in compliance with the settlement agreement and provide relevant evidence. The OFO will issue a decision on whether the agency has or has not failed to comply with the terms of the settlement agreement. If the OFO finds the agency was not in compliance with the agreement, you can recover any additional attorney fees you incurred bringing the enforcement action.

Can I enforce my settlement in court?

If your settlement agreement provides that you will receive monetary relief which the agency has failed to pay to you, or if the breach of the settlement agreement has resulted in monetary loss, you may seek enforcement of those provisions that relate to monetary relief in the U.S. Court of Federal Claims. You cannot seek enforcement in court of any provisions of the agreement that relate to equitable (non-monetary) relief (such as changes to a performance rating, restoration of leave, etc.).[2]

TIP

If you feel the Agency has not complied with an EEOC order, or has not met the terms of a settlement agreement DO NOT WAIT – immediately seek advice on initiating a petition for enforcement, and make sure the petition is submitted by the deadline.

The No FEAR act

The No FEAR Act (The Notification and Federal Employee Antidiscrimination and Retaliation Act of 2002) imposes reporting requirements on federal agencies but provides no substantive rights to federal employees. Among other requirements, the No FEAR Act requires that agencies reimburse the federal judgment fund for payments made to employees for findings of discrimina-

2 *See Cunningham v. United States,* 748 F.3d (Fed. 2014).

tion and retaliation. It also requires that agencies provide EEO and whistle-blower training to its employees and managers and post information on their public websites regarding EEO complaints filed against the agency.

TIP

Due to potential future changes in Part 1614 of the EEOC's regulations, when pursuing an EEO complaint, make sure you have the current version of the regulations, MD-110, and relevant case decisions. They are available on the EEOC website—EEOC.gov—under Federal Sector Information.

Final Thoughts

This chapter has addressed the various forums available to federal employees with discrimination claims. The obvious advantage of going to federal court is the right to a jury trial and the possibility of greater compensatory damages, although the statutory cap is still $300,000.

On the negative side, the cost of litigation in federal court is much greater, the opposition (generally U.S. Attorneys) is better, and procedural issues are often more difficult. In addition, many cases are lost on summary judgment and never get to a jury, and it may take another two to three years for a final resolution, assuming there is no appeal. There is always the possibility of going to federal court at any time during the administrative process, but filing in U.S. district court will cause the EEOC to dismiss your administrative case. Weigh the alternatives carefully before proceeding with your case.

7

Whistleblowing and Prohibited Personnel Practices

Dodging the Bullets When They Shoot the Messenger

In This Chapter You Will Learn:

- what whistleblowing is
- what you can do if you blow the whistle and there is retaliation against you
- what you can do if someone acts against you for other reasons

Contents Chapter Seven - Whistleblowing and Prohibited Personnel Practices

Introduction

When government employees observe abuse, wrongdoing, and corruption in government, they are encouraged to report it to management. Yet, all too often these public-spirited "whistleblowers" are retaliated against for their disclosures. This chapter will explain the Whistleblower Protection Act and the prohibited personnel practices, two of the most powerful—and underenforced—laws protecting federal employees. It will also discuss the role of the Office of Special Counsel ("OSC"), the agency designed to investigate complaints of this type.

Although complicated, you must not let the administrative "hoops" here deter you. The types of claims discussed in this chapter can be a very exciting way to reveal corruption in the federal government and seek justice. Use this chapter as a guide and reference tool, find experienced legal advice, and get strong and well-organized witness and documentary support.

What is whistleblowing?

Whether you are a current or former federal employee or only a job applicant, you are a whistleblower if you report what seems to be wrongdoing to your appropriate authorities. To be precise, to qualify as whistleblowing the wrongdoing you report needs to be "a violation of law, rule, or regulation, gross mismanagement, a gross waste of funds, an abuse of authority, or a substantial and specific danger to public health or safety,"[1] and you should have a reasonable belief that your disclosure is accurate. You are

---

1 *See* 5 USC § 2302(b)(8).

also protected if management takes action against you because they believe you blew the whistle, even if you didn't.[2]

What is whistleblower protection?

Illegal reprisal for whistleblowing occurs when an agency official takes, or threatens to take, a personnel action against a whistleblower. In the case of some personnel actions, such as promotions or raises, the reprisal can also take the form of not taking the action you had been looking forward to, and merited. The Whistleblower Protection Act of 1989 ("WPA")[3] forbids retaliation against a whistleblower. Reprisal for whistleblowing is one of the 13 prohibited personnel practices that will be described in this chapter and is a violation of the WPA, an amendment to the Civil Service Reform Act of 1978.

The WPA applies only when a personnel action is taken against the whistleblower at least in part because of the protected disclosure. Reprisal for making a protected whistleblower disclosure need not be the sole or major motivation for the action. A personnel action is illegal as long as the protected disclosure was "a contributing factor." Whistleblower protection is explained here separately from other prohibited personnel practices because many federal employees want or need to learn more about this protection, and because there are special procedures involved in prosecuting such complaints of reprisal.

What is the Office of Special Counsel?

The OSC is an independent federal investigative and prosecutorial agency. The OSC interprets, investigates, and prosecutes cases of prohibited personnel practices brought by government employees and enforces the Hatch Act. (See Chapter 23.) In addition, the OSC:

- operates a confidential whistleblower hotline
- has the authority to take part in other cases which enforce employee rights and remedies before the MSPB
- investigates certain claims denying veterans employment benefits under the Uniformed Services Employment and Reemployment Rights Act of 1994 (see Chapter 19)

---

[2] *See, e.g., King v. Dept. of Army*, 116 MSPR 689 (2011).

[3] *See* 5 USC § 2302(b)(8).

How do I "blow the whistle?"

There are three common methods of whistleblowing.

Report to a supervisor Probably the most common and least formal method is reporting to your supervisor or a higher level agency official conduct which you reasonably believe is a violation of law or evidence of government waste or fraud. You may not even consciously think of yourself as a whistleblower. But if you subsequently suffer adverse consequences after reporting wrongdoing, you should investigate your right to protection from retaliation.

Contact the Inspector General ("IG") A potential whistleblower may also contact the Inspector General's office at the agency where the wrongdoing takes place. Raising such a complaint will not necessarily protect your confidentiality, despite assurances, because of the interrelationship between the IG's office and agency management. The IG's office may or may not investigate the allegations. You do not lose protected whistleblower status if the IG's office fails to investigate. It may simply mean that fraud, waste, and abuse will go unchecked. If you suffer retaliation for having made the disclosure, you still retain your right to pursue a personal remedy, based upon a reasonable belief that your allegations constituted whistleblowing.

Contact the Office of Special Counsel You may also contact the Office of Special Counsel ("OSC") on the OSC Whistleblower Disclosure Hotline (1 800/572-2249) or by mail.[4] There are several advantages to making the report through OSC:

- Confidentiality is provided by law
- The OSC is empowered to order an agency to investigate and report on the information disclosed
- Following receipt of an agency report on the information disclosed, the OSC must send the report, with any comments regarding it by the whistleblower and by the OSC, to the President, Congress, and the Comptroller General
- If the OSC does not send the disclosed information to your agency for an investigation and report, it must return the disclosed

[4] Exceptions apply for some particular subgroups of federal employees (for example, Postal Service employees, FBI employees, and intelligence agency employees), who may be required to direct whistleblowing disclosures to agencies other than OSC. See discussion below for details.

information to you with an explanation of why no referral to the agency was made
- The OSC must also advise you of any other avenues for disclosure of the information

Again, even if the OSC finds no fraud, waste, or abuse, you may still pursue a whistleblower claim.

If you are extremely concerned that a disclosure will result in retaliation, you should take steps to protect the confidentiality of the disclosure. For a confidential whistleblower, it could be hard to prove retaliation if the offending management officials persuasively testify that they did not know of your whistleblowing. On the other hand, if you are a well-known whistleblower, adverse consequences are more easily attributable to the report you made. It is easier to establish that the official taking the action knew of your whistleblowing. The best advice is to be prepared in advance to identify retaliation and quickly take steps to assert your rights in opposition to any retaliation.

Essential to your status as a protected whistleblower is that you have a "reasonable" belief that what you disclosed was a violation of law, rule, or regulation, gross mismanagement, gross waste of funds, abuse of authority, or a danger to public health or safety. Even if your belief is ultimately proven wrong—that is, if no wrongdoing is found upon investigation—as long as you have a *reasonable* belief in the nature of the disclosure, you are protected from retaliation. However, mere speculation or subjective belief, without evidence, may not be enough to give you protection as a whistleblower.

How do I bring my whistleblower retaliation case?

There are three options in pursuing a whistleblower retaliation case. The choice of how to proceed will affect where to file your complaint, how it will be investigated, and the amount of time it may take to come to fruition. Be sure to consider the options carefully, as the choice is a procedural election that generally cannot be undone later, and it may dictate what claims can be raised later. [5]

Option one: affirmative defense in MSPB appeal If the agency takes an adverse action against you which is directly appealable to the MSPB (an Otherwise Appealable Action ("OAA")), you should raise your claim of

---

5 *See, e.g.*, 5 CFR § 1209.2(d).

reprisal for whistleblowing as an "affirmative defense" in an MSPB appeal. (See Chapter 4 for more information on MSPB appeals and asserting affirmative defenses.) Personnel actions which you may appeal directly to the MSPB along with your whistleblower reprisal claim are generally:

- Adverse actions (removals, suspensions of more than 14 days, reduction in grade or pay, and furloughs of 30 days or less) (see Chapter 4)
- Performance-based removals or reductions in grade (see Chapter 3)
- Denials of within-grade increases (see Chapter 13)
- Certain reduction-in-force ("RIF") actions (see Chapter 9)
- Denials of restoration to duty or reemployment rights
- Removals from the SES (see Chapter 29)
- OPM determinations in employment suitability and retirement matters (see Chapter 4 and Chapter 18)

Option two: Individual Right of Action If you suffer a personnel action other than one of the appealable actions listed above, you may file an appeal with the MSPB—called an Individual Right of Action ("IRA")—but only after going through a complaint procedure with the Office of Special Counsel. You are required to initiate and exhaust the OSC complaint process before filing an IRA case with the MSPB. In cases where you have a choice between an IRA and an OAA, choosing an IRA has a tradeoff: you gain the chance of the OSC possibly agreeing to seek a "stay" (discussed below), but if your case goes to the MSPB, you can only raise the whistleblower reprisal claim and cannot separately challenge the merits of the underlying adverse action. Note that a proposal for an adverse action is a "threatened" adverse action, and so the proposal can be separately challenged as whistleblower reprisal.

A common strategy is to:

1. file an IRA complaint against the proposal for the adverse action and seek a stay from the OSC, before the adverse action is finalized, and then also
2. file a separate OAA appeal of the final adverse action decision, citing whistleblower reprisal as an affirmative defense.

Option three: union grievance If you are a unionized employee, you may file a grievance alleging reprisal for whistleblowing under the grievance and arbitration procedure of the union's collective bargaining agreement with the agency. You cannot file a union grievance and an MSPB appeal or OSC complaint over the same act of reprisal. See Chapter 8 for a discussion of union grievances.

WHAT PROOF DO I HAVE TO PROVIDE?

In your MSPB appeal (whether by an OAA appeal or by an IRA), you must establish by a "preponderance of evidence" that:

- You made a protected disclosure and had a "reasonable belief" about the wrongdoing.
- The agency took, threatened to take, or failed to take the personnel action in question. The same elements of proof apply in a grievance under your union contract.
- If you are filing an IRA case with the MSPB, you must also establish by a preponderance of evidence that you raised the whistleblower issue before the OSC.
- You filed an IRA with the MSPB within either:

  a. *65 days* of getting your dismissal letter from the OSC, or
  b. *120 days* after filing your complaint with the OSC, if the OSC has not yet completed action on your complaint

---

TIP

Use certified, return receipt mail, facsimile, or some other personal delivery which provides proof that the MSPB actually received your appeal on a certain day. You can also use the MSPB's online filing option. www.mspb.gov

---

Regardless of the method of appeal, you need to know how to meet your "burden of proof." You must consider how much evidence and what type of evidence you will have to supply to the MSPB or an arbitrator to win. This is not an easy task, but bear in mind that a handful of good evidence is better than a roomful of weak evidence. Evidence is either direct, or else indirect (that is, "circumstantial"). It would be great if an agency official said to you, "Stacey, I'm firing you because you blew the whistle on the agency by reporting wrong-doing to the IG's office." However, that will rarely happen. If it does, it is direct evidence of retaliation in violation of the WPA. The more common case is that you have indirect or circumstantial evidence pointing to wrongdoing by an agency official. You may pursue your appeal with indirect evidence in addition to, or instead of, direct evidence of reprisal if necessary.

The most important piece of circumstantial evidence is the length of time between your whistleblowing disclosure and the adverse consequences. If there is a relatively short period of time between disclosure and the adverse action, the MSPB may presume there was retaliation. Because the two events are closely connected in time, the Board can infer an improper motive. Showing this connection gets harder as the period between the disclosure and the adverse action gets longer, especially once a year passes between the disclosure and the adverse action.[6] The agency may attempt to rebut that presumption by establishing other reasons for the adverse action.

The standard for evidence in an IRA case requires demonstrating that your act of blowing the whistle (the disclosure) was "a contributing factor" in the personnel action you are challenging.

You can show that the disclosure was a contributing factor by using circumstantial evidence to establish that:

- the official taking the personnel action knew of the disclosure, and
- the personnel action occurred within a period of time such that a reasonable person could conclude that the disclosure was a contributing factor in the personnel action

If you have direct evidence ("a smoking gun") that the disclosure motivated the personnel action, present it in your MSPB case first, then follow up with other, indirect evidence which also points to the disclosure as the real reason for the personnel action against you.

How will my agency respond?

Once you submit evidence that your disclosure was a contributing factor in an adverse action against you, the agency is entitled to defend itself. If the agency persuades the MSPB by "clear and convincing evidence" that the agency would have taken the same action against you even if you had never

6 *See, e.g., Gonzalez v. Dept. of Transportation,* 109 MSPR 250 (2008); *Cosgrove v. Dept. of the Navy,* 59 MSPR 618, 623 fn. 5 (1993) (citing S. Rep. 100-413 (July 6, 1988) at 14); *accord Russel v. Dept. of Justice,* 76 MSPR 317, 323 (1997); *Smith v. Dept. of Agriculture,* 64 MSPR 46, 65 (1994).

made the disclosure, the agency wins. Generally, the agency will attempt to prove that your protected disclosure was not in any way a contributing factor to your adverse consequences.

Can I rebut my agency's response?

You must challenge the agency's evidence by offering evidence and argument which show that agency officials would not have taken the same action in the absence of the whistleblowing disclosure. In some cases this may simply involve a rehashing of the initial proof, but usually it requires a new and reasonable explanation of why the agency's contention is misleading or wrong. You can offer this type of argument in rebuttal to the agency's defense. For example, you can show that the agency's argument is contrary to usual practice or is contradicted by other testimony or documents, that the specific managers in question had a strong personal motive to retaliate in your particular case, that the decision-maker had a motive to protect the agency, or that a pattern exists in how whistleblowers are treated versus non-whistle-blowers by the manager in similar circumstances.

TIP

Since an agency always argues that it would have made the same decision in the absence of your whistleblowing disclosure, you should anticipate this argument and simply include it in your initial case rather than wait to refute it on rebuttal.

What if my agency engages in other prohibited personnel practices against me?

"Prohibited personnel practices"—which include retaliation against a whistle-blower—is the special name for illegal personnel actions. To determine if what has happened to you qualifies as a prohibited personnel practice, you must identify both the action and the reason why it was taken.

The law explaining prohibited personnel practices contains two lists.[7] The first list, known as 2302(b), is a list of illegal reasons for taking action. The second list, known as 2302(a)(2), is a list of personnel actions. If you can pinpoint the reason for the action taken against you on the first list and

---

7 *See* 5 USC § 2302.

what the action was on the second, then keep reading to find out how to deal with the problem.

Illegal reasons for taking personnel actions

Section 2302(b) prohibits any employee who has the authority to take, direct others to take, recommend, or approve any personnel action from acting based upon:

1. unlawful discrimination (race, color, religion, sex, national origin, age, disability, reprisal, marital status, political affiliation)
2. solicitation or consideration of improper background references (this means an agency shall not consider a recommendation or statement concerning a candidate for a personnel action unless it is based on the personal knowledge or records of the person providing it and consists either of an evaluation of work performance, ability, aptitude, general qualifications, or an evaluation of the individual's character, loyalty, or suitability)
3. coercion of political activity
4. obstruction of the right to compete (this means agency officials shall not interfere with the fair consideration of a candidate during a competitive selection process)
5. influencing the withdrawal of applicants from competition (agencies shall not prevent the consideration of candidates, such as by failing to mail them inquiries concerning their availability for a position or falsely reporting their employment status during the competitive selection process)
6. unauthorized preferences (agencies shall not intentionally take a personnel action in such a way as to give preference to a particular individual for the purpose of improving her prospects for employment at the agency, such as hiring under a temporary appointment to circumvent a competitive selection process)
7. nepotism
8. retaliation for whistleblowing
9. reprisal for the exercise of an appeal right (including a whistleblower reprisal claim), for being a witness in another employee's complaint, for cooperation with the OSC or an agency IG's office, or for refusing to obey an order that would require you to violate the law
10. discrimination based on non-job related conduct (including sexual orientation)

11. knowingly taking, recommending, or approval—or failure to do so—of any personnel action if the taking of or failure to take such action would violate a veterans preference requirement (see Chapter 19)
12. taking or failure to take any other personnel action if doing so would violate any law, rule, or regulation implementing or directly concerning the merit system principles[8]
13. require an employee to sign a nondisclosure agreement without certain mandatory language being included. This mandatory language prevents the settlement agreement from interfering with future permitted whistleblowing, such as disclosures to Congress or to the Inspector General.

Retaliation for whistleblowing is one particularly well-known type of prohibited personnel practice. A claim alleging that you have suffered retaliation for making disclosures protected by Section 2302(b)(8) is called a whistleblower retaliation or reprisal case. It offers aggrieved employees the opportunity to file an IRA appeal with the MSPB, when the Board would normally not entertain other types of complaints, as discussed at the beginning of this chapter.

IRA appeals are also available for violations of Section 2302(b)(9), except that IRAs in cases of reprisal for your exercise of an appeal right are limited to retaliation for a prior whistleblower reprisal complaint.

If you are claiming a violation of Section 2302(b)(1)—unlawful discrimination—you will have to pursue that claim through the EEO procedure described in Chapter 6. The OSC will normally not investigate such claims of discrimination.

The list of personnel actions

The second list is the Section 2302(a)(2) list of personnel actions:

1. an appointment
2. a promotion
3. an adverse action or other disciplinary action or corrective action (see Chapter 4)
4. a detail, transfer, or reassignment
5. a reinstatement

---

8 *See* 5 USC § 2301 for merit system principles.

6. a restoration
7. a reemployment
8. a performance evaluation (see Chapter 2)
9. a decision concerning pay, benefits, or awards, concerning education or training if the education or training may reasonably be expected to lead to an appointment, promotion, performance evaluation, or other action
10. a decision to order psychiatric testing or examination
11. implementation or enforcement of any nondisclosure policy, form, or agreement
12. any other significant change in duties, responsibilities, or working conditions.[9]

If you are the target of one (or more) of the above "personnel actions" and the action is caused by one of the listed "prohibited personnel practices," you are eligible to raise a complaint, through the OSC, against the responsible person(s).

The OSC is the designated place—but not the only place—you can file complaints about alleged prohibited personnel practices. Some claims, as discussed, may be appealed directly to the MSPB, if the Board would already have jurisdiction over your appeal. The OSC defers processing of all discrimination claims other than marital status and political activity to the federal sector discrimination complaint procedures available under the regulations of the EEOC. (See Chapter 6.) Complaints of discrimination based upon veteran status can be raised in several ways, including at the OSC. (See Chapter 19.)

Besides the OSC and the EEOC processes, the negotiated grievance process is an available option for members of a collective bargaining unit to challenge prohibited practices. You should thoughtfully decide where you want to pursue your claim. Your choice is binding. After filing in one forum you cannot change your mind and file your claim elsewhere at a later time. Consult with a union representative or lawyer to investigate your options.[10]

How do I file an OSC complaint?

You should obtain a form from the OSC which is available online at www.osc.gov, but there is no required format for a complaint. A mere letter

---

[9] The MSPB has also held that "any other significant change in duties, responsibilities, or working conditions" includes retaliatory harassment of whistleblowers. *See, e.g., Covarrubias v. Social Security Administration,* 113 MSPR 583, 589 fn. 4 (2010).

[10] *See* 5 USC § 7121(d and g) and 5 CFR § 1201.3(c)(1).

stating the issues will suffice to initiate the complaint process. Along with your complaint, you should include:

- an organized report on what happened to you
- what types of personnel actions are at issue
- which prohibited personnel practice is at issue
- what evidence supports your belief that the prohibited personnel practice was a contributing or motivating factor in the adverse action against you.
- any relevant documents (identify them in your report and attach them)
- a list of witnesses, their full names, work addresses, phone numbers, and a short statement of the relevant information they may possess
- if the witnesses are cooperative, obtain and attach a brief affidavit from each witness, sworn under oath or "under the penalty of perjury," testifying to information the witness knows in support of your claim
- sign your report "under the penalty of perjury" so that it is a sworn statement (see Appendix E for a sample affidavit format and oath)

If it sounds like you are doing the job of an investigator at the OSC, you are. There are not enough investigators to go around. A complete report detailing evidence will greatly enhance the possibility of a reviewing official finding merit to your claim. Otherwise, you can almost assure yourself of a dismissal letter, often issued quickly.

TIP

It is always in your best interest to make your complaint as understandable as possible to someone unfamiliar with your situation. Do not use a lot of jargon and acronyms. Make the complaint as simple, but as thorough as possible.

You have probably heard the expression that one who "sits on his rights" loses them. This is not so with your right to be free of prohibited personnel practices. There is no time limit within which you must bring your claim of a prohibited personnel practice to the OSC. However, you should not dawdle. Quick action shows you are concerned. Delay will hurt your case as witnesses' memories fade.

TIP

Complaints of prohibited personnel practices should be directed to the "OSC Officer of the Week" at the following address:

> ***Complaints Examining Unit***
> ***U.S. Office of Special Counsel***
> ***1730 M Street, N.W., Suite 218***
> ***Washington, DC 20036-4505***

Complaints can be filed by fax to:

> ***202/544-3711,***

or filed electronically online at the OSC's website (https://www.osc.gov/oscefile/).

See Chapter 4 for discussion of electronic filing at the MSPB.

> ***Telephone (TDD equipped): 1 800/872-9855***
> ***or 202/254-3670***

As with other important legal matters, it is important to have proof that you filed the complaint and the date you filed it.

TIP

If you mail your complaint, send it by certified mail, return receipt requested. The green card you receive later will verify the date and the name of the person who accepted delivery of your complaint.

What can I expect during an OSC investigation?

Once you have filed a complaint alleging a prohibited personnel practice, the OSC will send an acknowledgement letter identifying the Examiner assigned to the matter. At this stage, the OSC refers to the person filing the complaint or request for information as the "requester" or "complainant." The Examiner may contact you to clarify the allegations. Provide as much relevant information as possible in response to a request for information, but do not overload the Examiner with a ton of paper and expect him or her to read it all. Narrow down the claim to its essence. Highlight documents which verify the connection between the agency's personnel action and the prohibited personnel practice.

The Examiner's initial task is to determine whether your allegation describes a violation of law deserving additional investigation. The OSC must make the initial determination within *240 days*. You can agree to an extension of time, which will likely be sought by the OSC if the office cannot meet the deadline. If the allegation does not appear to raise a matter over which the OSC has authority or otherwise merit further investigation, the Examiner will notify you in writing of the findings and intent to close the file in 13 days. You will then have an opportunity to supply the OSC with comments on the findings before the file is closed.

If appropriate, the Examiner, or an investigator, may refer a complainant to another forum where the claim may be more appropriately brought, such as the EEOC. Also, the Examiner may close the file if the OSC has already resolved the matter by obtaining corrective action from the agency.

If the allegation warrants further scrutiny, the matter will be sent to the OSC Investigation and Prosecution Division for field investigation. If the issue includes a whistleblower disclosure, the information may be sent to the OSC Disclosure Unit for processing through the agency.

The OSC Investigation and Prosecution Division reviews completed field investigations to determine:

- whether the inquiry has established a violation of law, rule, or regulation, and
- whether the matter warrants corrective or disciplinary action, or both

If the evidence is insufficient to establish a violation in the view of the OSC, the Investigation and Prosecution Division will notify you of its findings and invite comments *13 days* before closing the file.

Once the file is closed you cannot appeal. You may only pursue a whistleblower claim, with or without the assistance of counsel, as an appeal to the MSPB. But if you do not have a whistleblower reprisal claim, there is no further appeal to the MSPB or to the courts.

If the evidence sufficiently establishes a violation of law, rule, or regulation, the OSC reports its findings to the agency head and seeks agency certification that the agency is taking specific corrective action. If the OSC finds a possible criminal violation, it is reported to the Department of Justice. If the agency does not cooperate and take corrective action, the OSC may press a claim on behalf of the aggrieved employee (complainant) before the MSPB seeking "make-whole" relief, such as money damages or restoration of your position.

If the OSC obtains corrective action for you, it may then initiate disciplinary action against the government official who committed the prohibited personnel practice. However, you are powerless to compel the OSC to seek disciplinary measures. The agency may initiate the disciplinary action with the OSC's prior consent, or the OSC may prosecute the disciplinary action against the government official before the MSPB. Your testimony and cooperation may be essential to the OSC's effort to pursue disciplinary action against the responsible officials. Employees who commit prohibited personnel practices are subject to:

- removal
- reduction in grade
- debarment from federal employment for up to five years
- suspension
- reprimand, and/or
- a fine of up to $1,000

What about emergency situations?

In rare instances, the OSC or the MSPB may be willing to stop an agency from taking a proposed action, because the agency appears to be doing something that is "too bad to be true" so to speak. For example, if the agency proposes to remove someone and states that the reason is that the employee had filed or supported a complaint at the OSC, the OSC or the MSPB will probably want to stop the agency in its tracks, because of its blatant retaliation for protected activity. If the retaliation or illegality of the agency action is not so obvious, the OSC and the MSPB will normally let the proposed action run its course and, if you bring a complaint, rule on it and provide you a remedy if you prove your case.

When you want the OSC or the MSPB to stop an agency action before it is final, you must ask them to "stay" the action. You must convince the OSC or the MSPB that the personnel action is, or will be, the result of a prohibited personnel practice. You must give them reasonable grounds to believe this. Stays are like temporary restraining orders or preliminary injunctions—

designed to keep things the way they are until your charge of a prohibited personnel practice can be heard by the MSPB or investigated in its entirety by the OSC.

Generally, stays will prevent further substantial damage to you pending a resolution of the contested claim. Typically, the agency will voluntarily stay the contested action if the OSC convinces the agency that, otherwise, the OSC will ask for a stay through the formal process before the MSPB. In the case of a whistleblower retaliation case, stay requests may be filed directly with the MSPB once you are eligible to file your whistleblower appeal with the Board. Once you, or the OSC on your behalf, asks the MSPB for a stay, the MSPB has only *10 days* to respond.

Is it possible to settle my claim with the help of the OSC?

At any time, the OSC may attempt to get the agency to cooperate with the OSC's directives, by negotiating with you, as the aggrieved employee, and with the agency to resolve the dispute in a mutually satisfactory outcome short of lengthy and expensive litigation. Settlements can be "win-win" situations, as long as the parties are knowledgeable concerning the processing of claims and the alternatives to settlement. Therefore, you should seek independent legal counsel and seek the recovery of legal fees and costs before agreeing to a settlement. It is of the utmost importance that you understand your rights and possible remedies before signing a settlement agreement, which will compromise your rights. (See Chapter 32.)

Except for IRA cases as discussed above, the OSC decision to close your case is final—whether the OSC based it upon a determination of insufficient evidence, or the fact that it believes the agency has already taken sufficient corrective action. There is no avenue to challenge the OSC decision, which may leave an affected employee feeling dissatisfied.

Do not let a dismissal letter deter you if you allege reprisal for whistleblowing—a 2302(b)(8) case—or a violation of 2302(b)(9) for which an IRA appeal is available. Along with a dismissal letter, the OSC will inform you of your right to file an IRA appeal before the MSPB either on your own or with an attorney. This option is only available to those who allege reprisal for whistleblowing or certain violations of 2302(b)(9). The right to pursue an IRA is governed by MSPB regulations.[11]

---

[11] *See* 29 CFR § 1201, 1209.

One final thought about the OSC. It has historically not been regarded as a very effective agency for aggressively protecting employees' rights. If you can raise your prohibited personnel practices complaint directly with the MSPB or to an arbitrator, give serious consideration to doing so.

What remedies are available for victims of prohibited personnel practices?

The remedy for a victim of a prohibited personnel practice is through corrective action. Until 1994, corrective action was defined somewhat restrictively, considering the consequences that such practices, and the complaint process, have on an employee. In 1994, Congress amended the definition of corrective action to include the following possibilities:

- job restoration
- attorney fees and costs
- back pay and related benefits
- medical costs
- travel expenses
- reasonable and foreseeable monetary damages caused by the prohibited practice ("consequential damages")
- Compensatory Damages (for example, monetary payments for personal and emotional injuries) [12]

Security Clearance Reprisal and Intelligence Agency Whistleblowers

In addition to the OSC/MSPB/Union remedies discussed above, a separate set of whistleblower reprisal mechanisms are being created under Presidential Policy Directive 19 ("PPD-19"), which was issued in 2012. Under PPD-19, agencies are to develop procedures to handle:

(a) whistleblower reprisal claims from intelligence agency employees, and

(b) claims from all individuals who believe that they have been denied a security clearance in retaliation for whistleblowing.

These new complaint procedures were supposed to take effect in 2013, but the policies are being drafted separately by each affected agency. If

[12] Compensatory damages for whistleblower reprisal claims were only first allowed by the Whistleblower Protection Enhancement Act of 2012. The MSPB has held that compensatory damages are not available in cases where the whistleblower reprisal predated the 2012 amendments, although other money damages such as back pay and consequential damages are still available. *See King v. Dept of the Air Force,* 119 MSPR 663 (2013).

you have a claim that would fall within the scope of PPD-19, check your agency-specific policy for details on how to file your complaint. Following PPD-19, Congress passed Pub.L 113-126, Sections 601-603, covering many of the sames issues as PPD-19. The implementing regulations for Sections 601-603 were not yet written when this Guide went to press. When looking at possible PPD-19 claims, check out Sections 601-603 as well.

If you work for the Postal Service or one of the other agencies which are not specifically covered by prohibited personnel practices law[13] or the Whistleblower Protection Act, you should consult with an attorney, union representative, or labor relations expert to learn more about bringing your case.

Final Thoughts

Congress was concerned enough about protecting those who blow the whistle that it enhanced the Whistleblower Protection Act in 2012. It is still not easy to go against management by reporting something you believe is wrong to those who hopefully can do something about it. It is, however, good to know that if you do, the law usually provides protection for you—even if it turns out your reasonable concerns were unfounded. Through this whistleblowing legislation and the law outlining prohibited personnel practices, you have the weapons to fight back and protect your job when you think that you are wrongfully under attack. Of course, you should never proceed with a complaint based merely on suspicion or office gossip. It is important to check your facts carefully before initiating a complaint process.

---

[13] *See* 5 USC § 2302.

8

Unions and Collective Bargaining

All for One, and One for All...

IN THIS CHAPTER YOU WILL LEARN:

- what collective bargaining is
- what you should consider in determining whether to join a union
- what rights will be available to you as a union member
- which agencies govern union activities
- what union grievance procedures are

Contents Chapter Eight - Unions and Collective Bargaining

INTRODUCTION

At some point in your federal career, you may wish to consider the option of joining a union. Whether or not you decide to do so is totally up to you. You may do so because you have a family history of union involvement. You may feel threatened by aspects of your work environment. You may feel the union will give you protection from management or that you will achieve greater rights through the union. You may feel pressure to join a union from your coworkers or you may not want to be thought of as a freeloader who gets all the benefits a union brings, but doesn't pay union dues. Whatever the reason, your choice of whether or not to join will benefit from knowing something about how unions in the federal government work. That is what we will talk about in this chapter.

WHAT ARE UNIONS AND WHO CAN JOIN THEM?

Unions are organizations of workers who join together for the purpose of negotiating as a group with management about workplace issues. Who can be in the union and the issues it can negotiate with management are governed by collective bargaining statutes. This area is called labor law. In the federal sector, collective bargaining is governed by the Federal Service Labor-Management Relations Statute ("FSLMRS").[1] The Federal Labor Relations Authority ("FLRA" or "the Authority") administers the statute governing collective bargaining and unfair labor practices in the federal government. The Department of Labor ("DOL") is responsible for the standards of conduct for labor unions and the Federal Mediation and

[1] The Federal Service Labor-Management Relations Statute (FSLMRS) governing unions and collective bargaining is set forth in Chapter 71 Title 5 of the U.S. Code. The "FSLMRS" is one chapter of the Civil Service Reform Act of 1978.

Conciliation Service ("FMCS") provides mediation assistance for bargaining, and occasionally for grievance disputes.

TIP

The FSLMRS grants most federal employees the "... right to form, join, or assist any labor organization, or to refrain from any such activity, freely and without fear of penalty or reprisal, and each employee shall be protected in the exercise of such right." The decision to join or not join a union is yours to make.

Although the law governing collective bargaining and union activity of federal employees is similar to the law regulating the private sector, there are significant differences. As a federal employee, you do not have a right to strike. There is also a more limited scope of bargaining, as discussed later in this chapter. In the federal sector, you are not required to join a union or pay the equivalent of union dues.

Unions have the right to designate a representative, usually a union steward, to represent them in dealings with your agency and to engage in collective bargaining about the terms and conditions of employment.

Employees who represent unions in the negotiation of a collective bargaining agreement and in impasse procedures are normally paid for their time at their usual hourly rate by the agency they work for. This is called "official time." Unions may also negotiate for official time for employees who engage in other union representational activities, including grievance handling. However, internal union activities such as membership recruitment or union meetings may not be conducted on "official time."

Some employees are excluded from coverage under the FSLMRS. Excluded employees are:

- supervisors
- managers
- confidential employees (such as secretaries in the labor relations office or to agency policymakers)
- personnelists
- members of the Foreign Service (they have their own law)
- members of the uniformed services
- certain other agencies engaged in national security functions

A "supervisor" is defined as someone who consistently exercises independent judgment in his job—who has the authority to take certain personnel actions, to adjust grievances, or to effectively recommend such action. Any federal employee may belong to a labor organization. However, if the employee is excluded from coverage under the FSLMRS, the union may not represent the employee in job-related matters.

What is the role of the union in collective bargaining?

Collective bargaining is the process by which unions and management meet to consult, negotiate, and bargain in good faith to reach a written agreement on the terms and conditions of employment. Before a union can be recognized as the exclusive representative for any group of government employees, there must be a representation election supervised by the FLRA. In that election, a majority of the employees must vote in favor of union representation in order for the union to win the right to represent the bargaining unit. Unlike the private sector, in the federal sector there is no law permitting the voluntary recognition of a union by an agency without an election. Once recognized, only the union can negotiate with management.

After being certified as the exclusive representative by the FLRA, the union has the right to bargain over the terms and conditions of employment, including personnel policies and practices, and matters affecting working conditions with certain exclusions, such as broad management rights. The union can also bargain for employees' union dues to be automatically deducted from their paychecks and turned over to the union. The period of dues deduction is automatically renewable, unless such withholding is revoked by the employee.

The contract bargained between management and the union is called a "collective bargaining agreement" ("CBA"). The CBA is also sometimes simply referred to as the "union contract." The CBA will typically cover a variety of work rule issues affecting your employment. For example, your CBA may contain rules governing the requesting and granting of sick leave, the procedures management must follow when competing a vacancy for promotion, the criteria for receiving a career-ladder promotion, how long certain employment records must be retained, whether an employee gets higher pay when placed in a temporary promotion, health and safety provisions, as well as the grievance process employees must follow to challenge various violations of agency rules, policies, and the CBA. If you do not have a copy of your CBA, request one from your agency personnel office or your union steward.

The union is allowed to be present at "formal discussions" between the agency representatives and you concerning any grievance, personnel policy or practice, or other general condition of employment even if you choose to represent yourself rather than let the union represent you.

The union may also be present if you are interviewed by an agency representative in connection with an investigation if you reasonably believe that the interview may result in disciplinary action and you request representation. This right to union representation is known as the "Weingarten" right, based upon a major Supreme Court decision. The union representative usually takes an active role in advising you when you are under investigation.

Normally, it is up to you to request union representation and not to participate in an investigative interview until the union representative is available. However, you are required to respond to the agency concerning all matters which have to do with employment unless there is a possibility that a crime has been committed. If you are being interviewed about a potentially criminal matter, you may assert your Fifth Amendment right to be silent and to be represented by an attorney unless you are given immunity from criminal prosecution.

If you are challenging a disciplinary or adverse action under a statutory appeals system, such as an MSPB appeal or EEOC complaint, you may retain a private lawyer to represent you. However, if you would rather pursue your complaint under the labor agreement's grievance process, only the union may invoke arbitration if you are unsuccessful in obtaining relief in the grievance procedure or have received a final disciplinary or adverse action. It may be possible for your lawyer to represent both the union and you in arbitration, but only if the union consents to representation by a private attorney. At times, you will have to be prepared to pay part or all of the arbitration costs if you insist on private counsel.

Should I join the union?

Although unions are obligated by law to represent all employees of a bargaining unit regardless of union membership, as a practical matter, it may be more difficult to obtain union representation if you are not a member.

Even if you have not previously joined, it is a good idea to do so prior to or shortly after requesting the union's assistance in providing representation. If you are not satisfied with your union representative, you can request assistance from higher level union officials, and you can appeal to the membership at a union meeting. You can also file an unfair labor practice (ULP) charge if the union fails to properly represent you, i.e., violates its duty of fair representation, especially if it is due to your lack of union membership or internal union politics. See the section later in this chapter on ULPs.

Does the union have greater access to information I may need?

As the exclusive representative of employees, the union also has the right to obtain from the agency necessary information for which there is a "particularized need,"[2] without charge and without using the Freedom of Information and Privacy Acts. This right to information is very important in preparing for contract negotiations and in representing employees in grievances, arbitration, and in replying to proposed disciplinary and adverse actions.

The union may obtain relevant documents "normally maintained by the agency in the regular course of business" which are "reasonably available and necessary" in regard to matters within the scope of collective bargaining. This is especially important in obtaining information favorable to your case which the agency may not otherwise reveal, including how comparable employees were treated.

The union is not entitled to agency information which "constitutes guidance, advice, counsel, or training provided for management officials or supervisors."

What is the role of the Federal Labor Relations Authority ("FLRA")?

The FLRA is composed of three members who decide representation and election issues, ULP cases, negotiability appeals, and exceptions (appeals) to arbitration awards. For more information, go to FLRA.gov. Only FLRA final decisions in ULP cases and negotiability appeal cases can be appealed to the courts by the union or agency involved. The General Counsel of the

---

2 The union may not merely ask for the information, but must explain why it needs the information to represent the employee(s).

FLRA investigates alleged ULPs, issues ULP complaints, and prosecutes ULP complaints before the administrative law judges ("ALJs") and the FLRA.

Certification and decertification

Before a labor organization can file for exclusive recognition, it must first obtain a minimum 30 percent showing of interest from employees in an "appropriate bargaining unit." An "appropriate bargaining unit" is determined by such factors as the similarity of employees' jobs, what part of an agency's organization the unit comprises (small, fragmented units are not favored), whether the employees are under a common personnel office and appointing authority, and whether employees in the unit have a community of (common) interest. Also, professional and nonprofessional employees may not be placed in the same bargaining unit unless the professional employees specifically vote to be included in the same unit.

It may be necessary for the FLRA to hold a hearing if there is a dispute as to the appropriateness of the unit. In order to be certified as the exclusive bargaining agent for the employees, the union must prevail in a secret ballot election where it receives the majority of votes cast. There is a similar provision for the decertification of unions if the members no longer want the union to be the exclusive bargaining representative. Other labor organizations may seek to displace the current bargaining agent by requesting an election at periodic intervals. The FLRA administers the election and certification procedures.

Unfair labor practices (ULPs)

Both agencies and unions commit ULPs when they violate an employee's right to join and support, or not join and support, a union. Your agency commits a ULP when it engages in the following conduct.[3]

1. interfering with, restraining, or coercing employees who exercise their rights
2. encouraging or discouraging membership in any labor organization by discrimination in connection with hiring, tenure, promotion, or other conditions of employment
3. sponsoring, controlling, or assisting a labor organization other than furnishing upon request customary and routine services and facilities which are also furnished on an impartial basis to other labor organizations having equivalent status

---

[3] These agency ULPs are set out at 5 USC § 7116(a)(1)-(8).

4. disciplining or otherwise discriminating against an employee because the employee has filed a complaint, affidavit, or petition or has given any information or testimony under the FSLMRS
5. refusing to consult or negotiate in good faith with a labor organization
6. failing or refusing to cooperate in impasse procedures
7. enforcing any rule or regulation which is in conflict with any applicable collective bargaining agreement if the agreement was already in effect, or
8. otherwise failing to comply with any other provision of the FSLMRS

The first category is the most common and is included in all ULP charges. A violation generally involves your agency trying to prevent you from engaging in protected union activities. The second category will typically involve discrimination against you if you are a union representative or employee who participated in protected union activities such as filing grievances. The third category usually means an agency favoring one union over another. The fourth category usually means discrimination against you because of your participation in an FLRA matter. The fifth and sixth categories involve bad faith bargaining by agency management.

If a union, agency, or you as an employee believe that you have been subject to a ULP, you have *6 months* in which to file a formal complaint, using the FLRA's charge form, with the Regional Director of the applicable FLRA Regional Office. It is only necessary to simply state:

- what happened
- when it happened
- the relevant sections of the statute violated
- the names, addresses, and telephone numbers of the applicable parties

The FLRA Regional Director then conducts an investigation and may issue a complaint if he finds "probable cause" to believe a violation has occurred and the case is not settled.

If a complaint is issued, an FLRA attorney represents you, as the charging party, before an administrative law judge ("ALJ"). If the Regional Director of the FLRA refuses to issue a complaint, you may file a request for review by the FLRA's General Counsel. If the General Counsel does not overrule the Regional Director, there is no further appeal or judicial review.

Wrongdoing can occur on both sides of the labor-management equation. Unions may also commit unfair labor practices, which are also divided into eight separate categories: [4]

1. interfering with, restraining, or coercing employees who exercise their rights
2. causing or attempting to cause an agency to discriminate against any employee who exercises his/her rights
3. coercing, disciplining, fining, or attempting to coerce a member of the labor organization as punishment, reprisal, or for the purpose of hindering or impeding the member's work performance or productivity
4. discriminating against an employee with respect to terms or conditions of membership in the labor organization on the basis of race, color, creed, national origin, sex, age, civil service status, political affiliation, marital status, or handicapping condition
5. refusing to consult or negotiate in good faith with an agency
6. failing or refusing to cooperate in impasse procedures
7. calling or participating in a strike, work stoppage, or slowdown or picketing which interferes with agency operations, or
8. otherwise failing to comply with any other provision of the FSLMRS

Strikes by government employees are illegal, and you can be terminated for striking. However, peaceful informational picketing is a protected First Amendment right and can be engaged in by unions and employees who are off duty, provided that the picketing does not interfere with employees coming to or leaving work or with the performance of their duties. Unions representing federal employees that willfully and intentionally engage in a strike, work stoppage, or slowdown may be subject to severe penalties, including the loss of their recognition as the exclusive bargaining agent of the employees.

Contract negotiations

There are both mandatory and "permissive" subjects of bargaining. Agency management is required by law to negotiate concerning mandatory subjects. However, there is a limited scope of bargaining in the federal sector. There are a variety of management rights over which a union may not legally

---

[4] These union ULPs are set out at 5 USC § 7116(b)(1)-(8).

bargain. Agency management often refuses to negotiate on such "illegal" subjects as management's right to control the agency's:

- mission
- budget
- organization
- number of employees agency-wide, and
- internal security practices

Even if management does bargain and reach agreement with the union concerning one of these issues, the agreement is not enforceable. For example, the union may not bargain over management's right to assign work, determine training requirements, discipline employees, or determine internal security matters. The union may negotiate over "procedures" used by management in making these decisions, but cannot dictate the ultimate decision. For example, in the promotion process, the union could negotiate that the "best qualified list" of eligible candidates be comprised of the employees having the five highest scores from all applicants. But the union could not negotiate that the highest rated employee be selected for the promotion. Also, unions may not bargain over matters set by statute, like pay rates and retirement benefits. However, the parties may mutually agree to negotiate over what are known as "permissive" subjects—the numbers, types, or grades of employees assigned to a particular work unit or task. The scope of bargaining here is quite different from what unions may bargain over in the private sector where almost all issues affecting wages and working conditions are bargainable between the union and management.

During contract negotiations between a union and an agency, disputes often arise over the scope of bargaining. Negotiability appeals, which are unique to the federal sector, may be filed by unions that believe agency management is refusing to negotiate on a matter which comes within the scope of collective bargaining. Unions may appeal agency written determinations of non-negotiability to the FLRA and, if necessary, to the courts, although this a time-consuming process which often greatly delays collective bargaining.

Are there other agencies involved in union matters?

The FLRA is not the only agency that is involved in federal labor law matters. While the FLRA has general, overall responsibility for federal sector labor law, there are a few other agencies with more limited responsibilities, as well.

Federal Mediation and Conciliation Service ("FMCS")

Sometimes a union and management are unable to reach agreement in their collective bargaining negotiations. When this happens, they are required to seek mediation assistance from the FMCS. Mediators of the FMCS are federal employees stationed in various FMCS offices who provide assistance to the parties in settling negotiation impasses. Mediators attempt to bring the parties together in an agreed-upon solution reached by the parties themselves. The mediators cannot impose or mandate a settlement. The theory is that since the union and management are the ones who must live with the agreement they reach, they should be the ones to create it. The FMCS attempts to help them when they reach a snag in that process.

Federal Service Impasses Panel ("FSIP" or "the Panel")

Even after the parties engage the help of the FMCS, sometimes they still cannot agree on what goes into their collective bargaining agreement. They are stuck in their negotiations, with neither party willing to move. They have reached what is called an impasse. They can now ask for the assistance of the FSIP. However, they can only do so after they have exhausted the matter with the FMCS.

The FSIP is generally composed of neutral outsiders who work part-time for the Panel along with a small permanent staff. The FSIP, or an outside arbitrator if ordered by the FSIP or agreed to by the parties and approved by the FSIP, may issue final decisions on negotiation impasses. The Panel uses different methods, including reviewing written submissions of positions, mediation, arbitration, and holding hearings to resolve bargaining impasses. The FSIP's final decision is binding upon the parties with no right of further review, except for any FLRA challenge that the FSIP has included a "nonnegotiable" subject in its decision.

Department of Labor ("DOL")

Besides laws governing their bargaining activities, there are also laws unions must follow in conducting their internal business. The U.S. Department of Labor enforces the standards of conduct for unions. For more information, go to dol.gov. Under the law,[5] unions are required to:

- file copies of their constitution and bylaws and annual financial reports with the DOL

---

5 *See* 5 USC § 7120.

- be free from corrupt influences and influences opposed to basic democratic principles
- have certain fiduciary responsibilities to act for the benefit of members
- hold periodic election of officers
- provide that members are able to participate in the union's internal affairs
- assure that members receive fair and equal treatment and due process in union disciplinary proceedings, and
- hold proper elections

Union members have the right to free speech and assembly and an equal right to vote and participate in meetings.[6]

Complaints of violations by unions may be filed with the Department of Labor. The agency within the DOL assigned to enforce the law is the Office of Labor Management Standards ("OLMS").

The Department of Labor will insist that complaining union members exhaust internal union remedies before appealing to the DOL. Thus you will have to consult your union's constitution and file a timely internal union appeal within the deadlines set forth in the constitution. If the OLMS decides your complaint has a "reasonable" basis, there will be a hearing before an administrative law judge of the DOL. If there is a violation, the DOL has the responsibility of bringing the matter to court. There are special procedures for appealing unfair internal union elections to the DOL. The major difference between the rights of members of federal and private sector unions is that enforcement for federal employees is primarily through the DOL rather than through the courts.

Are disputes handled differently if there's a union?

Throughout this book we have made references to the alternative appeal procedures you may be able to follow if you are represented by a union. Often, the union has negotiated a different set of procedures for resolving disputes between the employer and unionized employees which are not available to employees not represented by a union.

---

[6] The standards of conduct for federal unions are comparable to the requirements of the Labor-Management Reporting and Disclosure Act, which apply to the private sector.

Virtually all collective bargaining agreements contain provisions for deciding disputes through grievances. The process is known as the negotiated grievance procedure because it has been negotiated by the parties and put into an agency-union collective bargaining agreement. Federal-sector collective bargaining agreements must provide for binding arbitration as part of the process for resolving disputes. The scope of the grievance and arbitration procedures—what matters can be grieved—may be negotiated by the parties.

Any union, agency, or employee in a bargaining unit with a collective bargaining agreement may file a grievance under the negotiated grievance procedure on any matter falling within the collective bargaining agreement's scope or coverage. However, there are certain disputes which by law are excluded from the scope of the grievance process. Excluded disputes are those concerning:

- prohibited political activities
- retirement
- life insurance or health insurance
- suspensions or removals due to violations of national security
- any employment examination, certification, or initial appointment, and
- the classification of any position which does not result in a reduction in grade or pay

Whether or not you are covered by a union-negotiated grievance procedure, you may also have the independent statutory right to file administrative appeals over:

- a prohibited personnel practice, including reprisal for whistleblowing
- an adverse action, or
- discrimination

These are referred to as "statutory appeals."

If you are covered by a negotiated grievance procedure which also covers these statutory appeals, you may file either a grievance under the CBA or file a statutory appeal/complaint to the appropriate agency, but not both. Generally, whichever procedure you first reduce to writing will be considered the one elected. Once made, this election is irrevocable. This is called an "election of remedies." However, if your negotiated grievance procedure covers reductions-in-force or denials of within-grade increases, these claims may *only* be pursued under the union grievance procedure.

Usually you do not know whether the union will agree to take the case to arbitration at the time an initial grievance is filed. Therefore, it is important to try to obtain the union's written agreement to arbitrate before filing a written grievance. This is especially true if you expect to be represented by private counsel. If the union is unwilling to commit to invoking arbitration, then you should consider filing an appeal with the MSPB or the EEOC, as applicable.

TIP

Often it is necessary to reach a financial understanding with the union as to the division of the expenses before the union will agree to invoke arbitration. The union may request that you pay for all or part of the union's legal fees and expenses.

Arbitration

After an agency issues its final response to a grievance, if the grievance is not satisfactorily resolved, the union may invoke arbitration. Unless the agency and union have already agreed on a permanent panel of arbitrators, a request is made for a panel or list of arbitrators, who are independent parties experienced in labor-management relations. The request is usually made to the FMCS or the American Arbitration Association. The union generally requests that the panel of arbitrators be limited to those in the relevant geographical area with federal sector experience, which may include members of the National Academy of Arbitrators who are very experienced but more expensive arbitrators.

Upon receipt of the list of arbitrators, the parties will normally alternately strike names or rank each arbitrator according to their preference. By these methods the parties will then select an arbitrator to hear the case. Depending upon the arbitrator's schedule, a hearing is normally scheduled within one to three months.

A typical arbitration hearing will last one day but may take longer if there are complicated issues, including adverse actions or claims of discrimination or reprisal. Each party may present witnesses and exhibits at the hearing. There may be a court reporter present if a transcript is needed.

At the closing of the hearing, the parties may make oral or written closing arguments and request to submit written briefs. The arbitrator will normally issue the decision (called an "award") within *30-60 days* after the close of the hearing or receipt of the written briefs.

TIP

A transcript is recommended for statutory appeals which have the possibility of judicial review, such as:

- ***suspensions of more than 14 days***
- ***demotions***
- ***removals***
- ***reductions-in-force***
- ***cases alleging discrimination***

The arbitrator's fees are usually split between the parties, unless they agree otherwise. The fees generally range from $1,500 - $2,000 or more per day, and include the hearing days and additional days for reviewing the record and preparing a decision and award.

Remedies Because grievance procedures frequently cover statutory appeals, arbitrators in the federal sector often have greater authority than those in the private sector in awarding remedies to prevailing unions. For example, the arbitrator may award reasonable attorney fees under the Back Pay Act,[7] under various civil rights acts, or the Fair Labor Standards Act for unpaid overtime. In the case of discrimination under the Civil Rights Act of 1964, and the Rehabilitation Act of 1973 (see Chapter 5), there is the possibility of compensatory damages of up to $300,000 per case. Where the arbitrator finds that the agency has committed a prohibited personnel practice, the arbitrator may order the agency to initiate disciplinary actions against the offending supervisors and management officials.[8]

Appeals An agency is required to take the actions ordered in the arbitrator's final award, including payment of back pay with interest. If either of the parties is not satisfied with the arbitration award, it may file an appeal to the arbitrator's award with the FLRA within the *30-day* period beginning

---

7 *See* 5 USC § 5596.
8 *See* 5 USC § 1215(a)(3).

on the date the award is served on the parties. This appeal is called an "exception." This statutory time limit of *30 days* cannot be waived. The FLRA will review the parties' written submissions and issue a final decision which is binding upon the parties with no right of judicial review, except for cases involving discrimination or ULPs.

However, not all appeals of arbitrators' decisions can be taken to the FLRA. If the grievance was over an adverse action otherwise appealable to the MSPB, you must instead file for review of the award with the United States Court of Appeals for the Federal Circuit.

Judicial review

If the arbitrator's award involves a "mixed case," which is an adverse action coupled with an allegation of discrimination, there is no review by the FLRA. The employee, not the union, may appeal to the MSPB, the EEOC, and then to the appropriate U.S. district court for a jury trial *de novo* on the discrimination issues. As mentioned earlier, if the arbitration award involves a statutory appeal, such as a suspension for 15 days or more, demotion, or a removal, there is no review by the FLRA. As noted above, you, not the union, may file a petition for appeal of the award with the U.S. Court of Appeals for the Federal Circuit.

In the case of ULPs, if there is an egregious case, upon the issuance of a ULP complaint, the FLRA may file a petition in the appropriate U.S. district court for temporary relief, including a restraining order to immediately stop the illegal practice. This is an extraordinary remedy which is rarely granted and only when there will be irreparable harm if the matter is not immediately resolved.

In addition, the FLRA may petition any appropriate court of appeals for enforcement of its final orders in ULP cases. Where the union or agency receives an adverse final decision from the FLRA involving unfair labor practices or negotiability appeals, it may request judicial review by the appropriate regional U.S. court of appeals.

Final Thoughts

Unions play an important role in obtaining and enforcing workplace rights for federal employees. Over one-third of the federal workforce is covered by collective bargaining agreements. Unions frequently have serious disputes with management concerning a variety of subjects affecting working terms and conditions. Union agreements often provide greater rights for employees than are possessed by employees in non-unionized agencies. For example, employees who are covered by union agreements can use grievance and arbitration procedures to enforce their rights. Unionized employees, through the union, also have more say about agency policies and practices. Being part of a collective bargaining unit can provide you with more options for obtaining and pursuing important job rights. Executive Order 13522, Creating Labor Management Forums to Improve Delivery of Government Services, has encouraged unions and management to work cooperatively to resolve outstanding issues without resort to litigation.

9

Reductions-in-Force and Furloughs

When Uncle Sam Streamlines

In This Chapter You Will Learn:

- what a reduction-in-force is and when it can be done
- what rights you have if you are caught in a reduction-in-force
- what you can do if you think you were the wrongful subject of a reduction-in-force

Contents Chapter Nine - Reductions-in-Force and Furloughs

Introduction

Reduction-in-force. The very words can send chills down the spine of the coolest federal employee. At one point, most of us thought that federal government employment was the safest job imaginable. There would always be a need for our services, and bureaucracy always gets bigger, not smaller. Or so we thought. But with wavering economic conditions, taxpayers calling for curbs on government spending, technology taking over positions once held by people, and other factors, this is simply not true anymore. One of the most disturbing things that can happen in your federal employment career is to be the victim of a reduction-in-force, or "RIF." Even if you've heard rumblings, it still generally takes you by surprise and turns your world inside out—at least temporarily. Suddenly you're out of a job. How will you feed yourself or your family? How will you pay your mortgage? What about your insurance? Will you ever be called back? What had once been security, is now nonexistent. What are you to do?

In this chapter we will discuss what a RIF is, what your rights are, and how you can turn the world from chaos back into sanity.

What is a Reduction-in-Force ("RIF")?

A reduction-in-force, or RIF, occurs when an agency decides to reduce staffing. RIFs can result from a variety of circumstances, such as lack of work, shortage of funds, lowered personnel ceilings, or reorganizations. You may also be riffed if subjected to a furlough of 30 days or longer. Please see below for details on furloughs. RIFs are not related to your conduct or performance.

However, your performance on the job may affect your retention rights, which are explained in this chapter. RIFs result in separations, demotions, furloughs for more than thirty days, or employee reassignments which, in turn, often result in the displacement or separation of other employees.

Federal agencies enjoy tremendous discretion in executing RIFs. For the most part, you will rarely be able to successfully challenge your agency's decision to conduct a RIF. Whether you are impacted by a RIF and separated from the agency, or displace another employee in the same or lower grade, depends on a complex series of "retention rights," which are also called "bump" and "retreat" rights. These rights are regulated and are explained later in this chapter. Agencies may, in their discretion, allow affected employees to fill vacancies not impacted by the RIF.

Agencies have total discretion to decide when to carry out a RIF. However, they must follow certain rules when implementing a RIF. You can reverse a RIF action when your agency fails to properly follow the RIF regulations.

Where can I find RIF regulations and procedures?

The regulations on RIFs issued by OPM can be found at 5 CFR 351. This chapter discusses the most important aspects of RIFs and how you can protect your rights. If you still have questions about the agency's duties and your rights and responsibilities, you should look directly at the regulations. If you ask your agency for a copy of these regulations, the agency must give it to you. If your agency is conducting a RIF, the agency personnel office should be able to provide you with additional agency-specific information, such as guidelines, policies, or procedures.

Who is covered by OPM's RIF regulations?

Most federal employees may be subject to a RIF and have RIF appeal rights, which are explained below. Generally, employees in the executive branch are covered by OPM's RIF regulations, as are many others who are specifically identified by Congress, such as administrative law judges. To determine whether you are covered, check the Code of Federal Regulations.[1]

Is it possible for me to stay on after a RIF?

It is possible for you to stay on even if there is a RIF in your agency. Whether you do or not usually depends upon your retention rights. Retention rights

---

1 *See* 5 CFR § 351.202.

are the rights you may have to remain employed with your agency even though the agency is undergoing a RIF. This area is heavily regulated by OPM and your agency. Know the rights well. They may make the difference between you getting on the bus in the morning and going to work, or getting on the bus and going to the unemployment agency.

Retention standing

Retention standing in a RIF determines whether you will be separated, demoted, or remain unaffected by the RIF. In a RIF, your agency determines the retention standing of each competing employee based upon the employee's competitive area and competitive level. The criteria for the competitive level, and your retention rights, are determined by OPM's regulations.

Competitive area Each agency is supposed to establish competitive areas in which employees compete for retention in the event of a RIF. A competitive area can be all or part of an agency and can be defined by organizational structure and by geographical boundaries. Organizationally, the minimum competitive area is a bureau, major command, directorate, or other equivalent major subdivision of an agency. The geographical boundary is usually the local commuting area. In the field, the minimum competitive area is an activity under separate administration within the local commuting area. Recent court cases interpret the regulations to read that the competitive area can be quite small.

The agency must make readily available for review descriptions of all competitive areas. This is very important to you because the competitive area identifies the organizational boundary in which you compete for a position. As soon as an agency announces its intention to conduct a RIF or that it is considering a RIF, you should talk with an agency personnel specialist and ask to review the competitive areas to see where you are identified.

Competitive level Each competitive area can have several different competitive levels. The goal of a competitive level is to identify a pool of similar positions so that the people in those positions can easily move within the pool. Employees assigned to the same competitive level compete for available positions according to their retention rights. All the positions in the competitive level should:

- be in the same grade or occupational level
- have the same classification series, and
- should be similar in:

1. duties
2. qualification requirements
3. pay schedules, and
4. working conditions

The similarities of the positions facilitate the reassignment of employees within the competitive level without undue interruption. Undue interruption occurs when the transferring employee is unable to perform the functions of the new job after ninety days.

Competitive level determinations are based on each employee's official position, not the employee's personal qualifications. Separate competitive levels must be established for positions in the competitive service. In the excepted service, levels must be established for positions under different appointment authorities (See Chapter 1). An agency must also establish separate competitive levels according to:

- positions under different pay schedules
- positions under different work schedules, and
- positions filled by trainees

Retention register The retention register is the single most important document in a RIF. Before releasing employees from a competitive level, agencies must establish a separate retention register for that competitive level. The register ranks all employees in a competitive level in order of their retention standing. The register identifies each employee in the competitive level by name. This list includes people who have been temporarily promoted or detailed from the competitive level, and therefore are expected to return to the competitive level at the end of the temporary promotion or detail. The register also identifies all temporary employees, and those on a time-limited appointment.

Your place on the retention register will tell you whether you will still have a job with the agency at the end of the RIF and if so, in what position. Like the descriptions of your agency's competitive areas, you should get a copy of the retention register as soon as possible. Review the retention register carefully to make sure that all the information used by the agency to place you on the register is accurate. Do not pass up this opportunity to ensure your proper placement on the retention register. Correcting an error at this stage may save you from the distress of being improperly RIFd.

Two retention registers are created, one for the competitive service and one for the excepted service. Employees in each service are separated into three groups based upon the employees' tenure with the government. In the competitive service, the three groups are:

- Career
- Career-conditional and probationary
- Indefinite or temporary appointments pending establishment of a register (TAPER), status quo appointments, term appointments and some other non-status non-temporary appointments

In the excepted service, the three groups are:

- Permanent employees whose appointments have no restriction or condition such as conditional, indefinite, specific time limit or trial period
- Employees serving trial periods or whose tenure is equivalent to career-conditional appointments in the competitive service
- Employees with indefinite tenures, time-limited appointments over one year, or in a temporary appointment but who have completed a continuous year of service

Each of these groups is then divided into three subgroups:

1. veterans with at least thirty percent service-connected disability;
2. veterans with less than thirty percent service-connected disability; and
3. non-veterans

Employees are further classified within these subgroups based upon their:

- tenure of employment
- veterans preference
- length of service, and
- performance

The retention register tells you which subgroup you are in. You then compete with other employees within the subgroup for retention. As discussed below, a person in a higher subgroup may displace a person in a lower subgroup.

Release from competitive level If your position is abolished, you are not automatically released from your competitive level. Instead, you compete with other employees in your group or subgroup for retention in the competitive level. First, the agency releases non-competing employees from a competitive level. If this first round of releases does not eliminate sufficient positions, the agency then releases competing employees according to their retention rights as identified on the retention register.

Retention rights

Again, a RIF does not automatically mean that you will be released from service. Even if you are chosen for release, you may have other rights that save your job.

Assignment involving displacement If you are released from your competitive level, you may be able to be assigned to a position in another competitive level. The position must meet the following criteria:

- be in the competitive service
- be in the same competitive area
- last at least three months
- have a representative pay rate (basic pay) no higher than the position from which you are released
- be one for which you are qualified
- be occupied by another employee subject to displacement, and
- have the same work schedule

If an assignment is available, your agency must offer you, rather than furlough or separation, an assignment to another competitive position which requires no reduction, or the least possible reduction, in your grade. If you accept an offer of assignment and displace another employee, you retain the same status and tenure in your new position. Your agency should not consider the promotion potential of the position which you are being offered when considering your assignment rights.

Bumping rights Bumping occurs when you are allowed to take a position in the same competitive area which is occupied by an employee in a lower tenure group in another competitive level. If you are given the opportunity to "bump," the employee occupying the position must be in a lower tenure group or subgroup than you. Also, the position cannot be more than three grade levels lower than your current grade.

Retreat rights Retreat rights allow you to retreat to a position that is the same or virtually the same as one you previously held, rather than being released from employment. The position to which you retreat must be the "same" position or an "essentially identical position" to one which you previously held. This means that your agency can offer you an assignment to a position very similar to a position you occupied in the federal government many years ago. The assignment offered does not need to be similar to the position you occupy when the agency initiates the RIF.

Your retreat rights may enable you to displace an employee in the same tenure subgroup in a different competitive level in the same competitive area. If you are given the opportunity to retreat into a position in the same subgroup, the employee occupying that position must have a lower retention standing than you and the position cannot be more than three grades below your RIFd position. This second limitation can be five grade levels if you are a veteran with a thirty percent service-connected disability. Also, if your performance rating is minimally successful (Level 2 or equivalent) or lower, you can displace only another employee whose performance rating is no higher than minimally successful (Level 2 or equivalent).

Qualifications for Assignment To be qualified for an assignment to another position, you must meet OPM qualification standards and requirements for the position, including any minimum educational requirement and any selective placement factors established by your agency. You must also be physically qualified to perform the duties of the position, meet any special qualifying condition which OPM has required, and have the capacity, adaptability, and special skills needed to satisfactorily perform the duties of the position without undue interruption. An undue interruption exists where it takes you over *90 days* before you are able to perform all the duties and responsibilities of the position. The physical ability to do a job may, depending on the job, mean with or without a reasonable accommodation for any handicap you may have. (See Chapter 5.)

There are special considerations for veterans with at least thirty percent service-connected disabilities. These veterans are entitled to notice if they are being denied a position because of their disability and are entitled to respond to that notice. Then, OPM determines whether the veteran is entitled to the position.[2]

Agencies are given wide latitude in conducting RIFs and in making offers of reassignment. For example, your agency may choose to offer a vacant other-than-full-time position to a full-time employee or to offer a vacant full-time position to an other-than-full-time employee instead of requiring separation by reduction-in-force. There are some limitations, however. Although your agency can offer RIFd employees assignments to positions with the same or lower grade levels, you cannot be offered or assigned to a

---

[2] For more information, see 5 CFR § 351.702.

position with a higher grade or with higher promotion potential. Furthermore, a non-full-time employee cannot displace a full-time employee.

What kind of notice of a RIF am I entitled to?

Amount of notice Prior to separating you by RIF, your agency must give you and your union representatives, if applicable, at least *60 calendar days* notice. Some union contracts require longer notice periods. There may be exceptions to these deadlines. When a RIF is caused by unforeseeable circumstances, an agency may ask OPM to approve a notice period of less than *60 days*. The shortened notice period must cover at least *30 full days* before the effective date of release.

Contents of notice The notice must inform you of the following:

- the action to be taken
- the reasons for the action
- the effective date
- your competitive area
- your competitive level
- your subgroup
- your service computation date
- your three most recent ratings received in the last four years
- the place where you can inspect the regulations and relevant documents
- the reasons for retaining any lower-standing employee in the same competitive level
- information on reemployment rights
- your right to appeal to the MSPB under the provisions of the Board's regulations or to grieve under a negotiated grievance procedure

Your agency must provide copies of OPM's RIF regulations upon request. However, the agency's RIF notice to you does not have to mention or identify these regulations at all, much less your right to a copy of the regulations.

TIP

Carefully review your RIF notice and immediately notify your personnel office of any inaccuracies.

The single most important thing you can do to preserve your rights in the event of a RIF is to ensure that the RIF notice is complete and accurate. The notice contains the information that the agency uses to place you on the retention register. The information in the notice will determine your retention standing. If any of the information in the notice is inaccurate, you should notify the agency immediately. Your failure to correct inaccurate information could adversely affect your retention standing and result in your separation from the agency.

Agencies must also issue a separate notice to employees who are entitled to reemployment or replacement assistance. Alternatively, the RIF notice itself can include reemployment and placement information. Qualified employees must be given information concerning the right to reemployment consideration under the Reemployment Priority List and/or the Career Transition Assistance Programs, if applicable. The notice must also contain information concerning how to apply for unemployment compensation through an appropriate state program. The agency must also give the employee an optional release to sign, which would let the agency give the employee's resume to State employment agencies and public and private sector employers.

Your agency must not take the action specified, such as demotion or separation, before the effective date in the notice. During the notice period, the agency should try to retain you on active duty status. If the agency decides to take an action more severe than first specified, it must issue a new notice of *60 days*, as appropriate. However, an emergency may require the agency to place you on a leave status during the notice period. Under emergency circumstances, your agency may place you on annual leave with or without your consent, leave without pay with your consent, or in a nonpay status without your consent.

Certificate of Expected Separation If it is reasonably certain that you will be separated, your agency may also issue you a Certificate of Expected Separation. This certificate will allow you, if you are eligible, to be considered for participation in a dislocated worker program under the Work Investment Act administered by the U.S. Department of Labor. This certificate may be issued:

- only when employment opportunities in the same or a similar position in the local commuting area are limited or nonexistent
- when placement opportunities within your own or other federal agencies in the local commuting area are limited or nonexistent, and

- when you have not filed a retirement application or otherwise indicated in writing an intent to retire

This certificate must identify the following:

- expected date of RIF
- a statement that each factor, above, has been satisfied
- a description of the Workforce Investment Act of 1998, title I programs, the Interagency Placement Program and the Reemployment Priority List

This certificate may be issued up to 6 *months* prior to the effective date of the RIF. Your agency's determination of eligibility for certification may not be appealed to OPM or the MSPB. If you are eligible, your agency can also enroll you in the Reemployment Priority List ("RPL") up to 6 *months* before the date of the reduction-in-force. For a discussion of the RPL, see page 208 of this chapter.

Are there other ways I can be RIFd?

Not all RIFs are undertaken for the same reasons. With the difference may come a difference in the rights that you have as a result of the RIF. That difference in rights may make the difference between you having a job or not.

Transfer of function RIFs

Your agency may sometime transfer certain agency functions from one geographical area within the agency to another. In a "transfer of function," the function must stop entirely in the first area and continue in an identical manner in the new area. When this happens, as an employee in the first area, you may be transferred with the function to the new area without any change in your tenure or status. You are entitled to a transfer only if the alternative would be separation or demotion. If you choose not to transfer, then you will be faced with separation or demotion. Your agency is then entitled to implement RIF procedures.

What are the notice requirements for this type of RIF? When your agency transfers functions, it must fully inform you of your option to be either RIF'd or transferred. The agency must tell you what entitlements you may have in either situation. If you choose separation, the separation cannot occur before the function transfers to the new area. If you accept a transfer, you can later change your mind and choose separation. But if you accept separation, you cannot change your mind later and be transferred.

How can I best protect myself in the event of a RIF?

Although the following guidelines may not save your job, these points could improve your chances of retaining a job with your agency.

- Keep your official personnel file ("OPF") complete and accurate. This is important before a RIF is even considered, because your OPF contains much of the information that will be used by the agency to determine your RIF rights and retention status.

- Maintain a current, complete, and up-to-date copy of your SF-171, your job application. Your SF-171 should identify all the positions you have occupied in the federal government. A full description of the duties and responsibilities you performed in these positions, as well as their series and grades, will help you maximize your possible retreat rights.

- As soon as you receive the RIF notice, examine it very carefully for accuracy. If the notice contains any mistakes or inaccuracies, have the agency correct it immediately.

- Ask to review the competitive areas to see where you are identified in the RIF.

- Request and acquire all the agency RIF records to which you are entitled. See 5 CFR 351.505.

- Request a copy of the complete retention register which will list your retention standing as well as that of other employees. The register also tells if you will be able to retain a position with the agency, and if so, what position. Review the retention register carefully to make sure that all the information is accurate.

- Keep your performance ratings up! If your performance rating is minimally successful (Level 2 or equivalent), you can retreat to another position *only* if the incumbent of that position has a performance rating no higher than minimally successful (Level 2 or equivalent). To help keep your performance ratings high, if you feel that you have been given an unfair performance evaluation, grieve it through the available procedures, such as a union grievance, internal agency grievance, or EEO process (if discrimination is involved).

- As soon as you receive any indication that the agency is conducting a RIF, go to your Official Personnel File (OPF) which is kept by the personnel office. When reviewing the OPF, check that all information is accurate and complete. In particular, you want to make sure that the criteria that determine your retention standing are accurate and complete:

1. your service computation date
2. your SF-171 (which identifies all prior federal positions to which you have retreat rights)
3. your performance evaluations (which help determine your rating on the retention register)
4. your veteran's status (particularly if you have a service-connected disability and, if so, the extent of the disability), and
5. your current position description and series (which could affect potential positions into which you could have bump or retreat rights)

Do I have any right to an appeal or other corrective action?

Even if you are RIFd, there may still be a way to save your job. As with most actions involving your federal employment, you have some right to appeal certain aspects of the RIF. Since not all aspects of a RIF are subject to appeal, carefully review the information to see if your situation is covered.

What procedures apply to RIFs?

An employee who has been furloughed for more than *30 days*, separated, or demoted by a RIF has a right to challenge the action. If you are represented by a union, the collective bargaining agreement will specify whether you are allowed to grieve the action. If the agreement or union contract does not specifically exclude RIFs from its grievance procedures, you cannot challenge the RIF by appealing to the MSPB; you must appeal through the union grievance process.

If you are not covered by a collective bargaining agreement, you may challenge the RIF by a grievance through the MSPB. You must file your MSPB appeal within *30 days* of the effective date of the RIF.

TIP

Be careful of the time limits for challenging a RIF. Each collective bargaining agreement has a different period of time for filing grievances, usually ranging from seven to twenty-one calendar days.

When a RIF action is unjustified or unwarranted, you should be entitled to be returned to the same situation you would have enjoyed if the RIF had been properly executed. This means that you may be entitled to retroactive reinstatement, back pay with interest and benefits, and payment for any reasonable attorney fees you incurred.

If you believe that your RIF action is based upon unlawful discrimination, you may also use the EEO complaint procedure. (See Chapter 5.) Because a discriminatory RIF action is appealable to the MSPB, it is a "mixed case" and you can choose to challenge it first through the EEO procedure or through the MSPB. If you are successful in your EEO allegation, you may be entitled to compensatory damages, including for emotional distress, in addition to the remedies identified above.

The procedures for challenging a RIF are very complex, especially for individuals who are covered by collective bargaining agreements. For these reasons, you should discuss your legal options with a union representative, if applicable, or an attorney. The chart on page 213 helps identify potential options for bargaining unit employees.

Is it possible for me to successfully challenge a RIF?

Because agencies enjoy so much discretion when conducting RIFs, it is very difficult to successfully challenge a RIF action. But it is not impossible. Your agency bears the burden of proving that its RIF decision was based on legitimate reasons described in the RIF regulations. Based on MSPB decisions of the past, this is not hard for agencies to prove. They also have to prove that the RIF was properly implemented. Your chances of challenging your agency's actions are best if you can show that they failed to properly identify your retention standing or improperly determined that you are not qualified to bump or retreat to a particular position.

Can you give me any pointers on negotiating an informal resolution?

If you are subject to separation from your competitive level because of a RIF, and if you challenge that action, you should try to reach an informal resolution with the agency. Overall, settlements are strongly encouraged, are faster and, unlike a legal challenge, will result in a predetermined outcome. When dealing with RIFs, talk with the agency representative assigned to your case frequently and from the beginning of the proceedings. Identify your most important goals, and let the agency know what is most critical to you.

For example, in a RIF reassignment to a lower grade in a different series, you may have reason to believe that the series assignment was wrong. You may also think the series assignment will seriously injure you because you know that the series will become obsolete and fully abolished in the next RIF. This means that although you may have a job right now, you are relatively certain that you will not survive the next RIF. Although you are also unhappy with the grade assignment, you would prefer to have a lower graded position than lose your job entirely at the end of the next RIF. In addition, you know that you will have "saved pay" (be able to retain your present salary—see pages 214-215 of this chapter) for two years and that you will probably be able to be promoted to a higher grade during that time if you can just keep your job.

OPTIONS FOR BARGAINING UNIT EMPLOYEES

IF:	THEN:
The negotiated union contract grievance procedure covers RIFs or is silent on RIFs;	Only grievance procedures apply.
and covers discrimination claims or is silent on discrimination claims:	You must elect to pursue the discrimination charge through the grievance procedure ***or*** through the EEO process, but not both.[3]
but excludes discrimination claims.	You can challenge the use of RIF procedures only through the grievance procedures. ***And*** you can challenge that the action was discriminatory only through the EEO procedure.[4]
The negotiated grievance procedure specifically excludes RIFs	Only the MSPB procedures apply.
and if you allege discrimination:	The discrimination allegation may be pursued through either the MSPB or EEO procedures, in which case the "mixed case" procedures apply. (See Chapter 6.)

[3] Initiating the informal EEO complaint procedure does not constitute an election. You have not elected to use the EEO complaint procedure until you file a formal complaint. (See Chapter 6.)

[4] The law is not clearly established, but it seems you may be entitled to a hearing before an EEOC administrative judge on the discrimination allegations.

Under these circumstances, in settlement the agency may be willing to change your series, which will insulate you from the next RIF. In exchange, you will not challenge the grade assignment. In the end, you have saved your job without the possibility of losing everything at a hearing.

What benefits am I entitled to if I am RIFd?

Federal employment is accompanied by many benefits, including salary, life insurance, health insurance, participation in the Thrift Savings Plan for FERS-covered employees (see Chapter 18), and, perhaps most important, retirement benefits. If you are separated, demoted, or reassigned due to a RIF, your entitlement to these benefits of employment will change.

Priority consideration

If you are separated or downgraded because of a RIF, your agency can give you priority consideration for reemployment or repromotion. Executive agencies create reemployment priority lists ("RPLs," also known as "PPPs," priority placement programs) for each commuting area that suffered a RIF. Within *30 days* of your RIF date, you must complete an application and inform your agency of any significant changes in the information provided. Your application should include the criteria under which you are willing to return to work for the agency, for example:

- the grade(s)
- series
- occupation(s)
- minimum hours of work per week, and
- work schedule(s)

If you have priority consideration, and if you qualify for a competitive position, you may be offered a position without competing for it. Priority consideration does not mean that you will automatically be selected for the position. The agency is still allowed to use its discretion in selecting a candidate. You may not be the only employee with priority consideration applying for the position. If you believe that another employee was improperly appointed to a position that you should have been given through the RPL, you may appeal to the MSPB under its regulations. (See Chapter 4.)

What is my salary in the event of a downgrade?

If you are demoted in a RIF, you are entitled to grade and pay retention, or "saved pay" for two years. Under "saved pay," you receive the same salary that you earned prior to being demoted. This benefit lasts for two years, at the end of which you will begin earning the salary of the position to which you are reassigned. At that time, if the saved pay you have been getting is higher than the highest pay rate of your new position, you will continue at the saved pay rate as long as it is not higher than 150 percent of the new position's highest pay rate. For example, assume that after the RIF you maintain saved pay for two years. At the end of those two years, your saved pay is still higher than the highest pay rate (Step 10) of the grade of your new position. You will continue to be paid at the higher salary (your saved pay), but you will not be paid more than one hundred fifty percent of the highest pay rate (Step 10) of your new (lower) grade. Thereafter, you will only receive 50 percent of the annual comparability pay until the maximum pay rate of the new job catches up with your saved pay salary. The two years of saved pay are considered for most benefit purposes, including the calculation of your "high-three" years of salary which are used to determine your retirement benefits. (See Chapter 18.)

Are there any entitlements in the event I am separated?

Even if you are separated due to a RIF, you are still entitled to certain things upon your separation. You may have rights to severance pay, insurance, or other things that will make the financial burden on you a bit lighter while you seek another position. Below are the entitlements you may qualify for.

Severance pay

You are entitled to severance pay if you meet three criteria:

- you are separated
- you have not refused an offer to be placed into a position within two grades of your current position, and
- you have served at least twelve months continuously

Severance pay is calculated at one week's pay for each year of service prior to separation. If you have worked for the federal government for at least ten years, you receive two weeks of pay for each additional year after the first ten. You receive an additional ten percent of severance pay if you are over forty years old. Your total severance pay cannot be more than one year's salary. You may also be entitled to unemployment compensation through your state. (See Chapter 17.)

Leave

After being separated, you can cash out all of your unused annual leave, but not unused sick leave. If you are reinstated, you are allowed to have your sick leave recredited. If you are under the Civil Service Retirement System ("CSRS"), unused sick leave is considered when calculating retirement and determining your service dates. Under the Federal Employee Retirement System ("FERS"), it is not.

Health insurance

You are entitled to be covered by your health insurance at government cost for *31 days* after the effective date of separation. Thereafter, you are allowed to enroll in the same insurance program at a cost of the insurance premium, plus two percent, for *18 months*. If you retire instead of separate, however, and if you have been continuously enrolled or covered for the five previous years, the government will continue to make the same health insurance contributions it did prior to your retirement.

Life insurance

Federal Employees Group Life Insurance ("FEGLI") covers life insurance premiums for *31 days* after separation. At separation, you may convert your insurance to an individual policy without taking a medical examination, but you are responsible for the premiums under the conversion policy. Retirees, however, are allowed to continue their same life insurance or can choose to continue with a percentage of the basic coverage after age sixty-five, assuming they have been enrolled for the five years immediately prior to retirement.

Retirement

Some RIFd employees are entitled to discontinued service retirement giving them an immediate annuity. Employees who have been informed of separation may retire at any time *prior to the effective RIF* date if they qualify for retirement. To qualify for discontinued service retirement, you must be:

- at least fifty years old with twenty years of creditable service, or
- any age with twenty-five years of service.

Under CSRS, you may retire after meeting either of these benchmarks, but your retirement annuity will be reduced by two percent for each year you are under age 55. If you choose to retire, rather than be separated, your retirement does not prevent you from appealing the RIF action. If you inform the agency that you want to retire, and then you withdraw your retirement prior to the RIF date, under most circumstances you are not required to retire. Your separation is then considered involuntary, and you are allowed to appeal to the MSPB.

Before choosing to take the discontinued service retirement option, consider the whole retirement package available to you. For example, ask yourself the following questions:

- **WILL YOU EVER GO BACK TO WORK?**

If you decide to work in the private sector or for a state or local government, you can continue to receive your retirement annuity and your new, private-sector salary. Plus, a cost-of-living adjustment is applied to your annuity every year.

- **WILL YOU GO BACK TO WORK FOR THE FEDERAL GOVERNMENT?**

If you return to government service, your salary will be reduced by the amount of your annuity or your annuity will stop. If your annuity stops, you will have to apply for retirement again in the future. Upon your next retirement, your annuity might be reinstated. If you want your new salary to increase your "high-three" and give you a higher retirement annuity when you finally retire for good, you will have to work for five more years.

- **WILL YOU GET SEVERANCE PAY PLUS AN ANNUITY?**

If you take discontinued service retirement, then you are not entitled to severance pay.

- **WHAT ARE YOUR HEALTH INSURANCE OPTIONS?**

If you take discontinued service retirement, and if you meet the five-year eligibility requirement mentioned earlier, you may continue with the same health insurance coverage at the same cost to you. Over the long term, this could be a very significant benefit.

TIP

Talk with your personnel office to learn all of your financial considerations, including what your annuity will be, and what your severance pay would be, if you are not eligible for discontinued service retirement.

- **What is the RIF date and does it give you a full year of service?**

If your RIF date forces you to retire prior to finishing a year of service, your annuity might be reduced. Talk to your personnel office to find out this information. And, if you are covered by CSRS or a FERS/CSRS combination, every month of early retirement may result in a reduction of your annuity by one-sixth of a percent (or two percent per year).

- **What about your spouse?**

Your discontinued service retirement does not affect your spouse's (or sometimes former spouse's) survivor annuity. But, if your annuity is insufficient because of early retirement, you and your spouse can agree to lower your spouse's survivor annuity to increase your annuity.

What is a furlough?

A furlough" is "the placing of an employee in a temporary nonduty, non-pay status because of lack of work or funds, and other nondisciplinary reasons."[5] Fortunately, the law requires a 30-day notice of furloughs lasting 30 days or less (22 calendar days for most employees), and employees are entitled to respond to the proposals orally or in writing, entitled to a representative or attorney, and may appeal an adverse ruling to the Merit Systems Protection Board (MSPB).

As a practical matter, employees have few grounds to challenge furloughs, unless the Agency failed to give proper notice or committed another due process violation. The MSPB evaluates the furloughs under the standard of "promoting the efficiency of the service," an easy burden for an agency to meet by showing that the furlough was a reasonable management solution to financial restrictions and that the agency fairly selected the employees to furlough. An Agency must, however, show that the furlough was applied uniformly and consistently, and that the Agency did not use the furlough to target employees for personal reasons, and may not attempt to exempt certain employees from the furlough without legitimate management reasons.[6]

The MSPB does not typically reverse furlough decisions, and has ruled that it will not second-guess management's discretion in conducting a short-term furlough unless an employee can show disparate treatment

---

5 *See* 5 USC § 5711(a)(g); 5 CFR § 752.402.

6 *See Chandler v. Dept. of the Treasury,* 120 MSPR 163,172 (2013).

among similarly situated employees. Clark v. OPM, 24 MSPR 224, 226 (1984). A 2013 MSPB decision regarding furloughs did provide limited grounds for challenging furloughs by arguing that their Agencies failed to conduct the furlough in a uniform and consistent manner.[7] The MSPB allowed a group of Treasury employees to request information through the discovery process relating to overtime decisions, stating that information about overtime and bonuses might be "relevant" because if the information revealed that "the agency used overtime payments and bonuses to relieve certain employees but not others of the financial consequences of the furlough, this may be sufficient to show that the furlough did not meet the efficiency of the service standard."[8]

The Board also allowed employees to gather information to support their claim that an Agency violated due process and committed harmful procedural error in executing the furlough.[9] An employee might also challenge the furlough by asserting affirmative defenses of discrimination if the facts support such a claim.

Agencies must identify which employees are affected by the furloughs. SES and political appointees are subject to administrative furlough; "leave-exempt" Presidential appointees are not subject to furlough. Some Presidential appointees may be subject to furlough yet not be entitled to adverse action procedures. The decision whether to furlough employees is not a subject of collective bargaining, but unions may bargain over impact and implementation of furlough proposals. Career SES appointees are entitled to a 30-day advance written notice of a furlough of any length, but SES noncareer, limited term and limited emergency appointees and reemployed annuitants holding career SES appointments are not entitled to a 30-day advance written notice, opportunity to respond, or a separate decision notice.

Probationers, employees under temporary appointments, and others without appeal rights, also have no entitlement to notice or an opportunity to respond to a proposed furlough. Retirement, life insurance, and health insurance coverage continues, and employee contributions for their Federal Employee Health Benefits shares will be paid during pay status, or resumed after duty status if the salary is insufficient for the payments during furlough.

---

7 *See* 120 MSPR at 171.

8 *See* 120 MSPR at 173; 176.

9 *See* 120 MSPR at 178.

Administrative law judges (ALJs), however, may only be subject to a shortened furlough notice of 30 days or less "for good cause established and determined by the MSPB on the record after opportunity for hearing before the Board." However, the MSPB held in 2013 that ALJs are not entitled to any greater protection than non-ALJ employees in a furlough situation, and "have no entitlement to receive favorable *substantive* treatment in a furlough." [10]

The furloughs need not be scheduled for consecutive days. Employees may not volunteer to do his or her job during the furlough time off; may not accumulate religious compensatory time off; may not work to earn credit hours; and may suffer some delays in the award of within-grade and step increases based on length of service and individual performance. OPM publishes specific guidance for employees who might otherwise reach the biweekly cap on premium pay, and also has guidance for federal employees on military duty, and on Leave Without Pay for Family Medical Leave Act purposes.

Furloughs extending beyond 30 calendar days or more than 22 discontinuous work days must be handled under Reduction-in-Force (RIF) procedures. (See above). Employees who are furloughed under RIF procedures also have MSPB appeal rights. The RIF procedures are also triggered when an administrative furlough of 22 workdays or less is extended for budgetary reasons.

Some employees may be eligible for unemployment benefits during furloughs, but the rules are state-specific, and employees should consult their appropriate State or District of Columbia office. The Department of Labor also has a website with information regarding unemployment compensation for federal employees.
http://workforcesecurity.doleta.gov/unemply/unemcomp.asp.

---

[10] *See Dept. of Labor v. Avery, et al.*, 120 MSPR 150,155 (2013).

Final Thoughts

Being caught in a RIF or a furlough can be a very scary situation. We depend on our jobs for both physical and emotional sustenance. You can't prevent a RIF or furlough if circumstances are such that your agency must undergo one. But you can certainly make sure you do all you can to exercise your rights and put yourself in the best position to preserve what you can. And who knows? That may mean you end up with your job intact.

10

Security Clearances and "Sensitive" Positions

For Your Eyes Only...

In This Chapter You Will Learn:

- how security clearances are revoked
- whether you can challenge a security clearance determination
- the rights of employees who occupy non-critical sensitive positions

?

Contents Chapter Ten - Security Clearances and "Sensitive" Positions

Introduction

As in our own lives, there are some things the government has a need to keep secret. Generally the reason is based on national security. To help assure this secrecy, the government grants limited access to some of its operations and information. Employees in positions who have a need to deal with such secret operations and confidential information are granted a security clearance from the government. In such jobs, loss of your security clearance most likely will result in the loss of your job. It is therefore important that you understand your rights and how to protect against a threat to your security clearance. That is what we will discuss in this chapter.

Do not underestimate the importance of fighting an agency's proposal to revoke your security clearance. Administrative and court review of agency decisions to revoke security clearance is extremely limited; so you want to do your best to avoid losing the clearance in the first place. When presented with a threat to your security clearance, your goal is to persuade your agency that keeping your security clearance is consistent with "national security." National security issues have only heightened since 9/11.

This matter is so important that you should consult an experienced lawyer at the start.

At the outset, it is important to know that you do not have a "right" to have, or keep, a security clearance. Your need and eligibility for a clearance is for the agency to decide. Often, an agency will hire an employee into a position needing a clearance before all of the background investigations have been completed. Not surprisingly, the agency may decide the employee is not worthy of a clearance after the employee has already been working in the position for some time. If an employee fails to receive the required clearance, and is terminated because of that during his or her probationary period, there is little the employee can do because an agency has wide latitude to fire employees during the probationary period anyway. Most disputes arise after an employee has previously been granted a security clearance, and the agency now wants to revoke it. Most of this chapter concerns attempts to revoke a security clearance that an employee has already been granted.

What is the procedure for revoking a security clearance?

Executive Order 12968 and Executive Order 13467

For most federal employees, the process of deciding to revoke a security clearance is governed by Executive Order 12968, signed by President Clinton on August 2, 1995, and Executive Order 13467, signed by President Bush on June 30, 2008. A key feature of Executive Order 12968 is your right to have a "personal appearance" (hearing) before an administrative judge, hearing officer, or hearing panel, comprised of multiple individuals. Because your rights are provided only by an executive order, and not by statute, they can be rescinded at any time by any President who may modify or revoke the order.

Section 5.2 of Executive Order 12968, entitled "Review Proceedings for Denials or Revocations of Eligibility for Access," contains the procedures agencies must follow when deciding to deny or revoke a security clearance. Section 5.2 provides that employees who do not meet the standards for access to confidential information shall be:

1. provided as comprehensive and detailed a written explanation of the reason for the denial as national security interests and applicable law permit
2. provided documents, records, and reports on which the denial is based to the extent they would be provided under the Freedom of Information Act (FOIA) and the Privacy Act. (See Chapter 22.) These things must be provided within thirty days
3. informed of their *right to counsel* or other representative, to request documents, and to request the entire investigatory file. If requested, these materials shall be promptly provided prior to the time set for written reply
4. provided a reasonable opportunity to reply in writing to the determination, and to request a review of that determination
5. provided written notice of and reasons for the results of the review, the identity of the deciding official, and *written* notice of the right to appeal
6. provided an opportunity to appeal in writing to a high-level panel appointed by the agency head. The panel shall be comprised of three members, two of whom shall be selected from outside the security field. Panel decisions are to be in writing and are final, and
7. provided an opportunity to appear personally and to present relevant documents, materials, and information at some point in the process before an adjudicative or other authority, other than the investigative entity, as determined by the agency head. A written summary or record of such appearance shall be made part of the employee's security record, unless the appearance occurs in the presence of the panel

Executive Order 13467 makes some modifications to Executive Order 12968, namely, by appointing the Director of National Intelligence to serve as Security Executive Agent, and by adding a "continuous evaluation" standard, whereby, "an individual who has been determined to be eligible for, or who currently has access to, classified information shall be subject to continuous evaluation under standards (including, but not limited to, the frequency of such evaluation) as determined by the Director of National Intelligence."

At most agencies, the revocation process starts with issuance of a written notice, often called an "Intent to Revoke Access Eligibility," or something similar-sounding. Usually, the notice will come with another document informing you that your access to classified information has been temporarily suspended pending the outcome of the proposed revocation. Read this written notice very carefully, as the notice will typically describe: any agency regulations that govern the proposed revocation of your security clearance; how many days you have to respond to the proposed revocation; and the details of your personal appearance and any written response rights afforded to you, including the individual from the agency designated as the administrative judge, hearing official, or in some cases, hearing panel. For example, for most Department of Defense employees, personal appearances are heard by administrative judges at the Defense Office of Hearings and Appeals (DOHA). However, other agencies, like the Department of Energy, for example, have their own Office of Hearings and Appeals, or other offices. This may be challenged in writing, but will become final if no challenge is submitted. You may be represented by counsel at your personal appearance. Furthermore, you must be provided with the supporting adverse information and personnel security guidelines used in the preliminary decision.

At this time, you may also request a copy of the investigative file, which the agency is relying upon to support the proposed revocation. This almost always makes necessary a request for an extension to reply to the proposed revocation. However, your access to classified information is suspended during this time.

After your personal appearance and/or reviewing any written response, the administrative judge, hearing officer, or hearing panel issues a written decision. The decision will apprise you of whether or not the agency has decided to allow you to continue to possess a security clearance. Read the decision very carefully, particularly in cases where the agency decides to revoke your security clearance. The decision will inform you of any appeal rights you have. Usually, appeal rights at this stage are limited to a written appeal to a second-level deciding official or panel.

THE PERSONAL APPEARANCE

The "personal appearance" will normally be held at your duty station, or a nearby location. The nature of the personal appearance will often vary, depending on the agency. Personal appearances are not always adversarial. You may be represented by an attorney or other personal representative. The personal appearance is usually not an adversarial hearing where witnesses testify subject to cross-examination. Rather, you may make an oral presentation, respond to questions posed by your representative, and respond to questions posed by the administrative judge, hearing officer, or hearing panel (or other designated official if you are not employed by the Department of Defense). However, at other agencies, the personal appearance takes on a more adversarial nature, more like a trial. In these types of hearings, you will have the opportunity to cross-examine the agency's witnesses, and the agency representative will have the opportunity to cross-examine you and your witnesses. Typically, a verbatim transcript will be made of the personal appearance hearing.

You may submit documents or affidavits in support of your case to the administrative judge, hearing officer, or hearing panel. Please refer to the procedures governing exhibits in the notice(s) you received from the agency regarding your proposed revocation.

TIP

What you want in an affidavit are facts relevant to the reason the agency is questioning your clearance, not impressions and opinions. Firsthand information is best. People with responsible positions, ideally higher up in your chain of command, make good witnesses for this purpose.

You or your representative may make a closing statement. The final decision as to whether you will lose or retain your security clearance is made by application of "adjudication factors" which contain aggravating and mitigating factors related to the reasons for the revocation.

The main thing to establish in your personal appearance is that the adjudication factors as applied in your situation warrant that you maintain your security clearance. Make sure you address those factors throughout your presentation and in your closing statement. Emphasize the factors that mitigate against the loss of your clearance and explain why the aggravating factors do not apply.

The Adjudicative Guidelines

Most federal employees requiring security clearances are employed by the Department of Defense. If you are employed by another agency, however, such as the Department of Justice or the Central Intelligence Agency, ask your agency for a copy of its own regulations issued to implement the requirements of Executive Order 12968.

Aside from the agency-specific regulations governing security clearances, on December 29, 2005, President Bush approved the "Adjudicative Guidelines For Determining Eligibility For Access To Classified Information."[1] These regulations are applicable to all agencies, and are used either exclusively or in concert with an agency's own regulations, to make security clearance determinations.

The Adjudicative Guidelines require that the administrative judge, hearing officer, or hearing panel take a number of factors into consideration when making a determination about security clearances. Together, consideration of these factors constitute what is called the "whole-person concept."

The factors are:

1. the nature, extent, and seriousness of the conduct;
2. the circumstances surrounding the conduct, to include knowledgeable participation;
3. the frequency and recency of the conduct;
4. the individual's age and maturity at the time of the conduct;
5. the extent to which participation is voluntary;
6. the presence or absence of rehabilitation and other permanent behavioral changes;
7. the motivation for the conduct;
8. the potential for pressure, coercion, exploitation, or duress; and
9. the likelihood of continuation or recurrence.

In addition, the Adjudicative Guidelines classify security concerns into a number of different guidelines, including:

---

1 *See* 32 CFR § 147.

1. GUIDELINE A: Allegiance to the United States;
2. GUIDELINE B: Foreign Influence;
3. GUIDELINE C: Foreign Preference;
4. GUIDELINE D: Sexual Behavior;
5. GUIDELINE E: Personal Conduct;
6. GUIDELINE F: Financial Considerations;
7. GUIDELINE G: Alcohol Consumption;
8. GUIDELINE H: Drug Involvement;
9. GUIDELINE I: Psychological Conditions;
10. GUIDELINE J: Criminal Conduct;
11. GUIDELINE K: Handling Protected Information;
12. GUIDELINE L: Outside Activities;
13. GUIDELINE M: Use of Information Technology Systems

Each guideline contains a number of factors which aggravate the security concern(s), and a number of factors which mitigate the security concern(s). You should focus your presentation in your personal appearance on the mitigating factors applicable to your case, and pointing out why the aggravating factors do not apply.

Can I lose my job because my security clearance is revoked?

If you lose your security clearance, your agency is not required by law to find you another job which does not require a clearance. By regulation or policy, some agencies give you the right to be considered for a vacant position not requiring a clearance. You must request the rules from your agency to know if it is one that requires that you be considered for a non-sensitive position before they take harsh action like removal.

Unfortunately, most federal employees who lose their security clearances will also be removed from their positions. If you have MSPB appeal rights, however, your agency must follow the adverse action procedures before terminating your employment.[2] (See Chapter 4.)

Can I appeal to the MSPB or Court?

Even if you have MSPB appeal rights, MSPB review of the agency decision is limited. The MSPB cannot review the correctness of your agency's decision to revoke your clearance. That is, the merits or wisdom of your agency's decision to revoke your security clearance is not reviewable.

---

[2] *See* 5 USC Chapter 75.

The MSPB does play some role, however. The MSPB has the authority to determine if the agency actually decided a security clearance was required for your job, and whether your agency followed the proper procedures in revoking your clearance. If no clearance was required, or the agency failed to follow proper procedures in revoking your clearance, then your removal will be reversed. If your agency is one of the agencies which requires that you be considered for reassignment to a vacant non-sensitive position prior to removal, the MSPB will also decide whether your agency met its obligation to consider you for such a vacant position.

The MSPB has no authority to decide whether your agency was correct in determining that your position required a clearance. The decisions as to what positions require security clearances are for the agency, which cannot be second-guessed on this issue.

There may be one exception to nonreviewability of your agency's decision to remove you based on revocation of your security clearance. If you believe that your clearance was revoked in violation of some Constitutional right, for example because you exercised your freedom of speech, the Supreme Court has suggested that the decision to revoke your clearance might be judicially reviewable.[3]

If you intend to make this type of claim, you must do more than make a bare claim in your MSPB appeal. You must support this claim with facts to make a *prima facie* case of a Constitutional violation. But be prepared for the MSPB to refuse to consider your claim of a Constitutional violation. You will then have to raise the argument again in the United States Court of Appeals for the Federal Circuit, which reviews MSPB decisions. As of this writing, however, the Federal Circuit has yet to accept such an argument from a federal employee.

Now that you see how limited the review is of an agency's decision to revoke a security clearance, you can also see why it is so important to attempt to persuade the agency not to revoke your clearance *before* that decision is actually made.

What if the revocation of my security clearance is discriminatory?

In past years, the EEOC had held that, in certain situations, it had jurisdiction to determine whether the decision to subject you to a security clear-

---

[3] *See Department of Navy v. Egan*, 484 US 518 (1988).

ance review was discriminatory. However, several court decisions have made it increasingly clear that the EEOC may play no role in the review of decisions with respect to security clearances. Therefore, if you believe the decision to review or revoke your clearance is discriminatory, you should raise it during the review process. However, the EEOC will not have jurisdiction over the issue if you file an EEO complaint.

CAN I BE SUSPENDED IMMEDIATELY IF MY CLASSIFICATION IS REVOKED?

Your agency has the right to suspend you immediately without pay if the agency head considers that a suspension is required in the interest of national security.[4] This provision is little used, but does exist. In this case, you are entitled to a statement of reasons within *30 days* of the start of the suspension, and to a hearing by hearing officials designated by the agency from a roster of officials maintained by OPM. The hearing board will issue a recommendation to the agency head as to whether you should be returned to pay status. The agency head's decision is generally final, absent some claim of procedural irregularity or Constitutional violation. Most agencies indefinitely suspend employees after the 7-day notice requirement discussed in Chapter 4.

Not all agencies must follow the procedures described in this chapter. Some agencies have been given special authority to make determinations about your retention based on national security. You should request copies of all statutes and regulations applicable to your situation if the agency threatens to revoke your clearance or takes action to remove you from federal service.

TIP

How can you help protect your security clearance or keep it from being called into question? Do not disclose sensitive information to anyone, not even your nearest and dearest friends or relatives. Be careful what you say, as well as what you write, about classified topics. This goes for any "professional" speeches you may give anywhere, too. Stay current with your personal financial obligations. Don't do drugs, or overdo the use of alcohol. Report any contact you have with foreign nationals to your supervisor or your agency's security office.

---

4 *See* 5 USC § 7532.

WHAT IF I DON'T HAVE A SECURITY CLEARANCE BUT OCCUPY A NONCRITICAL SENSITIVE POSITION?

Due to recent court decisions, employees who do not possess security clearances, but who occupy "noncritical sensitive" positions, where they possess access to sensitive information, have limited appeal rights to the MSPB to challenge adverse personnel actions based upon this access to sensitive information.[5] Unfortunately, as of the writing of this book, employees who occupy these noncritical sensitive positions arguably have even fewer rights than employees with security clearances, as there is not yet any mandatory agency-level reply or appeal process to challenge a proposed removal, demotion, indefinite suspension, or other action based upon the agency's concerns about whether or not the employee is eligible to occupy a sensitive position. In other words, there is no framework, such as the one mandated by Executive Order 12968 and Executive Order 13467 (discussed above) to challenge such adverse personnel actions. Although employees occupying these sensitive positions may gain more rights through a Presidential executive order in the future, the fact remains that employees in sensitive positions remain very vulnerable to adverse actions, particularly when their agencies base the action on a national security rationale.

---

5 *See Kaplan v. Conyers*, 733 F.3d 1148 (Fed. Cir. 2013), cert. denied.

Final Thoughts

A challenge to your security clearance or to your access to sensitive information, is a challenge to your job, pure and simple. Take care to reply accurately and adequately to a proposal to revoke your clearance. Your best chance of maintaining your clearance is to never have it revoked in the first place. If revoked, appeal and put forth the best case possible in your personal appearance. Support your case with affidavits or other witness statements. You have the right to be represented throughout this process. At a minimum, representation by a personnel expert or attorney experienced in security clearance matters should be seriously considered.

11

Overtime and Other Special Pay

When You Can Get More Than an Hour's Pay for an Hour's Work...

In This Chapter You Will Learn:

- the different categories of premium pay that exist in the federal government
- how you are paid for overtime
- what rights you have if you encounter a pay dispute

Contents Chapter Eleven - Overtime and Other Special Pay

Introduction

Money. That's the main reason most of us work. Of course, we get satisfaction from a job well done, and we appreciate the company of our coworkers (well, most of them...) as well as the gratification that comes with making a contribution to society. But the bills still need to be paid and we'd like a little extra for savings and those little amenities that make life more worthwhile and interesting. Federal employees can earn quite a good salary, but we could all find good uses for a fatter paycheck. In this chapter, we will discuss ways federal employees may be able to earn more money than their usual wages, and what to do if you earned it but didn't receive it.

What kind of pay can I earn beyond my regular wages?

In addition to receiving your regular wages, as a federal employee,[1] you may be entitled to "premium pay" over and above your usual salary. Premium pay is a catch-all term for the various kinds of pay federal employees receive in addition to their basic rate of pay. Premium pay is generally due when an employee works extra hours or takes on unusual

1 For historical reasons, certain executive branch agencies are carved out of the overall executive branch pay system. For example, certain civilian Department of Defense employees working in intelligence-related divisions are covered by the Defense Civilian Intelligence Personnel System (DCIPS). Some employees of the Federal Aviation Administration (FAA) and the Transportation Security Administration (TSA) are covered by Core Compensation systems. DCIPS uses its own grade/step tables, while Core Compensation uses a 'pay band' system which gives management discretion on setting pay levels for individual employees within specified ranges. Both DCIPS and Core Compensation have provisions for forms of premium pay such as overtime. Administrative Law Judges, emplloyees in the Senior Executive Service, Postal Service employees, Title 38 employees at the Department of Veterans Affairs (typically medical professionals), or Title 42 employees at the National Institutes of Health (typically scientists and researchers), and legislative and judicial branch employees also ordinarily fall outside of the GS/WG system; premium pay at those agencies is governed by their agency-specific policies. However, some agencies which have pay-setting authority independent to the General Schedule have chosen to duplicate the General Schedule (for example, the Government Printing Office).

work assignments, such as hazardous duty or night work. The general types of premium pay are discussed below.

Sunday premium pay

If you are a full-time General Schedule (GS), Wage Grade (WG) employee,[2] Defense Civilian Intelligence Personnel System (DCIPS) employee, or FAA/TSA Core Compensation employee whose regular schedule requires you to work on a Sunday, you are entitled to your regular hourly pay rate, plus premium pay computed at a rate of twenty-five percent of your basic pay rate. Generally, Sunday premium pay does not apply to overtime hours, i.e., anything more than an eight-hour shift on a Sunday. Part-time and intermittent employees are not entitled to Sunday premium pay.

Holiday pay

If you work on a holiday during hours that correspond to your normal hours of work, you are entitled to holiday premium pay equal to your basic rate of pay. In other words, you get twice your regular rate of basic pay for working on a holiday. However, if you work more than eight hours on a holiday, you are only entitled to your regular overtime rate for those additional hours.

Night differential pay

Wage Grade federal employees are generally entitled to receive a seven and a half percent differential rate for working on a second shift, that is, a shift between 3:00 p.m. and midnight, and a 10 percent differential for working on a third shift, i.e., a shift between 11:00 p.m. and 8:00 a.m. General Schedule employees are generally entitled to a 10 percent increase in their regular rate of basic pay as night differential pay for night work between 6:00 p.m. and 6:00 a.m.

Environmental differential pay

Wage Grade employees are entitled to environmental pay rates when they are exposed to working conditions or hazards that fall within one of the categories approved by OPM.[3] The amount of the differential for all appro-

---

[2] Federal employees may be appointed and paid under different laws. "Blue collar" workers tend to be paid on the "Wage Grade" pay scale, which attempts to reflect prevailing wage rates in the labor market. Most other federal employees are appointed and paid under the General Schedule or "white collar" pay system. See Chapter 1.

[3] A list of the exposures for which differentials may be paid can be found at 5 CFR Part 532, Subpart E, Appendix A.

priated fund WG employees is equal to the percentage rate approved by OPM for the particular job category, multiplied by the rate of pay for a WG-10, Step 2, which is the multiplier for all appropriated fund WG employees. One example is that a Wage Grade system worker performing ground work beneath a hovering helicopter is eligible for a fifteen percent differential.[4]

Hazardous duty pay

If you are a GS employee whose work involves unusual physical hardships or hazards that have not already been accounted for in your job classification, you are entitled to a hazardous duty pay differential ranging from four to 25 percent of your basic pay. Examples of physical hardships include exposure to extreme temperatures for a long period of time or arduous physical exertion. Hazards include job duties that involve risks of physical injury or death.

Administratively uncontrollable overtime ("AUO")

If you work in a job that requires you to perform substantial amounts of unpredictable, irregular, or occasional overtime, and in your job you are generally responsible for recognizing, without supervision, circumstances that require you to remain on duty, as a GS employee other than a criminal investigator, you may be granted AUO premium pay. AUO premium pay is granted if your job requires substantial amounts of irregular or occasional overtime work that cannot be controlled administratively.

AUO premium payments are set as a percentage of your annual base pay, but cannot be less than 10 percent or more than 25 percent. If you are receiving AUO pay, you are not eligible for any other kinds of premium pay, for example, overtime. For purposes of computing your retirement annuity, AUO overtime pay is considered part of your basic rate of pay.

Law Enforcement Availability Pay ("LEAP")

Law Enforcement Availability Pay (LEAP) is the annual premium pay granted to certain law enforcement personnel who have criminal investigation responsibilities. LEAP is the equivalent of administratively uncontrollable overtime (AUO) pay for criminal investigators. If you are a criminal investigator who qualifies under the law, you are entitled to LEAP, which is a fixed 25 percent of basic pay, including locality pay.[5] Higher graded law

---

[4] The fifteen percent Environmental Differential pay percentage for someone working under a hovering helicopter is the actual percentage called for by OPM's regulation for that work. *See* 5 CFR Part 532, Subpart E, Appendix A (1998).

[5] Locality pay is extra pay to compensate for the higher cost of living in some communities.

enforcement officers may be entitled to a lesser amount if their LEAP causes them to exceed the maximum earnings limitation for law enforcement officers, which is 150 percent of the minimum rate of GS-15 pay including locality pay.

To qualify, you must fill out a certification form annually, and also receive a certification from your supervisor that you perform criminal investigations and that you are available to work an annual average of two hours of unscheduled duty per regular work day, as requested by your agency. If you are a criminal investigator receiving availability pay, you are exempt from the minimum wage and overtime pay provisions of the Fair Labor Standards Act ("FLSA"). However, you remain eligible for night differential, Sunday, and holiday premium pay. You are not eligible for standby duty pay, which is discussed below.

Standby duty pay

Standby duty pay is overtime paid to certain employees, such as firefighters, whose jobs require them to remain on standby at or near their duty stations in excess of eight hours a day or forty hours a week. If you are an FLSA covered employee, as discussed later in this chapter under FLSA overtime, on standby duty, you are entitled to be paid one and one-half times your regular hourly rate of base pay for each hour spent in standby status. However, if your shift is more than 24 hours long, an agency may deduct up to eight hours from each of your 24-hour shifts for sleep and meal periods.

If you are an FLSA exempt employee, you are eligible to be paid one and one-half times your regular rate of base pay as long as your position is not graded above the GS-10, Step 1 level. Employees graded above GS-10, Step 1, receive one and one-half the GS-10, Step 1 rate as standby duty pay. As a GS employee, you may be eligible for annual standby duty pay if your tour of standby duty is established on a regular and recurring basis over a substantial period of time (generally at least a few months).

Annual standby pay rates range from five to twenty-five percent per year of an employee's basic pay that does not exceed the GS-10, Step 1 cap, including any locality pay, depending on the nature of your standby schedule. If you receive annual standby duty pay, you are not eligible for overtime, night, or holiday pay, other than pay for irregular or occasional overtime work.

Call-back pay

Call-back pay is premium pay that you receive when you get called to work on a day when you were not scheduled to work, or when you are required to return to work extra hours after completing a tour of duty. If you are called back, you must receive a minimum of two hours of overtime pay or compensatory time off (see p. 250), even if you are sent home before that time. Call-back pay rights extend to overtime work performed after hours on your scheduled day off. If the call-back occurs during regularly scheduled non-overtime work on a holiday, you must be paid two hours of holiday premium pay instead of overtime pay.

However, if you are a full-time employee called back on a holiday outside of your normal tour of duty, either before or after it, you are entitled to at least two hours of overtime pay.

What are my rights to overtime pay?

In addition to extra pay that you may receive for working under what we will term "abnormal" conditions or circumstances, as a federal employee, you may also be entitled to receive extra pay if you work more than forty hours in a week. Whether you are entitled to overtime pay, and how much, is governed by a federal statute. Read on.

The Fair Labor Standards Act ("FLSA")

As enacted in 1938, the Fair Labor Standards Act or FLSA applied only to the private sector. By two amendments, one in 1966 and the other in 1974, Congress extended FLSA coverage, first to state and local government employees, and then to federal employees like you. In the 1974 amendments, Congress gave the Civil Service Commission (now OPM) authority to administer the provisions of the FLSA "with respect to any individual employed by the United States."

In addition to requiring payment of minimum wage rates, the FLSA requires that employers pay one and one-half times the regular hourly rate of pay to employees for any work performed in excess of 40 hours in a given workweek. However, the FLSA does not apply to everyone. The statute identifies several categories of employees exempted from (not covered by) the minimum wage and overtime provisions of the Act. The group of exempt personnel includes those "employed in a bona fide executive, administrative, or professional capacity."

FLSA exemptions are to be "narrowly construed," and limited to those employees plainly and unmistakably within their terms and spirit. The FLSA, in effect, presumes non-exempt (covered) status. Your agency clearly has the burden of establishing an exemption, if it is claiming one. This means that the agency must prove each element of a claimed executive, administrative, or professional exemption or it is forced to pay time and one-half overtime pay.

OPM's regulations

OPM has issued regulations which supplement the FLSA and should be read in conjunction with this chapter.[6] Your agency must exempt from FLSA overtime provisions any employee who meets the exemption criteria set forth in those regulations. The regulations state that if you are properly classified at the GS-4 level or below (or the equivalent level in other white-collar pay systems), you are nonexempt, which means you are entitled to overtime pay at the rate of one and one-half times your regular rate of pay. If you are properly classified at the GS-5 through GS-10 levels (or the equivalent levels in other white-collar pay systems, such as excepted service appointees), you may be exempt only if you are an executive, administrative, or professional employee.

Executive exemption Do you have an executive exemption from FLSA overtime pay? According to OPM, an "executive" employee is a supervisor, foreman, or manager who manages a federal agency or any subdivision of an agency, including the lowest recognized organizational unit with a continuing function, and regularly and customarily directs the work of at least three subordinate employees, excluding clerical support employees, and meets all the following criteria:

a. Your primary duty consists of management or supervision. The primary duty requirement is met if you—

1. have authority to select or remove and advance in pay and promote, or make any other status changes of subordinate employees, or have authority to effectively suggest and recommend such actions, and

---

6 *See* 5 CFR Part 551.

2. customarily and regularly exercise discretion and independent judgment in such activities as work planning and organization; work assignment, direction, review, and evaluation; and other aspects of management of subordinates, including personnel administration

b. In addition to the primary duty criterion that applies to all employees, if you are a foreman-level supervisor in the federal Wage System (or the equivalent in other wage systems), a law enforcement employee at GS-7 through GS-9, or an employee classified at the GS-5 or GS-6 levels (or equivalent in other white-collar pay systems), you must spend 80 percent or more of the worktime in a representative workweek on supervisory and closely related work in order to be exempted.[7]

Administrative exemption Under OPM's regulations, you are an FLSA exempt administrative employee if you are an advisor, assistant, or representative of management, or a specialist in a management or general business function or supporting service. Examples of management support work include management consultants, systems analysts, personnel management specialists, and budgeting and financial management specialists. General business functions include negotiating and administering contracts, determining the acceptability of goods or services or authorizing payments. Supporting services include automated data processing, communications, or procurement and distribution of supplies.

To be exempt as an administrative employee, you must meet *all* of the following criteria:

a. Your primary duty consists of work that—

1. significantly affects the formulation or execution of management policies or programs, or
2. involves general management or business functions or supporting services of substantial importance to the organization serviced, or
3. involves substantial participation in the executive or administrative functions of a management official

b. You perform office or other predominately nonmanual work which is—

1. intellectual and varied in nature, or

---

[7] *See* 5 CFR § 551.205.

2. of a specialized or technical nature that requires considerable special training, experience, and knowledge

c. you must frequently exercise discretion and independent judgment, under only general supervision, in performing your normal day-to-day work

d. in addition to the primary duty criterion that applies to all employees, if you are a General Schedule employee classified at GS-5 or GS-6 (or the equivalent in other white-collar systems) you must spend 80 percent or more of the worktime in a representative workweek on administrative functions and work that is an essential part of those functions[8]

Professional exemption Professional employees, teachers, and school administrators are exempt from the FLSA. You are considered to be an exempt professional employee if:

a. Your primary duties consist of—

1. work that requires knowledge in a field of science or learning customarily and characteristically acquired through education or training that meets the requirements for a bachelor's or higher degree, with major study in or pertinent to the specialized field as distinguished from general education; or performing work, comparable to that performed by professional employees, on the basis of specialized education or training and experience which has provided both theoretical and practical knowledge of the specialty, including knowledge of related disciplines and of new developments in the field, or
2. work in a recognized field or artistic endeavor that is original or creative in nature (as distinguished from work which can be produced by a person endowed with general manual or intellectual ability and training) and the result of which depends on your invention, imagination, or talent

b. your work is predominately intellectual and varied in nature, requiring creative, analytical, evaluative, or interpretive thought processes for satisfactory performance

---

8 *See* 5 CFR § 551.206.

c. you frequently exercise discretion and independent judgment, under only general supervision, in performing your normal day-to-day work[9]

Title 5 overtime

If you are exempt from the overtime pay provisions of the FLSA, you are compensated for your overtime under Title 5 of the United States Code or other existing pay laws. Under Title 5, overtime pay is computed at a rate of one and one-half times your basic pay or the GS-10, Step 1, rate of basic pay, whichever is lower.

Please note that many agencies have policies requiring employees to get management authorization (usually, prior authorization) before they may work overtime. An employee's failure to get management authorization may not necessarily limit their entitlement to overtime pay for the hours worked. However, by working unauthorized overtime, the employee separately risks disciplinary action for violating agency time and attendance policies. See Chapter 4 for further discussion of disciplinary adverse actions.

Can I challenge a denial of overtime?

There may come a time when you need to challenge an overtime determination. Perhaps you worked more than your scheduled 40 hours in a workweek and you were not paid for the extra time. Perhaps your employer exempted you from overtime pay status, and you think that was a mistake. Or, perhaps you were given one kind of overtime pay when you think it should have been another, higher paid type. Whatever the nature of your disagreement, you generally have a right to file a grievance or claim with the appropriate agency or court, depending on the circumstances.

Grievances

If you have not received the proper amount of overtime pay under the FLSA or Title 5 and you are employed in a union bargaining unit covered by the provisions of a collective bargaining agreement, you must file your overtime claims as a grievance under the negotiated grievance procedures contained in that agreement.[10] If the union takes the case to arbitration, an arbitrator will decide the matter. See Chapter 8 for further details on the union grievance and arbitration process.

---

9 *See* 5 CFR § 551.207.

10 *See* 5 CFR § 551.703(a).

If FLSA or overtime claims are specifically excluded from coverage under your collective bargaining agreement's negotiated grievance procedures, you may not file your overtime claim as a grievance under your union contract. However, other complaint procedures exist that you can use to complain about your overtime issues as discussed below.

Agency and OPM claims

Agencies may adopt procedures for processing FLSA claims, such as administrative grievance procedures. Generally, if you are not covered by a collective bargaining agreement, you may file FLSA claims with either your agency or with OPM, but not with both at the same time. OPM encourages you to obtain a decision on the claim from your agency before filing the claim with OPM. However, you are not required to do so, and may use either avenue to pursue your claim. Going to the agency first may give you "two bites at the apple," but generally, OPM will side with the agency.

OPM claims must be in writing and must include:

- the position (job title, series, and grade) you occupied during the period of time covered by the claim
- a statement of the nature of the claim
- copies of the evidence supporting the claim, and
- a statement of the time period covered by the claim

TIP

You are responsible for providing all relevant evidence to the OPM in a timely fashion! Make sure you submit your time sheets, pay stubs, and any personal notes or calendars showing that you worked overtime but were not paid properly.

You have the right to designate a representative to assist you in presenting your OPM overtime claims. This must be done in writing and accompany your claim. As an OPM claimant, you may request that your identity remain confidential during the claim process.

Agencies have the burden of proving FLSA exemptions and are required to provide you with information relevant to your claim, if you so request.

If you receive an unfavorable decision, you may seek to have OPM reconsider it by showing that important information was not considered or there was a significant error of law, regulation, or fact in the original OPM decision. A final decision by OPM is binding on all parties and agency officials. OPM claims must be filed with OPM's "Oversight Division" office serving the area where the basis of your claim occurred.

You may appeal an adverse agency decision to OPM, but you may not appeal an adverse OPM decision to your agency. OPM's FLSA claim decisions are final and not subject to further administrative review. If you receive an adverse OPM decision on your overtime claim, you may file a court complaint.

Court claims/Statute of limitations/Relief

If you are not covered by a collective bargaining agreement, you can file complaints under the FLSA with the United States Court of Federal Claims in Washington, DC, or an appropriate U.S. district court. However, the district courts can only hear your claim if it is less than $10,000. If your court claim is more than $10,000, then it must be filed in the Court of Federal Claims. Moreover, filing a claim with an agency or with OPM does not stop the running of the statute of limitations governing FLSA claims filed in court. Also, OPM will not decide an FLSA claim that has been filed in court.

Regardless of whether you file an FLSA claim with your employing agency or OPM, or file a claim in court, the claim must be filed within *2 years* from the date that the claim arose. If the violation was willful or intentional, then the claim can be brought within *3 years* of when it arose. The date on which the employing agency, OPM, or the court *receives* the claim is the date used to determine whether the claim is timely. Retain documentation to prove when the claim was received—for example, file the administrative claim using certified mail, return receipt requested.

If your claim for back pay is successful, you will be entitled to double pay (called "liquidated damages") for a period of up to two years (three years for a willful violation) back from the date the claim was received, plus an award of attorney fees.[11]

[11] For administrative claims before OPM, OPM itself does not award the attorneys fees. Instead, these are payable by the employing agency under the Back Pay Act and must be sought separately after the OPM decision.

Can I challenge my agency's determination of exempt status?

Just as you can challenge overtime pay issues, you may also challenge your agency's determination that you are exempt from the provisions of the FLSA by either:

1. filing a grievance under an appropriate collective bargaining agreement or agency administrative procedure, and/or
2. filing an administrative claim with OPM, or
3. filing a claim in the U.S. Court of Federal Claims

Any of the above must be filed within the applicable time limits for bringing such actions.

Must I be paid for overtime with money?

At your request, the head of your agency may grant compensatory time off from your tour of duty instead of overtime pay for an equal amount of irregular or occasional overtime work. This is usually referred to as "comp time." If your agency has "alternative work schedules" such as "flex time with credit hours," you may use the credit hours earned from overtime for compensatory time off, even though your overtime is not irregular or occasional in nature. Under the FLSA, you may be deemed to have agreed to mandatory comp time if provided by the applicable provisions of a collective bargaining agreement, memorandum of understanding, or any other agreement between the agency and your union. If you were hired prior to April 15, 1986, the agency's regular practice in effect on April 15, 1986, with respect to comp time constitutes an agreement or understanding with you.

Except as stated above, your agency may not require that you be compensated for overtime work with an equivalent amount of comp time. The head of your agency may fix time limits for you to request and take comp time. If comp time is not requested or taken within the established time limits, you must be paid for overtime work at the overtime rate in effect for the work period in which it was earned.

Final Thoughts

As employees, we want to get everything that is coming to us. As a federal employee, you have several types of premium pay available that will compensate you over and above your regular wages if you fit within the requirements, as well as the option of comp time if your agency offers it. Make sure you are getting the pay you qualify for. If you have been wrongfully exempted from overtime pay, or denied pay for overtime you worked, there are at least three avenues open for you to challenge such actions. Use them to get what you deserve.

12

Classification Appeals

Do They Really Know What I Do?

In This Chapter You Will Learn:

- what to do to challenge your grade, pay level, title, or classification series

Contents Chapter Twelve - Classification Appeals

Introduction

You're in a position for a while, and one day it dawns on you that something isn't quite right. You look around at what others are earning or doing, and it occurs to you that your position may be misclassified. Sounds like it might be time for you to consider a classification appeal.

Classification appeals are appeals to your agency or to OPM challenging the classification of your position—your grade or pay level, your title, or the classification series assigned to your position or job. Most often, employees filing classification appeals believe that the work they are actually performing is at a higher grade than they are being paid.

Sometimes, an appeal to the MSPB or EEOC may involve a look at the classification standards and whether or not you are performing a certain job or being paid appropriately, but those are not direct appeals of the classification of your position.

You may also consider appealing the classification of your position or seeking pay or grade retention benefits if you are subject to a demotion in pay or grade by an agency, sometimes as a result of a reduction-in-force. (See Chapter 9.) This chapter will outline the right way to appeal directly the classification of your position.

What if I don't agree with my position classification?

If you hold a position in the General Schedule ("GS"), you may request that your agency or OPM's Classification Appeals Office review your classification and decide the appropriateness of your occupational series or grade. This is called a "classification appeal." You may file your appeal directly with OPM and skip the agency review process, but it is not advisable as OPM is generally more conservative.[1]

There is no time limit within which to raise your appeal with the agency unless it involves a reclassification that resulted in a downgrade, in which case you must appeal within *15 days* to preserve your right to back pay. There is no right to a hearing at any point in the process—before your agency or before OPM. A desk audit, which should include an observation of you and your actual duties and interviews with you and your supervisor, will be the most convincing proof of your case.

TIP

Your agency is not required to conduct a "desk audit" or study of your job as a part of deciding your appeal, but if the agency does not do one for you prior to your appeal, you should insist on it during the appeal!

Your initial appeal to your agency (or OPM) must be in writing and state the reasons why you think your position is not properly classified in terms of its series or grade, or why it should be included or excluded from the General Schedule. In crafting your arguments in support of your appeal, compare your job's classification to OPM's classification standards. You will need to obtain OPM's classification standards and compare your actual duties against the standards. A favorable desk audit will provide you with most of the necessary information.

Although showing inconsistent series and grades between you and coworkers may help establish that your series or grade is wrong, OPM will look at the classification standards to judge what your series and grade should be. OPM is prohibited from classifying positions on the basis of position-to-position compari-

[1] *See* 5 CFR § 511 F.

sons.[2] OPM can also decide that your coworkers' series and grades do not match the classification series and grades and change your coworkers' series or downgrade them!

TIP

You will not win your case by simply comparing your work to that of your coworkers.

You are not permitted to appeal:

- a position title (unless a specific OPM standard determined the title)
- the classification standards of another person
- classification of a position to which you are detailed
- the classification of a temporary promotion (unless the temporary promotion is for a period greater than two years)
- your position description

If you believe your position description is flawed, you must go through an internal agency grievance (or a union grievance) to resolve it before filing a classification appeal. If you dispute your position description during a classification appeal before OPM, OPM will make its decision based upon your actual duties, and not your position description.

Your agency must forward your appeal to OPM within *60 days* if

- the decision is unfavorable to you
- you request an OPM appeal, or
- the agency has no authority to decide (or fails to decide) your appeal

If the decision of OPM is unfavorable to you, you may request that OPM reconsider its decision within *45 calendar days* after its issuance. The Director of OPM, at his or her discretion, may reopen and reconsider any decision based upon written new evidence or argument raising a "reasonable doubt" about the technical accuracy of the decision.

---

2 *See* 5 USC § 5107 F.

If your agency does not forward your appeal to OPM, you should do so to protect your interests. You need to draft a new appeal and reasons for your appeal, but you should include a detailed statement of why you disagree with the agency's analysis and provide any relevant information which the agency ignored or misconstrued. OPM maintains a database of classification appeal decisions by occupational series and grade which can be accessed on opm.gov.

TIP

Don't expect your agency or OPM to look favorably upon your appeal unless you present them with all the information and analysis they will need to find in your favor. You may want to retain a professional classification expert to support your appeal.

If the result of the classification appeal is a determination (by your agency or OPM) to change your title, series, grade, or pay, a personnel action is required. The personnel action must take place within a "reasonable" period of time (usually several weeks) following the date of the final classification action.

If you prevail and receive a ruling involving no reduction in grade or pay, the personnel action making the change cannot be made effective earlier than the date of the classification action "certificate" or later than the beginning of the fourth pay period following the date of the certificate. You will not have a right to any back pay or retroactive benefits. The relief will affect future benefits only.

Unless there is illegal motivation, a reduction in grade (demotion) caused by a reclassification is not an adverse action entitling you to MSPB appeal rights. Demotion appeals should follow receipt of the written Notification of Classification Decision.[3] You must appeal within *15 days* of the effective date of the new, lower grade to preserve your right to retroactive relief. If the demotion action is sustained, demotion actions cannot be made retroactive. They will become effective not earlier than the date of the new certificate or later than the beginning of the fourth pay period following the date of the certificate.

---

[3] *See* 5 CFR § 511.

If you are placed in a lower-graded position following a reclassification action (regardless of whether you or the agency initiated the classification review process) or due to a reduction-in-force, you have certain rights to claim grade or pay retention.[4] Under these circumstances, OPM's regulations entitle eligible federal employees to retain for a period of *2 years* the grade held immediately before the placement into the lower-graded position. You can retain the pay of that grade, too, when your rate of basic pay would otherwise be reduced and when you do not meet the eligibility requirements for grade retention. If you have been placed in a different occupational series, the rate schedule for the new occupational series will apply. In any case, the agency is obligated to place in your Official Personnel Folder (OPF) a letter describing the circumstances warranting the grade and/or pay retention and the nature of that retention.

You will lose entitlement to grade or pay retention if you move to a grade equal to or greater than your retained grade or if you become entitled to a higher rate of basic pay due to other circumstances. You will also lose eligibility for grade or pay retention if you have a break in service of one workday or more, you are demoted for cause or at your request, or you reject a "reasonable offer" of another position which is graded at or above your retained grade.

Appeal of terminated grade/pay retention

If your right to grade or pay retention is terminated due to your rejection of a reasonable offer, you have the right to appeal the agency decision to OPM.[5]

TIP

File the appeal of terminated grade or pay retention in writing to OPM within 20 calendar days after being notified of the termination of benefits.

You must state in the appeal why you believe the offer of a position was not a reasonable offer. OPM may or may not investigate your appeal or hold a hearing to ascertain the facts of your case before issuing a decision. An

4 *See* 5 CFR § 532 G.

5 *See* 5 CFR § 536.302.

OPM decision is final and may only be revised if OPM agrees to reconsider it upon your request. OPM will reconsider its decision if, within *30 calendar days* of the date of the original decision, you establish and offer in writing new and material evidence which proves that there is "a reasonable doubt" as to the appropriateness of the original decision. You must convince OPM that the evidence was not available when you originally presented your appeal.

If you are in a union collective bargaining unit, you may have the right to have the termination of your grade or pay retention benefits reviewed under the union negotiated grievance and arbitration procedures. If the negotiated grievance procedure is available to you, you have *no* right to appeal to OPM.

TIP

The regulations are very detailed. Check them before proceeding to determine if you are eligible for grade and/or pay retention, and to find out what exceptions, if any, may apply in your case.

What if I think my job grading is wrong?

If you are in a Wage Grade job, you have the right to appeal the classification of you position to the appropriate regional office of OPM's Classification Appeals Office, but you must first seek redress from your agency.[6] There is no right to a hearing before your agency or OPM. The appeal procedures for Wage Grade employees are almost identical to the appeal procedure described earlier for General Schedule positions. So read both sections, especially the advice about how to prepare your appeal and argue your points.

If you are a Wage Grade employee and you are dissatisfied with an agency decision, you can file an appeal with OPM. Whether submitted to your agency or to OPM, your appeal can challenge only your occupational series, grade, or title. It cannot challenge your job standards, critical elements, job description, rate of pay, or the propriety of a wage schedule rate.[7]

Your agency is required to create and publish a system for processing requests for review of the series, grade, or title of jobs within it. In no case, however,

---

6 *See* 5 CFR § 532 G.

7 *See* 5 CFR § 532 G.

will there be more than one level of review over your appeal within an agency. So check with your agency's personnel office to get a copy of your agency's regulations or guidance.

Your appeal must be in writing and state the reasons why you believe your classification should be changed. There is no time limit for appealing your occupational series, grade, or title to your agency unless a demotion is involved. If you have been demoted in grade or pay, you have only *15 days* from the effective date of the lower grade to appeal if you want to preserve your right to retroactive relief, that is, back pay at your higher grade.

As part of your appeal to your agency (sometimes called a request for review), your agency must compile a "job-grading review file" (known as the "record") containing only information and documents which you have been given the opportunity to review. You must furnish any requested information and cooperate fully. You and your representative, if any, are entitled to a reasonable amount of time to present the request for review. You also may withdraw your request at any time, and the agency may cancel it if you fail to cooperate or leave the agency (unless retroactive benefits are at issue).

Your agency is obligated to decide your request for review "promptly." The agency decision must be based on the record, be in writing, and include the reasons for the decision, including an analysis of your job.

If the decision is not in your favor, the agency must also inform you in writing of your right to appeal to OPM and the *15-day* time limit, if applicable because of a reduction in pay or grade, for filing the appeal with OPM.

An appeal to OPM must be in writing and identify specifically the erroneous parts of the agency decision and analysis. OPM may make its decision based on documentation or may investigate or audit the job. Your representative, if any, may not be in attendance during any audit. OPM must notify you and your agency in writing of its decision and compute any relief, if appropriate.

OPM may reopen and reconsider a decision by a regional office upon your request or the agency's request if new key facts become known, if there is "reasonable doubt" as to the appropriateness of the decision, or if the decision potentially has a significant impact upon similar positions. Likewise, any OPM decision may be challenged if new important facts become available, an erroneous application of law or policy is involved, or the decision is of a precedential or exceptional nature.

What factors should I consider before appealing to OPM?

The above appeal processes through the agency and then to OPM sound like a fair and open avenue for potential relief. But beware. Many OPM classification appeals result in a downgrading—and not just of your position, but also of the coworkers to whom you have compared your work. OPM has frequently determined that an agency has overgraded positions. For this reason, it is always advisable to seek a reclassification action through your agency and, if possible, get the full support of your supervisor. If you are seriously considering an appeal to OPM, you should get a second opinion from a professional—a personnel consultant with federal government classification expertise or an attorney with experience in this area—before you file your appeal.

Another important avenue to consider is the union grievance procedure if you are covered by a collective bargaining agreement. Generally, the union contract will prohibit you from grieving the classification of your position except for a reduction in grade or pay, but you may be able to grieve your job performance standards, critical elements, or the accuracy of your job description. Moreover, the union can be aggressive in negotiating classification-related issues, such as your access to classification standards and reports, the creation of career ladders, pay equity within and among series and grades, and access to training opportunities for career growth. By utilizing union-supported negotiation or grievance avenues, you may achieve what you are looking for without engaging in a classification appeal and without risking a downgrade for your coworkers and yourself.

Also bear in mind that if you think your series or grade is wrong because of discrimination or a violation of the Equal Pay Act (equal pay for men and women for substantially equal work), you must file your complaint under the negotiable grievance procedure, if applicable, or in accordance with the EEO procedures developed by the EEOC. (See Chapter 6.) This may be a more effective way to get meaningful review of an improper classification.

Final Thoughts

With a classification appeal, all you really want to do is make sure you are getting paid and classified in accordance with the work you are performing. The procedure is in place for you to be able to do this. However, unlike some of the other aspects of your federal employment that can be appealed, this issue has potential land mines. If your appeal determines that your agency has classified you too high, as well as your comparators, you won't be very popular if they are also downgraded because of your appeal. Investigate fully before you make a move.

13

Promotions and Within-Grade Increases

Show Me the Money!

In This Chapter You Will Learn:

- what promotions are based on
- how you qualify for within-grade increases
- what to do if you don't get what you think you deserve

Contents Chapter Thirteen - Promotions and Within-Grade Increases

Introduction

Okay. You were appointed to service in the federal government. You've been here a while, you've kept your nose clean, and you've done a good job. Eventually you look around and realize that you'd like to reap some of the more tangible benefits from your efforts. You think it's time for some sort of step up the ladder. This chapter will explain how such decisions are made and the system for being promoted in the federal government. It will examine the three main ways of obtaining promotions: 1) by applying and competing for a position; 2) through a career-ladder promotion; and 3) by having the duties you are now performing raised to a higher grade. It will also discuss the standards the federal government uses to award within-grade increases, known as step increases. Finally, it will outline the reconsideration and appeals processes—how and where to challenge the denial of a promotion, either through an agency's internal grievance procedure, the MSPB, a union contract, or the EEO process.

How long do I have to wait for a promotion?

Before even looking at your performance as it relates to promotion, you must meet what are called "time-in-grade" requirements. Time-in-grade requirements are determined by the position to which you want to be promoted.

- To advance to positions at GS-12 or above:
  you must have completed a minimum of *52 weeks* in a position no more than one grade lower than the promotion position.
- To be promoted to a position in GS-6 through GS-12:
  you must complete a minimum of *52 weeks* in the next lower graded

position. The grade of the next lower graded position depends on how the position is classified:

1. when the position is classified at two-grade intervals (for example, positions classified at GS-7/9/11), you must have this experience no more than two grades lower;
2. no more than one grade lower when the position is classified at one-grade intervals (for example, GS-5/6/7);
3. or no more than one or two grades lower as determined by the agency, when the position is in a line of work properly classified at one-grade intervals but has a mixed interval promotion pattern.

- To advance to positions up to GS-5, you might not need to meet the time restriction. If the position is no more than two grades above the lowest grade that you held within the last 52 weeks, you have met the requirements.

There are some exceptions to the time-in-grade requirements.

- positions that are filled by direct-hire authority or by competitive examination
- non-competitive appointments that are authorized by law or executive order
- permanent positions you have previously held
- promotions from non-General Schedule positions
- temporary appointments
- promotion through a training agreement (maximum of 2 promotions in 52 weeks)
- promotions to avoid hardship to an agency or inequity to an employee (maximum of 3 grades in 52 weeks)

What are competitive promotions?

A competitive promotion is a change to a higher grade which you receive by competing with other employees. A promotion is not a within-grade increase or a quality step increase, both of which are explained below. A non-competitive promotion also can be acquired through a career-ladder position, also explained below.

Does my agency have some sort of merit promotion plan?

OPM requires that agencies adopt and administer merit promotion plans which are designed to be systematic means of selection for promotion according to merit. Merit promotion plans are designed to facilitate and encourage fairness. They apply to many circumstances which ultimately result in promotion-related actions, including:

- competitive promotions
- temporary promotions which last longer than *120 days*
- details to higher grades which last longer than *120 days*
- selection for training which is part of an authorized training agreement, part of a promotion program, or required before an employee may be considered for promotion
- reassignment or demotion to a position with more promotion potential than the position presently held by the employee
- transfer to a position of a higher grade or with more promotion potential
- reinstatement to a permanent or temporary position of a higher grade or with more promotion potential

Your agency's merit promotion plan must meet several important requirements designed to make sure you are given a fair and equal shot at promotion:

- The plan must promote employees based on merit and must be published and available to agency employees.

- All elements of the promotion process (for example, identification, qualification, evaluation, and selection of candidates) must be made without regard to political, religious, or labor organization affiliation or non-affiliation, marital status, race, color, sex, national origin, non-disqualifying physical disability, or age, and must be based solely on job-related criteria.

- The areas from which candidates are considered must be broad enough to guarantee a highly qualified pool of candidates.

- All qualified employees should be informed of the possible promotion, even if they are not in the area of consideration due to being on detail, on leave, in training, in the military service, or service in public international organizations or on Intergovernmental Personnel Act assignments.

- Candidates must meet the minimum qualification standards as identified by OPM. The selecting officials must also give proper consideration to performance appraisals and incentive awards.

- The plan must state that the selecting officials may select from the group of the best qualified candidates, but that the officials are not required to make such a selection. Managers may select from other appropriate sources, such as reemployment priority lists, reinstatement, transfer, disabled or Veterans Readjustment Act eligibles or candidates identified on an appropriate OPM certificate. Agencies may decide which of these sources are most appropriate, and most likely to fulfill the agency's mission and satisfy affirmative action policies.

- Your agency must keep records of each promotion, showing how candidates were rated and ranked. These records must be available to employees and the public, but must also ensure that employees' right to privacy is protected. The agency can destroy these records after two years or after the program is evaluated by OPM (whichever comes first), but may not do so before time limits for filing grievances lapse. If an EEO complaint is filed over a promotion action, the agency must retain the file until the EEO matter is completed.

Knowing that your agency's plan must meet these requirements is an important tool. If you do not think that your agency has complied with these requirements in making its promotions or creating and using its system for promotions, you may be able to use such deficiencies as part of any grievance or appeal you decide to bring.

Is it possible to be temporarily promoted?

Agencies generally may also make time-limited promotions to temporary positions to accomplish specific projects or to meet other needs that will not exist for more than five years. In such cases, your agency must give you advance written notice of the all conditions of the promotion, including the duration, the reason for the time limit, and that competition is required for any promotion which lasts more than *120 days*. They must inform you that you may be returned at any time to your former position or to a different position of equivalent grade and pay, without appeal rights to the MSPB.

Temporary promotions may be provided for in collective bargaining agreements. A temporary promotion that will last longer than 120 days must be done through competition. The agency may convert the temporary promotion to a permanent promotion without any additional competition if all candidates were notified that the position may become permanent.

What are non-competitive promotions?

Competitive procedures do not apply to certain types of promotions where agencies may promote you at their discretion. Many promotions may occur without competition. For example:

- Career-ladder promotions which are promotions without current competition of an employee who was competitively appointed with the express intent that the position would prepare the employee for promotion to a higher grade
- Position reclassification
- Accretion of duties
- Details or temporary promotions of 120 days or less
- Promotion to a previously-held position no longer held due to separation or demotion for other than performance or conduct-related reasons
- Promotion or reassignment to a position with a higher promotion potential, as long as the employee previously occupied a position with a similar higher promotion potential
- Consideration of a candidate who was not given proper consideration in a competitive promotion
- Appointments of SES appointees with reinstatement eligibility to any position for which they qualify, at any grade or salary level.

Where's the career-ladder around here?

The federal government has career-ladder promotions. Career-ladder positions have automatic promotion potential to a certain grade. You are initially selected for the position competitively. After successfully handling the duties and responsibilities of the position for an appropriate period of time and completing training, you may be promoted to a higher grade if you meet the requirements. OPM's requirements for career-ladder promotions are minimal, and agencies generally identify their own specific requirements.

Under OPM guidelines, you must meet the time-in-grade requirements discussed earlier to qualify for a career-ladder promotion. You also must receive a rating of "Fully Successful" (Level 3 or equivalent) or higher. (See Chapter 2.) If you receive a rating below "Fully Successful" on a critical element of the job, you are not qualified for a career-ladder promotion.

Agencies often identify their own requirements in their regulations or policies and procedures. Agency guidelines are often more strenuous than the minimum requirements identified by OPM. Agencies usually require:

- that time-in-grade requirements be satisfied
- that you have demonstrated the ability to perform at the next higher grade, and
- that there is sufficient work available to be performed at the next higher grade

Often, unions may negotiate the criteria for career-ladder promotions, which will then be included in the union contract.

What if I take on more duties?

A promotion through an accretion of duties is one resulting in the upgrading of a position due to a gradual change in your duties and responsibilities, the issuance of a new classification standard or the correction of an initial classification error. Under a promotion through accretion, you are already working at the higher grade, and then get promoted to that higher grade. If you are denied a promotion through accretion of duties, you have three primary options:

1. file a request for reclassification (a desk audit) with your agency, though this could also result in a downgrade of your position
2. file a complaint through the EEO process (if discrimination is present), or
3. file a grievance if permitted by the union contract or agency grievance procedure

If the refusal to promote you was reprisal for protected whistleblowing, you may ultimately have an appeal to the MSPB, after first complaining to the OSC.

Are there any other non-competitive promotions?

There are several other types of promotions which are also non-competitive.

- Temporary promotions or details for 120 days or less are non-competitive. These promotions are to higher graded positions with known promotion potential.

- Promotion to a higher grade you previously held on a permanent basis in the competitive service is allowed as long as you were not separated or demoted from that grade for performance or misconduct reasons, e.g., downgraded because of a reduction-in-force.

- Agencies can also non-competitively promote you or provide you with priority consideration in the future if you were not given proper consideration in a competitive promotion action. Many MSPB and EEOC non-selection or non-promotion cases are settled through non-competitive placement or promotion.

How much will my raise be when I'm promoted?

After being promoted in the General Schedule into a higher grade, your new salary must be the equivalent of at least a two-step increase in the grade from which you are being promoted.

How do I get a within-grade increase ("WIGI")?

In addition to grade promotions, agencies also grant within-grade increases (WIGIs). These are also called "step" increases. You are entitled to a WIGI if you meet the minimum eligibility requirements, also known as the acceptable level of competence determination. If you are in a permanent position under the General Schedule, and if you are paid less than the maximum rate for your grade, you are eligible to receive a WIGI. SES employees and presidential appointees are not allowed to receive WIGIs.

To receive a WIGI, three requirements must be met:

- your performance must be at an acceptable level, at least Fully Successful (Level 3). The rating system under which you demonstrate acceptable performance must be current and from the most recently completed performance appraisal period

- you may not receive more than one such increase in one waiting period (see below)

- you must have completed the mandatory waiting period for advancement. The length of the waiting periods is based upon your step

Does everyone have to meet the minimum wait rules?

Under certain circumstances, WIGIs must be granted even if you have not served in any position for the minimum period under an applicable performance appraisal program. The following reasons mandate a WIGI:

- absences that are "creditable service," see 5 CFR 531.406
- you have been on paid leave
- you have been granted a retroactive promotion
- you were detailed to another agency and no rating was issued
- you have not had enough time to demonstrate an acceptable level of competence because of "authorized activities of official interest to the agency, not subject to appraisal"
- you have been receiving long-term training

For more examples of absences that count towards creditable service, see 5 CFR 531.409.

Mandatory Waiting Periods

For employees with a scheduled tour of duty:

Promotional Step Sought	Waiting Period Since Last WIGI
2, 3, or 4	52 weeks of creditable service
5, 6, or 7	104 weeks of creditable service
8, 9, or 10	156 weeks of creditable service

For employees without a scheduled tour of duty (for example, intermittent employees[1]):

Promotional Step Sought	Waiting Period Since Last WIGI
2, 3, or 4	260 days of creditable service within 52 weeks
5, 6, or 7	520 days of creditable service within 104 weeks
8, 9, or 10	789 days of creditable service within 156 weeks

[1] Employees with a scheduled tour of duty have their schedule of working hours established in advance. An example of an intermittent employee without a scheduled tour of duty is an emergency worker used in hurricane relief work.

CAN MY WIGI BE DELAYED?

Within-grade increases are not automatic. Your WIGI can be delayed. WIGIs will be delayed when the agency delays in making a determination that you are performing at an acceptable level. This may happen only when:

- you have not been informed of the minimum elements required to meet the acceptable level of competence and you have not been given a performance rating within *90 days* prior to the end of the time period, or
- you have been downgraded because of unacceptable performance, in which case you are not entitled to a WIGI at your new grade until you have completed the minimum time in the lower-graded position

If your agency delays your WIGI, it must specifically inform you of the reason, and the specific requirements for performance at the acceptable level for competence so that you can receive the WIGI in the future. You should be reevaluated for a WIGI at the end of that period. If your performance then meets the acceptable level of competence, the agency must give you a WIGI, retroactive to the beginning of the pay period following the completion of the applicable waiting period.

CAN MY WIGI BE DENIED?

Your agency may also deny your WIGI. A denial must be in writing and must state the reason for the negative determination, tell you how you can improve in order to receive a WIGI, and inform you of your right to request reconsideration of the determination.

If you are denied a WIGI to which you believe you are entitled, you should request reconsideration and follow the procedures for reconsideration identified at 5 CFR 531.410. Ask your agency if it has issued its own regulations relating to WIGIs. Your written request for reconsideration must be filed within *15 calendar days* after receiving the negative determination. It should outline all of the reasons why you think the denial was wrong. Your agency must then create a file which contains:

- the negative determination and the basis for it
- your written request for reconsideration
- a report of investigation (if an investigation is conducted)
- a written summary of the transcript of any witness statements, and
- a final determination

You are entitled to all the documents in the file. You are also entitled to a reasonable amount of time, as determined by the agency, to prepare your reconsideration request and to respond to documents in the file. If your agency denies your request for reconsideration, it must inform you in writing and notify you that you have a right to appeal to the MSPB.

TIP

There is no specific deadline for the agency to respond to your request for reconsideration, so it can drag on or even fall through the cracks. Be diligent about checking to see if the matter has been decided and always follow up in writing.

Appeals under labor agreements

If you are covered by a collective bargaining agreement that does not specifically exclude WIGIs from its coverage, you are not allowed to pursue an appeal at the MSPB. Rather, you must file a grievance through the collective bargaining process.

If you allege discrimination as a basis for the WIGI denial, and if discrimination claims are not specifically excluded from the collective bargaining contract, you may pursue your discrimination claim either through the union contract or through the EEO process. The chart below helps identify the procedural avenues you can pursue in challenging your agency's denial of your request for reconsideration.

TIP

Be careful of your deadlines under the collective bargaining contract, because they are often shorter than the deadlines for appealing to the MSPB.

Challenges to WIGI denials for Employees Covered by Collective Bargaining Agreements

If:	Then:
The negotiated union contract grievance procedure covers WIGI denials or is silent on WIGI denials	Only grievance procedures apply.
and covers discrimination claims or is silent on discrimination claims	You must choose to pursue the discrimination charge through the grievance procedure or through the EEO process, but not both.[2]
but excludes discrimination claims	You can challenge the denial of the WIGI only through the grievance procedures OR you can challenge that the action was discriminatory only through the EEO procedure.
The negotiated grievance procedure specifically excludes WIGIs	You may only challenge the denial through MSPB procedures unless you are also alleging discrimination. (See Chapter 6.)
and if you allege discrimination.	The discrimination allegation may be pursued through either the EEOC or MSPB procedures, in which case the "mixed case" procedures apply. (See Chapter 6.)

What if I do my job exceptionally well?

Quality Step Increases (QSIs) are within-grade increases which are issued to employees because of exceptional performance. Your agency has discretion to issue QSIs which are designed to "provide appropriate incentives and recognition for excellence in performance by granting faster than normal step increases."[3] QSIs are not limited by the waiting period restrictions

2 Initiating the informal EEO complaint procedure does not constitute an election. You have not elected to use the EEO complaint procedure until you file a formal complaint. *See Chapter 6.*

which apply to step increases. QSIs are not frequently granted. Unlike within-grade increases, employees are not entitled to QSIs just because they meet the minimum requirements. You may not receive two QSIs in the same 52-week period. The denial of a QSI is not grounds for an appeal to the MSPB. (See below.)

What if I don't get the promotion or raise I think I deserve?

There are various avenues for you to challenge the denial of a promotion or other pay increase. Because there are so many different options, the road-map to relief can be confusing. It is important to fully understand each option that is available and its advantages and disadvantages. Moreover, some options are not allowed. If you mistakenly or wrongfully choose an incorrect option, you may not be able to choose the proper procedure at a later date.

Agency grievance systems

Agencies must institute internal grievance procedures that are available to you when you feel you have been improperly denied a promotion. Agency grievances may focus on whether the ranking and rating of candidates are properly conducted in conformity with the agency's merit promotion plan. However, if a group of candidates is properly ranked and certified, OPM's regulations provide that a resulting non-selection is not an appropriate basis for a grievance. Also, because the agency grievance procedure does not provide for review by a neutral party, this process is rarely one which would provide you with a successful outcome.

Negotiated grievance procedures

If you are covered by a collective bargaining agreement, the best avenue for challenging a non-promotion is generally the negotiated grievance procedure. If the procedure does not specifically exclude promotions from its coverage, non-promotions are considered covered by the collective bargaining agreement. If you are successful in a grievance, you may be entitled to retroactive placement into the position, back pay with interest and benefits, and attorney fees (if applicable). In pursuing a union grievance, focus on whether the agency applied its procedures or general practices to you differently than it did to other employees who were successfully promoted. Most importantly, show that you are qualified for the promotion.

---

[3] *See* 5 CFR § 531.503.

The deadlines for filing a complaint through the union's negotiated grievance process are identified in the labor agreement. Be careful of your deadlines.

TIP

Deadlines in a labor agreement are usually shorter than those for other avenues of redress. Often, they are as short as 7 days. Consult a union representative for assistance.

MSPB APPEALS

Under some limited circumstances, you may appeal an agency's decision not to promote you to the MSPB if you believe that the non-promotion was retaliation for whistleblowing, or failed to conform with OPM employment rules designed to examine and evaluate the qualifications for applicants for appointment in the competitive service. If the non-promotion resulted from reprisal for whistleblowing, the complaint should be filed as a prohibited personnel practice complaint with the Office of Special Counsel and then as an Individual Right of Action (IRA) with the MSPB. (See Chapter 7.) You may also raise an allegation of discrimination if you allege reprisal for whistleblowing. If the non-promotion resulted from improper implementation by OPM of its regulations in ranking and reviewing the candidates and analyzing the position, you should file an appeal with the MSPB. In this event, the procedures outlined in Chapter 4 for appeals to the MSPB apply.

EEO COMPLAINTS

If you believe that illegal discrimination resulted in your non-selection, you may initiate a complaint through the EEO process. The procedures identified in Chapter 6 apply to EEO complaints. If the case is "mixed," that is, if you allege that discrimination (which would normally go through the EEO process) played a role in a wrongful personnel action (which normally would fall under the MSPB's jurisdiction), "mixed case" procedures apply. (See Chapters 4 and 6.)

OPM appeals

You may appeal to OPM when you think that it has failed to properly implement its own regulations regarding ranking and rating candidates. However, OPM has no duty to investigate the grievance. It does so at its sole discretion.

Should I consider settlement?

Whenever you file a grievance, an appeal, or an EEO complaint, you should try to reach an informal resolution with your agency. Informal resolutions are almost always preferable to fully grieving actions because settlements are faster and you know exactly what the outcome will be. Overall, settlements are strongly encouraged—see Chapter 32.

Don't be afraid to mention informal resolution possibilities to the agency. Settlement discussions do not show weakness. Sometimes, agencies are afraid to be the first to mention settlement or are unaware of the merits of your case. Agencies are almost always relieved when they learn that you are a reasonable adversary who is willing to give them a means of resolving the dispute in an informal and mature manner.

When dealing with non-promotions and WIGI denials, talk with the agency representative assigned to your case. Discuss settlement frequently and from the beginning of the proceedings. If the agency refuses to negotiate a reasonable settlement, you can still follow through with the litigation. When you settle, you agree to drop your case in exchange for what you are really looking for. Usually, there are also written promises that neither you or the agency will disclose the terms of the settlement to anyone else.

TIP

The goal in informal resolution is to achieve your most critical goals by giving up other, less important objectives.

For example, when grieving a non-promotion to a higher grade, theoretically you might be able to get a retroactive promotion with back pay, interest, and full benefits (for example, retirement contributions). Often, your real goal is to reach your "high-three" as soon as possible, thus maximizing your retirement benefits calculations. (For a discussion of "high-three" calculations see Chapter 18.) You could spend lots of time and energy (and money!) going through full litigation, including a hearing, and risk losing your case entirely.

Alternatively, you could try to settle with the agency for a retroactive promotion, waiving the back pay entitlement. Usually, the back pay does not amount to a tremendous amount of money, especially if you filed your claim as soon as the agency denied you the promotion. But the back pay is money that comes from the agency's appropriations, and the agency is sometimes less inclined to settle with back pay payments.

In return for waiving the back pay, but having the agency make the necessary retirement contributions, the agency can still give you the promotion retroactively, so that it counts towards your "high-three" calculation and a higher retirement benefit. Generally, agencies do not mind doing this because the retirement benefits come from OPM's appropriations and do not cost the agency anything. In addition, you can agree with the agency that you will immediately begin performing at the higher level and be compensated at that higher level. The same theory applies to WIGIs.

Final Thoughts

Promotions and raises that you qualify for not only make you feel appreciated, feel good about a job well done, and fatten your paycheck; they are an important part of your federal employment rights. Knowing what promotions and raises are available, how you can qualify for them, and what to do when you don't receive them, are important tools for getting what you deserve.

14

Leave Issues

Gone Fishin'—That's Okay, Isn't It?

In This Chapter You Will Learn:

- what kind of leave is available to you
- whether you can be disciplined for leave-related problems
- what to do if you have a leave-related problem

Contents Chapter Fourteen - Leave Issues

Introduction

We are all human and have families and lives outside of work. From time to time we need to be absent from our jobs to tend to personal matters. Taking time off from work is known as "leave." Ideally, what you want is to be able to take leave without any adverse consequences such as loss of pay or being recorded as absent without leave (AWOL). This chapter will concentrate on the most common kinds of leave in federal employment—annual and sick leave, and the Family and Medical Leave Act.

What is annual leave and what can I use it for?

You are entitled to annual leave with pay. Annual leave is what is usually regarded as vacation leave. Annual leave is accumulated in accordance with regulations established by OPM.[1] You accrue annual leave at the following rates:

- one-half day for each full biweekly pay period if you have less than three years of service
- three quarters of a day for each full biweekly pay period if you have three but less than 15 years of service, with some exceptions, and
- one day for each full biweekly pay period if you have 15 or more years of service

Each agency usually issues its own set of rules (also known as regulations) regarding how it will permit employees to use annual leave. Annual leave may be granted at any time during the year as the head of your agency prescribes. You may only carry over 240 hours of annual leave from one year to the next. Leave in excess of 240 hours is referred to as "use or lose" leave, meaning that if you do not use that excess leave by the end of the calendar year, you will lose the right to use it.

---

[1] *See* 5 CFR § 630(C).

WHAT IS RESTORED LEAVE AND ADVANCE ANNUAL LEAVE?

There are a few exceptions to the "use or lose" rules, and in these cases, agencies may restore annual leave that was forfeited because it was in excess of 240 hours. These circumstances include when the agency believes the leave was forfeited due to administrative error, an exigency of the public business, or the sickness of the employee. Examples of situations where annual leave may be restored include: situations where the employee's services are deemed necessary in a national emergency; and in certain circumstances surrounding base closings. There are time limits for use of restored annual leave, and employees should check with their agency for specific policies and procedures for having leave restored.

Additionally, agencies may award employees advanced annual leave under certain circumstances. The amount of advanced annual leave is limited to the amount of annual leave an employee would accrue in the remainder of the leave year. Employees are not entitled to advanced annual leave, and each employee should check their agency's policies on advanced leave.

WHAT IS SICK LEAVE AND WHEN CAN I TAKE IT?

Just like annual leave, you earn sick leave. The rate at which you earn sick leave differs from that for annual leave. Specifically, you earn sick leave at the rate of one-half day for each full biweekly pay period you have worked. Unlike annual leave, sick leave that you do not use accumulates for use in succeeding years without limit. Sick leave unused at the time of your retirement from the federal government (for example, retirement) is added to your "service computation date."[2] Sick leave may be used to care for a family member who has an illness, injury, or any other medical condition which, if you had it, would justify the use of sick leave. You can use sick leave for time that you need in connection with the death of a family member, including making arrangements for or attending a funeral.

In general, an agency must grant sick leave when an employee:

1. receives medical, dental, or optical examination or treatment
2. is incapacitated for the performance of duties by physical or mental illness, injury, or childbirth

---

[2] The "service computation date" is the official measurement of your length of service with the federal government.

3. takes care of a family member who is incapacitated as a result of physical or mental illness, injury, pregnancy, childbirth or who receives medical, dental, or optical examination or treatment
4. makes arrangements necessitated by the death of a family member or to attend the funeral of a family member
5. would jeopardize the health of others by his or her presence on the job by exposing them to a communicable disease, or
6. must be absent for purposes related to adoption of a child

How do I apply for sick leave?

You must request advance approval for sick leave you use for planned examination or treatment, whether medical, dental, or optical. If you cannot request advance approval for sick leave due to the unplanned nature of the need for leave, then follow your agency's rules regarding notifying your supervisor and requesting sick leave after the need for leave arises. Otherwise, you must file an application for sick leave within the time limits set by the agency. Ask for a copy of your agency's rules regarding the use of sick leave and become familiar with them.

There are some limitations on the amount of sick leave an employee may take during any year. OPM's rules state that an agency may grant sick leave only when the leave is supported by "administratively acceptable" evidence. If it decides to, an agency may consider your own certification of the need for leave administratively acceptable. For absences *in excess of 3 days*, or a lesser period when the agency deems it necessary (e.g., because you are on leave restriction), the agency may also require you to provide a medical certificate or other administratively acceptable evidence. Usually, the medical information the agency needs is information that will show you were unable to perform your duties (incapacitated) during your absence from work.

You may object to providing your agency with medical information on the grounds that to do so would invade your privacy, but agencies have the right to request medical information about absences for which sick leave is requested. If you do not want your supervisor to know about your medical record, request that the medical information be sent to a doctor utilized by the agency for review, rather than to your supervisor. You take a risk if you refuse to provide medical information when requested by your agency. Among other things, your agency may discipline you for failure to comply with leave procedures, and place you in an AWOL status for the period of leave you requested.

What if I need more sick leave than I have earned?

There are a number of programs through which you may be able to use additional sick leave: the voluntary leave transfer program, the voluntary leave bank program, and recredit of leave.

Voluntary Leave Transfer Program The Voluntary Leave Transfer Program (VLTP) allows employees to donate unused accrued annual leave for use by another agency employee who needs such leave because of a medical emergency. Employees interested in applying to receive donated leave under the VLTP should do so in writing to his/her agency. If you are interested in donating annual leave under the VLTP, you should submit a written request to do so to your agency.

Voluntary Leave Bank Program The Voluntary Leave Bank Program (VLBP) is a program under which employees' unused accrued annual leave may be contributed to a leave bank for use by other leave bank members who need the leave because of a medical emergency. Employees who wish to either donate leave to their agency's leave bank or to become a leave bank recipient must submit a written application to their agency.

Recredit of leave When an employee transfers from one agency to another without a break in service, the employee's former agency must certify his/her sick and annual leave accounts to the employee's future employing agency for credit or charge. An employee who has had a break in service is entitled to recredit of sick leave if the employee returns to Federal employment.

Advanced Sick Leave In addition to these programs, agencies may grant advance sick leave for the same reasons it grants sick leave. An agency granting advanced sick leave is completely discretionary, and depending on the situation, there are ceilings on the amount of sick leave that may be granted. For example, an agency may grant up to 104 hours of advanced sick leave for medical, dental, or optical examinations, but may grant up to 240 hours of advanced sick leave for physical or mental illness, or injury. All told, an employee may not be indebted for more than 240 hours of advanced sick leave at any one time.

Employees interested in any of these programs should consult with their personnel offices for further information.

Leave use as a reasonable accommodation for a disability

In some circumstances, employees may also be able to use accrued leave, advanced leave, or LWOP as a form of reasonable accommodation for a disability. Among the reasons for an agency granting leave as a reasonable accommodation include, but are not limited to: obtaining medical treatment; recuperating from a disability; obtaining equipment repairs; avoiding temporary adverse conditions in the work environment; training a service animal; and receiving training in the use of Braille or sign language.

An agency must provide leave as a reasonable accommodation when there are no other effective accommodations and the leave will not impose an undue hardship on the agency. However, the employee must demonstrate a connection between the leave usage and disability. In other words, an employee is not entitled to leave as a reasonable accommodation solely because he or she is disabled. Lastly, the employee must be able to demonstrate that he or she can return to work in the foreseeable future. However, should an employee be granted leave as a reasonable accommodation, the agency may not penalize the employee for work missed during the leave.[3]

Can I be disciplined for leave-related misconduct?

Follow the rules carefully about how to request sick and annual leave. If you don't do it correctly, your leave requests can be denied, even if you would otherwise be entitled to leave. If your leave request is denied and you do not report to work during the period of the requested leave, you can be placed in an AWOL status. Moreover, you can be suspended for being placed on AWOL too many times and be disciplined for taking excessive leave, even if the leave is approved. For example, employees have been suspended and even removed for excess absenteeism and abuse of leave, such as taking sick leave when not really sick or falsifying medical information.

If you abuse your leave, you can be placed on leave restriction by your agency. Employees placed on leave restriction usually must follow more strict rules when requesting sick or annual leave. When you are on leave restriction, the agency can require you to provide medical documentation from doctors for absences as short as one day, and to call in any absences

---

[3] *See* EEOC Enforcement Guidance on Reasonable Accommodation and Undue Hardship Under the Americans with Disabilities Act (revised October 17, 2002), Question 19.

within one hour of the beginning of your tour of duty. Agencies can place an employee on leave restriction for extended periods of time such as six months or longer.

What should I do when I have a leave-related problem?

Depending on the leave-related problem—for example, being denied leave, or placed on leave restriction—and depending on the reason for the problem, there may be several ways to challenge the agency action which you believe to be unfair.

- If you believe that you are being treated differently than other employees with similar problems, and that the difference is because of your sex, race, color, age, religion, national origin, disability, or genetic information, then you may have a discrimination complaint. For example, if you were denied leave for some medical condition that amounts to a handicapping condition under the law, you may have a disability discrimination claim under the Rehabilitation Act. (See Chapter 5.)
- Under certain circumstances, the denial of sick leave may violate the Family and Medical Leave Act, which is discussed later in this chapter.
- If you are covered by a union contract, and you do not believe that discrimination was involved in your leave-related issue, then you may file a grievance under the procedures of the union contract. Check the time limits for filing a grievance with your union representative.
- If you are not covered by a union contract, and you do not believe any discrimination occurred, but you still believe the leave-related treatment was unfair or violated agency rules, then you may file a grievance under the agency's administrative grievance procedures. The deadline for initiating this kind of grievance varies from agency to agency. Consult your personnel office to find out how and when to file an administrative grievance. In both union and non-union situations, the filing deadline can be very short, such as *10 to 15 calendar days.*
- If you believe that the leave-related unfairness was due to the fact that you are a whistleblower, then you could file a claim with the Office of Special Counsel, which handles claims of whistleblower retaliation. (See Chapter 7.)

What leave rights does the Family and Medical Leave Act ("FMLA") provide?

The Family and Medical Leave Act (FMLA) gives an employee 12 workweeks of unpaid leave during any twelve-month period if the leave is needed for one or more of the following reasons:

A. to care for the employee's own serious health condition if that health condition makes the employee unable to perform the functions of his or her job
B. the birth of a son or daughter of the employee and to care for such son or daughter within one year of birth
C. the placement of a son or daughter with the employee for adoption or foster care or to care for the son or daughter within one year of placement
D. to care for the spouse, son, daughter, or parent of the employee if such spouse, son, daughter, or parent has a "serious health condition"[4]
E. any qualifying exigency arising out of the fact that the employee's spouse, son, daughter, or parent is a covered military member on "covered active duty"

TIP

Under the FMLA you have the right to 12 weeks of leave (without pay) during a 12-month period. Your agency cannot retaliate and punish you for requesting or taking FMLA leave.

Generally, the leave permitted by the FMLA is without pay. However, you may substitute paid leave for unpaid leave under the FMLA. You need not take your 12 weeks of FMLA leave all at once. For example, you may only need five days of leave because of a serious health condition, or two weeks of leave to care for the serious health condition of your child or spouse. The 12 workweeks of leave may also be taken intermittently. For example, if you require a periodic treatment for a serious health condition, you may take one day off every other week to receive the treatment.

[4] As of the date the 3rd edition of the *Federal Employees Legal Survival Guide* was sent to press, OPM proposed to revise the definition of spouse for FMLA purposes under 5 CFR § 630.1202 to permit Federal employees with same-sex spouses to use FMLA leave in the same manner as those with opposite-sex spouses. Consult a current version of the regulation for an up-to-date definition of spouse for FMLA purposes.

What kind of notice of leave must I give?

If you wish to take FMLA leave, you must comply with the rules for taking this type of leave. Generally speaking, if your need for FMLA leave is foreseeable and based on a planned medical treatment, you are required to provide the agency with at least *30 days* notice of your intention to take leave before the date the leave is to begin. In circumstances like these, you are required to make a reasonable effort to plan the treatment or the other activities involved so as to not unduly disrupt the agency's operations.

If you could not foresee the need for the leave, for example in emergency situations, then you must provide such notice "within a reasonable period of time appropriate to the circumstances involved." You are advised in these emergency situations to inform the agency of the need for leave *as soon as possible.*

OPM's rules concerning the FMLA do not require you to specifically state that you are requesting leave under the FMLA.[5] However, it is a good idea to mention the FMLA, if you believe the leave you need might be covered by the Act.

Do I need medical certification for FMLA leave?

If you take leave under the FMLA, agencies may require you to provide medical certification of the need for the leave. Agencies may also require certification if you request leave to take care of the serious health condition of a spouse, son, daughter, or parent.

Will my employment and benefits be protected in my absence?

If you take leave under the FMLA, upon your return to the agency, you are entitled to the same position you held when the leave started, or to an equivalent position, with equivalent benefits, salary, status, and other terms and conditions of employment. In addition, you are entitled to all the job benefits accrued before the FMLA began. You are also entitled to maintain your health benefits during the leave even if you are taking leave without pay under the FMLA. In this respect, if you are enrolled in the Federal Employees Health Benefits Program, your enrollment in that program may continue while on unpaid FMLA leave, so long as you arrange to pay the appropriate employee contributions to the health benefits fund.

---

5 *See* 5 CFR § 630(L).

How do I enforce my FMLA rights?

If you believe your FMLA rights have been violated, most Federal employees have limited avenues for redress.[6] You may file an administrative grievance or a grievance under a union contract, if you are included in the bargaining unit and the contract allows such grievances, or raise FMLA rights as a defense to a disciplinary or adverse action. You may also file an EEO complaint if you believe that the denial of your FMLA leave was due to discrimination. At least three courts have held that a federal employee may not bring a lawsuit against his/her agency for an FMLA violation.[7]

Final Thoughts

Unless you are a unique creature indeed, the need for leave from your federal job will inevitably arise. Federal employees earn or are otherwise entitled to leave that is appropriate for many different situations. Judicious use of your leave—using it only when truly necessary—and careful attention to your agency's rules will ensure that you do not run into trouble for leave abuse. However, if there is a problem, there are avenues of redress available.

---

6 For discussion of Federal employees with more expansive rights under FMLA, please see Chapters 25 and 29.

7 *See Mann v. Haigh, et seq.*, 120 F.3d 34 (4th Cir. 1997); *Bogumill v. Office of Personnel Management*, 1998 WL 486754 (Fed. Cir. 1998)(Unpublished); *Keen v. Brown*, 958 F. Supp. 70 (D. Conn. 1998).

15

Workers' Compensation

This Wasn't Exactly What I Had in Mind When I said I Needed a Break...

In This Chapter You Will Learn:

- what happens if you have a job-related injury or illness
- what rights you have to compensation for job-related injuries
- what rights you have to appeal Workers' Compensation determinations

Contents Chapter Fifteen - Workers' Compensation

Introduction

No matter how careful we are or what precautions we take, since we are only human, accidents and illnesses happen. With millions of people operating in the workplace every day, it is inevitable that some of those accidents and illnesses—or even deaths—will occur here. This can mean anything from a heavy-duty stapler that falls on your toe as you prepare some workplace document for distribution, to an accident involving other cars as you are driving an agency vehicle from one building to another, to an illness caused by exposure to chemicals in use at your job. If it is an on-the-job accident or illness, you may need time off, medical expense compensation, or even death benefits. In this chapter, we will discuss what you are entitled to if you are injured on the job or have a job-related illness or disease and meet the requirements for benefits. We will also discuss what options you have if you don't get the relief you think you should.

Can I receive benefits for job-related injuries or illnesses?

The Federal Employees Compensation Act (FECA)[1] provides compensation for a federal employee's disability or death resulting from any injury or illness sustained in the performance of duty. The Act is the exclusive means of compensation from the federal government. This means that as a federal employee injured on the job, you have no right to bring any other administrative or court action against the federal government or its employees.

---

1 *See* 5 USC § 8101, *et seq.*

You can, however, still receive proceeds from a personal insurance policy or a civil action against third parties who were responsible for your injury. An example would be a suit against a private company doing construction work on the premises, although you have to share the proceeds with the United States if you are a FECA beneficiary.[2]

The FECA covers civil service employees of all branches of the federal government, as well as:

- employees of government-owned corporations
- federal jurors
- volunteer civilian members of the Civil Air Patrol
- Peace Corps volunteers
- Job Corps enrollees
- National Teachers Corps members
- VISTA volunteers
- all non-federal law enforcement officers who are injured or killed while attempting to prevent a crime against the United States

The FECA is administered by the Office of Workers' Compensation Programs ("OWCP"), Employment Standards Administration, Department of Labor (DOL).[3] The OWCP telephone number is 866/692-7487, and its website is dol.gov/OWCP.

If you are not covered by the FECA, you may still be entitled to compensation benefits for work-related injuries under the Nonappropriated Fund Instrumentalities Act. See, infra.

What do Workers' Compensation benefits cover?

The FECA covers all medical care, including:

- hospitalization
- nursing service
- prosthetic devices, and
- medications

In addition to compensating workplace injuries or death, the FECA also covers any aggravation, during employment, of a preexisting medical condition and may provide for rehabilitation services, including retraining.

---

[2] *See* 5 USC § 8116.

[3] OWCP regulations are contained in 20 CFR § 10.

If you suffer a disabling traumatic injury as a result of your employment, you are entitled to *45 days* continuation of regular pay from your employer. Your regular pay must be continued during the *45-day* period unless the agency challenges the claim and is upheld by the OWCP. A disabling traumatic injury is a wound or other condition caused by external force (including stress or strain) within a single workday or shift.

What should I do if I have an on-the-job injury?

In order to receive continuation of pay after a traumatic injury, you must file a Form CA-1, "Federal Employee's Notice of Traumatic Injury and Claim for Continuation of Pay/Compensation," within *30 days* of the injury. You have the right to select a duly qualified private physician or hospital and be reimbursed for travel to and from them and should seek authorization from your immediate supervisor using a Form CA-16. In all cases reported to the OWCP, the attending physician must immediately provide a medical report.

What if I have an occupational illness or disease?

An occupational illness or disease is a "condition produced by the work environment over a period longer than a single workday or shift, including systemic infection, repeated stress or strain, exposure to toxins, poison, fumes or mental illness." If you suffer from an occupational illness or disease, you should file a Form CA-2, "Federal Employee's Notice of Occupational Disease and Claim for Compensation," as soon as possible after realizing that the disease or illness was caused or aggravated by your employment.

A Form CA-7 is used to claim compensation for all periods of disability not covered by continuation of pay.

The statute of limitations for all OWCP claims is *3 years* from the time you realized the injury, disease, or illness was caused or aggravated by your employment. You must file within this time, or you will not be able to pursue your claim.

What if I have an emotional illness rather than a physical one?

Although agencies may challenge traumatic injury claims and prevent continuation of pay until ruled upon by the OWCP, injury claims are much easier to prove than occupational illness cases. The DOL has seriously limited occupational illness claims by placing the burden of proof on you to establish that an illness is job-related. The Employee Compensation Appeals Board ("ECAB") has ruled that the disability must result from an employee's "emotional reaction to his regular or specially assigned work duties or to a requirement imposed by the employment."[4] When disability results from failure to receive a promotion, dissatisfaction with the structure of the work or position, or an involuntary transfer, it is generally not covered. The evidence in the record must clearly show that it could be reasonably concluded that the work environment caused your mental disability.

This narrow interpretation of the FECA has greatly limited emotional illness claims arising out of on-the-job discrimination. The OWCP almost always forces you to prove discrimination through corroborating witnesses and documents before it will approve a claim. Even a favorable settlement of an EEO case has been deemed to be insufficient proof of discrimination for OWCP purposes. While such narrow interpretations do save the government money, they are a disservice to employees who suffer occupational illness or disease, including mental illness, due to their treatment by their supervisors/managers. If you have an emotional distress claim, it is crucial to obtain the support of your mental health professional and to consult your Congressional representative who may be able to expedite the process.

What other options and considerations are important when it comes to Workers' Compensation?

In addition to whether you can receive benefits for on-the-job injuries or illnesses and what those benefits are, there are other matters that may arise when you are dealing with Workers' Compensation. For instance, you may have trouble getting your medical insurance provider to pay your insurance claims, you may have another related claim pending, or you may even wonder about your right to have your job back if you have been off work for an extended period. Check this section for Workers' Compensation related issues.

Can I receive Workers' Compensation and a disability annuity?

You cannot receive compensation for a job-related injury at the same time you are receiving a disability annuity under the retirement system, except for a "schedule award." This is an award which provides additional compensation for specified periods of time, i.e., a set number of weeks at an established rate, either 66 2/3 percent of salary with no dependents or 75 percent when the employee has one or more dependents, for the permanent loss, or

[4] *See* Lillian Cutler, 28 ECAB 125.

loss of use, of each of certain bodily members, organs, or bodily functions, for example, the loss of eyesight, hearing, or loss of use of a limb.[5] The OWCP regulations also provide for additional weeks of compensation for permanent injuries to certain organs, for example, breast, kidney, and lung, which range from 52 to 205 weeks and a payment not to exceed $3,500 for "serious disfigurement of the face, head or neck which is likely to handicap an employee in securing or maintaining employment."[6]

You are not entitled to receive disability retirement benefits in addition to a lump-sum compensation settlement from the OWCP.[7]

Should I choose Workers' Compensation or disability retirement?

If you suffer a job-related injury or illness which is believed to be permanent, it is a good idea to file not only for Workers' Compensation but also for disability retirement. You will not have to choose between Workers' Compensation benefits and a retirement annuity until after becoming eligible for both benefits. In most cases, it is better to elect Workers' Compensation which is nontaxable and more generous. If you recover from a compensable injury or illness, you are entitled to reemployment rights.

At the time you become eligible for both benefits, you must make an election by notifying the agencies in writing as to the benefits selected.[8] The OWCP pays:

- 66 2/3 percent of your salary if you have no dependents
- 75 percent if you have dependents.

TIP

You may be forced to make some tough decisions concerning which type of benefits to claim and where to file these claims. Ask the agency for complete information. When in doubt, you should also consider consulting your union, a financial or medical advisor, and/or a lawyer or some other professional.

OWCP payments are tax-free. Disability retirement payments are taxable with a small offset for your contributions to the retirement fund. If you have

---

5 *See* 5 USC § 8107(c).
6 *See* 20 CFR § 10.404.
7 *See* 5 USC § 8337.
8 *See* 5 USC § 8116(a).

been approved for both benefits and you elect Workers' Compensation, you can still elect disability retirement if Workers' Compensation is later cut off or reduced. However, you cannot rely upon this receipt of compensation from the OWCP to establish eligibility for disability retirement and vice versa, because the standards may be different.

What if I'm no longer able to earn as much because of my injury?

If you have a partial recovery, you may still receive compensation based upon your "loss of wage-earning capacity," i.e., the difference between your previous salary and what you can now earn with your injury or illness. If you are receiving compensation and you are not totally disabled, at some point, the OWCP will make a determination as to the loss of wage-earning capacity based on the medical evidence. The OWCP may request an additional medical examination. You will receive compensation based on the difference in salaries described above. You may also receive compensation for the recurrence of a disability, including any unused continuation of pay, if occurring not more than *45 days* after you have returned to work following your initial injury or illness.

Should I file for Workers' Compensation if I have an EEO claim pending?

It may not be as important to file an OWCP claim where there is a strong likelihood of success in the EEO case because as a federal employee, you can recover, compensatory damages and out-of-pocket expenses through the EEO process, including medical expenses, lost leave, etc.[9]

However, if your injury or illness is permanent or your EEO claim is not a probable winner, you should file for Workers' Compensation. Where there is any doubt, you should file regardless of the EEO claim. If you are facing absent without leave (AWOL) charges, you should file under the FECA because the receipt of Workers' Compensation means that you were not AWOL.

Do I get my job back if I recover from my illness?

In 1974, Congress amended the FECA to provide restoration to duty for civil service employees who have recovered from their job-related injuries or illnesses.[10] There are also reemployment rights for employees who have been subject to RIFs and for those employees who return from military service.[11]

---

[9] By statute, compensatory damages are available in all discrimination cases except age discrimination cases.

[10] *See* 5 USC § 8151.

[11] *See* 5 CFR § 353.

OPM has issued regulations which provide for restoration if you fully recover from compensable injuries within one year, as well as priority consideration if you fully recover after one year.[12]

- If you fully recover within one year from commencement of compensation, you are guaranteed the right to return to your former position or an equivalent one.[13]
- If your compensable disability exceeds one year, you are entitled to receive priority placement for two years, including "all reasonable efforts" from your former agency.

The regulations limit such entitlements to employees who were "separated or furloughed from a position without time limitations as a result of compensable injury."[14] Denial of these rights entitles you to a Merit Systems Protection Board (MSPB) appeal under 5 CFR 353.401. The Board has held that you are not entitled to such rights where the removal was clearly for cause unrelated to the injury.

There is no right to an MSPB appeal on the issue of eligibility to entitlement or continued receipt of benefits from the OWCP. OWCP cases must be adjudicated by the DOL. As to entitlement to OWCP benefits, the Secretary of Labor has exclusive jurisdiction to hear FECA claims. Courts may not review the Secretary's determinations, nor may the MSPB.

What if I don't agree with a Workers' Compensation determination?

When you submit a claim for benefits for an injury or illness, a determination is made as to whether you will be covered, what you will receive, and for how long you will receive it. You may disagree with the determination. If you do, there are steps you can take to appeal.

Do I have a right to an appeal?

The OWCP appeals process is cumbersome and time-consuming. After an initial turndown of your Workers' Compensation claim by the OWCP district office, you can obtain a short oral hearing or written review of the record. Unless you are planning to have witnesses testify, especially expert witnesses, a written review of the record may suffice. After reviewing the record, a hearing officer from Washington, DC will issue a recommendation.

12 Pursuant to its statutory authority under 5 USC § 8151(b)(1) and (2).

13 *See* 5 CFR § 353.303.

14 *See* 5 CFR § 353.103(c)(1).

If your review is unsuccessful, you may request a written review by the OWCP within *one year* of the date of its initial decision.

The request for reconsideration may contain additional evidence not previously submitted, such as medical reports, or new witnesses or legal arguments. If the decision is still negative, there is a right of final appeal within *90 days* to the Employee Compensation Appeals Board, which is part of the DOL. Appeals for good cause can be filed within one year. Review by the ECAB is limited to the evidence in the record. You cannot submit new evidence or testimony. Unfortunately, there is no right of judicial review.[15]

TIP

Be sure to keep track of deadlines. If you want continuation of pay, you must file a claim within 30 days of a traumatic injury. Otherwise, you have 3 years to file claims for injuries or occupational illnesses. You have 1 year to request the OWCP to review a turn-down decision and thereafter 90 days to appeal a negative OWCP decision to the ECAB.

What if my health plan won't pay my medical bills?

A problem can arise if, during a challenged OWCP claim, you are incurring medical/hospital bills that must be paid. On occasion, your federal health plan may refuse to pay for your medical care while the claim is still pending at the OWCP.

If you properly notify the health plan that your injury is job-related, your health plan should pay the outstanding bills and then be reimbursed by the OWCP if it approves the claim. It may be necessary to threaten to, or actually file a complaint with OPM (which monitors federal health benefit plans), or to contact your Congressional representative. When a claim is approved by the OWCP, you have the option to buy back any unused sick or annual leave used as a result of your injury or illness. As a practical matter, if you are continuing to be employed, it is advantageous to buy back the sick or annual leave used with the compensation you received because the unused leave will increase in value over time as your salary increases. However, if you are retiring or separating from federal service, you should not buy back your leave.

---

15 *See* 5 USC § 8128.

Can I recover attorney fees?

A major drawback in handling OWCP cases is that attorneys are not allowed to accept any fees for representation except for costs, until the fees are approved by the OWCP. The OWCP does not rule on attorney fees until the lengthy process of claim consideration is completed. This means that attorneys must wait for long periods of time before attempting to collect their approved fees. It is a criminal offense for an attorney to accept fees in advance of OWCP approval, except when paid into a third-party escrow account. Attorneys must submit an itemized statement showing the work done, and the client has the opportunity to review and comment on the statement submitted. The OWCP does not honor contingency fee agreements, direct the payment of attorney fees, or assist in their collection.

As a result of all of this, very few attorneys will handle OWCP cases. Some lawyers charge large sums to "review" potential cases in order to avoid the prohibition on collecting fees prior to OWCP approval. Be very careful before agreeing to a large fee to review your case. Make sure that you have a written fee agreement spelling out what legal representation will be provided.

Compensation for work-related injuries under the Nonappropriated Fund Instrumentalities Act

Morale, welfare and recreation (MWR) as well as base exchange workers on U.S. military installations in the U.S. and overseas are covered by the Nonappropriated Fund Instrumentalities Act and may be entitled to compensation benefits pursuant to the Longshoremen's and Harbor Workers' Compensation Act. If you are covered, and you have an occupational injury or illness, you must first notify your employer and the Longshore District Office of your injury within 30 days of the occurrence of the injury or 30 days of your becoming aware of the injury using Form LS-201 or in writing. If your employer does not begin paying compensation, you must file a claim for benefits using Form LS-203 within one year after the date of injury. However, if your occupational disease results in death or disability, you must file your claim within two years from the date you become aware of the relationship between the employment, the disease, and the death or disability, or within one year of the date of the last payment of compensation, whichever is later. For more information, see http://www.dol.gov/owcp/dlhwc/lsfaqs.htm.

Final Thoughts

If you are unfortunate enough to suffer an on-the-job injury or an illness or disease related to your employment with the federal government, you or your family may be entitled to compensation. For example, if the on-the-job injury or illness results in death and there is no child entitled to compensation, the employee's surviving spouse will receive 50 percent of the employee's monthly compensation until death or remarriage before reaching age 55. If there is a child entitled to compensation, then the percentage payments for children and the surviving spouse cannot exceed 75 percent of the employee's monthly compensation.[16] The intent of the law and regulations here is not to give you a windfall because of your unfortunate situation, but rather to provide you with compensation and services geared to either assisting you with your loss of income during the period, or providing some compensation for your family if you lose your life. It is important to be aware of your rights and the time lines in order to take advantage of these benefits.

---

16 *See* 20 CFR § 10.410.

16

Federal Employees Health Benefits Program

Let's Look at What the Cafeteria Offers...

IN THIS CHAPTER YOU WILL LEARN:

- how you can select, change, and continue your health benefits program
- your rights if a claim for coverage is denied
- when you can go to OPM and court concerning denial of health benefits

Contents Chapter Sixteen - Federal Employees Health Benefits Program

Introduction

Federal employees have a unique "cafeteria" type health benefits program. You can pick and choose which plans and benefits you want. You can choose between different health care carriers and providers such as HMOs and insurance companies. Unlike employees in the private sector, you are not covered by the Employee Retirement Income Security Act ("ERISA"). However, you have the right to have OPM and federal court review denial of claims by health carriers. In this manner you can enforce the promises made in the health plans.

This chapter uses the words "carrier," "provider," and "plan." A carrier is any association, corporation, or other organization that provides, pays for, or reimburses the cost of health services under group insurance policies. A provider is an individual or organization that provides medical health services, such as a doctor or hospital. "Carrier" is a broader term which may include providers. However, the terms "carrier" and "provider" are frequently used interchangeably. A "plan" is the document issued by the carrier listing the benefits and rules concerning coverage, service, payment, and claims.

What is the Federal Employees Health Benefits Program?

> The Federal Employees Health Benefits Program ("FEHBP") is the health benefits program the federal government provides for its employees and their families. The FEHBP offers employees a choice of health care delivery systems that include insurance companies, preferred provider organizations,

health maintenance organizations, point-of-service products, and managed fee-for-service plans.

There are over 250 different FEHBP plans. There are managed-fee-for-service plans where you choose your own physician, and the plan reimburses you or the health care provider. There are health maintenance organizations ("HMO"s) which designate certain physicians and hospitals covered by their plans which must be used by subscribers. Point of service ("POS") plans have features of both HMOs and managed fee-for-service plans. POS plans allow members to use both a designated network of providers and also out-of-network providers, which are more costly. There are also High Deductible Health Plans and Health Savings Accounts where usually a portion of the premiums are contributed.

Employees can choose a "self only" plan or a family plan covering the employee's spouse and unmarried dependent children under age 26.

Some of the plans are only open to residents of certain geographic areas. Some plans are union or employee association plans with restricted membership. One popular program is offered by Blue Cross/Blue Shield. There are also dental and vision benefits available, as well as long-term care.

When and how can I enroll in a health benefit plan?

Employees may elect to enroll in a plan within *60 days* after becoming eligible. Usually, employees become eligible to enroll in a health plan when they are first hired by the federal government or during what is called an "open season." You do not have to take a medical examination to be covered under the FEHBP, nor are there any age or medical requirements for enrollment. In addition, there are no waiting periods. You can be enrolled in a plan within *31 days* from the date you enter government service or become eligible to enroll. You can also choose coverage for you and your family or just for yourself.

When can I change plans or types of coverage?

If you are already enrolled in a federal health benefits plan, you may change plans only during "open season" or when you have a change in family status.

Open season

Generally, an employee can enroll in a health plan, or change plans or options, once each year during what is called "open season." Changes in options include changing from self-only to self-and-family, or from self-and-family to self-only. The open season usually occurs between November and December each year, or whenever OPM announces the open season. However, you do not have to wait for a change in family or employment status or an open season to change from self-and-family to self-only, or to disenroll from a plan.

Change in family status

You can enroll in a plan or change your plan when there is a change in your family status. Changes in your family status include changes in your marital status, the birth of a child, or the addition of a child as a new family member. When your family status changes, you can enroll, if you are eligible, change your enrollment from self-only to self-and-family, or change plans or options.

Change in employment status

In addition, you can enroll in a plan or change your plans or options when your employment status changes. Some examples of changes of this type include:

- a return to pay status following a loss of coverage due to
  a. the expiration of *365 days* in leave without pay status, or
  b. the termination of coverage during leave without pay status
- reemployment after a break in service of more than *3 days*
- restoration to a civilian position after serving in the uniformed services under conditions that would entitle the employee to benefits under OPM's regulations
- a change from a temporary appointment in which the employee is eligible to enroll under the FEHBP statute, which requires payment of the full premium with no government contributions, to an appointment that entitles the employee to receive the government contribution
- separation from federal employment when the employee or employee's spouse is pregnant and the employee supplies medical documentation of the pregnancy. But the employee who enrolls or changes enrollment under this category must do so during his/her final pay period
- a transfer from a duty post within a state of the United States or the District of Columbia to a post of duty outside a state or Washington, DC, or the reverse. Health plan changes or enrollments

in a situation like this must be done within the period beginning *31 days before leaving the duty post* and ending *60 days after arriving* at the new duty post

- a change, without a break in service or after a separation of *3 days or less*, to part-time career employment, or a change from such part-time career employment to full-time employment that entitles the employee to the full government contribution

How much does coverage in a FEHBP plan cost me?

Both you and your employing agency contribute to the cost of your premium for the FEHBP plan you choose. Your portion of the premium is deducted from your salary. The cost of your premium, and your share, depends upon the plan and type of coverage you choose. In general, the government will pay about 72% of the total cost of the premium, but not more than 75% of the total premium for any plan.[1] Your share of the premium is the balance of what the government does not pay.

TIP

For information concerning the costs of a particular plan, you can contact OPM, log onto OPM's website (www.opm.gov/insure/health), or contact the plan administrator.

Can I continue my coverage when I leave my employment with the federal government?

In general, there are several ways in which your coverage under a plan can continue if you leave your job:

Continued coverage during retirement, for former spouses, for your family after your death, or if you transfer/move or go on leave

Generally, the FEHBP provides for continuation of coverage:

- for you when you retire from the federal government

---

[1] The costs for temporary, part-time, and Postal Service employees are different.

- for a former spouse, if you divorce and your former spouse has a qualifying court order [2]
- for your family if you die, and
- for you and your family if you move, transfer, or go on leave without pay (some restrictions apply to these situations, and you should contact your personnel office to discuss these situations)

Temporary extension and conversion

If you are enrolled in a health plan under the FEHBP and your enrollment is terminated, other than by cancellation of the enrollment or cancellation of the plan, you are entitled to a temporary extension of your coverage for *31 days* for yourself or yourself and your family. The 31-day extension period also applies to any covered family members. Your employing agency must notify you of your right to convert to an individual policy within *60 days* after the date your enrollment terminated.

Temporary continuation of coverage

You may receive additional temporary continuation of coverage under your plan for *18 more months after separation from service.* During this period, you must pay the total premium plus two percent for administrative expenses. You may be entitled to this temporary continuation of coverage if:

- you are separated from service, voluntarily or involuntarily, under any circumstances (unless your involuntary separation is due to gross misconduct), and
- you are not otherwise eligible for any benefits through the FEHBP (for example, if you are not covered by a FEHBP plan in retirement)

In addition, your children may receive temporary continuation of coverage if their coverage ends because they stop meeting the requirements of being considered unmarried dependent children (for example, they get married). Also, under some restricted circumstances, former spouses may receive temporary continuation of coverage.

Your agency is required to notify you of your right to temporarily continue your coverage no later than *30 days* after the end of the expiration of the *31-day* temporary extension of coverage discussed above. For a child who is eligible to elect temporary continuation of coverage, you should inform your former employing agency of the change in the child's status within *60 days*

---

[2] For information on "qualifying court order," see 5 CFR § 838 and OPM Handbook RI 83-116.

of that change and request information concerning temporary continued coverage for the child. If your former agency receives the notice regarding the change in your child's status within that *60-day* period, the agency must notify the child of his/her rights to temporary continuation of coverage within *14 days* after receiving your notice.

Your election of temporary continuation of coverage can be by letter, written statement, or by use of Standard Form 2809. If you wish to elect temporary continued coverage, you must notify your agency in writing of your election no later than *60 days* after the later of:

- the date of your separation, or
- the date you received the notice from your employing agency of the right to temporary continuation of coverage

When your employing office doesn't give you the required conversion notice within *60 days*, or you aren't able to request conversion on time for reasons beyond your control, you can request a late conversion by writing directly to the carrier of your plan within *6 months*. The temporary continuation of coverage for former federal employees lasts *18 months* from the date of the separation from federal service. In the case of covered children of former federal employees, the temporary continuation of coverage lasts *36 months* from the date the child ceases to meet the requirements for being considered an unmarried dependent child.

You are *not entitled* to temporary continuation of coverage if you are removed from employment due to "gross misconduct." If your agency decides that you are being terminated for gross misconduct, it must notify you in writing that it intends to deny you temporary continuation of coverage. The notice from your employing agency must give you the reasons for denying you temporary continuation of coverage and give you a reasonable amount of time to reply to the notice. You must be given at least *7 days* to respond either orally or in writing or both, and you are entitled to be represented by an attorney or other representative in your response. The agency will issue a written final decision which is not reviewable by OPM. Finally, if you resign after you have received notification of your agency's intent to separate you involuntarily for gross misconduct, but before the scheduled separation date, your separation is still considered involuntary and you are not entitled to continued coverage.

What can I do if my claim for coverage or service is denied?

All claims for service or payment are submitted to your health carrier. If your health carrier denies a claim, or even a portion of a claim, you can ask the carrier to reconsider. You must submit your reconsideration request to the carrier within *6 months* of the date of the notice that your claim was denied. This time limit may be extended under certain circumstances, such as where you were prevented from filing due to events beyond your control. A request for reconsideration must be in writing and provide the reasons that the denied claim should have been approved.

The carrier has *30 days* after it receives your reconsideration request to either:

- affirm its original denial in writing
- pay the bill or provide the service originally denied, or
- ask you to provide additional information

If your carrier requests that you provide information, it must clearly state what additional information is needed. Then you have *60 days* to provide the carrier with the information requested. The carrier has *30 days* after it receives the additional information to make a decision to either pay the claim, provide the service, or affirm its original denial. You should be aware that if you do not provide the carrier with the requested information, it will make a decision based upon all the information it then has.

Your carrier's decision regarding your request for reconsideration must be in writing. If the carrier simply affirms its original decision to deny coverage or a service, the carrier's reconsideration decision must inform you of:

- the specific and detailed reasons for the denial
- your right to request review of the decision by OPM, and
- the requirement that a request for OPM to review the carrier's decision must be received by OPM within *90 days* after the date of the carrier's denial notice

OPM review

If you are not satisfied with the carrier's decision, you may ask OPM to review the carrier's decision. OPM reviews claims that the carrier did not comply with the provisions of the plan. You should review the disputed claims section of your plan brochure for further information.

As discussed in the next section, it is important to request review by OPM because you cannot bring a denial of benefits claim to court unless you have first asked OPM to review the carrier's denial. Your request to OPM must be filed by one of the following applicable deadlines:

- no later than *90 days* after the date of the carrier's notice to you that its original denial was affirmed. For example, if your provider denied your claim on May 1st, you requested reconsideration on June 1st and on June 30th your carrier affirmed its original (May 1st) decision, you have *90 days* from June 30th to file a request for review with OPM
- if the carrier failed to respond to your request for reconsideration, then OPM must receive your request to review no later than *120 days* from the date that you asked the carrier to reconsider its original denial decision. For example, if your carrier denied a claim on May 1st, 2013, and you filed a reconsideration request with the carrier on May 31st, 2013, but the carrier did not respond, you have *120 days* from May 31st, 2013 to submit your request for review to OPM
- no later than *120 days* after the date the carrier asks for additional information from you, or
- no later than *120 days* from the date you are notified that the carrier is requesting information from another health care provider

OPM can extend these deadlines if the carrier failed to tell you about the deadline for requesting OPM review or if you were prevented from filing your request with OPM due to circumstances beyond your control. OPM must issue a decision regarding your request for review or notify you of the status of your request within *90 days* after it receives your request.

Review by Federal Court

You may seek review of a final decision by OPM on the denial of a health benefits claim in either U.S. district court or the U.S. Court of Federal Claims. If you wish to have a federal court review OPM's decision on a denial of benefits, you must first have exhausted OPM's review process described earlier. If you decide to have OPM's decision reviewed by a court, you must bring that claim to federal court no later than December 31st of the *3rd year after the year in which the care/service was provided/denied*. For example, if your claim was denied on June 1, 2013, you must bring your court claim no later than December 31, 2016. If you want to have OPM's decision reviewed in court, you must name OPM, not the carrier, as the defendant.

What can I do if I am denied enrollment in the FEHBP?

If your employing agency has denied you enrollment in a FEHBP, you have certain appeal rights. You may request your employing agency to reconsider its initial decision denying you enrollment or a change in enrollment. The agency decision ("initial decision") must be in writing and notify you of the right to request an independent review of the initial decision. Your request must be filed in writing and within *30 calendar days* from the date of the written decision denying you enrollment. Your agency must issue a final written decision on your request for reconsideration, in which it explains the findings and conclusions supporting its final decision. If you are not satisfied with your agency's final decision, you may have that decision reviewed in federal court. That court case must be filed against your employing agency.

For more information about the FEHBP

For more information concerning the FEHBP or regarding specific plans offered through the FEHBP, you can contact OPM, log onto OPM's website (www.opm.gov), or contact your agency's human resources office. You can also review OPM's regulations, 5 CFR Part 890, concerning the FEHBP.

Final Thoughts

Federal employees have a unique "cafeteria" type program of health benefits. You can pick and choose which you want. There are important rules and regulations concerning enrollment and changes in coverage. Fortunately, you have the right to protest and appeal if your claims concerning coverage are denied by your health provider. You can pursue these claims through OPM and all the way to federal court if necessary.

17

Unemployment Compensation

Will the Government Help Out When My Paycheck Stops?

In This Chapter You Will Learn:

- how federal employees qualify for unemployment compensation
- what unemployment compensation pays
- what to do if you disagree with an award decision

Contents Chapter Seventeen - Unemployment Compensation

Introduction

It can happen in federal employment, too—suddenly you find yourself without a job. If this occurs and you thereby lose your primary source of income, you may need financial assistance while you search for a new job. Federal employees, like those in the private sector, are entitled to such assistance. There are, however, requirements that must be met. In this chapter, we will discuss your right to unemployment compensation upon separation and what to do if you need to challenge determinations about it.

Am I entitled to unemployment compensation?

Unemployment compensation for former federal civil service employees and ex-servicemembers is provided by federal law.[1] Although the responsibility for both programs is delegated to the Secretary of Labor, the actual payment of unemployment compensation benefits is made by the state unemployment security agencies from funds provided by the federal agencies. Federal employees are not taxed to provide for unemployment compensation.

Each federal agency is billed for, and deposits quarterly, an amount equal to benefits paid by state agencies to former employees of that federal agency. These deposits are made into a special Treasury account. State agencies draw funds from this account as needed to pay benefits to eligible claimants.

Your entitlement to unemployment benefits rights will generally be determined by the law of the state where you had your last official duty station, regardless of your state of residence. This is also true of the District of Columbia, Puerto Rico, and the Virgin Islands.

The standards states must follow in processing unemployment compensation for former federal employees are set forth in the Department of Labor (DOL) regulations.[2] There is an exception for former federal employees

---

1 *See* 5 USC § 8501, *et seq.*

2 *See* 20 CFR § 609.

(U.S. citizens only) who were employed outside of the United States and former federal employees who worked in the private sector in their state of residence and established a claim after termination of federal service.

For these former federal employees, the law of the state where they reside will determine their entitlement to unemployment compensation. Overseas employees must first return to the state of their residence before they can file a claim for unemployment compensation benefits.

Can I contest the reasons given for my separation?

Before a 1976 amendment to the law, you could not challenge the reasons for termination from federal service in state proceedings, and were bound by the findings of your agency or the Civil Service Commission on the merits of contested terminations.[3] Since the amendment, findings by federal employers as to the reasons for separation are not entitled to be given special weight.

Unemployment compensation determinations are not binding on arbitrators or the MSPB, which adjudicates terminations, but the documentary evidence and testimony introduced during the unemployment proceedings may be valuable in an MSPB or arbitration appeal of the underlying personnel action.

TIP

You have the right to protest if the agency gives incorrect information concerning the circumstances of your termination.

You are entitled to procedural due process and must be treated the same as a private sector employee seeking unemployment benefits. The law and procedures vary from state to state. While the various state laws and procedures have some similarities, review the applicable statutes and regulations of the employment security agency in the state in which your case arises. This information is usually available in your local public library, and the nearest state unemployment office, online or on the internet. In this chapter, we focus on the law and procedures in the District of Columbia (DC) as an example.

---

3 *See* 5 USC § 8506(a).

Must I have worked for a certain time period to collect benefits?

You must have had sufficient qualifying employment or earnings during the time specified by state laws as the "base period." All civilian service for the federal government during the base period, whether for one agency or more than one, is considered employment with a single employer for purposes of state unemployment compensation law. In the majority of states, a 12-month period beginning less than 18 months before the claim is filed is considered the base period.

In DC, the "base period" means the first four out of the last five completed calendar quarters immediately preceding the first day of the benefit year. To qualify for benefits in DC, you must have been:

1. paid wages of at least $1,300 in one quarter in your base period
2. paid wages of not less than $1,950 in not less than two quarters in such period, and
3. received total wages equal to at least one and one-half times the amount of your wages actually received in the highest quarter or be within $70 of that amount

In DC, paid annual leave is included in the definition of wages, but not self-employment income subsequent to the termination of other employment.

Are there things that can reduce the benefits I might receive?

Leave payments

The law of the state determines whether you are eligible for unemployment benefits during the period covered by lump-sum payments for unused annual leave or severance pay. Some states deny or reduce unemployment benefits to you if you are receiving such payments. Other states disregard leave payments and severance pay periods in determining eligibility for benefits.

Pension benefits

States must deduct pension benefits from unemployment benefits if the federal government made contributions.[4] The law requires the states, as a minimum, to reduce the weekly benefit amount by the amount of any governmental or other pension, retirement pay, annuity, or any other similar periodic payments which are based on the previous work of the employee.

---

4 *See* 29 USC § 3304(a)(15)(A).

States may disregard pension payments if the base-period employment did not affect eligibility for or increase the amount of the pension. Social Security and Railroad Retirement benefits must be deducted regardless of whether pay or service for a base-period or chargeable employer affected eligibility or increased the amount of the pension. States are permitted to limit the amount of any reduction to take into account contributions made by the individual to the pension plan. State laws for pension offsets may exceed these federal minimums, and deductions vary from state to state.

How much can I expect to receive in unemployment benefits?

Benefits vary from state to state depending upon the amount of the employee's earnings during the base period. In some states, weekly amounts are increased by allowances for dependents. The number of weeks benefits will be paid ranges from 26 to 30, with 26 being the norm. Benefits may be extended under various state programs when unemployment reaches specified levels. Benefits may also be extended during periods of high unemployment by 50 percent, up to 13 additional weeks, under the federal-state Extended Compensation Program.

How do I qualify for unemployment benefits?

In general, to qualify for benefits, you must:

- be physically able to work
- must be available for work, and
- must have registered and regularly inquired for work

You must register and inquire for work at the employment office or on-line as designated by your unemployment compensation agency. You must continue to register and inquire for work if there is an initial dispute and delay as to your eligibility. Otherwise, your benefits may be denied, or you will be penalized by a delay in receiving benefits when your claim is later approved.

"Available for work" means that you must be in active touch with the labor market and making adequate contacts with prospective employers. However, you do not have to accept wages, hours, or working conditions "substantially less favorable to you than those prevailing for similar work in the locality."[5]

---

[5] *See* 26 USC § 3304(a)(5)(B).

TIP

In most states you will not lose your unemployment benefits if you turn down a job that is substantially inferior to your prior position. You can hold out for a position similar to the job you had before.

To prove that you are available for work, you must actively seek employment and not unreasonably restrict your job search. You must be able to demonstrate that you have conducted an active search for work.

The inability to accept full-time work does not automatically render you ineligible for benefits, especially if you have previously worked part-time.

TIP

If you enroll in school, your class schedule may negatively impact your eligibility for unemployment compensation.

But, if you are in school during the period, you want to collect unemployment, you may not be penalized if you are able to prove that suitable positions were not available during the hours you were available or that you would be willing to switch or drop classes to accept a job with conventional hours.

Former employees in DC are also not disqualified if they become self-employed after their termination.

Applicants in DC who obtain unemployment benefits and then are employed on a part-time basis receive an additional $20 weekly benefit. 80 percent of their earnings are then subtracted from their benefits.

How do I file for benefits?

Regardless of whether there is a waiting period, you should file your unemployment compensation claim as soon as possible after your separation from federal employment, with the nearest office of the state, online, or by telephone or on the internet, if permitted. Bring with you:

- your Social Security number

- a copy of your SF-50 (Notice of Personnel Action), SF-8 (Notice to Federal Employee About Unemployment Compensation), or other documents showing that you were separated from federal employment

Within four workdays after receipt of a request from a state agency, a federal agency should complete and return to the state agency the forms showing your service and wages in the specified tentative base period.

You may not be able to receive benefits immediately. Some states impose a waiting period of up to one week after the filing of a claim before you can receive benefits. While filing late will not disqualify you from receiving unemployment compensation or lessen the total amount of compensation, it can result in an additional waiting period because there is no retroactivity. To avoid delays, be sure to file in the state where you were last employed, not the state you reside in. However, you may file in a different state which will act as an agent for the benefits claimed and will process the claim, but the state law where you last worked will govern eligibility, disqualifications, and the amount and duration of benefits.

TIP

If you have questions or need help, contact the unemployment compensation office of the state where you were formerly employed for assistance in filing your claim.

How is my unemployment claim processed?

Shortly after you have filed a claim for benefits and your former employer has provided the necessary information, a state claims examiner assigned to the claim will hold a "predetermination fact-finding interview" to determine whether you are subject to disqualification. The claims examiner will initially determine whether benefits are payable, and if payable, when they commence, their maximum duration, and the weekly benefit amount. The examiner will then send the initial determination to both your agency and you.

Is it possible for me to be disqualified from unemployment benefits?

The receipt of unemployment benefits upon separation from your agency is not automatic. It is possible that your claim will be disqualified. If your claim is totally or partially denied, the reasons for the denial will be checked in the relevant box of the initial determination you receive. The major reasons for disqualification under DC law are because an employee:

1. voluntarily left most recent work without good cause connected with the work
2. was discharged for misconduct occurring in most recent work
3. failed to apply for or accept suitable work
4. failed to attend an approved training or retraining course, or
5. was unemployed as a direct result of a strike or other labor dispute (except for a lockout)

A termination for performance-related reasons is usually not disqualifying.

If your claim is disqualified, it usually means that you are not able to collect benefits for a certain period of time. Due to the drain on unemployment compensation funds caused by a large number of claims in recent years, the period of disqualification has been increased in a number of states, and also in DC.

If you are an employee in DC who left your most recent work voluntarily without "good cause" connected with the work, or have been discharged for misconduct occurring in the course of your most recent work, you are not eligible for benefits unless you:

- have been employed in each of 10 subsequent weeks, and
- have earned a salary equal to not less than 10 times the weekly benefit amount to which you would have been entitled

This means that if you are a disqualified employee, you will first have to find other employment before becoming eligible for unemployment compensation. A 10-week disqualification is also imposed if you fail to apply for new work when notified of a job vacancy in suitable employment.

Benefits cannot be denied "solely on the basis of pregnancy or termination of pregnancy."[6] Benefits for any claimant who is or has recently been pregnant are determined under the same standards and procedures as for any other

[6] *See* 26 USC § 3304(a)(12).

claimant, and there is generally no presumption that a woman who is pregnant is physically unable to work.

Will I still be able to receive benefits if I resign?

Remember that you can be disqualified from benefits if you leave your employment without good cause. So if you leave on your own, it therefore becomes important to show that you had good cause for doing so. Good cause for resignation in DC is defined as "what a reasonable and prudent person in the labor market would do in the same circumstances." The following constitute good cause for resignation in DC:

1. racial or sexual discrimination or harassment
2. failure to provide pay for employee services
3. working in unsafe locations or under unsafe conditions
4. illness or disability caused or aggravated by the work, provided that the claimant has previously supplied the employer with a supporting medical statement, or
5. transportation problems arising from the relocation of the employer, a change in the primary worksite, or transfer of the employee to a different worksite; provided that adequate, economical, and reasonable transportation facilities are not available

The following reasons are *not* considered good cause for resignation:

1. refusal to obey reasonable employer rules
2. minor reduction in wages
3. reasonable and necessary transfer from one type of work to another
4. marriage or divorce resulting in a change of residence
5. general dissatisfaction with work
6. desire to attend school or training, or
7. personal or domestic responsibilities

If you resign under threat of imminent termination, the separation is considered a "constructive discharge for misconduct" in DC, and a determination is made under regulations governing misconduct terminations. Check the rules in your state to determine what constitutes good cause for resignation. An employer that alleges you engaged in misconduct has the responsibility of presenting evidence supporting such a finding. On-the-job misconduct includes, but is not limited to:

1. willful violation of employer's rules
2. intoxication
3. repeated disregard of reasonable orders
4. sabotage
5. gross neglect of duty
6. insubordination, or
7. dishonesty

Again, you must check the rules in your own state concerning what constitutes misconduct. Most states deny benefits when an employee is dismissed for just cause.

TIP

"Just Cause" or "good cause" are the standards used by most states to award or deny benefits. If you are terminated without "just cause" or have "good cause" to resign, you will probably receive benefits.

Is it possible to challenge an unemployment determination?

If you or your employer disagree with the initial determination of your eligibility for unemployment benefits, either of you may appeal. Appeals of unfavorable determinations must be filed in a timely manner. The short time limits for example, *10 calendar days*, are usually strictly applied for both you as the claimant, and the employer. An appeal in DC results in a hearing before an "appeals examiner." Notice of the time, date, and place of the hearing is mailed to each party. Telephone hearings may be conducted but are generally less desirable than in-person hearings. Continuances (postponements) may be granted for good cause and should be requested as early as possible with an explanation of the reasons.

Take the hearing seriously. You may want to retain private counsel, especially if you have challenged the underlying personnel action (for instance, your claim was denied because you were terminated for misconduct, but you do not agree that you engaged in misconduct). Subpoenas are generally available to command the presence of witnesses and production of documents.

It is of critical importance to you whether the employer appears in person to represent its interests and brings at least one witness who has firsthand knowledge of the events which led to the termination of your employment. If not, you as a claimant may win by default if you present a *prima facie* case of entitlement to unemployment benefits, i.e., that you were dismissed through no fault of your own.

If you do not prevail in the examiner's written decision, you must usually file at least one administrative appeal before you can take your claim to a court of law. In other words, you must exhaust the administrative procedures before going to court. Filing in court is often time-consuming and expensive, and usually requires hiring a lawyer. There are also provisions for appeals to higher courts if the initial court decision is negative. The courts will review the record to see if there have been errors of law in the administrative proceedings, but will not permit additional evidence or a hearing with witnesses.

Final Thoughts

The time may come when you are terminated from your job with the federal government and must seek employment elsewhere. If you need financial assistance during the interim period, you may file a claim for unemployment benefits. If you do file, you want to do all you can to make sure you receive the benefits you deserve. If your claim is wrongfully denied by the unemployment agency, you can challenge that finding, up to and including a judicial review.

18

Retirement

I'm Outta Here... Or Am I?

In This Chapter You Will Learn:

- what is available to employees who would like to retire
- what benefits an employee who retires can expect
- what you need to know about disability retirement

Contents Chapter Eighteen - Retirement

Introduction

After many years in the federal service, you've managed to get through not just the day-to-day work but performance appraisals, wage issues, promotions, even disciplinary procedures or injuries on the job. It's now time to say goodbye to all of your coworkers and start living the life you've dreamed of for the past decades. In other words, retire. But how will you do it? What are the rules about it? What laws govern it? How will you make it financially? What if you want to come back to work? In this chapter, we will discuss these and other issues surrounding the matter of separating from your employment with the federal government after your illustrious career.

What retirement options are available to me?

Federal employees have a variety of retirement benefits available to them, which are administered by OPM. Federal employees and their agencies contribute 7% of their salaries to their retirement funds.

The Civil Service Retirement System ("CSRS") covers all appointed and elected officers and employees in or under the executive, judicial, and legislative branches of the federal government and certain employees of the District of Columbia, except those excluded by law or OPM regulations. For those federal employees hired after January 1, 1984, who are covered by Social Security, a new retirement system was developed, the Federal Employees Retirement System ("FERS").

What is the difference between the Civil Service Retirement System (CSRS) and the Federal Employees Retirement System (FERS)?

CSRS is a straight retirement plan with the benefits dependent upon your years of service and "high-three" salary years. High-three average pay is the highest average pay produced by your basic pay during any three consecutive years of service, including within-grade increases, but not overtime or other allowances, with several exceptions.

FERS is a three-tiered retirement system containing three benefits:

- The first tier is Social Security
- The second tier is a Basic Annuity plan less generous than CSRS
- The third tier is an optional Thrift Savings plan

If you are a FERS employee, you may contribute up to 10 percent of your pay to the thrift plan with full matching by the agency on the first three percent and half matching on the next two percent. These contributions are credited to your own account. If you are in the Thrift Savings Plan, there are a number of investment vehicles to which you can direct your funds. Because of the volatility in the stock market, FERS employees may have concerns about their retirement.

What is disability retirement?

Disability retirement is a benefit available to federal employees subject to the retirement system funded by the Civil Service Retirement System and the Disability Trust Fund ("the Fund"). The Fund is supplemented by agency contributions and appropriations used to pay retirement and death benefits.

If you are seeking disability retirement, you must show that you became disabled and/or were separated while in a job subject to CSRS or FERS. A preexisting medical condition commencing prior to federal employment is not a bar to disability retirement, and it does not matter if the illness or injury occurred while you were off duty. There is no requirement that you became disabled in the current federal position from which you are retiring. You are eligible for disability retirement even if you are separated for misconduct or poor performance or voluntarily resign from federal employment. If separated, you must prove that you were disabled at the time of your separation.

Employees who are age 62 are not eligible for disability retirement if they are also eligible for regular retirement. There is no financial advantage for older employees in obtaining disability retirement.

What is the basic eligibility for disability retirement under CSRS? To qualify for disability under the CSRS, you must have been employed for a minimum of five years and no longer be able to effectively perform at your current grade or pay level due to a medical condition.

What is the basic eligibility for disability under FERS? The FERS pays disability benefits to you if you become disabled after completing at least 18 months of service. Under FERS, if you apply for disability benefits, you must also apply for Social Security disability benefits or show that you are not eligible for those benefits.

Are there other retirement options I should know about?

"Discontinued service retirement" is available if you are involuntarily separated without cause, or on account of poor performance, before becoming eligible for optional retirement. There is also early optional retirement due to major reorganizations, major RIFs, or major transfers of function as determined by OPM.

If you are under age 55 at the date of retirement, under the CSRS, an annuity is reduced by:

- one-sixth of 1% for each full month,
- 2% per year.

There is no similar penalty or reduction under FERS based on age. If you are separated for cause or resign from federal employment with a minimum of five years service and do not obtain a refund of your retirement contributions, you may wait until age 62 for deferred retirement.

When can I retire?

Optional voluntary retirement under the CSRS is available when you reach:

- age 55 with at least 30 years of service
- age 60 with at least 20 years of service, or
- age 62 with at least five years of service

You must have been employed under the CSRS for at least five years, including one year out of the last two years immediately preceding your separation. In addition, you must have been employed in a position covered by CSRS where retirement deposits were or should have been made, except for disability retirement benefits.

You may retire under FERS at age:

- 60 with at least 20 years service with reduced benefits, and
- 56 with a minimum of 10 years service with greatly reduced benefits

Early retirement will cause benefits to be reduced by five percent for each year you are under age 62 when you retire. There is also a gradual extension of the minimum age of 56 for retirement under FERS for employees born in 1948 and thereafter.

How do I compute the amount of my annuity?

One of the first things you'll want to know when you begin to think about retirement is how much money you will receive if you retire. How much you receive depends on several factors, including the system under which you retire.

CSRS

The general formula under CSRS provides retirement benefits not to exceed 80% of the high-three average pay as follows:

- take 1.5% of your high-three average pay and multiply the result by your years of service up to five years;
- add 1% of your high-three average pay and multiply the result by all your years of service over five years up to 10 years;
- add 2% of your high-three average pay multiplied by all service over 10 years.

A simple way to estimate your CSRS annuity is to:

- multiply your high-three average pay (which is usually your last three years);
- times 2%;
- multiplied by your years of service;
- minus 4%.

For example: If your high-three average earnings were $50,000 and you have 30 years service at age 62, your annuity will be $28,000 per year ($50,000 x 60% - 4%, or 56%).

If you retire under CSRS, you receive a cost-of-living allowance ("COLA") based upon the rise in the Consumer Price Index ("CPI"). Under CSRS, you also receive credit for unused sick leave and payment for any unused annual leave.

FERS

Under FERS the formula consists of:

- taking 1% of the high-three average pay and multiplying the result by years of service, or

- taking 1.1% of the high-three average pay times years of service if retiring at age 62 with 20 years of service

For example: If you retired under FERS with 30 years of service at age 62 and had high-three average earnings of $50,000, your annuity would be $16,500 ($50,000 x 30 x 1.1% or 33%).

Under FERS, you receive a reduced COLA based upon the increase in the CPI, but there are no COLAs until you reach age 62. You also receive payment for any unused annual leave and credit for unused sick leave.

Disability retirement

Under CSRS there is a minimum guaranteed disability retirement annuity based on the lesser of the following:

- 40% of the high-three year average pay, or
- a computed amount under the general formula based on years of actual service plus remaining years to age 60

FERS has a different formula for disability retirement. During the first year after disability, you receive an amount equal to:

- 60% of your high-three average salary
- reduced by any Social Security benefits payable

The FERS disability retirement plan after the second year is:

- 40% of your high-three average salary
- reduced by 60% of any Social Security benefits payable

The FERS disability retirement is indexed by the FERS COLA, generally the change in the CPI minus one percentage point. At age 62, the FERS disability benefit is recomputed in accordance with changes in the cost of living. [1]

Civilian retirement based on military service

If your civil service retirement annuity is increased because of military service, it is offset by your eligibility for Old Age or Survivors Insurance

[1] The Federal Medical Evidence of Record (FEDMER) program (www.opm.gov/retire/pre/fedmer) allows employees to apply for both FERS and Social Security disability through their employing agencies. OPM and SSA receive the same medical records at the time of application and, once a decision is made by either, it contacts the other with the determination.

benefits ("OASI") under the Social Security Act ("SSA"),[2] whether or not you actually receive OASI benefits. OPM is also required either to exclude certain military service from its calculations or to reduce your annuity by the amount of the Social Security benefits attributable to your military service, whichever results in the small or annuity reduction, unless you have made a deposit with interest for your military service.[3]

What do I need to know about disability retirement?

Disability retirement is more involved than the usual optional retirement at the end of your federal career, and the following section explains it in detail.

Qualifications

To qualify for disability retirement, you must be disabled not only for your current position, but also for any vacant positions at the same grade or pay. Your agency must certify to OPM that it has reviewed all vacant positions under its jurisdiction at the same grade or pay level and tenure in the commuting area and there are no vacant positions for which you meet the minimum qualification standards. What is the official definition of disability?

An employee shall be considered to be disabled only if the employee is found by the Office of Personnel Management to be unable, because of disease or injury, to render useful and efficient service in the employee's position and is not qualified for reassignment under procedures prescribed by the Office, to a vacant position which is in the agency at the same grade or level and in which the employee would be able to render useful and efficient service. [4]

There is no requirement that you be totally disabled, only that you are unable to perform "useful and efficient service" which is defined as:

- either acceptable performance of the critical or essential elements of the position or the ability to perform at that level, and
- satisfactory conduct and attendance, or [5]
- incompatible with either useful and efficient service or retention in the position [6]

---

2 *See* 5 USC § 8332(j).
3 *See* 5 USC § 8332(j); 5 USC § 8334(j).
4 *See* 5 USC § 8337(a); 5 USC § 8451(a).
5 *See* 5 CFR § 831.1202; 5 CFR § 844.102.
6 *See* 5 USC § 8451; 5 CFR § 844.103(a).

Eligibility for disability retirement will not be denied if you reject reassignment to a position at a lower grade or pay level, but if you voluntarily accept a lower-grade position, you are deemed to have withdrawn your application for disability retirement.

If you are an employee who has withdrawn retirement contributions from your last federal employment, you are ineligible for disability retirement until those contributions are repaid with interest. If you have withdrawn your contributions from prior employment, you will receive reduced benefits. If a refund was taken for prior CSRS service which ended before October 1, 1990, you can either repay the outstanding amounts plus interest before retiring, or elect to have a reduced annuity.

A disability retirement is appropriate when your service is less than fully successful because of a medical condition or if you are unable to go to work because of your medical condition. Normally, OPM will not approve an application for disability retirement if there is a reasonable expectation that recovery will occur within one year after the onset of the disabling condition.

Medical documentation

Medical documentation is necessary to demonstrate whether the criteria for disability retirement have been met. This medical documentation consists of the following information from the examining physician:

1. the history of the specific medical condition(s), including reference to findings from previous examinations, treatment, and responses to treatment
2. the clinical findings from the most recent medical evaluation, and tests, such as x-rays, EKGs
3. an assessment of the current clinical status and plans for future treatment
4. a diagnosis
5. an estimate of the expected date of full or partial recovery
6. an explanation of the impact of the medical condition on your activities both on and off the job
7. an assessment of the degree to which the medical condition has or has not become static or well stabilized and an explanation of the medical basis for the conclusion
8. an assessment of the likelihood that you will suffer sudden or subtle incapacitation associated with the medical condition and the medical basis for this conclusion

9. an assessment of the probability that you will suffer injury or harm if you are not restricted or accommodated and the medical basis for this conclusion
10. the medical basis for the decision to recommend or not recommend restrictions that prohibit you from attending work altogether or from performing specific duties of your position [7]

Federal policy under the Rehabilitation Act of 1973 and the Americans with Disabilities Act, as amended requires that "reasonable accommodation" be made to disabled employees.[8] Your agency must exhaust all reasonable efforts to alleviate any deficiencies in your ability to serve through accommodation, including reassignment, before it counsels you to seek disability retirement or supports your request for disability retirement.

Filing

If possible, you should personally complete and sign the application for disability retirement. If you are unable to complete and file a disability retirement claim form due to circumstances beyond your control, some other legally responsible person may complete and submit the claim form on your behalf. This person may be a court-appointed guardian, a spouse, or some other member of your immediate family.[9] There are also very limited circumstances where your agency must apply for disability retirement on your behalf. One example is when a disabled FERS employee who has 18 months of service eligibility is removed from service and has no personal representative or immediate family. [10]

You may apply for disability retirement at *any time* before separation from service and up to *one year* after separation.[11] Your application must be received by OPM or your agency before the *one-year* deadline. There is an exception to this deadline for cases of mental incompetence. The same time limits apply to employees receiving Workers' Compensation under FECA for work-related injuries. These employees, if they meet the requirements, should also file for disability retirement within *one year* following separation from federal service.

---

7 *See* 5 CFR § 339.104.

8 *See* 29 USC § 791, *et seq.*

9 *See* 5 CFR § 831.1204; 5 CFR § 844.201.

10 *See* 5 CFR § 844.202.

11 *See* 5 USC § 8453; 5 CFR § 844.201.

A completed disability retirement application should be submitted to the agency personnel office by you or some other legally responsible person.

TIP

- *Standard Form 2801, **Application for Immediate Retirement**, is the OPM form used to apply for optional, discontinued service, or disability retirements under CSRS.*
- *Standard Form 3107 is used for FERS employees.*

The agency reviews the form you send in and all supporting documents for completeness, including the

- supervisor's statement
- physician's statement(s)
- agency Certification of Reassignment and Accommodation Efforts
- job description
- performance standards
- critical elements
- latest performance appraisal, and
- Disability Retirement Application Checklist

Your agency then sends the package to OPM.

TIP

*Standard Form 3112c, **Documentation in Support of Disability Retirement Application**, is used for both CSRS and FERS disability retirement. CSRS employees also need Standard Form 2824, while FERS employees also need Standard Form 3105.*

It is a good idea to notify your personnel office that you intend to file for disability retirement so that your Official Personnel File (OPF) is retained rather than being sent to permanent storage.

When all documentation is evaluated, OPM's Disability Claims Division will issue a decision either allowing or disallowing your disability application. OPM has the authority, which is rarely utilized, to offer you a medical examination if it determines that additional medical evidence is necessary to make a decision on your application. Your refusal to submit to an examination is grounds for disallowance of the application.[12] Notice of either the allowance or disallowance decision will be sent to both your agency and you.

TIP

If you initiate an application for disability retirement after having been separated from federal service for a period of 31 days or more, send your application and all supporting documentation by certified mail, return receipt requested, to:

OPM
Retirement Operations Center
Employee Service and Records Center
P.O. Box 45
Boyers, PA 16017-0045

EFFECTIVE DATE

On receiving a notification of approval of your disability retirement from OPM, your agency must not delay in establishing a date of separation. If you are retiring due to a disability, your annuity begins:

- on the first day of the month after separation from the service, or
- the day after pay ceases and the disability requirements are met[13]

The annuity cannot start until you separate from your civil service position, but may be retroactive to the last day in a pay status.[14] This means that the annuity will retroactively cover any final period of leave without pay upon approval of the disability retirement.

---

12 *See* 5 CFR § 831.1206(a)(4); 5 CFR § 844.203(b).
13 *See* 5 USC § 8345(b)(2)(B); 5 CFR § 831.701(b); 5 CFR § 844.301.
14 *See* 5 USC § 8345(b).

APPEAL TO OPM If your request for disability retirement is denied, you may appeal to OPM. It is first necessary to complete the internal OPM appeal procedure, including the filing of a request for reconsideration, before filing a disability retirement appeal with the MSPB. It is important to raise all possible issues during the initial appeal to OPM and following, in any request to OPM for reconsideration. The MSPB will not consider appeals on new matters that were not raised before OPM, although it will review new medical evidence. The initial OPM decision is sent to both you and the agency and informs you of your right to request reconsideration and how to file it.

REQUEST FOR RECONSIDERATION Your request for reconsideration of OPM's initial decision must be in writing and must include your:

- name
- address
- date of birth
- claim number
- basis of the request; for example, erroneous finding of fact or error of law

The reconsideration request must be received by OPM within *30 calendar days* after receipt of the initial decision, unless you have requested an extension and it has been granted by OPM. You may obtain a waiver of the time limit by showing that you were not notified of the limit or otherwise aware of it, or were prevented by circumstances beyond your control from timely filing.[15]

When you request reconsideration of the initial OPM decision, OPM will review your retirement file and any additional evidence of disability submitted with the request for reconsideration. However, your agency is not required to wait for a final OPM decision or Board action on a disability application before terminating your employment because of disability.

After reconsideration, a final written decision on disability retirement will be issued to you and to your agency, setting forth the findings and conclusion of OPM and informing you and your agency of your right to file an appeal to the MSPB.[16] OPM's reconsideration decision must articulate any reason or basis for denying your disability retirement claim.

---

[15] *See* 5 CFR § 831.109(e)(2).

[16] *See* 5 CFR § 831.109(f); 831.110.

Appeal of OPM decision to the MSPB After receipt of the OPM final reconsideration decision, you may appeal directly to the MSPB regional or field office in accordance with the Board's procedures for filing petitions of appeal. An appeal of an adverse final OPM decision must be filed with the appropriate MSPB office within *30 days* after the date the decision was received.[17] For a more detailed description of MSPB procedures see Chapter 4.

TIP

When filing an MSPB appeal of a final OPM denial of disability retirement, if the 35th day falls on a Saturday, Sunday, or federal holiday, the filing period will include the first workday after that date.

The Board treats disability retirement appeals the same as other appeals. Waivers of the timely filing requirement may be granted for good cause. You must show that you exercised due diligence or ordinary prudence under the particular circumstances of the case.

You have the right to discovery and a hearing with a transcript (now audio recording). You must request a hearing within *10 days* of the MSPB administrative judge's acknowledgment order and initiate discovery within *30 days* of the date of the acknowledgment order.

When an appeal for disability retirement is successful, there is also the possibility of reimbursement of attorney fees and costs under the Back Pay Act.[18] A nonfrivolous allegation of involuntary retirement based upon misleading information given to you by your agency also entitles you to a hearing. (See the discussion of constructive removals in Chapter 4.)

TIP

It is a good idea to hire an experienced lawyer since MSPB hearings require detailed knowledge of the rules and procedures, as well as litigation skills.

---

[17] *See* 5 CFR § 1201.22(b)(1).

[18] *See* 5 USC § 5596.

PRIMA FACIE CASES The U.S. Court of Appeals for the Federal Circuit has held[16] that in cases where you have been separated for physical inability to perform your duties and there was no other position that you qualified for and were physically able to do, you are deemed to have met the initial *prima facie* burden of proof of disability retirement. The burden then shifts to the government to come forward with evidence sufficient to support a finding that you are not disabled. However, the ultimate burden of proof still rests with you. You will prevail only if you establish entitlement by a preponderance of the evidence.

MSPB HEARING The administrative judge will usually schedule a hearing within *65 to 90 days* after the filing of an appeal. It is a good idea for you to request an on-site hearing as it is more difficult to conduct a telephone or video hearing, although an expert witness may find it more convenient.

TIP

It is not unusual for OPM to fail to show up at a retirement hearing. OPM is not required by law or regulation to be present.

It is critical that you have your physician(s) testify, as disability retirement cases are almost always dependent upon medical testimony. Both parties will normally make closing arguments at the end of the hearing. The administrative judge will usually issue a decision within 120 days of the filing of the appeal.

MSPB INITIAL DECISION In the initial decision,[20] the administrative judge is required to set forth a statement of facts, including your medical condition, your position and duties, and the nature of the disagreement between you and OPM. It is important that there be a well-reasoned initial decision to give the Board a complete understanding of how the judge reached his/her conclusions, especially if there is subjective evidence of a disability. If you allege disability discrimination in connection with the denial of disability retirement, the judge is required to decide both the issue of disability discrimination and the merits of the disability retirement claim.

---

19 *See Bruner v. OPM*, 996 F.2d 290 (Fed. Cir. 1993).

20 *See* 5 CFR § 1201.111(b)(1).

Petition for review to full board If the initial MSPB appeal is unsuccessful, a petition for review ("PFR") may be filed with the full Board in Washington, DC [21] within *35 days* of the date of the initial MSPB decision.

In seeking review by the full Board of an administrative judge's decision, you are limited to two bases:

1. the existence of new important evidence which was not discoverable before the PFR, and
2. a demonstration that the initial decision was based on an erroneous interpretation of law or regulation

The PFR is filed in writing with the Board and the opposing party may file a response. There is now a right to a reply brief. The standards of review are the same in a disability retirement case as in any other PFR.

Appeal to the U.S. Court of Appeals A final MSPB decision should be issued within *one year* in most cases, and sometimes may only consist of a short summary affirmance approving the decision of the administrative judge. If still unsuccessful, you may file an appeal with the U.S. Court of Appeals for the Federal Circuit within *60 days* after receipt of the adverse decision. However, such appeals are limited to the question of whether there has been a substantial violation of important procedural rights, a misconstruction of the governing legislation, or some like error going to the heart of the administrative determination.[22] In other words, the Court of Appeals will not review the merits of disability retirement appeals.

Termination of disability retirement

The MSPB has held that you must demonstrate continued disability by a preponderance of the evidence.[23] OPM has the right to request that you, as an annuitant, provide current medical information and/or undergo a medical reevaluation annually until you reach age 60.

If you are under 60 years of age, you must report to OPM your annual income from wages and self-employment. Earning capacity is considered restored, ending entitlement to an annuity, if, in any calendar year, your income from wages or self-employment or both equals at least 80% of the current rate of pay for the position you occupied immediately prior to

---

21 *See* 5 CFR § 1201.114.

22 *See Lindhahl v. OPM*, 470 US 768 (1995).

23 *See* 5 USC § 7701(c).

retirement. If you are a formerly disabled employee whose annuity has been terminated, you may nevertheless have your disability retirement restored if you suffer a recurrence of the disability before age 62 when you would be eligible for a regular annuity.

WHAT HAPPENS TO MY RETIREMENT BENEFITS IF I DIE?

Death benefits are available to your surviving spouse and children when you elect a reduced annuity and die while employed by the government after completing 18 months in federal service. A lump-sum benefit is payable immediately if you had less than 18 months of civilian service, or if you had completed 18 months of creditable service and leave no spouse. The lump-sum benefit is payable to a designated beneficiary or, in the absence of a designated beneficiary, in an established order to next of kin. If you want to designate a beneficiary, you must so advise OPM before your death.

Under FERS, your widow is entitled to lump-sum benefits if you die after completing at least 18 months of credible service. If you leave government service before you are eligible for an immediate annuity and then die before becoming eligible for a deferred annuity at age 62, your spouse will only receive a lump-sum benefit and not an annuity.

CAN MY SPOUSE OR CHILDREN RECEIVE MY ANNUITY IF I DIE?

When you are about to retire, you must elect the type of retirement annuity you want. Unless you elect an annuity without survivor benefits, or you are not married when you retire, a survivor annuity based upon 55% of the annuity before reduction will be payable to the spouse to whom you are married at the time of retirement, if death occurs after retirement under CSRS. The election of a survivor annuity is irrevocable once received by OPM.[24] The survivor annuity under FERS is based upon 50% of your annuity, and there is a greater reduction in the amount of your annuity—10% versus 7-8%. The survivor annuity will reflect all cost-of-living adjustments up to the time of your death. The annuity terminates when the surviving spouse dies or remarries before becoming 55 years of age.

You may name a new survivor beneficiary within *two years* after the date of remarriage or revert to a full life annuity if:

- the spouse you named at time of retirement predeceases you

---

24 *See* 5 USC § 8339(j)(5)(C)(i); 5 CFR § 831.613(b)(4)(i); 5 CFR § 843.301, *et seq.*; 5 CFR § 843.401, *et seq.*

- you later marry or remarry, or
- the marriage is otherwise dissolved and you remarry

To be eligible for a survivor benefit in such a case, the spouse must be married to you for at least nine months immediately before your death or be the parent of a child born to the marriage.[25]

To qualify for a survivor annuity, a child must be:

- under age 18
- unmarried, and
- dependent upon you, i.e., you either lived with the child at the time of your death or contributed to his/her support[26]

A child over 18 may qualify for a survivor annuity up to age 22 if she/he is a full-time student or if he/she is incapable of self-support because of a disability incurred before age 18.

An adopted child is entitled to a survivor annuity provided that you and your spouse file a petition for adoption prior to your death and, after your death, your surviving spouse adopts the child. There are also benefits for acknowledged children of unwed parents and for stepchildren, the latter being required to have lived with you.[27]

A number of statutory and regulatory provisions are based on your marital status at the time of your retirement. "Marriage means a marriage recognized by the law of the state with the most significant interest in the marital status of the employee" unless it is contrary to the public policy of the United States.[28]

Because there is no federal law governing domestic relations, it is necessary to look to the applicable state law as interpreted by the state courts. The validity of a marriage under applicable law must be determined by the appropriate local judicial body, not by OPM or the MSPB. OPM will recognize only one marriage for purpose of a survivor's annuity and will defer to the local courts to determine which marriage should be recognized.[29] Same-sex domestic partners benefits which were limited by the Defense of Marriage Act are now available in states that recognize same-sex marriages.

25 *See* 5 USC § 8341(a)(1); 5 CFR § 831.618(a); 5 USC § 8441.
26 *See* 5 USC § 8341(a)(3); 5 USC § 8441(4); 5 CFR § 405-406.
27 *See* 5 CFR § 831.615-617; 5 CFR § 843.401-410.
28 *See* 5 USC § 831.603; 5 CFR § 843.406.
29 *See* 5 CFR § 831.603.

Can I give part of my retirement to someone else?

The law provides that a former spouse is entitled to a portion of your retirement benefits to the extent that the division of those benefits is "expressly provided for" in a "qualifying court order."[30] The court order, most commonly a divorce decree or property distribution order, must specifically:

- divide the federal retirement benefits
- award a payment from the federal retirement benefits, or
- award a former spouse an annuity

The Board has interpreted the "expressly provided for" requirement in the Spouse Equity Act[31] as precluding OPM from undertaking its own determination of spousal entitlements and awarding survivor benefits based on uncertain or ambiguous state court orders.

OPM also will not honor state court orders made after the primary beneficiary's death. In addition, OPM regulations will not allow the garnishment of attorney's fees, interest, or court costs as part of child support and alimony unless a court order defines them as part of child support or alimony.[32]

TIP

It is essential that a divorcing employee or spouse ensure that the lawyer handling the divorce be aware of the requirements of federal law concerning spousal entitlement.

What if I'm overpaid?

If you receive money you are not entitled to, the government can require you to repay the overpayment. The government can forego or waive its right to overpayment when:

30 *See* 5 USC § 8345(j)(1); 5 USC § 8445.
31 *See* 5 USC § 8341(h)(1).
32 *See* 5 CFR § 581.102, 581.307.

- you are without fault, and
- recovery would be against equity and good conscience [33]

Recovery is against equity and good conscience when: [34]

- it would cause financial hardship to you;
- you can show (regardless of your financial circumstances) that, due to the notice that such payment would be made or because of incorrect payment, either you had relinquished a valuable right or changed your financial position for the worse, i.e., you have changed your financial position because of the money you received; (for example, purchased an automobile on credit), or [35]
- recovery could be unconscionable under the circumstances.

A request for a waiver of the interest on the overpayment may also be considered by the MSPB.[36]

If you are an annuitant receiving retirement benefits and you claim that you are entitled to a waiver of overpayment, you will normally receive an initial decision from OPM stating your right to reconsideration. A request for reconsideration must be received by OPM within *30 calendar days* from the date of the original decision,[37] and include your:

- name
- address
- date of birth
- claim number, and
- the basis for the request

After reconsideration, a representative of the Associate Director of Compensation, OPM, will issue a final decision setting forth the findings and conclusions and spelling out the right to appeal to the MSPB. [38] OPM has the burden of proof by a preponderance of the evidence that an overpayment actually occurred. The burden of proof is on you as an annuitant to establish that you are eligible for a waiver, including the absence of fault.[39]

For more information about waivers of overpayment, see Chapter 27.

---

[33] *See* 5 USC § 8346(b); 5 USC § 8470.
[34] *See* 5 CFR § 831.1403; 5 CFR § 845-303.
[35] *See* 5 CFR § 831.1401.
[36] *See* 5 USC § 8347(d)(1).
[37] *See* 5 CFR § 831.109; 5 CFR § 845.204.
[38] *See* 5 CFR § 831.110; 5 CFR § 845.204.
[39] *See* 5 CFR § 831.1402 and 831.1407; 5 USC § 8470(b); 5 CFR § 301-305.

Are there any special retirement issues?

Federal law enforcement officials and firefighters already contribute 7.5% of their salaries to their retirement systems. They are entitled to greater benefits while retiring at an earlier age. Retirement is optional at age 50 and is mandatory at age 55 with at least 20 years of law enforcement or firefighter service, although it may be extended to age 60 by the agency head.[40] Military service as a firefighter or law enforcement officer may not be credited toward the minimum 20-year civilian service requirement under CSRS.[41]

Annuities for law enforcement and firefighting personnel are computed by taking:

- 2.5% of the high-three average pay;
- multiplying the result by 20 years of law enforcement or firefighter service;
- plus 2% of the high-three average pay for all service after 20 years;
- multiplied by all service over 20 years.

Annuities for air traffic controllers, law enforcement and firefighting personnel and nuclear materials couriers under FERS are computed at 1.7% of high-three average pay for 20 years and 1% per year of service thereafter.[42]

Firefighters

The definition of "firefighter" is limited to those who are engaged in the control and extinguishment of fires or the maintenance of firefighting apparatus and equipment. If your primary duties are the performance of routine fire prevention inspection, you are excluded from this definition.[43]

Primary duties are those duties that are paramount in influence or weight, occupy a substantial portion of your working time, and are assigned on a regular and recurring basis. A primary position is one directly involved in the above duties while a secondary position has supervisory or administrative duties in the firefighter or law enforcement field. Your service in a primary position that has been approved by OPM or your agency is automatically covered under the special retirement provisions of the law.[44]

---

40 *See* 5 CFR § 831.901-911.

41 *See* 5 USC § 8336(c)(1).

42 *See* 5 CFR § 842.405.

43 *See* 5 CFR § 831.902.

44 *See* 5 USC § 8336(c).

You are considered a law enforcement officer ("LEO") if you are engaged in the investigation, apprehension, or detention of persons suspected or convicted of offenses against the criminal laws of the United States. The definition does not include an employee whose primary duties involve maintaining law and order, protecting life and property, guarding against or inspecting for violations of law, or investigating persons who are not suspected or convicted of offenses against the criminal laws of the United States.

TIP

The OPM regulations for CSRS employees are contained in 5 CFR 831.901-911, while the regulations for FERS employees are contained in 5 CFR 842.801-809.

The definition of "primary duties" was amended, effective December 5, 1990, to include duties performed at least 50% of the time.[45] However the law indicates that there may be rare instances where special circumstances allow a position to meet the paramount duties standard even though it does not meet the 50% standard.

Secondary law enforcement officer (LEO) coverage is granted to you if you transfer directly without a break in service of more than *3 days* from covered positions to supervisory or administrative positions that require primary law enforcement duties. There is no difference in benefits for LEOs with primary and secondary coverage.

If you are a CSRS employee, coverage in a LEO position or credit for past service will not be granted for a period greater than *one year* prior to the date the request for coverage is received by your agency.

If you are an FERS employee, you must file a request for coverage with your agency within *six months* after entering your position or after any significant change in your position or by showing that you were unaware of your status or were prevented by circumstances beyond your control from requesting a change of official status.

---

45 *See* 5 CFR § 831.902.

Federal police officers who are performing criminal investigation, apprehension, and/or detention duties for more than 50% of their job should apply for LEO coverage. OPM has tried to exclude employees who are classified as police officers from LEO coverage, but there is no legal bar to coverage. However, the MSPB has applied the "basic reasons for the existence of the position" test, which has limited LEO coverage for police officers.[46]

Final Thoughts

When we look ahead to retirement, there are a number of things we want to think about, including whether we qualify for retirement under CSRS or FERS rules, when we want to retire, and whether we can afford to live on our retirement annuity. Phased retirement is now an option. What can we do now, while we are still employed, to put ourselves in the best possible position at retirement? We often want to investigate, too, whether there are special provisions for our retirement situation, whether we could retire on disability, and who would receive our benefits if we die. Careful consideration of these issues in advance will give our retirement a much better chance of being a time of true relaxation rather than worry.

[46] *See Watson v. Dept. of the Navy*, 262 F. 3d 1292, 1304 (Fed. Cir. 2001).

19

Veterans' Rights

I Love America—and It Loves Me Back

In This Chapter You Will Learn:

- what employment protections the law provides for veterans
- what you can do if you do not receive the protection the law provides
- what the reemployment rights of returning veterans are

Contents Chapter Nineteen - Veterans' Rights

Introduction

The law contains many protections, as well as certain benefits, for veterans and those who have served in the uniformed services, particularly those who have incurred service-connected disabilities. This chapter discusses veterans preferences, the Veterans Employment Opportunities Act ("VEOA"), the Disabled Veterans Affirmative Action Program, and various other protections and benefits for veterans and/or disabled veterans. In addition, this chapter gives a detailed review of the Uniformed Services Employment and Reemployment Rights Act of 1994 ("USERRA" or "the Act") and its procedures, which are designed to protect employees from discrimination because of their uniformed service, as well as provide employees with rights to return to civilian employment after service.

Does the government give me preferential treatment if I'm a vet?

Because of the value the government places on military and other uniformed service, and because of problems veterans have at times encountered in either employment or reemployment, there are certain preferences in place for veterans. What they are and what protection they provide is discussed below.

Who qualifies for veterans preference?

The law provides a very broad and inclusive definition of individuals who are "preference eligible" because of their own or a family member's veteran status. A "veteran" is generally someone who served on active duty in the armed services during a war or other military activity. A "disabled veteran" is someone who suffered a service-connected disability or is receiving benefits through the Department of Veterans Affairs. The term "preference-eligible veteran" includes not only veterans and disabled veterans but also unmarried widows or widowers of preference-eligible veterans, spouses of disabled veterans, and, in some cases mothers of veterans.

What does "veterans preference" mean?

A preference-eligible veteran is entitled to certain benefits and advantages in federal employment.

Preference eligibles are entitled to have 5 to 10 points added to their scores in a federal civil service examination. 5 points are added to your examination score or rating if you are a veteran who served:

- during a war
- during the period April 28, 1952 through July 1, 1955
- for more than 180 consecutive days, other than for training, any part of which occurred after January 31, 1955, and before October 15, 1976
- during the Gulf War from August 2, 1990, through January 2, 1992,[1] or
- in a campaign or expedition for which a campaign medal has been authorized, for example, any Armed Forces Expeditionary medal or campaign badge, including El Salvador, Lebanon, Grenada, Panama, Southwest Asia, Somalia, and Haiti
- for more than 180 consecutive days, other than for training, any part of which occurred during the period beginning September 11, 2001, and ending on the date prescribed by Presidential proclamation or by law as the last day of Operation Iraqi Freedom.

You are entitled to 10 points if you are:

- a disabled veteran
- an unmarried widow or widower of certain veterans
- the spouse of a veteran who has a service-connected disability who has been disqualified for a Federal position along the general lines of his or her usual occupation
- the mother of an individual who lost his or her life under honorable conditions while serving in the armed services (the mother may qualify under certain circumstances—for example, if her husband is disabled or she is no longer married), or
- the mother of a veteran who suffers from a service-connected total disability (the mother may qualify under certain circumstances—for example, if her husband is disabled, or she is widowed or divorced).[2]

---

1 A campaign medal holder or Gulf War veteran who originally enlisted after September 7, 1980, (or began active duty on or after October 14, 1982, and has not previously completed 24 months of continuous active duty) must have served continuously for 24 months or the full period called or ordered to active duty.

2 For more details, see 5 USC § 2108(3).

Applicants who have qualified for appointment to the competitive service are entered onto registers in rank order, with preference eligibles ranked ahead of others who obtained the same rating. [3] When filling a position, the agency will select from the highest three eligibles available. An agency must select a preference eligible before a non-preference eligible in the applicable group of three. If an agency wants to pass over a preference eligible in order to select an individual who is not a preference eligible ("passover"), the agency must file written reasons with OPM for the passover and obtain OPM's approval.[4] OPM's approval may be obtained because of medical qualifications, unsuitability for federal employment, or for other reasons considered by OPM to be disqualifying for the particular position.[5] There is no obligation for the agency to notify the applicant that it is seeking passover authority; nor does the applicant have the right to object to the passover. If OPM sustains the passover, there has (thus far) been little success in challenging the agency's action as a violation of Veterans' Preference. In addition, under current case law, an agency may even cancel a vacancy announcement in order to avoid hiring a preference eligible, and this does not violate the applicant's veterans' preference.

These rules are slightly different if an agency proposes to passover a disabled veteran (with a 30% disability or more), or to disqualify a disabled veteran based on the physical requirements of the position. In that case, the agency must notify both OPM and the disabled veteran of the reasons for the passover and of the veteran's right to respond to OPM within 15 days of the date of the notification. OPM must take into account any information provided by the veteran. OPM will notify the agency and the disabled veteran of its decision, with which the agency must comply. OPM is prohibited by law from delegating this function to any agency.[6]

Veterans are also given a higher retention standing in the event of a reduction-in-force in the Federal service. (See Chapter 9). OPM has ruled that a veteran is not allowed any preference for the purposes of "in service actions such as promotions."[7] However, OPM has also instituted the Disabled Veterans Affirmative Action Program, which encourages "recruitment, hiring, placement and advancement" of disabled veterans and is discussed below.

---

[3] *See* 5 USC § 3313.

[4] *See* 5 USC § 3318(b)(1).

[5] *See* 5 CFR § 332.406.

[6] *See* 5 USC § 3312, 3318.

[7] *See* 5 CFR § 211.102(c).

Veterans Employment Opportunities Act ("VEOA")

In October 1998, Congress passed the Veterans Employment Opportunities Act (VEOA), which expanded veterans' employment rights.[8] The VEOA was amended by Section 511 of the Veterans Millennium Health Care Act (Pub. Law 106-117) of November 30, 1999. The VEOA expands the definition of a "prohibited personnel practice" to include the following:

- [to] knowingly take, recommend, or approve any personnel action if the taking of such action would violate a veterans preference requirement, or
- [to] knowingly fail to take, recommend, or approve any personnel action if the failure to take such action would violate a veterans preference requirement[9]
  (See also Chapter 7, on "prohibited personnel actions.")

In addition, the VEOA expands employment opportunities for veterans by the following:

- regardless of whether a veteran has competitive status, a preference eligible or veteran who has served at least three years of continuous active service and received an honorable discharge is entitled to compete for federal vacancies where the agency seeks outside applicants. Veterans who were released shortly before completing a 3-year tour are also considered eligible.[10]
- federal vacancy announcements issued under agency merit promotion principles must state that veterans are eligible to apply
- OPM must establish an appointing authority to appoint preference eligibles and veterans
- for certain purposes (for example, affirmative action mandates for government contractors), Congress has expanded the definition of "veteran" to include all "veterans who served on active duty during a war or in a campaign or expedition for which a campaign badge has been authorized," and not limit the definition to just disabled or Vietnam era veterans
- agencies are prohibited from hiring contractors who fail to make annual reports regarding their affirmative action responsibilities to hire qualified veterans, and

---

[8] VEOA does not apply to the TSA. *Morse v. MSPB*, 621 F.3d 1346 (Fed. Cir. 2010).

[9] *See* 5 USC § 2302(b)(11).

[10] OPM's interim regulations use the term "substantially completed an initial 3-year term." Agencies will then decide, in individual cases, whether a candidate has met this standard.

- veterans preferences may now apply to many jobs in the judicial and legislative branches.

Veterans who were appointed before the 1999 amendments to the VEOA were given Schedule B appointments in the excepted service. Those veterans who actually competed under merit promotion procedures are, pursuant to the amendments, converted to career conditional appointments retroactive to the date of their original VEOA appointments. Those who did not compete and were appointed noncompetitively will remain under Schedule B until they do compete.

What do you do if you think that an agency has violated your veterans preference rights under the VEOA? The VEOA created an avenue of redress for a preference eligible who alleges that an agency violated his or her veteran's preference rights. To seek such redress, a preference eligible must contact the Department of Labor ("DOL"), Veterans' Employment and Training Services ("VETS") and file a *written* complaint within *60 days* after the date of the alleged violation. You must show that you provided a summary of the allegations forming the basis of the complaint so that the Dept. of Labor can conduct an investigation.[11] The DOL enjoys subpoena authority to investigate the complaint by reviewing the agency's documents and inter-viewing its witnesses. If VETS finds that the agency has violated the VEOA, it must try to ensure that the agency complies with the applicable statute or regulation. If VETS is unable to resolve a complaint within 60 days, it must provide notice of the unsuccessful effort to the complainant. You must also show that you have either received written notification of the results of DOL's investigation of the complaint, or, if DOL does not resolve the complaint within 60 days, that you provided written notification to DOL of your intent to file a Board appeal.[12]

Although, as discussed in Chapter 7, the Office of Special Counsel ("OSC") has the authority to investigate and remedy prohibited personnel practices, OSC defers to VETS regarding allegations of violations of veterans' preference rights for corrective action purposes. Although OSC will still investigate such allegations for possible disciplinary action against agency officials, OSC recommends filing your complaint with VETS.

---

[11] *See* 5 USC § 3330a(a); *Gingery v. OPM and Dept. of the Treasury*, 119 MSPR 43 (2012) (citing *Burroughs v. Dept. of the Army*, 115 MSPR 656.9, aff'd, 445 Fed. Appx. 347 (Fed. Cir. 2011)).

[12] Additional information about VETS can be found at http://www.dol.gov/vets. *Gingery v. OPM and Dept. of the Treasury,* 119 MSPR 43 (Dec. 11, 2012) (citing 5 USC § 3330a(d)(1)-(2); *Burroughs v. Department of the Army,* 116 MSPR 292.10 (2011)).

You may also pursue your complaint at the Merit Systems Protection Board or in federal court. But if you choose to go to the Board, you must *first* file your written complaint with the DOL within 60 days as described above, and give the DOL a 60-day opportunity to investigate the complaint. DOL must close out the investigation, either on its own accord or at the behest of the employee.[13] You *must* exhaust this administrative remedy prior to filing with the Board. After the 60th day, you may file an appeal with the Board. If the DOL issues a negative decision on your complaint, you must file an appeal with the MSPB *within 15 days* after you receive the DOL's decision. An appeal may be filed electronically by using the Board's Internet filing option available at the Board's website https://e-appeal.mspb.gov/. The regulations governing VEOA appeals at the Board are found at 5 CFR 1208.

After filing an appeal with the MSPB, you may also make an election to move your case to U.S. District court if two conditions are met:

1. the Board has had the opportunity to process your case for *120 days*, and
2. the Board has not yet issued a judicially reviewable decision on the merits. (See Chapter 4, for judicially reviewable decisions of the Board).

You must file your election with the Board, and the Agency, and you must file your complaint in U.S. District Court within *60 days* after you make your decision. The Board will stop processing your case when it receives the election.

If you are successful under the VEOA, the Board or the court will order the agency to comply with the law, and may order the agency to award you lost wages and benefits, reasonable attorney fees, expert witness fees, and other litigation expenses. If you prove that the agency's violation was willful, that is, that the agency knew that it was violating the law, the Board or court may also award you special ("liquidated") damages equal to the amount of the back pay.

If you think that your agency has violated VEOA and discriminated against you (e.g., failed to hire you because of your race, sex, or other bases), you must pursue your action with two separate places. The MSPB has found that it does not have jurisdiction to hear claims of EEO discrimination along with claims that an agency violated VEOA. The discrimination claim must be filed pursuant to the EEOC's regulations. (See Chapter 6.)

---

[13] *See* 5 CFR § 1208.21

ARE THERE SPECIAL PROVISIONS FOR DISABLED VETERANS?

The Federal government has a Disabled Veterans Affirmative Action Program ("the Program"), designed to promote "federal employment and advancement opportunities for qualified disabled veterans." The Program places certain requirements upon agencies in an effort to accomplish this goal. Agencies are responsible for instituting and providing "adequate resources" to an affirmative action program for the recruitment, hiring, placement, and advancement of disabled veterans. Agencies have reporting and planning requirements in this regard under the Rehabilitation Act of 1973.

The plans must include instructions for each agency component promoting employment and advancement of disabled veterans. OPM is responsible for monitoring and reviewing the agency's programs and conducting on-site evaluations of their effectiveness. Agency and OPM responsibilities are covered in 5 CFR Part 720, subpart C, and 38 USC 4214.

An agency may give a noncompetitive temporary appointment or term appointment to any veteran who is retired from active military service with, or rated by the VA within the preceding year with, a disability rating of at least 30 percent. The agency may convert the employee, without a break in service, to a career or career-conditional appointment at any time during the employee's temporary or term appointment.[14]

As discussed above, disabled veterans are also given extra protection if an agency seeks to pass over their application and hire a non preference eligible.

WHAT IS A "VETERANS RECRUITMENT APPOINTMENT?"

The Veterans Readjustment Appointment was a special authority by which agencies could appoint (without competition) an eligible Vietnam era or post-Vietnam era veteran to positions which would otherwise be in the competitive service. The Jobs for Veterans Act ("Act"), enacted November 7, 2002, revised the eligibility requirements for a Veterans Readjustment Appointment, and redesignated these appointments as "Veterans Recruitment Appointments" ("VRA").

The VRA authorizes agencies to appoint eligible veterans (without competition) to positions at any grade level through General Schedule (GS) 11 or equivalent.[15] As of the time of this printing, OPM had not revised 5 CFR

---

[14] *See* 5 USC § 3112; 5 CFR § 316.302(a)(4) also, 5 CFR §§ 316.302(b)(4), 316.402(b)(4) and 315.707.
[15] *See* 38 USC § 4214.

Part 307, which applied to the prior statute, and, thus, to the extent the regulations are not in accordance with the new law, the new law governs.

To be eligible for a noncompetitive VRA appointment, you must be qualified for the position, as well as meet one of the following criteria:

- be a disabled veteran
- have served on active duty in the Armed Forces during a war, or in a campaign or expedition for which a campaign badge has been authorized
- while serving on active duty in the Armed Forces, participated in a military operation for which an Armed Forces Service Medal was awarded; or
- be a veteran last separated from active duty within the past 3 years

If the agency has more than one VRA candidate for the same job and one (or more) is a preference eligible, the agency must apply the Veterans' preference procedures in making VRA appointments. After two successful years of continuous employment, these positions are converted to career-conditional or career employment. (See Chapter 1.) Employees appointed under a VRA can appeal adverse actions to the MSPB if they have at least one year of continuous service and are preference eligible.[16] If the veteran is not preference eligible, he or she is not allowed Board rights until converted to the competitive service.

What is the Uniformed Services Employment and Reemployment Rights Act ("USERRA") and how does it work?

USERRA is an anti-discrimination act for people who have served, or are serving, in the uniformed services. In 1994, Congress replaced the Veterans' Reemployment Rights Act of 1968 (VERRA) with USERRA. USERRA attempts to eliminate the disadvantages to civilian careers and discrimination resulting from a person being in the uniformed services.[17] USERRA was designed to clarify VERRA's complex and sometimes confusing language and to expand its coverage. Regulations designed to inform members of the uniformed services and assist them with their rights and obligations may be found at 32 CFR 104.

---

16 *See* 5 CFR § 752.401(c)(3).

17 *See* 38 USC § 4301(a)(1) (1998 Supp.).

Who is covered by USERRA?

The Act includes broad protections and coverage. Unlike many anti-discrimination acts, USERRA provides that individuals can be personally sued for violating the Act. Consistent with the Act's broad proscriptive efforts, it also has a broad definition of "service in the uniformed services," which is:

> the performance of duty on a voluntary or involuntary basis in a uniformed service under competent authority and includes active duty, initial active duty for training, inactive duty training, full-time National Guard duty, a period for which a person is absent from a position of employment for the purpose of an examination to determine the fitness of the person to perform any such duty, and a period for which a person is absent from employment for the purposes of performing funeral honors duty.[18]

You are not covered by the Act if you are separated from uniformed service with a dishonorable or bad conduct discharge, separated "under other than honorable conditions," dismissed, or dropped from the rolls.[19]

Discrimination and retaliation under the Act

The Act prohibits discrimination on the basis of uniformed service status. Discrimination includes the denial of "initial employment, reemployment, retention in employment, promotion, or any benefit of employment by an employer on the basis of" service in the uniformed service.[20] Like many other discrimination and employment-related statutes, USERRA also forbids an agency from retaliating against employees who have tried to protect their own rights or someone else's rights under USERRA.

The test for establishing discrimination is different than for a claim under Title VII of the Civil Rights Act. Under Title VII, you always maintain the burden of proving that an agency has discriminated or retaliated against you. Under USERRA, you, as an individual in the uniformed service, bear the initial burden of proof of showing that your military service was "a substantial or motivating factor" in the adverse employment action. However, if you do so, then the burden shifts to the agency to come forward with evidence to show that it would have taken the adverse action anyway, for a valid reason.

---

18 *See* 38 USC § 4303(13).

19 *See* 38 USC § 4304.

20 *See* 38 USC § 4311(a).

Your initial burden of proof for a retaliation claim includes showing that the agency knew that you had engaged in an activity protected under the Act, that the agency took an adverse personnel action, and that there is causal connection between your activities under USERRA and the agency's action. The connection can be demonstrated if the personnel action (for example, termination or demotion) took place shortly after the protected activity (for example, testifying on behalf of another employee who has raised a USERRA claim). Again, after you meet your initial burden, the agency must come forward with evidence to show that it would have taken the adverse action anyway, for a valid reason.

If you think that your agency has discriminated against you because of your military service *and* another reason (e.g., your race or sex, or other bases) you must pursue your action in two separate ways. The MSPB has found that it does not have jurisdiction to hear claims of EEO discrimination along with claims of USERRA discrimination. Therefore, you have to file an EEO complaint to challenge the discrimination claim. (See Chapters 5 and 6).

REEMPLOYMENT RIGHTS

If you have been absent from employment because of your service in the uniformed services, you may be entitled to reemployment and benefits if you meet certain requirements. To qualify for these rights you must:

- give advance written or verbal notice to the agency of your intended absence
- have been absent due to service for less than five years in total
- report to or submit an application for reemployment to the agency in a timely manner, and
- not have disqualifying character of service

TIP

To protect your rights, give your agency advance written notice of your absence for military purposes.

Under certain circumstances, the notice requirement may be waived. For example, "military necessity" or other circumstances may prevent notice from being possible. When notice is impossible, the agency cannot deny reemployment.

The total period of absence cannot be more than five years. For example, if you are gone for two years, return for two years, and then are gone for two years again, you are entitled to reemployment and benefits. The five-year period does not include an initial period of obligated service or a period when, due to no fault of your own, you were unable to obtain orders releasing you from service before the end of the five-year period. The law also outlines special circumstances where service may not count towards the five-year maximum.[21] You can find a sample of how to write a notice of uniformed service at Appendix B of the Department of Defense's USERRA regulations at 32 CFR 104.[22]

WHEN AN AGENCY IS NOT REQUIRED TO REEMPLOY Agencies are not always required to reemploy members of the uniformed services. An agency does not have to reemploy you if:

- the agency's circumstances change to such a degree that reemployment is impossible or unreasonable
- you incurred a disability that prevents you from being able to perform your job and cannot be accommodated
- you are no longer qualified for the position or any other position of lesser status after a reasonable effort to qualify you for an alternate position
- the position was for a brief, non recurrent period
- you were separated with a dishonorable or bad conduct discharge, were separated under other than honorable conditions, or were dismissed or dropped from the military rolls,[23] or
- your cumulative length of service exceeds five years.

NOTICE REQUIREMENTS The length of time that you served in the uniformed service controls the type of notice of reemployment you must give the agency.

- if you were absent for less than *31 days* or for a fitness for duty examination, you are entitled to have an *eight-hour* period at home after the end of the service period. Then, you must report to the agency on the *next regularly scheduled workday*.

---

[21] *See* 38 USC § 4312(c)(3) and (4).

[22] OPM's regulations are contained at 5 CFR § Parts 213, 353, 870 and 890.

[23] *See* 38 USC § 4304.

- if you were absent for more than *30 days* but less than *181 days*, you must submit an application for reemployment within *14 days* after the end of the period of service.
- when you are in the service for more than *180 days*, you must submit your application for reemployment to the agency within *90 days*.

There are also exceptions when you are recuperating from an illness or injury which was incurred or aggravated during the performance of uniformed service. Under these circumstances, the time period for notifying the agency begins to run as soon as you have recovered. However, the recovery period cannot exceed two years. There are limited exceptions to these deadlines if you were prevented from giving such notice due to circumstances beyond your control.

TIP

Don't miss your deadlines for notifying the agency of your return.

If you fail to follow the reporting and notice requirements required by the Act, you do not necessarily lose all reemployment and benefit rights under the Act. Rather, you become subject to the disciplinary and conduct rules for absences from scheduled work.

When you notify your agency that you seek reemployment, it may ask for proof that you are qualified to receive the benefits of the Act. Your agency may request documentation proving three things:

- that the notice is timely
- that you have not exceeded five years of service, and
- that you remain eligible for reemployment benefits (see above)

Maintain all documents regarding your service so that you can produce them upon request.

Your agency may not delay or deny your reemployment or try to escape a reemployment obligation by demanding documentation that does not exist or that is not readily available. If the requested documentation does not exist or is not available when your agency asks for it, it may not deny your reemployment rights. However, if documentation becomes available after reemployment, and if that documentation shows that you did not meet one or more of the three requirements, the agency may terminate your employment. Your failure to provide the requested documentation may result in a break in service for pension purposes, however.

Reemployment positions You are entitled to prompt reemployment after serving in the uniformed services. The Act's goal is clear: return you to the same circumstances you would have been in if you had not served in the uniformed services, or as close to that as possible. This goal is balanced against the agency's rights to have qualified and productive employees. The Secretary of the DOL, through its Veterans Employment and Training Service, is responsible for providing assistance to you if you wish to invoke your USERRA reinstatement rights.

You are not entitled to reinstatement to any position you desire. You are entitled to a position similar to what you would have occupied if you had not served in the uniformed services. The law does not, and cannot, force an agency to retain an unqualified or incapable employee in any specific position. The duration of your period of uniformed service and any related disabilities may affect your reinstatement rights.

If you are absent due to uniformed service and you notify the agency in writing that you do not intend to return to the agency, you give up all reinstatement rights. If the agency tries to deny employment on these grounds, the agency must produce the written notice and prove that you knowingly waived your rights under USERRA.

If you are returning following an absence of more than 30 days, you are entitled to be restored as soon as possible, but in no event later than 30 days after receipt of your application to return.

Service for 90 days or less If you were absent from work for 90 days or less due to service in the uniformed services, then you must be reemployed in the position that you would have held if your employment had not been interrupted by uniformed service. In certain circumstances, this position may not be the same position you occupied when you left to engage in uniformed service.

For example, if you were in training as a systems analyst, the agency may have a standard policy of promoting "systems analysts" to "senior systems analysts" within 30 days after being employed. The promotion to "senior" analyst might remove you from an introductory probationary period, raise your salary, and improve your benefits.

Under the Act, if you return from the uniformed service, you would be entitled to the "senior" position. This is known as the "escalator" position. But you may not be qualified for the escalator position because you lack training. Under these circumstances, your agency must take reasonable steps to qualify you for the position. If the agency cannot qualify you with reasonable efforts, then you are entitled only to be placed in the position that you occupied when you left for service in the uniformed services. In our example above, you would only be allowed reinstatement to the "systems analyst" position.

Service of 91 days or more If you are absent for 91 days or more, you are entitled to the escalator position (if qualified) or a position of comparable seniority, status, and pay for which you are qualified. As discussed above, if you are not qualified for the escalator position, the agency can return you to your original position, or one with comparable seniority, status and pay, after taking reasonable steps to qualify you for the escalator position.

Placement upon reinstatement These formulas do not always apply to every situation. Often, employees find that the Act does not answer the questions raised by their particular circumstances. To ease this problem, USERRA has identified several helpful factors.

- first, the Act asks: What position would you have had if you had not served in the uniformed services?
- second, the Act asks: Are you qualified to act in that position?

If you are not qualified, the Act orders your agency to use reasonable means to train you for that position. If you remain unable to perform the job after a reasonable effort to qualify you, then the Act requires that the agency give you the job you occupied when you left for uniformed service. If that position is also not available, or if you are not qualified for it (for example, due to a disability), and the agency cannot reasonably make you qualified, then you are entitled to the most similar job for which you are qualified.

There are two critical points which must always apply:

- the reinstatement position should be as close as possible to the position you would have had, but for the uniformed service
- you must be qualified for the reinstatement position

Under USERRA, if you cannot become qualified for either the position you would have occupied upon your return, or the position you occupied when you departed, you do not lose reinstatement rights. Instead, you should be placed in another position for which you are qualified. That position should be as similar as possible to the position you would have had if you had not served in the uniformed services. If such a position is not available, then you may be placed in the position most comparable to the position you occupied when you left for service. If your agency determines that it is impossible or unreasonable to reemploy you, the Director of OPM must identify a position of like seniority, status and pay at another federal agency that satisfies the reemployment criteria and for which you are qualified. OPM must ensure that you are offered such position.

Reasonable accommodation for service-related disabilities When your service results in, or aggravates, a disability, your agency has a duty to provide you with a reasonable accommodation so that you can perform the essential functions of your job, consistent with the Rehabilitation Act. (See Chapter 5.) "Reasonable accommodation" refers to an agency's obligation to make adjustments to your work situation or environment so that you can perform your job even with your disability. Reasonable accommodations could take the form of restructuring your job duties, providing you with different equipment to enable you to perform your job, altering your work schedule, or placing you in a vacant position for which you are qualified. Just what accommodations are "reasonable" depend on the circumstances of each case. Generally, the employee has the obligation to first request a reasonable accommodation and to suggest possible accommodations to management.

TIP

Requests for reasonable accommodation should be in writing so that you have a record of the request for any possible EEO complaint over the agency's failure to grant your request.

If you remain unable to perform the position after the reasonable accommodation, then USERRA entitles you to any other position equivalent in seniority, status, and pay for which you are qualified or for which you can become qualified with reasonable efforts by the agency. If you cannot become qualified for a position of equal status, then you are entitled to the next closest position in terms of seniority, status, and pay.

Reorganizations and downsizing The Act tries to solve problems raised by the Federal government's frequent reorganizations and downsizing. For example, due to reorganization and downsizing, an entire executive agency may be abolished or all of its functions may be transferred. As a result of the elimination or transfer of job functions, it may be impossible or unreasonable for the agency to reemploy a person.

Under these circumstances, the Director of OPM may determine that reinstatement to the person's former agency is impossible. In such a case, the Director must identify a position of comparable seniority, status, and pay at another federal executive agency that satisfies the Act's reinstatement requirements. As always, you must be qualified for that position. The Director then is charged with ensuring that you are offered the position.

When changes occur in the judicial and legislative branches, the agency, not OPM, determines whether reinstatement in another federal agency is possible or reasonable. Then, OPM must guarantee you an offer of a comparable position in another federal executive agency. When this occurs, you must apply for reinstatement in another federal agency to the Director of OPM.

Reemployment by certain federal agencies Some agencies are responsible for issuing agency-specific procedures implementing USERRA. These include the security and intelligence agencies (such as the FBI, CIA, and NSA), the GAO, and quasi-governmental corporations such as the FDIC. The procedures must identify a specific official within the agency who is charged with determining whether reemployment is possible or reasonable and informing OPM. You are not entitled to judicial review of the agency's conclusion. As with other federal agencies, you are entitled to submit an application to OPM, and you remain entitled to a position in another federal executive agency.

Leave of absence status While you are absent from your federal employment because you are in uniformed service, you are considered to be on furlough or leave of absence. If you are reemployed under USERRA, you must be treated the same as others who are furloughed or on a leave of absence. If you are reemployed under USERRA, you are not entitled to special treatment or benefits that your agency does not give to other employees.

Employment benefits When you are reemployed under USERRA, you are entitled to the same seniority, rights, and benefits that you enjoyed on the date you began your military service plus the additional seniority, rights, and benefits you would have attained if you had remained continuously employed. During your military absence, you are also entitled to whatever other rights and benefits unrelated to seniority that the agency generally gives to other employees who have similar seniority or status and who are on furlough or leave of absence. If the agency establishes new procedures during the period of uniformed service, those procedures apply to you. If you are absent due to uniformed service, you are responsible to pay any employee costs for funded benefits.

Federal employees enrolled in FERS who are reemployed may make-up contributions to the Thrift Savings Plan over a period of time. Employees covered by FERS are also entitled to employer contributions to TSP for their period of absence in an amount equal to 1% of basic pay. If the employee makes make-up contributions, the employing agency must make matching contributions. Federal employees enrolled in CSRS may also make-up contributions; however, no employer contributions are made.

Use of leave Your agency cannot require you to use sick, vacation, annual, or other leave while participating in uniformed service. However, you may use such accrued benefits if you make a written request. Agencies also provide for military leave. When you leave your civilian position to enter the military service, your agency must "certify" your leave account with a statement that you are serving in a uniformed service.[24]

Enforcement of employment or reemployment rights

You have several ways of enforcing your rights under the law. Which route you choose will depend largely upon your circumstances. The good news is that there is no time limit for filing a USERRA claim.

Department of Labor administrative procedures The Act provides an informal administrative complaint procedure through the DOL. If you believe that your agency is failing or refusing to comply with USERRA, you may file a complaint with the DOL. You may also file a complaint with the DOL if you are entitled to reemployment with the Federal government but your agency or OPM is not complying with USERRA. The complaint must be in writing and be consistent with OPM's and/or the DOL's regulations.[25]

---

[24] *See* 5 CFR § 630.504.

[25] *See* 5 CFR § 630.504.

The complaint must include the name and address of the agency and a summary of the relevant facts. Both you and the agency can ask the DOL for technical assistance in drafting the complaint.

The DOL is responsible for investigating the complaint. If it finds that your agency violated USERRA, the DOL must try to resolve the complaint by convincing your agency to reemploy you. If your agency refuses, the DOL must notify you of the results of the investigation and your rights to further pursue the matter.

The informal complaint procedure could be beneficial. For example, the DOL could encourage an agency to comply with USERRA before you have to file a formal complaint, which may result in protracted litigation. In addition, and as explained below, if you file the complaint with the DOL first, you could be represented by the Office of Special Counsel.

Merit Systems Protection Board appeals

If you believe that your agency or OPM is not complying with USERRA, you may either file a complaint with the DOL or directly with the MSPB.[26] If you file with DOL, you must exhaust the DOL investigative process before proceeding to the MSPB. If you file with the DOL, and if the DOL is unable to resolve the complaint, the DOL must inform you of your right to continue to pursue your complaint. You must then ask the DOL to refer the complaint for litigation before the MSPB. The DOL must also refer the complaint to the Office of Special Counsel ("OSC"). If DOL is unable to resolve the complaint, you may file a USERRA appeal directly with the MSPB or ask DOL to refer the complaint to OSC. If OSC agrees to represent you, OSC may file a USERRA appeal directly with the MSPB. If OSC does not agree to represent you, you may file a USERRA appeal directly with the Board.[27]

The Special Counsel may, but is not required to, represent you in your complaint against the agency. If the Special Counsel declines to do so, he or she must notify you of that decision. You are then entitled to retain a lawyer or other representative and file your own an appeal with the MSPB.

If the MSPB finds that a federal executive agency or OPM has violated USERRA, the Board will order the agency or OPM to comply with the Act and to compensate you for any resulting loss of wages or benefits. Compliance

---

[26] *See* 5 CFR § 1208.11(a).

[27] *See* 5 CFR § 1208.11.

may involve reinstating you or placing you in an appropriate position. The Board may also award reasonable attorney fees, expert witness fees, and other litigation expenses. The MSPB's regulations governing USERRA appeals are found at 5 CFR 1208.

If the MSPB does not rule in your favor, you may file an appeal to the United States Court of Appeals for the Federal Circuit to review the Board's final order or decision.

Other protections and appeal rights

If you believe that an intelligence agency (for example, the FBI, CIA, or NSA), GAO, or a quasi-governmental corporation has not complied with USERRA, you may submit a claim to the Inspector General of the agency. The Inspector General must investigate and resolve the allegation according to procedures prescribed by the head of the agency.

Final Thoughts

Veterans and other federal employees who serve in the uniformed services have important protections for their federal civilian employment. They are protected from discrimination. They may receive preferential treatment in civil service applications and in RIFs. They may benefit from affirmative action plans designed to make federal agencies take an active, rather than passive, role in their employment. When such employees temporarily leave their employment for service-related activities, they are entitled to be reinstated to the same or a similar position, with little or no loss in benefits, leave, and other rights. If this chapter applies to you, know your rights and exercise them to make sure you suffer no workplace disadvantage from serving your country in the uniformed services.

20

Ethics in Government

Do The Right Thing

In This Chapter You Will Learn:

- what your ethical responsibilities are as a federal employee
- what happens if you violate government ethics rules

Contents Chapter Twenty - Ethics in Government

Introduction

Whether or not you are already worried about complying with government ethics rules, this chapter is for you. One reason folks avoid the subject of ethics is because it sounds boring, or like stuff we were born or raised knowing, such as the Golden Rule. Ethics can be boring because it is a set of detailed rules—the "do's and don'ts." But ethics rules are not entirely instinctive, nor do they always seem logical. For instance, is it ethical under the rules to give your supervisor, whom you also consider a friend, a $20 birthday gift? No. Is it ethical to give your supervisor, whom you also consider a friend, a $50 wedding gift? Yes.

The U.S. Office of Government Ethics ("OGE") is the federal agency responsible for issuing government-wide regulations and overseeing the enforcement of ethical standards. There is one set of regulations called the "Standards of Ethical Conduct" which applies to all federal employees.[1] As you read this chapter, the appropriate regulatory reference will be shown in parentheses or in footnotes so that you can obtain and read the full regulation if necessary. In addition to these government-wide ethics rules, each agency is free to issue additional ethics rules, and many agencies do so. Therefore, it is always a good idea to ask your agency's personnel officer or ethics officer for a set of the agency's ethics rules.

---

[1] *See* 5 CFR Part 2635.

Are there any guiding principles I can use to determine ethical conduct?

The Standards of Ethical Conduct begin by explaining some general principles of ethics for government employees. There are many other rules that are far more specific about what you can and cannot do as a government employee. However, almost all of those rules are just applications of these general principles. So don't worry if you can't remember all of the rules that are discussed in this chapter. If you keep the general principles in mind, and apply them carefully, you should not find yourself in trouble for an ethics violation.

The first principle explains the reason all these rules exist. This principle says "Public service is a public trust, requiring employees to place loyalty to the Constitution, the laws and ethical principles, above private gain."[2] As an employee of the government, you are a unique individual—someone who is dedicating your career to protecting and defending the public interest. Every citizen in the United States trusts you to represent his/her interests, not your own. Most of the other general principles reflect this idea.

The other principles provide that government employees shall:

- not hold financial interests that conflict with the conscientious performance of duty
- not engage in financial transactions using nonpublic government information or allow the improper use of such information to further any private interest
- not [except as discussed below] solicit or accept any gift or other item of monetary value from any person or entity seeking official action from, doing business with, or conducting activities regulated by the employee's agency, or whose interests may be substantially affected by the performance or nonperformance of the employee's duties
- put forth honest effort in the performance of their duties
- not knowingly make unauthorized commitments or promises of any kind purporting to bind the government
- not use public office for private gain
- act impartially and not give preferential treatment to any private organization or individual
- protect and conserve federal property and not use it for other than authorized activities

---

2 *See* 5 CFR § 2635.101(b)(1).

- not engage in outside employment or activities, including seeking or negotiating for employment, that conflict with official government duties and responsibilities
- disclose waste, fraud, abuse, and corruption to appropriate authorities
- satisfy in good faith their obligations as citizens, including all just financial obligations, especially those—such as federal, state, or local taxes—that are imposed by law
- adhere to all laws and regulations that provide equal opportunity for all Americans regardless of race, color, religion, sex, national origin, age, or handicap
- endeavor to avoid any actions creating the appearance that they are violating the law or the ethical standards set forth above. Whether particular circumstances create an appearance that the law or these standards have been violated shall be determined from the perspective of a reasonable person with knowledge of the relevant facts[3]

It sure seems like a lot of principles. But they can be summarized like this:

- Do a day's work for a day's pay.
- Do your duty as a citizen by following the law.
- Do not use your position to benefit yourself, and stay out of situations where it might look like you are using your position for personal gain.
- Do not give preferential treatment to anyone or discriminate against anyone, and do not do anything that might look like you are giving preferential treatment or acting in a discriminatory way.
- Do use government resources only for government purposes.

You should try to apply these principles to everything you do. Think about these principles particularly hard when you are faced with a situation that is not specifically covered by the other Standards of Ethical Conduct. You can be disciplined for violating the regulatory standards. In extreme cases, where you know that you are violating ethical standards, you can even be charged with a crime. So be careful whenever you think there is a possible ethical question concerning your work or activities.

What should I do if I'm in doubt?[4]

When in doubt, talk to your agency's ethics officer. If you rely in good faith on the advice of the ethics officer, you cannot be subject to disciplin-

---

3 *See* 5 CFR § 2635.101(b).
4 *See* 5 CFR § 2635.107(b).

ary action. It is advisable to confirm all advice from an ethics officer in writing.[5]

Be cautious in your conversations with ethics officers. They are reliable resources you should consult before taking any step you think is questionable. However, you need to be careful about what you disclose if you think that you may have already committed an ethics violation. Your discussion with an ethics officer is not necessarily confidential. An ethics officer is required to report any information about criminal violations.[6] Consider consulting an attorney first if you think you may have committed a criminal ethics violation.

The Standards also point out there might be special rules for employees detailed or assigned to other agencies, other branches of the government, or to state or local governments or international organizations. If you are in one of these situations, talk to your agency ethics officer about what rules may apply to you.

What are the ethics do's and don'ts?

The general principles state that you should not use your position for personal gain. They also make it clear that you should not get yourself into situations where it looks like you might be tempted to give someone preferential treatment. As a result, there are a lot of specific rules governing the giving and receiving of gifts. These rules can be divided into two parts—rules concerning gifts from outside sources and gifts from other federal employees.

TIP

The rules state that "an employee shall not, directly or indirectly, solicit or accept a gift" either from a "prohibited source" or "given because of the employee's official position." [7]

---

5 If you violate a criminal statute in reliance an ethics officer's advice, this is no guarantee that you will not be criminally prosecuted.

6 *See* 5 CFR § 2635.107(b).

7 *See* 5 CFR § 2635.202(a).

The rules about gifts from individuals who are not government employees are called rules about "gifts from outside sources." The general rule concerning soliciting or accepting gifts from outside sources is:

> "Except as otherwise permitted, an employee shall not, directly or indirectly, solicit or accept a gift from a prohibited source or because of the employee's official position."

A "prohibited source" is a person or company or other organization that could be seriously affected (for good or bad) by an action for which you or your agency is responsible.[8] A "prohibited source" also includes organizations of which more than half of the members are themselves "prohibited sources." A prohibited source is also a person or organization that is seeking official action by your agency, or a person or organization that does business or is seeking to do business with your agency. A gift is "solicited or accepted...because of the employee's official position" if the gift exists only because of your position as a federal employee.[9]

Whenever you are thinking about asking for, or accepting, a gift, you should think about:

- whether the person giving the gift could possibly be interested in the outcome of something that you or your agency have authority over, and
- whether you would have received the gift if you had not been a federal employee

This rule applies not only to gifts given to you, but to gifts given with your knowledge to your family members or to charitable organizations at your suggestion.[10]

The term "gift" is defined[11] very broadly under this rule to include meals and nearly everything else of monetary value. There are a few exceptions. For instance, you *can* accept:

- "modest" items of food and refreshment, such as soft drinks or coffee and donuts, offered other than as part of a meal

---

[8] *See* 5 CFR § 2635.203(d).
[9] *See* 5 CFR § 2635.203(e).
[10] *See* 5 CFR § 2635.203(f).
[11] *See* 5 CFR § 2635.203(b).

- items with "little intrinsic value," like greeting cards, plaques, certificates, and trophies that are "intended solely for presentation"
- items that everyone receives on terms generally available to members of the public, including loans from banks and other financial institutions (as long as the terms for the loan are similar to those made available to the general public)
- prizes awarded in contests you enter for reasons other than your official employment
- favorable rates and commercial discounts made available to the public at large
- favorable rates and discounts if they are made available to all government employees or all uniformed military personnel
- pensions and other benefits that you earned from a former employer
- items paid for by the government "or secured by the Government under Government contract"
- items that are "accepted by the government under specific statutory authority,"[12] such as travel expenses accepted by an agency under the authority of 31 USC 1353 in connection with an employee's attendance at a meeting or similar function relating to his official duties which takes place away from his duty station, and other gifts provided in kind which have been accepted by an agency under its agency gift acceptance statute.

TIP

In general, "frequent flier" benefits earned on the basis of government-financed travel may be used for personal use, but not in all cases.

There are specific rules about keeping free flights and other benefits awarded to frequent fliers. Refer to the detailed notes provided with the regulation.[13]

---

[12] *See* 5 CFR § 2635.203(b)(8).

[13] *See* 5 CFR § 2635.203(b)(7) and 41 CFR Part 301-53.

Special rules apply to frequent flier miles, which have changed over the years. For example, while you are travelling on government business and at government expense, the flight attendant offers you an opportunity to register for the airline's frequent flier program. The attendant takes your name, verifies your destination, and asks you to sign a form. Prior to 2001, you would have been in violation of the ethics rules if you signed up to participate in your own name with the benefit going to you personally. Now it is permitted, but not in all cases. See 41 CFR Part 301-53 for details.

Some exceptions to the rules on accepting outside gifts One general exception permits you to accept any gift[14]—but only if you pay "fair market value" for it.

- If someone gives you a new jacket, you can accept it as long as you give them what it would cost to purchase an essentially identical jacket at a local store.

- If you receive a ticket to a nice dinner you would need to pay the face price of the ticket—not the actual price of the meal. For example, if someone gives you a $250 ticket to a charitable event consisting of a reception with refreshments and chamber music worth about $20, you would be obligated to pay the $250 face value of the ticket.

There are a number of other exceptions to the rule against accepting gifts. You may, for instance:[15]

- accept items from a single source as long as the gifts have a total market value of $20 or less per occasion, and as long as the total from that source does not go over $50 in a year. This exception does not apply to cash or investment interests, like stocks, bonds, or CD's
- receive a gift if it is "clearly motivated by a family relationship or personal friendship."[16] The agency may look at the history of the relationship to see if it is genuine and find out whether a family member or friend is paying for the gift to see if the purpose is work-related

If you receive a gift on one occasion worth $30, you cannot reimburse the source of the gift $10 and keep the gift. If you can divide the gift into

---

14 *See* 5 CFR § 2635.203(b)(9).

15 *See* 5 CFR § 2635.204.

16 *See* 5 CFR § 2635.204(a) and (b).

parts, for example, a $40 pen and pencil set, you can accept $20 worth of its parts (pen) and decline the remaining part (pencil).

As noted earlier, you can accept discounts as long as they are made available to all government employees. In some situations, you can accept discounts not made available to all government employees as long as they are based solely on:

- professional qualifications, or
- where the discount is "[o]ffered to members of an organization, such as an employees' association or agency credit union, in which membership is related to government employment if the same offer is broadly available to large segments of the public through organizations of similar size"

There is one catch, however. If you buy something with government money and get a bonus item or discount as a result of that purchase, that item or discount remains the property of the government.[17] This exception does not apply to frequent flier miles, flight upgrades and access to air carrier clubs as an accrued benefit from government travel, so long as the benefits accrue the same way as they do for the general flying public.[18]

There are a few other exceptions to the prohibition on receiving gifts from outside parties in connection with receiving awards.[19]

- You can accept gifts (except cash or investments) associated with awards as long as they have an "aggregate market value of $*200 or less*" and the awarder is not a prohibited source.

- You can accept awards *over $200* in certain limited situations. If the award is a regular event and made according to written standards, talk with your ethics officer about receiving a waiver. You will also need to talk with your ethics officer if you are to be awarded an honorary degree. You will need a "written determination by an agency ethics official that the timing of the award of the degree would not cause a reasonable person to question your impartiality in a matter affecting the institution." If you accept one of these awards or degrees, it is also permissible to accept meals and entertainment given to you, and to members of your family, at the event at which the award is presented.

---

17 *See* 5 CFR § 2635.204(c).

18 *See* 41 CFR § 301-10.123 note, 301-53.1 *et seq.*

19 *See* 5 CFR § 2635.204(d).

You can also accept meals, transportation, and other benefits from a non-prohibited source if it is due to your or your spouse's private employment or business relationships and as long as it is not really intended to influence you.[20]

For example, if you work for the FDIC and your spouse works for an FDIC-member bank, you may attend a theater event with your spouse even if the tickets, valued at $80 each, came from the member as an "employee appreciation" bonus. The gift is not meant to influence you. Your attendance is a result of your personal relationship.

If you have already disqualified yourself from involvement in work on certain projects due to an ethics conflict, as required under the ethics rules (discussed below) when you are looking for a job outside the federal government, you may accept gifts which are customarily provided as a part of "bona fide" employment discussions with a potential employer.[21]

There are other exceptions which permit you to accept meals, transportation, lodging, free attendance at concerts or events, and other benefits. Under the Hatch Act, if you are permitted to engage in political activities (for example, take an active part in political campaigns), you may accept meals and lodging, transportation, and other benefits in connection with these activities so long as these benefits are provided by a qualifying political organization.

If it is not a political activity, but a widely attended gathering (100 or more people) or other event, you may participate as a speaker or simply attend at no cost if the event's sponsor provides the benefit of free attendance, if your participation is a customary and necessary part of your job assignment, and if no other gift is involved. Your agency must make a prior determination that:

- your attendance is in the interest of the agency
- the fair market value is $250 or less, and
- the gathering will include persons with a diversity of viewpoints

If the sponsor of an event or a majority of the members of the organization extending an invitation have interests that may be substantially affected by your official duties, you must obtain a written agency determination that the agency's interest in your free attendance outweighs a number of

---

[20] *See* 5 CFR § 2635.204(e).

[21] *See* 5 CFR § 2635.204(e)(3).

the concerns discussed earlier. Again, if your spouse is also offered free attendance, the fair market value of what is offered must not exceed $250 for both persons.

If you do not qualify under these exceptions, check with your ethics official or an attorney about other specific laws which may establish your right to accept the above benefits, because there are a few other statutes and agency regulations which may give you that right. Some of those statutes include the Foreign Gifts and Decorations Act[22] and a provision based upon the sponsor's tax exempt, non-profit status.[23]

There is a broader exception for attending a widely attended gathering or event when your cost of attendance is provided by a sponsor who bears the cost without actually designating which employee in your organization will be attending. If the sponsor is an organization, your dues to that organization will not prevent you from qualifying for this exception.

You may attend a social event sponsored by a non-prohibited source if the event is attended by several people, none of whom are charged any fees. You are entitled to accept free food, refreshments and entertainment, but you may not accept travel or lodgings under this specific exception.

If you are in a foreign country, you are a bit less restricted in accepting food, refreshments and entertainment when it is in conjunction with a meeting during a meal or other event and the local market value does not exceed the per diem rate for the area. There are other specifications about the attendees and purpose of meetings and events, so it is best to check out such situations with the ethics officer before you leave on a trip.

Even if one of these exceptions apply, it is always unethical to accept a gift in "return for being influenced in the performance of an official act," to "[s]olicit or coerce the offering of a gift," or to accept so many little gifts from one source that it would lead a reasonable person to believe that "the employee is using his public office for private gain."[24] It is, of course, also always impermissible to accept a gift which violates any other law, not just the rules set forth in the Standards of Ethical Conduct.

How to deal with improper gifts If you receive an improper gift, you must dispose of it properly.[25] Generally, you should simply return the gift,

---

22 *See* 5 USC § 7342.

23 *See* 5 USC § 4111.

24 *See* 5 CFR § 2605.202(c).

25 *See* 5 CFR § 2635.205.

or if that is impossible, pay its fair market value. It is permissible to accept a questionable gift publicly to save the giver public embarrassment, and return it after an event. If the gift cannot be returned because it is perishable, your supervisor or agency ethics officer may authorize it to be donated to an appropriate charity, shared with the agency, or destroyed. For instance, a flower arrangement may be placed on a reception desk. Gifts from foreign governments or as a result of official travel must be handled according to other specific regulations. Check with your supervisor or agency ethics officer on how to handle such problems.

Gifts between federal employees

The Standards of Ethical Conduct contain a general rule banning gift-giving and gift-receiving between employees who are in a supervisory relationship or who earn different salaries. The rule makes it unethical and illegal to attempt to "buy" a good performance rating from a superior, or cooperation from an employee. As usual and as will be discussed later, a few exceptions to the rule exist.

TIP

Remember the prevailing rule: If you try in good faith to comply with the rules, or if you sought and followed the advice of an agency ethics officer, you will not be subject to discipline for an error. The agency should work with you to resolve the situation.

The broad definition of a gift here—which includes meals and nearly everything else of monetary value—is the same as the one described earlier in this chapter, including the exceptions described. The rule cannot be skirted by having a family member give the banned gift to the other person, or by having someone else give the gift and reimbursing that person.

Carpooling counts as a gift and is banned in some situations, but it is permissible in others. Carpooling is allowed between the employees in a supervisory relationship or who earn different salaries so long as the employees bear the fair market value for their respective benefit of the carpooling.[26] So, despite what some may say about federal employment, there is no such thing as a free ride!

---

[26] *See* 5 CFR § 2635.303(a).

TIP

In general, the ethical standards prohibit an employee from giving, donating to, or soliciting contributions for, a gift to an official superior and from accepting a gift from an employee receiving less pay than him or herself, unless the item is excluded from the definition of a gift or falls within one of the exceptions to this rule.[27]

An exception to the general ban on gifts between certain federal employees applies when two employees are not in a supervisory relationship, there is a personal relationship present, and when the gift is appropriate for the level of friendship present.

Another exception applies for gifts given by employees to someone in their supervisory chain when it is in the form of a contribution for a group gift, like a luncheon, reception, or the like. This is a situation that often arises among well-intentioned office personnel who want to celebrate various occasions.

The contribution is only permissible if the person is made aware of precisely what proportionate share of the cost is being requested, along with the statement that "*you may choose to contribute less or not at all.*" These are magic words! Do not solicit gifts unless you include this phrase verbally or in writing. The only time you do not have to add the magic words is when the cost of the gift is going to be included with the cost of a luncheon, reception, or similar event.

For example, if the gift is a luncheon and everyone agrees to attend and split the cost of the supervisor's lunch eight ways, you can do it and the magic words are not necessary. If you are soliciting contributions for a plaque to give to the supervisor at a luncheon, you need to ask for a contribution toward the plaque and the luncheon with the phrase that "you may choose to contribute less or not at all."

If someone chooses to contribute less or not at all, you must respect that decision. If you make derogatory comments about someone's choice to contribute less or not at all, it may appear that you are coercing or intimidating others to contribute, which is also unethical.

---

[27] *See* 5 CFR § 2635.301.

Some exceptions to the rules against gifts between employees Two big exceptions apply to situations where gifts are traditionally exchanged.

- If the situation is a special or fairly rare occasion, like a marriage, birth, illness, death, or anything ending a work relationship, like retirement, resignation, or transfer to a different supervisory chain, a gift of an appropriate value for the occasion may be given voluntarily. For example, a $70 china place setting may be given to your supervisor and her husband if you attend their wedding. A $30 flower arrangement may be given to someone who is retiring.

- If the event is not so traditionally special or rare, then a $10 limit applies. For example, you can purchase and share with your office and supervisor an $8 box of saltwater taffy from your seashore vacation.

Somewhere in the middle is the "hospitality" exception, whether at the home or office. You can give a gift which is appropriate to the hospitality event and the level of friendship. For example, you may take a $15 bottle of wine to your supervisor's home under typical circumstances. You can also accept or give refreshments to be shared by people at the office. Christmas is not an event which is rare or of personal significance between you and your supervisor; thus you cannot take up a collection to buy your supervisor a Christmas gift. If everyone wants to contribute for refreshments for a party —celebrating anything—that would be fine.

The general rule is that gifts to your supervisor are not allowed. If you believe the situation is subject to an exception, you are safest by limiting it to $10 or less. If you solicit contributions for a gift, keep the request for money minimal, in the range of $5-$10. Always tell others that the gift is purely voluntary and they may give less or nothing at all.

Conflicting financial interests

This rule also prohibits you from official participation in anything which will have a similar impact on the financial interest of your spouse, your general business partner, an organization in which you serve as an officer, director, trustee, general partner or employee, or person with whom you are negotiating prospective employment.[28]

The general rule broadly prohibits you from having any serious involvement in a task which you think would affect one or more of your investments,

[28] *See* 5 CFR § 2635.401 *et seq.*

one of your family's investments, or one of your business associates' investments. You are also prohibited from taking action on something which would affect the financial interests of an organization or person with whom you are seeking employment.

TIP

You are prohibited from participating personally and substantially in an official capacity in any matter in which you have a financial interest, if that matter will have a direct and predictable effect on your financial interest.

If you violate these prohibitions, you can be charged with a crime and receive jail time if convicted. Even if you are not charged with a crime, you could be disciplined and lose your job.

A "financial interest" can be almost anything of value.[29] Most frequently, you will find that stock ownership gives you a financial interest which might result in a conflict of interest on the job. There are numerous other financial interests which must be looked at for conflicts of interest, such as:

- any type of future or present interest in property
- business or employment relationships
- bonds
- partnership interests
- leases
- future stock options
- commodity futures

Future interests of other family members are excluded, as are rights in an unsettled estate.

Financial interests can also include volunteer or paid work for certain organizations or outside employers when the organization or outside employer has a financial interest in your work. An example is if you serve as volunteer vice-president for the local Rails-to-Trails biking organization, and your organization depends upon federal grants from the Department of the Interior. You may have a conflict of financial interest which will

---

[29] *See* 5 CFR § 2625.403(c).

prevent you from serving as a project manager at the Department of Interior where your job involves decision-making concerning your agency's grant program. In this example, you may be forced to give up your volunteer position because you cannot disqualify yourself while still performing your expected duties.

The regulatory language[30] splits hairs over the degree of involvement you are allowed to have in a task and whether it is probable that your task will have a direct enough effect on your financial interests to require you to remove yourself from the task.

- If you are not directly involved in the task, you may not have a conflict.
- If the impact on your financial interest is only speculative or subject to the flux of the general economy, you would not have to disqualify yourself.
- If the dollar amount of the impact is unknown, or even if you know it will be minimal, you still would have a financial conflict.

If your financial interest—or that of your family or business associates—is at stake you must inform you supervisor and disqualify yourself from further involvement in your assigned task. If the conflict concerns a prospective employer, you must follow the directions for disqualification described in a different section of the regulations (discussed below). Generally, this means that you simply remove yourself from involvement in the task.

Occasionally, a written statement of disqualification might be requested of you. You may decide on your own that it would protect your interests to write one and file it with your supervisor and ethics officer. You may also need to inform your coworkers or subordinates that, due to a conflict of interest, you should not be involved in a certain task. This notification will help ensure that you are not included in discussions or receive communications about the matter creating the conflict.

When you might receive a waiver of conflict In some instances when you have a financial conflict, you may be eligible to receive a waiver of the conflict.[31] There are specific guidelines in the regulations which describe when waivers may be an option. In general, you may be eligible for a waiver if your financial interest is "too remote or inconsequential to affect the integrity" of your services.[32] You can approach your agency's ethics officer

---

30 *See* 5 CFR § 2635.402(b)(1).

31 *See* 5 USC § 2635.402(d)(2).

32 *See* 5 USC § 2635.402(d).

for a waiver or go directly to the Office of Government Ethics. You are only eligible for a waiver if:

- you request one prior to engaging in the activity
- you make a full disclosure of your conflict, and
- the official finds that it is not a substantial conflict

If you receive a waiver, the government decided that your participation outweighs the concern that a reasonable person may question the integrity of agency programs and operations. If you have already participated in the matter and violated the law, it is too late to request a waiver.

If no waivers apply, however, and your financial interest would detract from your ability to carry out your job or the agency's mission, the agency can require that you sell or divest yourself of your financial interest.[33] You will have no more than *90 days* to carry out the order to divest.[34] The good news is that if you are directed to divest, you will receive a "certificate of divestiture" which will probably entitle you to special tax provisions which may remove any financial sting suffered from selling or otherwise divesting yourself of the financial interest.[35]

Some official duties are likely to create financial conflicts of interest. When you can identify a potential conflict ahead of time, the Standards of Ethical Conduct require you to notify your supervisor right away. Certain assignments and conflicts can then be avoided. When the government identifies certain financial interests which would cause a "reasonable person" to question the integrity of agency programs, the agency can prohibit or restrict you (and your family) from those financial interests. If the agency can determine ahead of time that your financial interest would detract from your ability to carry out your job or the agency's mission, the agency can prohibit you from obtaining certain financial interests.[36]

If you are unsure whether you should disqualify yourself, seek the advice of your supervisor and, if still unsure, from the agency's ethics officer. However, it is also a good idea to obtain a copy of the regulations and review your situation. When you are concerned about whether you have a conflict, or believe that you may have already violated ethics rules, you should seek legal advice for an independent assessment of your particular situation

---

33 *See* 5 CFR § 2635.402(e)(2).

34 *See* 5 CFR § 2635.403(d).

35 *See* 5 CFR § 2635.402(e)(3).

36 *See* 5 CFR § 2635.403(a).

and an analysis of the regulations. The agency's ethics official is only a good resource *before* something happens. Conversations between you and ethics officials are not confidential. Unlike lawyers, they have no duty to keep the information you provide them confidential.

IMPARTIALITY IN PERFORMING OFFICIAL DUTIES

Even if you analyzed your financial interests and decided you were not disqualified from a given undertaking, you still might have to disqualify yourself temporarily if someone who knew the facts would question your impartiality.[37] The agency can authorize you to continue your assignment despite this concern or appearance of bias if the agency determines that your service is more valuable to the agency than the possibility that someone would question the integrity of the agency's programs because of your participation.

TIP

You have an absolute duty to perform your duties impartially, meaning without any bias in favor of or against someone. If you realize that your participation might look biased, you have a duty to refrain from participating in the activity until you receive special authorization.

The factors that the agency would look at in determining whether to authorize an employee's continued participation include:

- the nature of the relationship involved
- the effect of the financial interest on you or others
- the type of responsibility you have for the work and whether you must exercise discretion
- the sensitivity of the task involved
- the difficulty in substituting another employee to carry out the work, and
- adjustments that could be made to eliminate the appearance of bias

One basis for alleging a bias would be a financial interest in the matter at hand. A possible conflict of interest due to financial interest should be dealt with as described above and may result in disqualifying you from that activity. But even if it is not technically a substantial financial interest

[37] *See* 5 CFR § 2635.501*et seq.*

conflict, if the appearance of such conflict is still present, you should get special authorization to continue your work.

TIP

When you are dealing with an organization which previously gave you a payment of over $10,000, you are banned for two years from working on matters related to that organization unless you obtain a waiver.

Another basis for alleging a bias would be prior severance or other "extraordinary" payment to you from a private sector entity.[38] This provision is also meant to prohibit you from working on a particular matter when your relatives, business associates, or other persons with whom you have a personal relationship, represent a party in that matter.[39] Normally, this results in the appearance of likely bias, and special authorization must be sought to continue your official duties.

Just as you are prohibited from working on a particular matter when it involves your relatives, you will also be disqualified from working on a matter which involves an organization in which you are an active participant. Active participation in a political party (defined in 26 USC 527(e)) will not disqualify you. Active participation means "service" in an organization such as being a committee chairperson, spokesperson, or directing activities.[40] For example, significant time devoted to promoting programs or coordinating fundraising would disqualify you from participating in a matter dealing with that organization. Simply paying dues or donating or soliciting financial support would not mean that you are an active participant, and hence, would not disqualify you.

Your political, religious, or moral views cannot disqualify you from working on a specific matter. For example, if the matter involves a decision regarding health care funding or programming, your moral, religious, or political views on abortion could not prevent your participation.

---

38 *See* 5 CFR § 2635.501 and 2635.503.
39 *See* 5 CFR § 2635.501.
40 *See* 5 CFR § 2635.502(b)(1)(v).

There is also a federal law which specifically prohibits you from seeking employment or having any arrangement concerning prospective employment with a prospective employer if you participate personally and substantially in decisions affecting that prospective employer.[41] You are subject to criminal penalties if found guilty of violating this ethical rule. You must disqualify yourself from any matters which would create this problem before you seek employment.[42] Again, speculative effects are not substantial enough to be worried about. But even if a substantial conflict does not exist, the appearance of a conflict could disqualify you.

"Seeking employment" includes sending out targeted resumes, having job interviews and conducting negotiations aimed at determining terms of employment. Seeking employment can also include networking through others. You will be banned from these job-seeking activities unless you disqualify yourself first from the particular matters creating the possible conflict. The disqualification will last until you are *no longer seeking employment* from the banned organization or until *two months* pass without any interest or activity related to your overtures for employment from the organization.[43]

TIP

You are banned from seeking any type of outside employment with any non-federal organization when you know it would have a direct and predictable effect on your financial interests.

If you already have an arrangement for future employment with an organization from which you would be banned from seeking employment, you must disqualify yourself or seek a waiver to carry on your duties. You *are* allowed to:

- reject an unsolicited job or a job possibility
- request a job application

---

41 *See* 18 USC § 208(a).
42 *See* 5 CFR § 2635.604.
43 *See* 5 CFR § 2635.603(b).

- send a resume or application to someone who is only generally affected by your work[44]

Generally, a job search "mass mailing" does not present a problem because those initial contacts are rather distant. If you get a follow-up call and begin interviewing and have more serious negotiations, you must analyze whether you fall within the prohibited area of seeking employment.

You may disqualify yourself by removing yourself from official duties relating to that prospective employer or seek a waiver to carry on your official duties during otherwise prohibited job search activities. If you are not in a position to remove yourself effectively from work related to that employer, you will need to discuss the problem with your supervisor or seek a waiver.

"Revolving door" restrictions There are specific ethical restrictions for the "revolving door" situation that may occur when you leave government for a private sector position. The restrictions are aimed at instances when you "switch sides" on a particular matter. These post-federal employment restrictions are governed by a government-wide post-employment law (18 USC 207) and implementing regulations (5 CFR Parts 1304 & 2641). In particular, you will find that there are many post-employment restrictions for federal procurement officials and Department of Defense employees. Attorneys also must abide by the "revolving door" restrictions which may exist in state law and legal ethics rules.

The basic prohibition of 18 USC 207 states that no former government employee, after terminating government employment, shall knowingly act as agent or attorney for, or otherwise represent any other person in any formal or informal appearance before, or with the intent to influence, make any oral or written communication on behalf of any other person:

- to the United States
- in connection with any particular government matter involving a specific party, and
- in which matter such employee participated personally and substantially as a government employee

Prohibited representation means acting as agent or attorney, or other representative in an appearance, or communicating with the intent to influence.

---

44 *See* 5 CFR § 2635.603(b)(1)(ii,iii).

The statutory prohibition on representation covers any other former employee. As a general rule, these restrictions take three forms: lifetime restrictions on representation on matters which the former employee was personally directly involved; restrictions (typically 2 years) on representation in matters which were in the former employee's scope of authority but for which there was no direct involvement; and restrictions (typically 1-2 years) on senior-level former employees engaging in representation involving their former agency on any topic or representing foreign entities.[45] A close look at the regulations or consultation with your agency ethics official is necessary before moving to that new job.

An example in the statute of a prohibited representation is the prohibition that will apply to a former employee against acting as an expert witness in a lawsuit involving a matter in which the former employee was involved absent a court order (although permitting testimony as a fact witness). The regulations contain many illustrative examples of how to apply these rules in various circumstances.

Prohibited appearances are any communications made with the intent to influence. A physical appearance in either a formal or informal setting is prohibited. An appearance by conveying material via correspondence, telephone calls, and e-mail, is also prohibited in most cases.[46] Although some exceptions do exist (for example, for some forms of public speaking), these exceptions are very specific. Careful review of the regulations or consultation with the agency ethics official is highly advisable before proceeding with any such event.

TIP

Do not use anything you learn from work or are officially entitled to for your own or others' personal gain.

---

[45] *See* 5 CFR § 2641.104 and 2641.201 *et seq.*

[46] *See* 5 CFR § 2641.201.

Misuse of position

The general standard of conduct concerning the use of your position, title, authority, and official information is logical. Do not try to peddle your influence with your government ID card or make endorsements or promises for others with your official position. Anything which is confidential or not subject to release to the public under the Freedom of Information Act cannot be disclosed to others because it is not public information. Protect and preserve government property and use it only for its intended purpose. It belongs to the taxpayers. Work an honest day's work on your official duties. Take leave to attend to your personal needs.

Misusing your position on or off "the clock" or misusing government property entrusted to you are some of the most common types of ethical violations. In most cases, such misuse of your position will result in disciplinary or adverse action being taken against you. Refer to Chapter 4 for more information on how to deal with such situations. But be smart. Avoid getting into bad situations by complying with your ethical obligations.

Restrictions on outside activities

If you want to hold a second job or hold an appointment or leadership-type position outside of your job, whether paid or unpaid, you must refrain entirely or in some instances from the following activities:

- working at a job or holding an appointment outside the government (whether paid or unpaid) that conflicts with your official duties or which would violate a law, rule, or regulation
- failing to comply with any agency requirement for prior approval of outside employment or activities
- earning outside income if you are a Presidential appointee or other 'covered non-career employee,' as defined in the regulations[47]
- testifying as an expert witness (not all such activity is banned—consult your agency's ethics officer)
- participating in professional organizations (not all such activity is banned—consult your agency's ethics officer)
- paid and unpaid teaching, speaking, and writing (not all such activity is banned—consult your agency's ethics officer)
- fundraising activities (not all such activity is banned—consult your agency's ethics officer)

---

47 *See* 5 CFR § 2636.303(a).

TIP

The Standards of Ethical Conduct prohibit and restrict many different kinds of activities which you may engage in outside of work because these activities may create or appear to create a conflict with how well or honestly you could perform your duties.

There are at least nine specific laws, rules, and regulations which prohibit you from holding certain types of outside jobs or appointments. The above Standards of Ethical Conduct by the Office of Government Ethics are one set of regulations which compel your disqualification from certain types of outside activities if performing them would violate a Standard of Ethical Conduct.

There are also criminal statutes which make it illegal to accept a "bribe" or inducement to do or not do something in your official capacity. The government also specifically prohibits you from appearing before or acting as a representative or attorney for someone who has a claim against the United States government—your employer—whether such representation would be in an executive branch, legislative branch, or judicial branch setting, with potential criminal consequences.[48] The U.S. Constitution Article 1, Section 9 says that you cannot become an agent of a foreign government or accept gifts from a foreign government because it makes you seem like a foreign agent. The Hatch Act, discussed in Chapter 23, specifically prohibits certain political activities, some of which would independently be a violation of the above Standards of Ethical Conduct.

Another very important area is your ethical obligation to satisfy in good faith all "just" financial obligations.[49] This means you are expected to honor your legitimate financial obligations, whether to a former spouse, to credit card companies, or to anyone else with whom you have a financial obligation. A judge's alimony or child support order must be obeyed. The intent here is basically to preserve the notion that federal employees are honorable in paying their debts. There are other provisions of law which provide for offsetting or garnishing of your wages and income, and even your tax refund. See Chapter 27 for a more detailed discussion of how this takes place.

48 *See* 18 USC § 205.
49 *See* 5 CFR § 2535.101(b)(12).

As a federal employee, getting into financial trouble is not just a personal concern, but an ethical one, as well. Consult the regulations for specific information on the other limitations listed above. In some cases, only your agency will have the agency-specific guidance you will need. If you are unsure about what course of action to take, consult with an agency ethics officer and get his/her advice in writing.

Are there other ethics rules I should be aware of?

The Presidential Executive Order which ordered the Office of Government Ethics to establish government-wide regulations also ordered OPM to issue supplemental ethics rules for areas not covered by the Office of Government Ethics. In February 1993, OPM published three more rules of ethics.

OPM's regulations prohibit gambling while on duty or on government property,[50] criminal or disgraceful conduct,[51] and preparing anyone for an OPM exam or the Foreign Service exam through teaching, lecturing, or writing.[52]

How do I handle charges of unethical conduct?

You may face charges of unethical conduct from your agency or from law enforcement officials in a criminal proceeding.[53] An agency can discipline you or propose adverse action based upon its finding of unethical conduct just as it could in cases of employee misconduct or non-performance. Some of the charges of unethical conduct can also be brought as criminal offenses, which raises the stakes quite a bit higher. If criminal charges are brought, you likely will also receive discipline if criminal wrongdoing is found. Refer to your agency's table of penalties for an idea of how severely your agency may punish verified charges of unethical conduct. Also refer to Chapter 4 for a discussion of your rights and defenses when facing discipline or proposed adverse action.

The Office of Government Ethics can order you to take corrective action regardless of what disciplinary actions your agency may or may not also impose. For example, if the Office of Government Ethics discovers that you are involved in a conflict of financial interest, it may order you to divest yourself of your financial interest. You must comply. If you do not, you surely would face stiffer penalties, perhaps even lose your job.

---

50 *See* 5 CFR § 735.201.

51 *See* 5 CFR § 735.203.

52 *See* 5 CFR § 735.202.

53 *See* 5 CFR § 2635.106.

The Office of Government Ethics cannot propose or carry out discipline against you for your unethical conduct or failure to abide by its orders to take corrective action, but the Director of the Office of Government Ethics can recommend to the agency that you be disciplined.[54] The Office of Government Ethics, like any federal agency, can also refer charges of unethical conduct to the appropriate U.S. attorney or other law enforcement official for consideration and processing of civil or criminal prosecution.

TIP

Have questions? Need advice? The Office of Government Ethics invites you to consult with your agency ethics officer, or contact their office at:

Office of Government Ethics
1201 New York Avenue, NW Suite 500
Washington, DC 20005
(202)482-9300

Final Thoughts

Whew! That was a big chunk to swallow, wasn't it?—especially learning that some ethical missteps could mean criminal charges being brought against you. Your best defense is a good offense. Know the ethical rules and abide by them. Some may seem silly or meaningless—that is, until you recall the powerful position you are in as a federal employee. You represent the federal government. From the clerk who opens the mail to the director who runs the agency, all are agents of the federal government and carry with them some semblance of the power of the federal government. Guarding against misuse of power is a must.

---

[54] *See* 5 CFR § 2638.501 *et seq.*

21

Constitutional Rights

I Got Rights!... Don't I?

In This Chapter You Will Learn:

- what Constitutional rights are afforded you as a federal employee
- what right an employer has to search or test you for drugs
- what to do if your rights are violated

Contents Chapter Twenty-One - Constitutional Rights

INTRODUCTION

As a federal employee, you are sometimes in a strange position when it comes to your status. On the one hand, you essentially are the government, since, as an employee, you are hired to conduct its business. On the other hand, you are also a citizen who has important Constitutional rights that cannot be infringed. But when are you the government and when are you a citizen, who enjoys the important freedoms the law grants? Sometimes it is difficult to determine. In this chapter we will inform you what Constitutional rights you have as a federal employee, and how you can ensure that these rights are not trampled.[1]

CAN I BE DISCIPLINED OR FIRED FOR SOMETHING I SAY OR WRITE? FREEDOM OF SPEECH.

Federal employees, like all United States citizens, have the right to freedom of speech under the First Amendment. So is it legal for your agency to take disciplinary measures against you because the agency disapproves of something you say or write? Yes, but with some important qualifications. The First Amendment of the United States Constitution provides that "Congress shall make no law...abridging the freedom of speech, or of the press." The term "speech" encompasses all types of communications. "Speech" includes words uttered by you as an employee, as well as writings produced by you.

But what exactly does "freedom of speech" mean? This is a difficult question to answer, but there is one thing for certain: "freedom of speech" does *not* give you, as a federal employee, the absolute right to say and write whatever you want. Certain types of speech are not protected by the First

[1] Please note that this chapter discusses free speech and other Constitutional rights outside of formal complaint procedures. For a discussion of your statutory rights in the context of protected whistleblowing or disclosures regarding discrimination, see Chapters 7 and 6, respectively.

Amendment. If you engage in "speech" which is not protected by the First Amendment, your agency can take disciplinary action against you.

To be protected, speech must relate to a matter of "public concern"

Only certain speech is protected by the First Amendment. To be protected, the speech must relate to a matter of "public concern." The determination of whether a particular matter relates to the "public concern" is based upon the individual facts of each case. As a general rule, speech is considered to be of "public concern" if it has to do with political, social, or other matters of community concern.

TIP

Freedom of speech has limits. You can't yell "fire" in a crowded theater, if there is no fire. Similarly, speech which is disruptive of government operations will generally not be protected by the courts.

Here are some examples to help you determine when speech is Constitutionally protected. The Supreme Court has determined that:

- a letter written by a teacher to a local newspaper, criticizing a proposed tax increase and the way the Board of Education dealt with proposals to raise new revenue for local schools, related to a matter of "public concern"[2]
- an employee's oral expression of disappointment that the assassination attempt on President Reagan failed, related to a matter of "public concern"[3]

As you can see from these examples, your criticisms of your employer may be protected as long as these criticisms are related to a matter of "public concern."

On the other hand, your speech about internal office matters or personal grievances will not be afforded the protection of the First Amendment because these internal or personal matters do not affect the "public concern."

---

2 *See Pickering v. Board of Ed. of Township High School Dist. 205, Will Cty.,* 391 US 563 (1968).
3 *See Rankin v. McPherson,* 483 US 378 (1987).

The Supreme Court determined that a questionnaire prepared by an agency employee which "pertained to the level of office morale" in a particular agency did not constitute a matter of public concern, and therefore was entitled to no protection under the First Amendment.

The balancing test

Establishing that your speech relates to a matter of "public concern" is only half the battle. If the court determines that your speech is a matter of public concern, then it might be protected under the First Amendment. However, it will not automatically be protected. Your speech will only be protected if your interest in commenting on a particular matter outweighs the government's interest in promoting the efficiency of the public service. Further, your speech will likely not be protected, if the speech is being made within the scope of your job duties.

TIP

Your speech about internal office matters or personal grievances will likely not be afforded the protection of the First Amendment. Be cautious when speaking about these types of matters in a way which is disruptive to the agency or your coworkers; you could be subject to disciplinary action.

In applying this balancing test, courts will analyze whether your speech affects your ability to perform the duties of your job, whether the speech is disruptive, and whether the speech is in your capacity as a private citizen versus as part of your job duties. To use a previous example, the words of the employee who wished that the attempted assassination of President Reagan was successful were protected by the First Amendment because the statements did not impact the employee's ability to do his job. In another example, speech by a court docketing clerk in a memorandum to his supervisor reporting possible misrepresentations in search warrant affidavits was found not protected, since it was speech in connection with his job duties rather than as a private citizen.[4] However, subpoenaed witness testimony has been found protected in some cases.[5]

---

4 *See Garcetti et al v. Ceballos,* 547 US 410 (2006).

5 *See Lane v. Franks et al,* 573 US __, No. 13-483(2014).

In addition, courts will examine the truthfulness of your statement. The importance of your interest in the speech is diminished if you knew that the statement was false when you made it.

Do I have to incriminate myself in an investigatory interview?

One of the most uncomfortable situations you will encounter as a federal employee is being subjected to questioning by management officials about misconduct you allegedly committed. Much like any other citizen charged with a crime, you have the "right to remain silent" if you are being interviewed about matters which could criminally incriminate you.

If you are questioned about alleged misconduct that you reasonably believe concerns a criminal offense, before answering you should inquire as to whether the misconduct could lead to criminal prosecution. If the agency refuses to answer your question, or answers "yes," then you can invoke your right against self-incrimination and refuse to answer. If the agency says "no," then you are required to answer the questions. However, you should ask for written notice which clearly informs you that the information you are asked about will not be used in any subsequent criminal proceeding against you. This notice is to ensure that a federal employee is not faced with a dilemma of "either answering and thereby subjecting himself to the possibility of self-incrimination, or of avoiding giving such help to the prosecution at the cost of his livelihood."[6] If the agency does provide the requisite notice, i.e., inform you that your answer will be used only for administrative purposes, you must answer the questions asked. Failure to answer or cooperate in the investigation under these circumstances may lead to discipline, including removal.

TIP

Before answering any questions from a management official about alleged misconduct, make sure you are assured that your answers will not be used in any subsequent criminal proceeding against you.

A second rule applies in cases of investigations which might lead to possible criminal prosecution, when the agency:

6 *See Kalkines v. United States*, 473 F.2d 1301, 1394 (Cl. Ct. 1973).

a. issues an employee an order that demands that the employee answers questions and expressly threatens an adverse action (such as removal) if the employee fails to these questions, and/or
b. issues an employee an order that demands that the employee answers questions and expressly states that the employee's responses cannot be used against employee for purposes of criminal prosecution.

In those situations, the testimony from the investigation cannot be used in a criminal prosecution. However, the employee can then potentially be disciplined if he or she fails to answer the questions, and cannot assert the 5th Amendment.[7] This area of law is extremely complicated, and so employees facing an agency order of this sort are strongly advised to seek legal advice.

Do I have a right to counsel/representation?

If you are a member of a bargaining unit represented by a union, you have the right to have a union representative present at an investigatory interview, if you have a reasonable belief that discipline may result.[8] However, you are not entitled to have a union representative present unless you specifically ask for one. If your representative is not available, ask for the interview to be postponed until a time when your representative is available. Your agency also has the obligation to *annually* inform all of its employees of their right to counsel.[9] Your agency is not required to inform you of your right to counsel prior to conducting an investigatory interview. As long as your agency provides annual notice, it has satisfied its legal obligation.

TIP

Always ask for a representative to be present during any investigatory interview. Although you are not entitled to one under all circumstances, many agencies will allow you to have one during any investigatory interview.

---

7 *See Garrity et al. v. New Jersey,* 385 US 493 (1967); *Kalkines v. United States,* 473 F.2d 891 (Cl. Ct. 1973); *Uniformed Sanitation Men v. City of New York,* 436 F.2d 619 (2nd Cir. 1970), *cert. denied* 406 US 961 (1972); *see e.g., Bucknor v. U.S. Postal Service,* 93 MSPR 271 (2003).

8 *See* 5 USC § 7114(a).

9 *See* 5 USC § 7114(a).

If you are not a member of a bargaining unit, you are still entitled to have a representative present during an investigatory interview if that interview is custodial. An interview is custodial if you are not permitted to leave the interview at any time. If, however, the agency official conducting the interview permits you to leave at any time, as a non-union employee, you are not entitled to have counsel present. In practice, though, many agencies will permit you to have a personal representative or attorney present at any investigatory interview.

Can agencies conduct searches without a warrant?

The Fourth Amendment to the U.S. Constitution provides that the government may not initiate any "unreasonable searches and seizures" against citizens of the United States. The two most common searches that federal employees face are physical searches of workspace, such as desks and lockers, and drug testing.

Physical searches

If an agency obtains a warrant from the court to search your workspace, the agency has the right to conduct the search. However, most of the time, your agency will not have a warrant before proceeding with the search. Searching without a warrant is called a warrantless search. Your agency does *not* have a right to conduct a warrantless search of your workspace if you have a "reasonable expectation of privacy" in your workspace, and if you can establish that the agency's search was unreasonable.

Proving that you have a reasonable expectation of privacy in your workspace could be a significant legal hurdle for you to overcome. If you work in a cubicle, as opposed to an office, you may have very little chance of convincing a court that you had a reasonable expectation of privacy in your workspace because the workspace is readily viewable by anyone who walks by. The agency would not need a warrant to conduct a search if this were the case. The Supreme Court has held that "some government offices may be so open to fellow employees or the public that no expectation of privacy is reasonable."[10] However, even in such open offices, contents of your personal luggage and bags, especially if closed (for example, a closed purse or briefcase) could not be searched without a warrant.

---

[10] *See O'Connor v. Ortega*, 480 US 709, 717-18 (1987).

Even if you can establish a reasonable expectation of privacy, you must still establish that the agency's search was unreasonable. In determining the reasonableness of a search in the workplace, a court will balance the invasion of your expectation of privacy with the agency's need for ensuring efficient operation of the workplace. In other words, in each individual case, the court must decide which is more important—the privacy of the employee or the efficiency of the agency. The Supreme Court made it difficult for employees to prevent searches of their workspace by agencies when it held that "work-related" searches generally "satisfy the Fourth Amendment reasonableness requirement."[11] Examples of work-related searches include:

- a search which the agency conducts to turn up evidence that the employee is guilty of work-related misconduct, such as theft of office supplies, and
- a search which is necessary for a non-investigatory work-related purpose, such as to retrieve a needed file.

It is important to note that if the search is "non-work related," an employer is generally required to obtain a warrant to conduct the search. An example of a non-work related search is a search which the agency conducts to turn up your private papers.

TIP

If an investigator wants to interview you or search your desk or requests a drug test, you should ask for representation. Request the opportunity to consult a union steward, a lawyer, or a higher agency official. There is no downside or risk to asking for a prior consultation before consenting to a procedure which could hurt you.

SPECIAL RULES FOR UNIONIZED EMPLOYEES If you are represented by a union, you may have more rights with respect to employer searches than do your non-union coworkers. Every agency has the absolute authority to determine the "internal security practices of the agency."[12] Examples of these practices include: when and how agency employees can gain access to agency facilities, and the formation of policies that are intended to secure or safeguard the

---

[11] *See O'Connor v. Ortega*, 480 US 709, 717-18 (1987).

[12] *See* 5 USC § 7106(a)(1).

agency's personnel and physical property from internal and external risks. A union cannot negotiate with management to get management to change their policies with respect to these practices. However, a union does have the right to negotiate certain procedures and an "appropriate arrangement for employees adversely affected by the exercise" of this authority. An arrangement is considered appropriate if it does not excessively interfere with the exercise of management's absolute right. Through collective bargaining, your union may negotiate added safeguards for you in the event of a search.

TIP

It is important for you to be aware of what types of arrangements your union representatives have negotiated for you with respect to searches of the workplace. One common arrangement is that the employee and a representative have the right to be present during the search. Before you permit your employer to search your workplace, you should contact your union representative to determine what arrangements, if any, have been negotiated.

Can my agency legally test me for drugs?

Under Executive Order 12564, dated September 15, 1986, President Reagan directed all federal agencies to develop a plan for achieving the objective of a drug-free workplace. This Order mandates that each agency must establish a drug testing program.

Every agency's drug testing program must comply with the Fourth Amendment because drug testing is considered a "search" of an employee. An employee subjected to a drug test undoubtedly has an expectation of privacy. Therefore, the key question is whether your agency's drug testing procedures are reasonable. If your agency's drug testing program is "unreasonable," then it is unconstitutional, and must be struck down. Generally, your agency may test you for drugs if it has a "reasonable suspicion" that you have engaged in drug use. In one case before the MSPB, the Board held that the agency had a reasonable suspicion that an employee was using drugs after the employee's brother told management officials about the employee's drug use.

Is random drug testing legal? It depends upon the nature of the job you have. Your agency does not need to have a reasonable suspicion about your drug use when "privacy interests implicated by the search are minimal, and where an important governmental interest furthered by the intrusion would be placed in jeopardy by a requirement of individualized suspicion."[13] Once again, the factfinder will balance your privacy rights with the rights of your agency to determine whether random drug testing is appropriate.

The MSPB has previously found random drug testing to be constitutional for air traffic controllers and electronics technicians working for the Federal Aviation Administration. The FAA employees occupying these positions are responsible for the safety of thousands of airline passengers every day. In these cases, the MSPB permitted the agency to give random drug tests to these employees because it determined that the safety of airline passengers was an important governmental interest that outweighed the privacy rights of the employees.

UNIONIZED EMPLOYEES: RIGHT TO REPRESENTATION? Several decisions by the Federal Labor Relations Authority have held that union proposals requesting that a representative be allowed to be present when the agency collects a urine sample from an employee are negotiable in collective bargaining. Your union contract may contain provisions giving you protection during drug testing. Contact your union representative for information on the rights that have been negotiated for you.

TIP

Before agreeing to submit to a drug test, contact your union representative to determine what rights, if any, have been negotiated for you. If you are not represented by a union, consider contacting an experienced employment lawyer for advice. However, be mindful that refusing to undergo a drug test may subject you to discipline, including termination, for "insubordination." The rule to follow: obey now, grieve later.

CAN I SUE THE FEDERAL GOVERNMENT FOR VIOLATING MY RIGHTS?

After reading through this book, you now probably realize that the procedures established for you to file a complaint against the federal government can be very confusing. You may be wondering why you cannot go into court and sue the federal government. The answer is simple: the federal government

---

13 *See Skinner v. Railway Labor Executives' Association,* 489 US 602, 624 (1989).

cannot be sued without its consent. This is known as *sovereign immunity*. We have previously discussed the areas in which the federal government has consented to being sued (EEO, whistleblowing, etc.), and we have also discussed the procedures established for federal employees to do so. If you want to sue the federal government, you must follow those procedures.

In addition, you should note that states do not have the authority to pass laws which apply to the federal government. Therefore, you should not rely on state law to bring a cause of action against a federal agency. For example, suppose the state in which you live has a law which says that a supervisor cannot spread false rumors about an employee. Further assume that you learn from a coworker that your supervisor has been spreading false rumors about you. Can you sue the agency under your state's law? No. Your state's laws provide you with no legal remedies for actions taken by a federal agency. Any state law purporting to provide such a remedy would be in violation of the Supremacy Clause of the U.S. Constitution.

In almost all employment-related matters, you are not permitted to sue federal officials in their individual capacities—you must sue the agency for which that government official works. So if a supervisor denies you a promotion, proposes your termination, or harasses you in the workplace, your best legal recourse is to take action against the agency, not the supervisor.[14]

Final Thoughts

Just because you are a federal employee does not mean that you no longer have any rights under the U.S. Constitution. In fact, in many instances you have more Constitutional rights than private employees. Your rights to free speech and freedom from unreasonable searches in particular, are significant. Make sure your rights have not been violated when you find yourself facing a difficult situation in this area.

[14] There are a few extreme occasions when a suit against a supervisor is permitted, such as when the supervisor is acting outside the scope of his/her duties. See Chapter 24.

22

Information and Privacy

Who Knew What When and Where?

IN THIS CHAPTER YOU WILL LEARN:

- what federal government information you can access
- how you can access obtainable information from the federal government
- what information about yourself you can keep private
- when can the government collect medical information from you
- who can the government disclose your medical information to

Contents Chapter Twenty-Two - Information and Privacy

Introduction

In order to function, the government often needs to make use of personal information regarding its employees. As a federal employee, there is information gathered about you from the time you apply for a position with the government until the time you quit or retire, and perhaps afterwards. We have a democracy that allows all citizens access to government information in order to help them participate in public affairs in an informed and intelligent way. But you are also a private individual with all of the usual concerns for privacy and confidentiality in your personal affairs.

Does the fact that you are a government employee mean that the public has a right to your agency's records on you? If you wish to obtain information to assist you in an appeal against your agency, do you have a right to obtain that information? In this chapter we will discuss your right to privacy, as well as your right to access government information.

What is the Privacy Act and what does it do?

According to Congress, the right to privacy is a personal and fundamental right protected by the Constitution of the United States. The Privacy Act of 1974, which is a very important statute for federal employees like you, became effective on September 27, 1975.[1] The main purpose of the Privacy Act is to protect the privacy of individuals such as yourself, who are identified in information systems maintained by federal agencies, by regulating

[1] *See* 5 USC § 552a.

the collection, maintenance, use, and dissemination of that information by such agencies.

What kind of information can I obtain under the Privacy Act?

Under the Privacy Act, your agency must permit you, or your representative, access to your records or to any information pertaining to you contained in its system of records.[2] You also have the right to receive a copy of all or any portion of your records in a form comprehensible to you. The agency may require that you furnish a written statement authorizing the agency to discuss your record in the presence of any personal representative you may have. Under the Privacy Act, agencies may establish fees charged to you for making copies of your records, excluding the cost of any search for and review of the records by the agency. A sample Privacy Act request can be found in Appendix E-5.

How does the Privacy Act protect me from improper disclosure of my records?

Under the Privacy Act, no federal agency may disclose any record contained in its system of records, which pertains to you, by any means of communication to any person or another agency, without your written request or prior written consent, unless disclosure of the record would be:

1. to those officers and employees of the agency maintaining the record who have a need for it in the performance of their duties
2. required under the Freedom of Information Act (FOIA), as discussed below
3. for a routine use, which is defined as the use of such record for a purpose compatible with the purpose for which it was collected[3]
4. to the Bureau of Census for purposes of planning or carrying out a census, survey, or related activity
5. to a recipient who has provided the agency with advance adequate written assurance that the record will be used solely as a statistical research or reporting record, and the record is to be transferred in a form that is not individually identifiable

---

2 *See* 5 USC § 552a(d)(1).

3 From time to time, a notice is published in the Federal Register for each system of records covered by the Privacy Act. This notice lists the identified routine uses for that system of records, among other details.

6. to the National Archives and Records Administration as a record with significant historical or other value to warrant continued preservation by the U. S. government, or for evaluation to determine whether the record has such value
7. to another agency or to an instrumentality of any governmental jurisdiction within or under the control of the United States for a civil or criminal law enforcement activity if the activity is authorized by law, and if the head of the agency or instrumentality has made a written request to the agency that maintains the record specifying the particular portion desired and the law enforcement activity for which the record is sought
8. to a person pursuant to a showing of compelling circumstances affecting the health or safety of an individual if upon such disclosure notification is transmitted to the last known address of such individual
9. to either house of Congress or, to the extent of matters within its jurisdiction, any committee or subcommittee thereof, any joint committee of Congress or subcommittee of any such joint committee
10. to the Comptroller General, or any of his or her authorized representatives, in the course of the performance of the duties of the Government Accountability Office
11. pursuant to an order of a court of competent jurisdiction, or
12. to a consumer reporting agency

Is certain information not available to me under the Privacy Act?

The Privacy Act exempts from disclosure to you the following systems of records:

1. investigatory material compiled for law enforcement purposes with certain exceptions
2. records maintained in conjunction with providing protective services to the President of the United States or other individuals
3. records required by statute to be maintained and used solely for statistical records
4. investigatory material compiled solely for the purpose of determining suitability, eligibility, or qualifications for federal civilian employment or promotion potential in the armed services, but only to the extent that the disclosure would reveal the identity of a confidential source of such information, or

5. testing or examining material to determine individual qualifications for appointment or promotion in the federal service, the disclosure of which would compromise the objectivity of the testing or examination process

In addition, the Privacy Act does not allow you access to any information compiled in reasonable anticipation of any civil action or proceeding.

Do I have a cause of action if my privacy is violated?

If you are adversely affected by an agency failing to comply with the Privacy Act, you may bring a civil action against the agency. The purpose of your action will be to stop the agency from committing further violations of the Act and to receive corrective relief. The action, brought in the appropriate U.S. district court, as described on page 380 of this chapter, must be filed *within 2 years from the date on which the cause of action arose.* In cases of failure to maintain accurate records or certain other violations of the Privacy Act (for example, improper disclosure of information or documents from Privacy Act records), if the court determines that the agency acted in a manner that was intentional or willful, the United States will be liable to you in an amount equal to the sum of:

- actual damages sustained by you, but in no case will you receive less than the sum of $1,000 if you are entitled to recovery, and
- the costs of the action together with reasonable attorney fees as determined by the court

Agency officials may be subject to criminal misdemeanor penalties for knowing and willful violations of the Privacy Act.

What about my privacy during a misconduct investigation?

The Privacy Act also protects you if you are the subject of a misconduct investigation. If you are the subject of an investigation, agencies that maintain a system of records must collect as much information as possible directly from you, when the information may result in adverse determinations about your rights, benefits, and privileges under federal programs.

Courts have interpreted this to mean, for instance, that if your agency is seeking objective information about you, such as whether you went on a trip on a particular date, the agency has the responsibility of collecting that information from you directly (and in many cases, first). If you find out that your supervisor asked coworkers or non-agency personnel about your conduct before questioning you, or if the investigation concludes with you not being contacted at all, you may have a cause of action against the agency for violating the Privacy Act.

In order to sue for a violation of the information collection section of the Privacy Act, you must prove that:

- the agency maintains a system of records
- the agency's violation of the Act was intentional or willful. You can show this by proving that the agency's act was committed either without grounds or with flagrant disregard for your rights under the Act
- the agency's contact with third parties, prior to questioning you, had an adverse affect on you
- you suffered actual damages (which do not include emotional pain and suffering; medical expenses related to emotional pain and suffering may be recoverable, however)

If you win, you are entitled to the greater of either $1,000 or the actual damages sustained in excess of that minimum amount, along with the costs of the action and reasonable attorneys' fees.

What assurance do I have that records about me are accurate?

Under the Privacy Act, each agency must maintain all records used in making any determination concerning you with such accuracy, relevance, timeliness, and completeness as is reasonably necessary to assure fairness to you in the determination. Prior to disseminating any record about you to any person other than an agency, unless the dissemination is made pursuant to the Freedom of Information Act, an agency must make reasonable efforts to assure that such records are accurate, complete, timely, and relevant.

What if there are inaccuracies in my records?

Your agency must permit you to request an amendment of any record pertaining to you. Within *10 days* (excluding Saturdays, Sundays, and legal public holidays) after the date of receipt of your request, the agency must acknowledge your request in writing and promptly, either:

- correct any portion of the record which you believe is not accurate, relevant, timely, or complete, or
- inform you of its refusal to amend the record in accordance with your request, and state the reason for the refusal. It must also inform you of the procedures established by the agency for you to request a review

of the initial agency refusal by the head of the agency or an officer designated by the head of the agency. The agency must provide you with the name and business address of that official

If you disagree with the agency's refusal to amend your record, the agency must permit you to request a review of the refusal. If your review is not successful, the agency must permit you to file with them a concise statement of the reasons for your disagreement with the refusal. They must also notify you of your right to have a court review their decision. Thereafter, the agency must clearly note any portion of the record that is disputed and provide copies of your statement of dispute. If the agency deems it appropriate, it must provide copies of a concise statement of the agency's reasons for not making the requested amendments, to persons or other agencies to whom the disputed record has been disclosed.

Can I sue the agency if it doesn't correct my records?

If the agency makes a determination not to amend your records as you request, or fails to make a review in accordance with the Act, you may bring a civil action against the agency, in the appropriate U.S. district court. The proper U.S. district to file a civil act can be located in:

- the district in which you reside
- the district court in which you have your principal place of business
- the district in which the agency records are situated, or
- the District of Columbia

If you prevail, the court may order the agency to amend your record in accordance with your request or some other method directed by the court. Attorney fees and other reasonably incurred litigation costs are also available if you prevail.

What is the Freedom of Information Act ("FOIA")and what does it do?

The Freedom of Information Act (FOIA)[4] is a federal law that permits people to obtain disclosable information from the federal government. The basic concept of FOIA is that all records maintained by federal agencies must be accessible to you, as a member of the public, unless the records are specifically exempt from that requirement. FOIA can be quite helpful if you are seeking information that may assist you with a grievance, appeal, or lawsuit. A sample FOIA request can be found in Appendix E-5.

---

4 *See* 5 USC § 552.

What kind of information is available to me under FOIA?

Under FOIA, agencies must make certain information available to you, as a member of the public. Specifically, each agency must separately state and publish in the Federal Register for your guidance:

- information as to where and how to request agency information
- statements of the general course and method by which its functions are channeled or determined
- rules of procedures, descriptions of forms available or the places where the forms may be obtained, and instructions as to the scope and contents of all papers, reports, or examinations
- substantive rules of general applicability adopted by the agency, as authorized by law
- statements of general policy or interpretations of general applicability formulated and adopted by the agency, and
- each amendment, revision, or repeal of these rules

If an agency fails to publish required information in the Federal Register, you cannot be required to adhere to that information, unless you have actual and timely independent notice of the information.

Under FOIA, each agency must also make available for your inspection and copying:

- final opinions, including concurring and dissenting opinions, as well as orders, made in the adjudication of administrative cases
- statements of policy and interpretations adopted by the agency not published in the Federal Register
- administrative staff manuals and instructions to staff that affect a member of the public
- indexes providing identifying information for the public as to any matter issued, adopted, or promulgated by the agency after July 4, 1967, and
- records on the final votes of each agency member in every agency proceeding, unless the materials are promptly published and copies offered for sale

To prevent clearly unwarranted invasions of personal privacy, an agency may delete identifying details when it makes available or publishes an opinion, statement of policy, interpretation, or staff manual or instruction. However, the justification for the deletion must be explained fully in writing. Many agencies make FOIA request instructions available online. Documents commonly requested under FOIA are often on the agency's website in an 'electronic reading room.'

What information is not available to me under FOIA?

Under FOIA, you cannot receive information that is, among other things:

- specifically authorized under criteria established by an executive order to be kept secret in the interest of national defense or foreign policy, and properly classified as such
- related solely to the internal personnel rules and practices of an agency
- trade secrets and commercial or financial information obtained from a person that is privileged and confidential
- inter-agency or intra-agency memorandums or letters which would not be available by law to a party other than an agency in litigation with the agency
- personnel and medical files and similar files, the disclosure of which would constitute a clearly unwarranted invasion of personal privacy
- records of information compiled for law enforcement purposes that would interfere with the enforcement efforts or constitute an unwarranted invasion of personal privacy or confidentiality or endanger personal safety of a person involved
- information that is contained in or related to examination, operating, or condition reports prepared by or for an agency responsible for the regulation or supervision of financial institutions, or
- geological and geophysical information and data, including maps, concerning wells

Any reasonably segregable portion of a record must be provided to you upon your request, after deletion of the portions exempt under FOIA.

Does it cost me anything to get FOIA information?

As noted earlier, some information is published by agencies, including rules and decisions. For this and other types of records you must submit a written request to the agency describing the records you desire and follow the agency's rules regarding such requests. The agency must then make the records promptly available to you.

Agencies must publish a fee schedule to inform you of costs. Under the regulations, when records are requested for commercial use and the like, fees must be limited to reasonable standard charges for document search, duplication, and review.

Documents must be furnished free or at a reduced charge if disclosure of the information is not primarily for commercial purposes and is in the public interest because it is likely to contribute significantly to public understanding of the operations or activities of the government. For example, there are no fees for requests by educational or noncommercial scientific institutions.

The agency may not require advance payment of fees unless you have previously failed to pay fees in a timely fashion, or the fee will exceed $250.

How do I obtain FOIA information?

Upon your request for records made under the FOIA, the agency must determine within *20 days* (excluding Saturdays, Sundays, and legal public holidays) after the receipt of any such request, whether to comply with your request. It must immediately notify you of its determination and the reasons for it, and of your right to appeal an adverse decision to the head of the agency. If you file an appeal, the agency must make a decision on it within *20 days* (excluding Saturdays, Sundays, and legal public holidays) after receipt of the appeal. Some agencies impose deadlines for filing such appeals (such as 30 days). If the denial of the request is partially or fully upheld on appeal, the agency must notify you of your right to have a court review the agency's denial. You must exhaust the administrative appeals process for all aspects of the request before filing a case in court.

TIP

If you want to obtain records from the government, you should prepare a letter stating, describing, and identifying exactly which documents you want. Address the letter to the head of the agency or whichever officer is responsible for FOIA information. Be sure to keep a copy of your letter for your own files.

Can I enforce my FOIA rights in court?

If you file a complaint in a U.S. district court with proper jurisdiction as set forth in the Privacy Act section above, the court may order the agency to stop withholding agency records and order the production of records improperly withheld from you. As with the Privacy Act, if you win, reasonably incurred attorney fees and other litigation costs are available. Although FOIA itself does not have a statute of limitations within which you must bring suit against an agency, courts have held that the general six-year statute of limitations for bringing civil actions against the United States applies to FOIA actions.

When can the government require me to provide my medical information?

In various circumstances, the federal government can ask employees to provide medical information in connection with normal federal personnel actions. Because of the sensitivity of medical information, the collection and handling of this information is subject to stringent restrictions on its use and distribution. Collection, use and distribution of medical information is not just restricted by the Privacy Act, but also by a variety of other regulations, including the regulations implementing the Rehabilitation Act (protecting persons with disabilities) and the Genetic Information Nondiscrimination Act (GINA).[5]

When is the government prohibited from demanding my medical information?

The default rule is that managers are not permitted to ask for medical or genetic information from an employee.[6] Many specific exceptions apply for a variety of situations (for example, reasonable accommodation requests or medical documents to substantiate sick leave requests), but they only apply if an express exception appears in federal statute or regulations.

Restrictions on government collection of genetic information concerning employees are also extremely strict. Agencies are only able to collect genetic information if discovered inadvertently, if provided voluntarily by an employee in connection with a voluntary wellness program or to substantiate a FMLA request for caring for a sick relative, from public news sources, when necessary to monitor employee health in workplaces where the employees work with toxic substances, or from DNA testing laboratory workers to help avoid sample contamination.[7]

Even stronger limitations apply to requests for medical information made to job applicants. Simply put, before a job offer is made, an agency is solely permitted to ask applicants if they need reasonable accommodation to complete the *job application process*; agencies are only permitted to

---

5 *See* Chapter 5 for further information on GINA and the Rehabilitation Act.

6 *See, e.g.*, 29 CFR §§ 1630.13, 1635.8.

7 *See* 29 CFR § 1635.8.

ask an applicant if they need reasonable accommodations to perform job-related functions (with or without reasonable accommodation) if the applicant volunteers that he/she is disabled or if the disability is obvious.[8] Any other inquiries into an applicant's disability status are prohibited, including questions which are designed to elicit information from an applicant which might indicate whether or not they are disabled. While some information concerning an applicant's disability status may be included with a job application if they are applying under special hiring preferences (for example, hiring preferences for disabled veterans or Schedule A hiring authority for disabled applicants), specific information concerning the applicant's medical status is not supposed to be provided to the selecting officials or interview panel.[9] Only after a job offer has been extended to a particular applicant may the employing agency ask if a reasonable accommodation is needed—and then only if all incoming employees are asked the same question, if the applicant volunteers that he/she is disabled, or if the disability is obvious.[10]

WHAT MEDICAL INFORMATION MUST I PROVIDE FOR SICK LEAVE AND FMLA REQUESTS?

Ordinarily, a federal employee has to be sick, seeking medical treatment, or treating a sick relative, in order to use sick leave.[11] Regulations permit most employees to self-certify that they are sick for sick leave requests. However, management is permitted to ask for a doctor's note to justify the leave, especially if the leave request is for more than 3 days or if special circumstances (such as a leave restriction notice) apply.[12]

A Family and Medical Leave Act (FMLA) leave request based on an employee's own medical condition or on the need to care for a relative must be substantiated by a doctor's certificate.[13] The Agency is restricted to requesting only the information needed to substantiate the cited reason for

---

[8] *See* 29 CFR § 1630.14(a); *EEOC Enforcement Guidance: Reasonable Accommodation and Undue Hardship Under the Americans with Disabilities Act* (October 2002) at § 12; EEOC *Enforcement Guidance: Preemployment Disability-Related Questions and Medical Examinations* (October 1995).

[9] *See, e.g., Jones v. Dept. of the Air Force*, EEOC Appeal No. 07A10033 (June 25, 2001).

[10] *See* EEOC *Enforcement Guidance: Reasonable Accommodation and Undue Hardship Under the Americans with Disabilities Act* (October 2002) at § 12.

[11] *See* 5 CFR § 630.401(a). Sick leave can also be used for funerals of relatives or for adoptions, but that sort of sick leave usage is not relevant to medical confidentiality issues. *See* Chapter 14 for a more detailed discussion of leave issues.

[12] *See* 5 CFR § 630.405(a).

[13] *See* 5 CFR § 630.1208. *See* Chapter 14 for a more detailed discussion of FMLA.

the requested FMLA leave.[14] The Agency is permitted to ask for a second or third medical certificate—at the Agency's expense.[15]

What medical information must I provide for reasonable accommodation requests?

When an employee requests reasonable accommodation for a disability, the government is entitled to request medical information concerning the employee's disability.[16] These inquiries as limited to only that information needed to demonstrate the existence of the disability requiring reasonable accommodation and of the necessity for the reasonable accommodation requested. Agencies are restricted from asking for an employee's full medical file, or for information on medical conditions unrelated to the disability requiring reasonable accommodation.

When can the government require me to take a fitness-for-duty medical examination?

As the Merit Systems Protection Board has noted, federal agency authority to order fitness-for-duty examinations of employees, in particular psychological examinations, has been sharply cut back over the years due to a history of agencies abusing this authority.[17] Under current regulations and MSPB precedent, an agency may only force an employee to undergo a medical examination in the following three limited circumstances:

1. when the employee's position in question has medical standards or physical requirements or is covered by an established medical evaluation program;

2. when an employee has applied for or is receiving workers' compensation; or

3. when an employee is reassigned as part of a reduction in force and the position to which the employee has reassignment rights has medical standards or specific physical requirements which are different from those required in the employee's current position.[18]

---

14 *See* 5 CFR § 630.1208(c).

15 *See* 5 CFR § 630.1208(d-f).

16 *See* EEOC *Enforcement Guidance: Reasonable Accommodation and Undue Hardship Under the Americans with Disabilities Act* (October 2002) at §§ 6-7; EEOC *Disability-Related Inquiries and Medical Examinations of Employees Under the Americans with Disabilities Act* (ADA) (July 2000) at § 7.

17 *See, e.g., Doe v. Pension Benefit Guarantee Corp.*, 117 MSPR 579 (2012).

18 *See* 5 CFR § 339.301; *Doe v. Pension Benefit Guarantee Corp.*, 117 MSPR 579 (2012).

An agency may offer a medical examination in any situation where the agency needs additional medical documentation to make an informed management decision (including on performance or conduct issues), but cannot order the employee to participate—although the agency can indefinitely suspend an employee pending management's receipt of information indicating the employee's renewed fitness for duty.[19]

WHAT ARE MY REMEDIES IF THE GOVERNMENT IMPROPERLY DEMANDS THAT I GIVE THEM MY MEDICAL INFORMATION?

If the government improperly asks for medical information, the request itself is technically a violation of the Rehabilitation Act or of GINA, depending on the specific information requested.[20] Because in many cases the damages for this violation are likely to be limited, this claim is less likely to be litigated separately, but instead can be raised as an additional claim as part of a larger discrimination complaint. Further, employees can cite to this possible claim in discussions with management prior to filing an EEO complainant, as a negotiating tool to get management to drop demands for medical information or to modify the information request into something less objectionable.

WHO CAN THE GOVERNMENT DISCLOSE MY MEDICAL INFORMATION TO?

Confidential medical information collected by the agency can only be disclosed to five categories of persons under regulations and EEOC guidance, and only for limited reasons.[21] Supervisors and managers may be informed of medical restrictions on an employee's work or duties and related reasonable accommodations. First aid and safety personnel may be informed, when appropriate, if the disability might require emergency treatment. Government officials investigating compliance with the Rehabilitation Act are permitted access to relevant information on request, as are disclosures to state workers' compensation offices or disclosures for insurance purposes. The mere fact that a recipient is allegedly involved with implementing an accom-

---

19 *See* 5 CFR § 339.302; *Doe v. Pension Benefit Guarantee Corp.*, 117 MSPR 579 (2012).

20 *See, e.g., Munford v. U.S. Postal Service*, EEOC Appeal No. 01A60384 (July 12, 2006) (unsubstantiated order for fitness for duty exam renders employee aggrieved); *Clark v. U.S. Postal Service*, EEOC Appeal No. 01992682 (November 20, 2001) (per se violation of Rehabilitation Act claim exists for improper for fitness for duty examination).

21 *See* 29 CFR § 1630.14; EEOC *Enforcement Guidance: Reasonable Accommodation and Undue Hardship Under the Americans with Disabilities Act* (October 2002) at fn.111; *Meadows v. Dept. of the Army*, EEOC Appeal No. 0120101541 (August 17, 2010).

modation for an employee does not give a 'need to know' if the recipient is not a supervisor/manager or a subject matter expert (such as a medical professional or personnelist) who is being specifically consulted by the manager as part of the specific deliberations on possible reasonable accommodations, even if the individual is involved in implementing a proposed accommodation.[22] Genetic information can only be disclosed in a few circumstances to persons other than the subject of the information: disclosures to health researchers under certain federal regulations, in response to a court order, to officials investigating GINA compliance, disclosures in connection with a FMLA leave request, and to public health authorities in the event of an epidemic.[23]

The requirements concerning nondisclosure of confidential medical information applies to confidential medical information obtained from any employee, and is not limited to individuals with disabilities.[24] Even information provided in connection with an ordinary sick leave request is covered by these nondisclosure requirements.[25] While not all medically-related information documentation is covered by these requirements, information concerning an individual's symptoms, past, present, and expected future diagnoses and treatment, and the fact that an applicant or employee has requested or received accommodation for a disability are all covered by these nondisclosure requirements.[26]

Does HIPAA or the Privacy Act protect medical information I have given the government?

Generally, the Health Insurance Portability and Accountability Act (HIPAA) does not affect information collection or disclosure by an employee's employing agency. HIPAA is focused primarily on patient information collection, storage and disclosure by those in the health care industry: doctors, hospitals, health insurance companies, etc…[27]

---

22 *See Skarica v. Dept. of Homeland Security*, EEOC Appeal No. 0120073399 (March 5, 2010); *Manns v. U.S. Postal Service*, EEOC Appeal No. 01A53044 (June 9, 2006); EEOC *Enforcement Guidance: Reasonable Accommodation and Undue Hardship Under the Americans with Disabilities Act* (October 2002) at § 42.

23 *See* 29 CFR § 1635.9.

24 *See Skarica v. Dept. of Homeland Security*, EEOC Appeal No. 0120073399 (March 5, 2010).

25 *See, e.g., Fisher v. Dept. of the Army*, EEOC Appeal No. 01A32251 (September 28, 2004), aff'd EEOC Request No. 05A50210 (January 14, 2005).

26 *See Meadows v. Dept. of the Army*, EEOC Appeal No. 0120101541 (August 17, 2010); *Skarica v. Dept. of Homeland Security*, EEOC Appeal No. 0120073399 (March 5, 2010); *Tyson v. U.S. Postal Service*, EEOC Appeal No. 01992086 (August 23, 2002).

27 *See, e.g.* 45 CFR § 160.102(a), 160.103, 164.500 *et seq.*

A Privacy Act claim is only possible if the confidential medical information is being disclosed from a Privacy Act-covered system of records. Further, the Privacy Act disclosure claim only works if the employee also suffers "actual damages" from the wrongful disclosure, such as back pay or medical expenses—emotional pain and suffering is not enough.[28]

WHAT ARE MY REMEDIES IF THE GOVERNMENT IMPROPERLY DISCLOSES MY MEDICAL INFORMATION?

If the government improperly discloses confidential medical information, the disclosure itself is a violation of the Rehabilitation Act or of GINA, depending on the specific information disclosed. An employee whose information is disclosed then has the option of initiating an EEO complaint based on the request, within the normal 45 calendar day deadline for federal sector EEO complaints.[29] While compensatory damages are available, no proof of harm is required for an improper medical information disclosure complaint.[30] Like claims for denial of reasonable accommodation, a complainant raising a claim of an improper disclosure of confidential medical information is not required to prove any intent to discriminate.[31] Instead, the fact that the medical information was disclosed is enough to give rise to a lawsuit.

In this context, a Privacy Act wrongful disclosure lawsuit[32] is inferior to a claim for violation of GINA or the Rehabilitation Act. A Privacy Act claim is only possible if the confidential medical information is being disclosed from a Privacy Act-covered system of records. GINA and the Rehabilitation Act apply whether or not the medical information was ever stored in a particular system of records. Further, the Privacy Act disclosure claim only works if the employee also suffers "actual damages" from the wrongful disclosure, such as back pay or medical expenses—emotional pain and suffering is not enough.[33] That limitation does not apply to either GINA or the Rehabilitation Act. Finally, the Privacy Act wrongful disclosure claim requires that the agency's disclosure be "intentional or willful." In contrast, GINA and the Rehabilitation Act require no particular level of intent to state a claim—any improper disclosure of confidential medical information is sufficient for a complaint.

---

28 *See Federal Aviation Admin. v. Cooper*, 132 S. Ct. 1441, 1451, 1451 fn.6 (2012).

29 *See* Chapter 6 for more information on the federal-sector EEO complaint process.

30 *See, e.g., Jones v. Dept. of the Air Force*, EEOC Appeal No. 07A10033 (June 25, 2001); *Hampton v. U.S. Postal Service*, EEOC Appeal No. 01A00132 (April 13, 2000).

31 *See Torres v. Dept. of Veterans Affairs*, EEOC Appeal No. 0120091384 (July 22, 2009).

32 *See* earlier in this chapter for discussion of this form of lawsuit under the Privacy Act.

33 *See Federal Aviation Admin. v. Cooper*, 132 S. Ct. 1441, 1451, fn.6 (2012).

Final Thoughts

We live in a big world where information is constantly being gathered about us, and information is constantly being created regarding government activities. If we know the rules and laws and fit within them, we can limit access to our own private personal information, and also gather the information we need from the government. Such information can be important if you are pursuing a grievance, appeal or lawsuit. However, you need to keep in mind that very often federal agencies do not respond to FOIA/Privacy Act requests in a timely manner. As a result, the information may not be available to use when pursuing a grievance or appeal with short deadlines.

23

The Hatch Act: Prohibited Political Activities

Please Tell Me I Don't Have to Campaign For My Boss

In This Chapter You Will Learn:

- what activities are considered political
- what restrictions there are on federal employees engaging in political activity
- the consequences of violating the rules

CONTENTS CHAPTER TWENTY-THREE - THE HATCH ACT: PROHIBITED POLITICAL ACTIVITIES

Introduction

Much of government is greatly impacted by the political process. Even though we tend to think of our agency, and others, as independent entities, they are still subject to politics. That means that there is a connection between agency employees and those who engage in politics. Congress wanted federal employees to be insulated from the political process. While the Hatch Act is generally thought of as restricting federal employees from engaging in politics, its main purpose is to protect them from being pressured to engage in political activity by someone on the job to whom they are accountable. The Hatch Act puts many limitations on federal employees' involvement in political activities.[1] Failure to observe these limitations may result in your termination from federal service.

In this chapter, you will find out what the Hatch Act covers, what you can and cannot do under the Act, and what to do when you run into trouble because of it.

Recent Improvements

Hatch Act penalties used to be draconian. A finding of violation most often meant automatic removal from employment. Fortunately, the Hatch Act Modernization Act of 2012 took effect January 19, 2013 , and substantially broadened the scope of government employee political activities as follows.

---

[1] *See* 5 USC § 7321, *et seq*; 5 CFR § 734.

The Act:

- Lifted the restriction on running for office previously imposed on state and local government employees whose programs were partly funded by federal loans or grants. The restriction still holds for state and local government employees whose salary is paid completely, either directly or indirectly, by federal loans or grants. The Act did not, however, lift the ban on coercive conduct or misuse of official authority for partisan purposes, irrespective of the level of federal funding of the employee's state or local program.

- Modified the penalties under the Hatch Act. Previously, removal was the automatic penalty, with the slight possibility of mitigation by the Board. Now the penalties include: "removal, reduction in grade, debarment from Federal employment for a period not to exceed 5 years, suspension, reprimand, or an assessment of a civil penalty not to exceed $1,000."

- Extended to District of Columbia employees the same Hatch Act provisions that apply to state and local government employees; and

- Extended to federal employees who reside in the District of Columbia the same right to participate in municipal political management and political campaigns already allowed to federal employees residing in nearby areas of Maryland and Virginia.

What activities are prohibited?

As a federal employee, you are prohibited from certain types of political activities and from engaging in others at certain times and places. For example, you are prohibited from:

1. using your official authority to interfere with an election
2. knowingly soliciting or receiving a political contribution from any person, except under the circumstances addressed in items 14-17 in the section "What activities are permitted?" that follows
3. running for the nomination or as a candidate for election to a partisan political office
4. allowing your official title to be used in connection with fundraising activities
5. knowingly soliciting or discouraging participation in any political activity of any person or persons who have an application for any

compensation or grant before your agency or are being audited by your agency

6. using your official title while participating in political activity
7. soliciting or accepting uncompensated individual volunteer services from a subordinate for any political purpose
8. signing a letter seeking volunteer services from individuals by using your official title
9. asking a subordinate employee to volunteer on behalf of a partisan political campaign
10. hosting a fundraiser at your home. However, a spouse who is not covered by the Hatch Act may host such a fundraiser and you may attend.

In addition, employees of certain government agencies (for example, the MSPB, the FBI, the CIA, and the Secret Service) may not take an active part in political management or political campaigns. Political management means directing or supervising a partisan political group or campaign for partisan political office.

Other prohibited political activities include engaging in political activity while on duty or while you are in any room or building occupied in the discharge of your official duties.

What activities are permitted?

Although the Hatch Act prohibits a number of political activities by federal employees, there are many such activities specifically permitted by law. For example, you may:

1. express your opinion privately and publicly on political subjects
2. be politically active regarding an issue not specifically identified with a political party, for example, constitutional amendments
3. participate in nonpartisan activities, such as civic, community, or professional organizations
4. participate fully in public affairs
5. be a member of a political party
6. serve as an officer of a political party or of a committee of such group
7. attend and participate fully in the business of nominating caucuses of political parties
8. organize a political party and participate in political conventions, rallies, or other gatherings

9. serve as a delegate to a political party convention
10. participate, including hold office, in any nonpartisan group
11. canvass voters by telephone on behalf of a political party or partisan political candidate
12. distribute campaign leaflets by hand to homes or parked cars, so long as you are not on duty
13. place in your yard a sign supporting a candidate for partisan political office
14. attend a political fundraiser
15. if you live in the District of Columbia, or certain municipalities in Maryland, Virginia, or other parts of the country identified by OPM, you may:
    a. run as an independent candidate for election to partisan office in elections for local offices of that municipality, and
    b. accept or receive political contributions in connection with local elections of that municipality. However, you may not solicit political contributions from the general public.
16. Solicit, accept, or receive uncompensated volunteer services from any person, and
17. Solicit, accept or receive a political contribution if:
    a. the person who is solicited for a contribution belongs to the same federal labor organization, or federal employee organization, as you
    b. the person who is solicited is not a subordinate to you, *and*
    c. your request for a contribution is for a multicandidate political committee of a federal labor organization, or to the multicandidate political committee of a federal employee organization in existence on October 6, 1993.

In addition to the independent candidacy for public office allowed in some localities as noted in the list above, you may run as a candidate in a nonpartisan election as well. Generally speaking, a nonpartisan election means an election where none of the candidates is to be nominated or elected to represent a political party, or an election involving an issue which is not specifically identified with a political party.

Subject to certain limitations, you may also:

1. display pictures, signs and stickers, and badges associated with political parties and candidates for partisan political office

2. circulate a nominating petition for a candidate for partisan political office
3. canvass for votes
4. endorse or oppose a partisan political candidate

However, you may not engage in these political activities while on duty. You are entitled to vote in any election and to make financial contributions to a political party.

The permitted political activities above are, however, not permitted during certain times and in certain places. In general, you may not participate in these activities while:

a. on duty
b. wearing a uniform or badge that identifies your agency
c. in a room or building occupied in the discharge of your official duties, or
d. using a government-owned or government-leased vehicle

For example, an employee of the General Services Administration may broadcast endorsements for a partisan political candidate by a public address system attached to his/her private automobile, but may not place a partisan political bumper sticker on any government owned or government-leased vehicle.

These rules are different for certain types of employees and employees of certain federal agencies. There are more restrictive rules governing political activities of employees of certain agencies, among others:

- the CIA
- the Secret Service
- the MSPB
- the FBI
- the National Security Agency
- the National Security Council
- the Defense Intelligence Agency
- the Office of Criminal Investigation of the IRS
- the Office of Investigative Programs of the U.S. Customs Service
- the Office of Law Enforcement of the Bureau of Alcohol, Tobacco, and Firearms
- the Central Imagery Office
- the Office of Special Counsel

If you are employed by any of these agencies you are precluded from engaging in many types of political activities. For example, you may not:

- be a candidate for partisan political office
- drive voters to polling places in concert with a political party or partisan political group
- take an active part in managing the political campaign of a candidate for partisan political office
- campaign for partisan political office
- canvass for votes in support of or in opposition to a candidate for partisan political office, if such canvassing is done in concert with such a candidate, or a political party or partisan political group
- endorse or oppose a candidate for partisan political office or a candidate for political party office in a political advertisement, broadcast, campaign literature, or similar material, if such endorsement or opposition is done in concert with such a candidate, political party, or partisan political group
- initiate or circulate a partisan nominating petition
- serve as an officer of a political party, or as a member of a national, state, or local committee of a political party, an officer or member of a committee of a partisan political group, or be a candidate for any of these positions
- organize a political party organization or partisan political group
- serve as a delegate, alternate, or proxy to a political party convention
- address a convention, caucus, rally, or similar gathering of a political party or partisan group in support of or in opposition to a candidate for partisan political office or political party office, if this address is done in concert with such a candidate, political party, or partisan political group
- solicit, accept, or receive political contributions
- organize, sell tickets to, promote, or actively participate in a fund-raising activity of a candidate for partisan political office or of a political party, or partisan political group

This is not a complete list of political activities employees of these agencies are barred from engaging in.

Working for these agencies does not preclude all political activity, however. For example, if you are employed by any of these agencies, you may still engage in the following political activities so long as the activity is not performed in concert with a political party, partisan political group, or a candidate for partisan political office:

1. express your opinions as an individual, privately and publicly, on political subjects and candidates
2. display political pictures, signs, stickers, badges, or buttons, so long as the display is in compliance with other rules on the display of badges and the like at work and on duty
3. sign a political petition as an individual
4. be politically active in connection with a question not specifically identified with a political party, such as a Constitutional amendment
5. register and vote in any election
6. take an active part, as a candidate or in support of a candidate, in a nonpartisan election
7. serve as an election judge or clerk, or in a similar position, performing nonpartisan duties as prescribed by state or local law
8. participate in nonpartisan activities of a civic, community, social, labor, or professional organization
9. be a member of a political party or other partisan political group and participate in its activities to the extent consistent with other federal law
10. attend a political convention, rally, fundraising function, or other political gathering
11. make a financial contribution to a political party, partisan political group, or to the campaign committee of a candidate for partisan political office

For example, you may address a political convention but not on behalf of or at the request of a political party, partisan political group, or individual running for partisan political party.

There are special provisions of the Hatch Act covering certain presidential appointees and employees paid from the appropriation for the Executive Office of the President. Generally, these employees may engage in political activities while on duty and in government buildings. For example, the head of an executive department may hold a partisan political meeting or host a reception which is not a fund-raiser in his conference room during normal business hours.

What happens if I violate the Hatch Act?

The penalties for violating the Hatch Act can be steep, but were lessened as a result of the Hatch Act Improvements of 2013. The Office of Special Counsel (OSC) investigates and prosecutes allegations that federal employees have violated the Hatch Act. If, after investigation, the OSC determines that corrective or disciplinary action is warranted, it will prepare a written complaint against you containing its determination, along with a statement of supporting facts. The complaint will then be presented to you and to the MSPB. However, the OSC usually first contacts the employee and his or her agency to see if the matter can be resolved—such as by the employee agreeing to accept some discipline—without formal MSPB litigation.

TIP

Under the Hatch Act, you cannot solicit political financial contributions or request a subordinate to engage in political activity. However, you can display political bumper stickers. You can become an active member of civic, community, and public organizations. You can, when off duty, distribute campaign leaflets and canvass voters by phone.

If you are presented with a complaint from the OSC alleging a Hatch Act violation, you have certain rights. You are entitled to:

a. a reasonable amount of time to answer the complaint orally and in writing, and to provide affidavits or other documents in support of your answer
b. be represented by an attorney or other representative
c. a hearing before the MSPB or an administrative law judge
d. a transcript of any such hearing, and
e. a written decision, including the reasons for the decision, at the earliest practicable date, including a copy of any order imposing disciplinary action

The MSPB may impose a range of penalties for Hatch Act violations. The Board may remove you from your position, suspend you, reduce you in grade, reprimand you, or impose a civil penalty of not more than $1,000. Finally, you may also be debarred from employment with the federal government for a period of no longer than *5 years*.[2] You can appeal the Board's decision to impose disciplinary action to the U.S. Court of Appeals for the Federal Circuit.

---

[2] This penalty structure applies to violations that occurred before, on, or after January 27, 2013, unless OSC has already initiated a complaint with the Board as of that date, or an employee has already entered into a settlement agreement with OSC.

Final Thoughts

The Hatch Act was put in place to protect you from political pressure in your job as a federal employee, as well as to protect others from you if you are exerting pressure. While there are a number of political activities you may engage in as a federal employee, there are many you cannot. If you are uncertain about a particular activity after you have read this chapter, you may wish to check on your own specific circumstances. For questions concerning the Hatch Act, contact the Office of Special Counsel. It is well worth taking the time to do this, since engaging in prohibited political activities may have severe consequences such as job loss and debarment from federal employment for a period of time, as well as a fine.

24

Personal Liability

Help! I've Been Sued!!! (Or I'm Suing!)

In This Chapter You Will Learn:

- when you can be sued for your acts at work
- what to do if you are sued for something you did at work
- when you can sue the federal government
- how you go about suing the federal government

Contents Chapter Twenty-Four - Personal Liability

Introduction

Do you feel you've been harmed by a federal employee or the government and want some kind of compensation? Maybe you want to sue your supervisor for ruining your reputation. Do you sue the supervisor himself, or the government? Or maybe it was you who harmed someone else while doing your job. Did you injure someone in a car accident while driving a government vehicle, for example? Can you be held personally responsible? In this chapter, we will discuss what right you have to sue another federal employee or the government and the rights others have to sue you (including your protections from those lawsuits), and how those rights are exercised.

What is the government's liability for my acts?

Under the Federal Tort Claims Act ("FTCA"), a person may bring claims for money damages against the U.S. government for injury to or loss of property, or for personal injury or death, caused by your negligent or wrongful act or omission as an employee of a federal agency acting within the scope of your office or employment. These are called tort claims.

If you are a federal law enforcement or investigative officer, then you will most likely not be personally liable for any injuries you cause unintentionally or through negligence, as long as you did so within the scope of your employment.[1] You will be defended by the Attorney General for claims of assault, battery, false imprisonment, false arrest, abuse of process, and malicious prosecution, as well as unintentional tort claims, brought against you if you were acting within the scope your employment when you committed the tort.

---

1 However, you can be personally liable if you knowingly violate an individual's Constitutional rights.

If you are not a federal law enforcement or investigative officer, you are personally liable for intentional tort claims, including claims of assault, battery, false imprisonment, false arrest, malicious prosecution, abuse of process, libel, slander, misrepresentation, deceit, or interference with contract rights. If you are accused of committing an unintentional tort (such as an act of negligence), then you will be personally liable if you were acting outside the scope of your employment when you allegedly committed the tort. If you were acting within the scope of your employment, then the FTCA applies and the United States will take over for you as the defendant; you will not be held personally liable for the alleged unintentional tort.

Does the Attorney General represent me if I'm sued?

Under the FTCA, the Attorney General is charged with defending any civil action brought against you as an employee of the federal government. Under the Westfall Act, the Attorney General can certify that you, as the employee against whom the civil action is brought, were acting within the scope of your office or employment when the claim arose. As a result of such certification, the United States is substituted as the defendant in place of you, and all pending claims brought against you in state court will be removed to federal district court for the district in which the state action is pending. In some circuits, the Attorney General's certification can be challenged; in others, it cannot.

If the Attorney General refuses to certify that you were acting within the scope of your employment at the time the cause of action arose, you may petition the court any time before trial to find and certify that you were acting within the scope of your employment. If the court agrees that you were acting within the scope of your employment, the U.S. government will be substituted as the defendant. If the court decides that you were not acting within the scope of your employment when the cause of action arose, the district court must send the case against you back to state court, and you are responsible for defending your actions.

Among other exceptions outlined in the statute, the FTCA protects you from any claim against you based upon your act if you exercised due care in executing a statute or regulation, whether or not the statute or regulation is valid. For example, if it was your job to execute Food and Drug Administration (FDA) health code regulations and, in doing so, you came across a violation at a meat packing plant that required you to shut down that plant, you could not be held responsible for any damage to the meat packing plant, its products, or to anyone working there that resulted from your shutting it down, because in doing so you properly executed the FDA regulations.

TIP

If an incident, accident, or event occurs where you might be liable for harm occurring to another, you should inform your agency immediately. In addition you should consider consulting with your own private lawyer.

The FTCA also protects you from claims based upon your exercise or performance, or failure to exercise or perform, a discretionary function or duty on your or your agency's part, whether or not the discretion involved was abused. For example, if your duty is to make determinations on contract bids, you cannot be held liable for failing to select a particular contractor.

If your job involves the use of discretion you cannot be sued for how you exercise your discretion. Furthermore, the FTCA prevents:

- claims based upon the transmission of letters or other postal matters;
- the collection or assessment of any tax or the detention of any goods by a customs or law enforcement officer;
- claims based upon combatant activities of the military during time of war; or
- any claim arising in a foreign country.

If you are individually sued for conduct that you engaged in while acting as an employee of the federal government, you need to inform your agency first, and then fully cooperate with your agency and the Attorney General's office to prove that the conduct for which you are being sued occurred in connection with your official duties as a federal employee. If you can show the Attorney General's office that you were acting within the scope of your official authority, the government will take over the case on your behalf and you will no longer be held personally liable for your conduct. However, if the Attorney General does not believe that you were acting within the scope of your job duties, and the court agrees, you may be held personally responsible for any harm caused by your conduct.

As the responsible party, can I be sued in any other way?

Generally, if you harm another person or her property you can be sued in state court. However, once an FTCA action is commenced (once the United States has become the defendant in a suit based on your actions), that law precludes victims from pursuing any other civil action or proceeding against you for money damages arising out of or relating to the act or omission which gave rise to the FTCA claim. Thus a civil action or proceeding, such as a state law personal injury case, cannot be brought against you personally. However, you can be sued for a violation of the U.S. Constitution (under the precedent set in Bivens v. Six Unknown Narcotics Agents, 403 U.S. 388 (1971)), or under a separate federal statute which authorizes such a personal suit. But you still may be immune from such Constitutional violations if you did not knowingly violate the Constitution.

What do I do if I have been harmed by the government or a government employee?

If you were harmed by a federal employee, getting compensation for that harm can be complicated. As you have read in the beginning of this chapter, for some kinds of harm, you cannot sue the individual federal employee who harmed you; you must sue the government instead. For other kinds of harm, you cannot sue the government, and must sue the federal employee who harmed you. Some claims can only be brought in state court, others only in federal district court. How do you know whom to sue and where?

When a person or the government unlawfully harms someone, it is called a tort. When you have been the victim of a tort committed by a member of the public, you can sue that person for damages to compensate you for the harm you have suffered. But what if the government is responsible for the tort? Generally, you can't sue the government – it's called sovereign immunity. The sovereign (the government) is immune from suit – unless it says otherwise. Thankfully, through the Federal Tort Claims Act (FTCA), the government allows itself to be sued for certain acts or omissions made by its employees.

Note that if you are injured in the course of your federal employment (while doing your job), you cannot bring an FTCA action against the United States. Your exclusive remedy from the government is to file a Workers' Compensation claim (see Chapter 15).

If you were harmed by an act or omission covered by the FTCA (i.e. an act or omission the government allows itself to be sued for), you must sue the government – you cannot sue the individual federal employee who actually caused the harm. You must also take certain steps to attempt to resolve your claim before you can file a suit in court. When you do file a suit, you can only sue the government in federal district court, not in state court. On the other hand, if you were harmed by an act or omission not covered by the FTCA (i.e. one that the government has not consented to be sued for), your only option is to file suit against the individual who harmed you (not the government) in state court.

WHOM DO YOU SUE AND WHERE?

Figuring out whom to sue and in what forum requires answering these questions:

- Who harmed you?
- What kind of claim are you making?
- Was the person who caused the harm acting within the scope of his or her employment?

WHO HARMED YOU AND WHAT KIND OF CLAIM ARE YOU MAKING?

Typical claims actionable under the FTCA include those based upon the following types of harm:

- a death
- personal injury, including pain and suffering
- injury to real estate or personal property, and
- loss of real estate or personal property

If you claim that you were harmed by an intentional tort such as assault, battery, false imprisonment, false arrest, abuse of process, slander, libel, interference with contract rights, or malicious prosecution, you must sue the wrongdoer individually, in state court, unless the wrongdoer was a federal law enforcement or investigative officer. If the person who you claim committed the intentional tort was a federal law enforcement or investigative officer, OR if you claim you were harmed by an unintentional tort, then your claim will be against the United States in federal district court, provided the wrongdoer was acting within the scope of her employment when she caused the harm. If the wrongdoer was not acting in the scope of her employment when she harmed you, then your claim will be against her individually, in state court.

Was the person who harmed you acting within the scope of his or her employment?

Determining whom to sue and where also depends on whether the act or omission that harmed you falls within the scope of employment of the person responsible for the harm. If the conduct that harmed you was within the scope of the wrongdoer's employment, then before you file suit in any court you must first make an administrative claim for relief with the Agency that employs the wrongdoer. If the administrative claim fails to resolve the matter, then you can bring suit against the United States in federal district court. If the conduct falls outside the scope of the wrongdoer's employment, then the claim is against the employee personally, in state court.

State law determines what kinds of conduct fall within the scope of employment, so if you are thinking about bringing a tort claim against a federal employee, you should certainly consult with an attorney in the state where the harmful or offensive conduct occurred. An attorney familiar with your state's employment laws will be able to tell you whether the conduct that resulted in your harm was likely within the scope of the employee's job or not, which will determine whom you can sue, and where.

If you decide that an individual federal employee was not acting within the scope of her employment when she harmed you, and you bring a tort suit against her in state court, the Westfall Act allows the US Attorney General to certify that the employee being sued was indeed acting within the scope of her employment when the alleged tort occurred. If the Attorney General makes this kind of certification, your case must be removed to federal district court, and the United States must take over for the employee as defendant. In many cases where this kind of removal to district court occurs, the case will be dismissed because the plaintiff has not exhausted his or her administrative remedies (by making an administrative claim with the employing agency) prior to filing suit. In some federal circuits, it is possible to challenge the Attorney General's certification that the alleged tort was committed within the scope of the employee's federal employment. In the other circuits, the Attorney General's certification cannot be challenged.

When can I bring an FTCA claim?

The laws of the state in which the negligent or wrongful act or omission occurred govern the date when the legal claim comes into existence, which is usually when the harm was suffered. Federal law controls the statute of limitations for bringing a claim under the FTCA. Under federal law, FTCA claims against the United States must be presented in writing to the responsible federal agency within *2 years* after the claim arises. If you are the one making a claim against the government under the FTCA, you cannot pursue the claim in court unless you have first presented the claim to the appropriate federal agency. If you fail to notify the agency of your claim, you will not be permitted to pursue your claim in court. You must wait until you have received a final denial of your claim from the agency in writing by certified or registered mail. If the agency fails to make a final disposition of a claim within *6 months* after it is filed, you may, at your option, treat the failure of the agency to make a timely final disposition under the FTCA as a final denial of your claim. If you wait to sue until after you receive the agency's denial of your claim, your lawsuit must be filed within *6 months* of the date of the mailing of the agency's final denial of your claim.

Claims against individuals acting outside the scope of their employment and duties brought in state court are governed by the appropriate state law governing the statute of limitations.

TIP

If you have a claim against the federal government under the FTCA you must first file a claim with the agency which caused the harm. Then you can file suit within six months after that agency denies the claim.

Relief under the FTCA

If you bring a suit covered by the FTCA in federal district court as described above, the government will be liable for tort claims under state law in the same manner and to the same extent as a private individual under like circumstances. However, although the United States is liable for actual and compensatory (pain and suffering) damages in a successful FTCA lawsuit, the government cannot be sued for punitive damages. Also, the government is not liable for interest on the money due for the period of time prior to judgment and if you owe anything to the government, they can deduct it from whatever damages are owed to you under the FTCA claim. You cannot institute any court action under the FTCA for a sum in excess of the amount of the claim presented to the federal agency, except where the increased amount is based upon:

- newly discovered evidence not reasonably discoverable at the time of presenting the claim to the federal agency, or
- allegations and proof of intervening facts relating to the amount of the claim, such as a worsened medical condition naturally occurring as a result of the government's original act.

Attorney fees are recoverable if a person is successful in prosecuting a FTCA claim. However, no attorney may charge, demand, receive, or collect for services rendered, fees greater than:

- 25 percent of any judgment rendered by a court or any settlement made by the Attorney General, or
- 20 percent of any award, compromise, or settlement made by an agency in the administrative process

Moreover, any attorney who charges, demands, receives, or collects for services rendered in connection with such a claim any amount in excess of that allowed under the FTCA, will be fined not more than $2,000 or imprisoned not more than one year, or both.

Final Thoughts

At some point, you may find that you either want to sue the federal government for harm that has occurred to you, or you are being sued as the one who did the harm while representing the federal government. Such claims are generally governed by the Federal Tort Claims Act. Since you can be either the plaintiff bringing the claim, or the defendant against whom the claim is brought, you would do well to be familiar with what liability the Act permits and exempts.

25

Postal Service Employee Rights

You Mean Dogs Chasing Me Isn't the Only Difference Between Me and Other Federal Employees?

In This Chapter You Will Learn:

- whether U.S. Postal Service ("USPS") employees have the same rights as other federal employees
- how USPS employee rights may differ

Contents Chapter Twenty-Five - Postal Service Employee Rights

Introduction

If you are employed by the U.S. Postal Service ("USPS"), you are in a unique situation. The Postal Service is a hybrid agency. For some purposes, it is a federal agency. For other purposes, it is a private company that functions like a commercial enterprise. As a result, your rights as a postal employee may vary greatly from those of other federal employees, depending upon the issue. For example, postal employees have rights as federal employees under the U.S. Constitution, but are not covered by the Whistleblower Protection Act or prohibited personnel practice laws. Recognizing these differences is important to understanding and protecting your rights. In this chapter we will discuss the differences and how they impact your rights as an employee.

Is the Postal Service's structure the same as other federal agencies'?

Before 1970, the United States Postal Service was known as the Post Office Department. In 1970, Congress passed the Postal Reorganization Act.[1] Under this Act, the old Post Office Department became the United States Postal Service. Rather than being simply a department, it became an independent executive agency. The Act reorganized the Post Office Department and created the structure that we know today.

The Postal Service is now governed by a nine-member Board of Governors. The Board of Governors selects a Postmaster General, who serves as the chief executive officer of the Postal Service.

Are most Postal Service employees covered by union contracts?

With more than 500,000 employees, the Postal Service is one of the largest employers in the United States. Most postal employees are covered by union

---

1 *See* Pub. Law. No. 91-375.

collective bargaining agreements. Under the Reorganization Act, Congress established a Postal Career Service and a labor-management system that expressly called for the setting of terms and conditions of employment through collective bargaining.

As a Postal Service employee, you are allowed to collectively bargain over wages and working conditions under laws applying to private industry. The National Labor Relations Board ("NLRB"), rather than the FLRA, has been given authority to enforce your collective bargaining rights, as it does in private industry. However, like federal employees, you are prohibited from striking. Many benefits afforded federal employees are also afforded to you as a postal employee, such as veterans preferences and coverage under the Federal Employees Health Benefits (FEHB) program, the Federal Employees Compensation Act (FECA), and the Civil Service and Federal Employees Retirement Systems (CSRS and FERS). (See Chapters 16-19.)

Is the pay different for Postal Service employees?

As you may be aware, the collective bargaining agreement covering you affects your pay. The collective bargaining history between the Postal Service and its unions has done much to improve postal pay practices since 1970. The Postal Service operates its own pay system. It is the policy of the Postal Service that the compensation and benefits provided to its employees should be comparable to those offered by the private sector for similar work. Under its system, there are two general types of salary structures, as well as a specialized structure for rural letter carriers. The two generalized pay structures are the:

- **PS (Postal Service) salary structure**—this covers bargaining unit employees such as most clerks and carriers, mailhandlers, nurses, and security personnel, and
- **EAS (Executive and Administrative Salary) structure**—this covers executives, professionals, supervisors, postmasters, technical and administrative employees, and other workers not covered by bargaining agreements

As a postal employee, your pay rates are based upon an 80-hour biweekly pay period. Hourly pay is calculated by dividing annual salary by 2,080 hours. Eligible employees in the Postal Service and eligible employees through EAS Grade 18 (EAS grades range from EAS-1 through EAS-26) may receive time-and-one-half overtime pay.

The Postal Service also employs part-time regular schedule employees and part-time flexible schedule employees, who are paid according to the number of hours worked. They receive overtime for working more than eight hours per day or 40 hours in the workweek.

Nearly every full-time non-exempt postal employee is entitled to:

- holiday pay
- Sunday pay
- night differential pay
- step pay increases based upon satisfactory completion of the required time in grade, as long as no equivalent raise was received during the required time in grade

As a Postal Service employee, you are also eligible for cost-of-living adjustments and you receive a five to 10 percent raise in your base pay upon promotion to or within the EAS. Supervisors and postmasters are provided special pay packages that affect their compensation. Check with your personnel office for more information on supervisor and postmaster pay packages.

TIP

Postal Service employees have their own separate pay system different from other branches of the government. Unions representing postal employees, unlike unions representing most other federal employees, can negotiate for terms relating to wages which are spelled out in labor agreements.

Do Postal Service employees have MSPB appeal rights?

In cases of adverse actions, the following Postal Service employees have appeal rights to the MSPB:

- postmasters
- managers
- supervisors
- confidential personnelists, and
- non-probationary preference-eligible employees (those with veterans preference)

Non-preference-eligible Postal Service employees who are covered under union contracts do not have MSPB appeal or any other rights under Title 5 of the United States Code, unless expressly granted by some provision of law not found in Title 5.

In order to have MSPB appeal rights, a preference-eligible or other qualifying Postal Service employee must have at least one year of continuous service in the same or a similar position. One year of continuous service means that you must either:

- have been employed in one position without a break of a workday, or
- have been employed in more than one position in the same line of work, i.e., positions that involve related or comparable work that requires the same or similar skills, without a break of a workday

Service in a temporary excepted service position may be counted toward the completion of the one-year current continuous service requirement.

On the important issue of whether positions are "similar positions" that would mean no break in service and thus appeal rights, the MSPB and the United States Court of Appeals for the Federal Circuit have held, for example, that Postal Service special delivery messenger positions and distribution clerk positions are "similar positions." On the other hand, the MSPB has held that a city letter carrier position and a general expediter position are not "the same or similar positions." Likewise, a distribution clerk position and a postmaster position are not "the same or similar positions."

In determining the similarity of positions, the MSPB will look at whether substantial training was necessary to go from one position to the other, and whether one involves supervisory authority that the other did not. Therefore, if you are a Postal Service employee with possible MSPB appeal rights and you change jobs through promotions or the like, that change in jobs could cause you to lose your MSPB appeal rights for a period of one year. (See Chapter 4 for a more complete explanation of MSPB procedures and jurisdiction.)

What if I have an EEO complaint?

The federal anti-employment discrimination laws apply to the Postal Service, but the procedures can be a little different. The collective bargaining agreements between the Postal Service and the unions that represent its eligible employees may provide that allegations of employment discrimination may be raised under the terms of a collective bargaining agreement's grievance procedure. Note, however, that there is no requirement that collective bargaining agreements provide for the processing of allegations of discrimination. In fact, the NLRB has held that a Postal Service employee covered under a collective bargaining agreement may pursue allegations of discrimination under *both* the negotiated grievance procedure and the Postal Service EEO complaint process.

Under the EEOC's regulations, the Postal Service has been given the option of holding EEO complaints in abeyance while processing a grievance over the same action. The Postal Service must notify you if it decides to hold your EEO complaint in abeyance under the EEOC regulation.

You have the right to file agency EEO complaints on your own, without resorting to the union. However, you cannot invoke arbitration of a grievance under a collective bargaining agreement without your union's participation and authorization. In any EEO settlement negotiation that purports to also settle a pending grievance, the union has a right to be involved. The Postal Service cannot cancel your EEO complaint based on the settlement of a union grievance unless the grievance settlement constitutes full relief for you under discrimination laws. Likewise, your union cannot settle your pending EEO complaint without your authorization and endorsement of the settlement.

Most Postal Service collective bargaining agreements provide that a terminated employee will remain on the Postal Service's rolls until the resolution of any grievance over the removal is reached. However, under EEO law, an employee is considered terminated on the last day on which he or she is allowed to come to work. Therefore, if you are terminated from your employment, you must contact an agency EEO counselor within *45 days* of your last workday for your complaint of discrimination to be timely, regardless of whether a grievance is filed on your behalf as well. (See Chapter 6 for a more complete explanation of the EEOC process.)

If your EEO complaint does proceed through the EEOC process, you will likely be provided the opportunity to participate in mediation through the Postal Service REDRESS program. REDRESS is a voluntary mediation program which utilizes non-postal, impartial, third-party mediators to resolve EEO complaints during the informal EEO process. Of course, reaching agreement is strictly voluntary between you and the Postal

TIP

If you are a unionized postal employee with a complaint of discrimination, you should consider protesting through both the EEO complaint process and the union grievance procedure. Sometimes your union can achieve good results, much faster than you can achieve on your own. However, unions are busy helping many people. You must continually press the union representatives to focus on your particular grievance. Remember, the "squeaky wheel" usually gets more grease.

Service. If mediation is unsuccessful at resolving your EEO complaint, you will then be given the opportunity to proceed to a hearing.

Do Postal Service employees have appeal rights in RIFs?

Unlike other federal employees, only those Postal Service employees with veterans preference have the right to appeal a reduction-in-force (RIF) action to the MSPB. Therefore, if you, as a postal employee, do not have veterans preference, you do not have the right to appeal adverse RIF actions, such as your separation from employment or your downgrade, to the MSPB. If you do have veterans preference, you have the same RIF appeal rights as a competitive service federal employee. (See Chapter 9.)

Final Thoughts

As a Postal Service employee, you are in the unique position of working for a federal agency that operates like a private corporation for some purposes. While many of your rights are the same as those of other federal employees, there are some significant differences. Always check to see whether your problems and issues are treated the same as other federal employees or are handled differently because you are a Postal Service employee.

26

Congressional and Presidential Employees' Rights

You Mean We Finally Got Some Protection?!!

In This Chapter You Will Learn:

- what protective employment laws apply to Congressional employees and employees in the Executive Office of the President
- what avenues are open for bringing claims for violations

Contents Chapter Twenty-Six - Congressional and Presidential Employees' Rights

Introduction

If you are a Congressional employee, or one of certain types of employees within the Executive branch of the U.S. government, at times you have probably thought you were in a netherworld (for more reasons than one...). You hear about exciting new legislation that provides greater protection for employees, including federal employees, only to later find out that you are not covered as a Congressional or executive branch employee. You may legitimately wonder why you seem to have second-class status when it comes to employment, with fewer rights than other federal or even private employees. This may strike you as particularly odd since you work for the very people who make the laws or are responsible for executing them.

Someone heard your lamentations. In 1995, several of the more important pieces of protective legislation for employees were extended to you. In this chapter, we will discuss what those laws are, when the legislation becomes effective for you, and what to do to enforce your rights under the laws.

What is the Congressional Accountability Act?

The Congressional Accountability Act ("CAA"), enacted on January 23, 1995, applies the following eleven workplace laws to you if you are employed by Congressional employers—i.e., offices of Senators and Representatives, and U.S. Congressional committees.

- Fair Labor Standards Act
- Title VII of the Civil Rights Act of 1964

- Americans with Disabilities Act
- Age Discrimination in Employment Act
- Family and Medical Leave Act
- Occupational Safety and Health Act
- Employee Polygraph Protection Act
- Chapter 71 of Title 5 of the United States Code (concerning labor-management relations)—the FSLMRS
- Workers Adjustment and Retraining Notification Act ("WARN" Act)
- Rehabilitation Act, and
- Chapter 43 (concerning veterans' employment and reemployment) of Title 38 of the United States Code

As described in other chapters of this book, these laws:

- prohibit discrimination against employees due to their race, color, sex, age, national origin, religion, or disability
- require employers to pay all employees the minimum wage and to pay certain employees overtime, and
- require the granting of time off to care for the birth of a child, or because of an employee's serious health condition

How do I enforce my rights under the CAA?

In order to file a complaint, you must follow the procedures established by the CAA. To pursue a claim the following steps *must* be taken:

1. counseling
2. mediation
3. filing of a formal complaint or a lawsuit in court

Each of these steps has deadlines which must be carefully observed.

Counseling

The first step in filing a complaint is to request counseling from Congress' Office of Compliance within *180 calendar days* of the date you become aware of the alleged violation of the CAA. The counseling period, which will last *30 calendar days*, is to be used to discuss your concerns and to attempt to resolve the matter at the earliest stage. Once counseling is completed the Office of Compliance will notify you that the counseling period is completed, and that you may request mediation if you are still dissatisfied.

MEDIATION

Mediation is a process in which you and your employing office attempt to resolve your complaint through the assistance of a third party, called a mediator. The mediator cannot impose a solution on the parties, but rather helps the parties reach their own solution. If you wish to continue pursuing your complaint, you must request mediation. To request mediation, you have *15 calendar days* from the date you receive the notice from the Compliance Office that the counseling period has been completed. The period in which mediation takes place lasts only *30 calendar days,* although extensions can be requested.

TIP

Try your best to get your complaint resolved by counseling and mediation. A speedy and fair compromise settlement is generally most advisable. However, if the agency is unreasonable, formal litigation procedures are available.

FILING A FORMAL COMPLAINT OR LAWSUIT IN COURT

If your complaint is not resolved during the mediation period, you will then be notified by the Office of Compliance of your rights to pursue your complaint further. You have two options. You can either:

- file a formal complaint with the Office of Compliance, or
- file a civil action (lawsuit) in a U.S. district court

You cannot do both. If you wish to pursue either of these two options, you must do so *between 30 and 90 calendar days* after the date on which you were notified of the completion of mediation. For example, if you were notified on January 1, 2014, that the mediation period was completed, you could not file your complaint or lawsuit until February 1, 2014, and it must be filed no later than April 1, 2014.

If you file a formal complaint with the Compliance Office, a hearing officer will be appointed to conduct a hearing concerning your complaint, and, thereafter, will issue a decision. Whichever option you choose—formal complaint or lawsuit—the decision of the hearing officer or of the U.S.

district court can be appealed to the U.S. court of appeals. The CAA provides attorney fees to prevailing parties, and can award compensatory damages if provided under the law alleged to have been violated.

What is the Presidential and Executive Office Accountability Act?

What the CAA does for Congressional employees, the Presidential and Executive Office Accountability Act ("PEOAA") does for employees of the Executive Office of the President. It applies the same eleven workplace laws to employing offices within the Executive Office of the President, the Executive residence at the White House, and the Vice President's official residence.

If you wish to allege violations of the PEOAA, you must follow the administrative procedures set forth in the law. These procedures are virtually identical to those applicable under the CAA (see above), except the administrative hearing is held by the Merit Systems Protection Board. Like the CAA, the PEOAA provides for attorney fees for prevailing parties, and awards of compensatory damages if provided under the law alleged to have been violated.

Final Thoughts

If you are a Congressional or Executive Office employee, you may not yet be aware that protective legislation which previously excluded you now applies. If you have any of the employment problems covered by the statutes which now provide coverage for you, look at those chapters to see what your rights are. Unfortunately, outside of these statutes, there is still no way to challenge other personnel actions, such as removals for misconduct or poor performance.

27

Waivers of Overpayment and Financial Claims Against the Government

Hey Uncle Sam! You Owe Me!

In This Chapter You Will Learn:

- what happens if the government overpays you
- what to do if you have a financial claim against the government
- how to exercise your rights under the law

Contents Chapter Twenty-Seven - Waivers of Overpayment and Financial Claims Against the Government

Introduction

Did Uncle Sam accidentally put a little extra money in your paycheck this week? If so, you may get to keep it! According to Congress, it may take more time and effort than it is worth to have the government take it back. If Uncle Sam, on the other hand, owes you money—to reimburse travel expenses, or for some type of pay or benefit—you will need plenty of patience. In this chapter, we will explain the procedures for seeking a waiver of a government overpayment to you, how to deal with a government collection action against you, and how to collect a debt the government owes to you.

How do I request a waiver of an overpayment to me?

The U.S. Code provides a small but significant opportunity for you to avoid having to repay Uncle Sam in certain instances when the United States makes an erroneous payment of pay or travel, transportation, or relocation expenses and allowances.[1] If the overpayment was toward your health benefits, the government generally is precluded from trying to recover it. If the overpayment was toward your retirement benefits, the government may fight vigorously to reclaim it. The procedures for seeking a waiver of overpaid annuities are discussed separately below.

General overpayments

You must determine where and from whom you should request a waiver of the overpayment. If the government overpayment to you is a total amount of *$1,500 or less*, you may be able to seek a waiver in whole or in part of the overpayment from the head of the agency which made the erroneous overpayment. You can seek a waiver from the head of the agency if your agency is one of the following:

- an Executive agency

1 *See* 5 USC § 5584(a).

- the Government Printing Office
- the Library of Congress
- the Office of the Architect of the Capitol, or
- the Botanic Garden

You may seek a waiver of an overpayment to you from the Director of the Administrative Office of the U.S. Courts even if the amount is as high as *$10,000*, if you are an employee or officer of:

- the Administrative Office of the U.S. Courts
- the Federal Judicial Center, or
- any court defined by 28 USC 610

Under 5 USC 5584(a)(2), the head of an Executive agency may waive an amount not more than $1,500 per individual claim while higher amounts must be waived by an "authorized official," which under § 5584(g)(2) is the Director of the Office of Management and Budget (OMB). The Director of OMB has delegated OMB's waiver authority to the Executive agency that made the erroneous payment in question, and there is no dollar limit. Each agency is responsible for establishing waiver policies and standards and determining levels of approval. It is not uncommon for agencies to provide for a two-tier review, but there is no appeal outside of the Executive agency that made the disputed overpayment.

While the Office of Personnel Management (OPM) is responsible for regulating various types of pay and allowances and also issues claims settlement decisions regarding compensation and leave matters (see 5 CFR Part 178, subpart A), it does not have authority under § 5584 to waive overpayment of debts resulting from erroneous payments of pay and allowances except for its own employees. OPM claims decisions may be involved in determining whether erroneous payments have been made, *i.e.*, whether an overpayment debt actually exists, but OPM generally will not become involved until after the employee has received a final agency-level decision. *See* HYPERLINK "http://www.opm.gov/Payclaims" www.opm.gov/Payclaims for additional information.

The General Services Administration (GSA) Civilian Board of Contract Appeals (CBCA) has authority to settle claims incurred by federal employees for official travel, transportation, and relocation, although GSA does not have authority under § 5584 to waive overpayment debts resulting from erroneous payments of travel, transportation and relocation expenses and allowances. Any waiver request involving such matters must be directed to the agency that made the erroneous payment, and any agency waiver decision is not subject to review by GSA.

TIP

Do not miss the 3-year time limit for seeking a waiver of an overpayment. For most overpayments, you will have only 3 years from the date you discovered the erroneous payment in which to request a waiver of the overpayment.[2]

In order to succeed in your bid for a waiver of an overpayment from the head of your agency, you must meet the "equitable" legal standard which determines whether you are entitled to a waiver of overpayment. You must convince the deciding official that the collection of the overpayment would be inequitable, unfair, against good conscience, and not in the best interests of the United States.[3] You must prove entitlement to the waiver under this standard by "substantial evidence." All the evidence in your case, the good and the bad, will be considered. If the evidence shows a rational basis for your position, then you can say that substantial evidence supports your case.

Annuities or Retirement Benefits

If you have been overpaid in annuities or your retirement benefits, you may be eligible for a waiver of the overpayment.[4] Although OPM may notify you of your right to request a waiver, you should not wait for this notice if you discover the overpayment on your own. Rather, prepare a written request for a waiver immediately and submit it to the Director of OPM.[5] You must convince OPM that you, the overpaid employee, are blameless for the overpayment and that recovery would be inequitable, unfair, and against good conscience.

If you are not successful in your OPM request, you must request reconsideration. If the final OPM decision is negative, you may file a petition for appeal to the MSPB as long as you do so within *30 days* of your receipt of an unfavorable OPM decision. Send your appeal in writing to the regional or field office of the MSPB which has jurisdiction over your area. That address

---

2 *See* 5 USC § 5584(b).
3 *See* 5 USC § 5584(a).
4 *See* 5 USC § 8546(b).
5 *See* 5 USC § 8546(b).

should be included in the final OPM decision. Also, you can go to mspb.gov or see Appendix L of this book.

TIP

OPM's denial of a waiver of overpayment in your annuity or retirement benefits may be appealed to the MSPB within 30 days of receiving OPM's denial of your request for reconsideration.

On appeal, you must convince the MSPB that equity and good conscience dictate that you should not have to repay the overpaid annuities or retirement benefits. You could also argue for a partial waiver if that is what makes sense, given the equities of the situation. The equities of the situation mean that, in balance, you are asking only for what is fair to you and to the government—no more. For example, you should consider seeking a partial waiver if the reason why you had no knowledge of the overpayment was due to a period of time when you were ill and not personally managing your assets. Once well again and competent to manage your assets, you may not have a good argument to waive overpayment. Or, for another example, perhaps your bank made an error on your account for a certain period of time during which it would have been impossible to determine there had been an overpayment. It would be appropriate to seek a partial waiver for the time when the bank made an error—something out of your control—but not for the remaining time when you simply failed to notice or seek a correction to a noticeable overpayment. See Chapter 18 for a fuller discussion of retirement-related overpayment and waiver issues.

STRATEGIES AND APPROACHES FOR FILING YOUR WAIVER REQUEST

First, investigate and if appropriate challenge the accuracy of the government's claim. The government's calculation of the amount overpaid may be inaccurate. Put the government on notice of your challenge.

To bolster your arguments of equity and good conscience, point out that you committed no intentional wrong. Establish that the agency created the error which led to the overpayment. Argue that the agency should bear the burden of its mistake, given the fact that it would create a financial hardship for you to repay it now. This is sort of a "finder's keepers" argument, but couple it with an earnest account of your good faith-reliance upon the government's payment —which you did not know was an overpayment— and the financial difficulties of your present situation. Describe the difficulties in detail. If it looks like you profited handsomely, if the overpayment was obvious, and if you have the money to repay it, these arguments may not be persuasive and you will have to repay the money.

A decision-maker might be swayed if you include evidence of failing physical or mental health, the complexity of the payment information sent to you, and your diligence in addressing the problem promptly when you noticed something was wrong. If pertinent, discuss how your financial position was worsened as a result of your innocent reliance upon the overpayment received.

If you are unable to get a waiver or partial waiver, your fall-back position should be a concern about the repayment terms. Ask for an extended repayment plan over a long period of time in order to preserve your standard of living. Try to come to an agreement on a repayment plan, such as an offset from your annuity rather than using other assets you may have. For more information on the government's right to collect its money, read the next section on government collection.

If you are not successful in your attempt to obtain a waiver from your agency head, you have no further appeal rights. The decision is not reviewable by any court or by any higher ranking executive branch official, except in cases of overpayment of retirement benefits, which cases are appealable to the U.S. Court of Appeals for the Federal Circuit.

If you seek a waiver of the overpayment, but the government collects it from you while you are seeking a waiver, don't give up! The employing agency which made the erroneous payment to you will be forced to refund you the amount of a subsequently approved waiver. You must apply to the employing agency which made the erroneous overpayment for your refund within *2 years* following the effective date of the waiver.

How do I deal with government collection?

When you are indebted to the federal government—whether because of an erroneous overpayment to you or your failure to pay the government for something—the government is entitled to recoup its debt by simply deducting the amount you owe them from monies they owe to you, including your tax refund! If the government does not seek a civil judgment against you, you must be given notice of the alleged debt and an opportunity to contest it in front of someone who does not report to the head of the collecting agency.[6]

The government's burden of proof

The government must establish the overpayment or debt and seek to collect it in a timely fashion. You should determine whether the amount has been correctly calculated and the demand for repayment made within the time limit. The government must declare its right to collect the debt within *10 years* of the debt or overpayment. If the government truly did overpay you wages, travel, transportation, relocation expenses and allowances, or retirement benefits, and begins collection procedures within *10 years* of the overpayment, you must pay, unless you are fortunate enough to get a waiver.

The government establishes its right to offset a debt from your pay (for example, if you do not pay charges for travel on a government credit card), through a mandatory administrative process. The government must notify you of:

- a debt due to the agency and the agency's intention to collect the debt by an offset from your pay
- your right to request reconsideration and/or a waiver of the debt, and
- your right to an administrative hearing before an official who is independent of the head of the agency collecting the debt, or if the agency chooses, before an administrative law judge

The government establishes its right to offset a lump-sum payment due to you by a similar administrative process, but one which provides different rights. The government must give you:

- notice of the debt and the intent to collect it by administrative offset
- an opportunity to inspect the records
- an opportunity for review of the debt within the agency, and
- an opportunity to reach a written agreement with the agency concerning the rate of offset

When the government has overpaid retirement benefits, the government may recover the overpayment by notifying you of:

---

6 For a fuller explanation of the government's collection standards and practices, refer to the Debt Collection Act of 1982, as amended, 5 USC § 5514; 31 USC § 3711-3702A (Claims of the U.S. Government); Federal Claims Collection Standards, 4 CFR § 101.1 *et seq.*, and 5 CFR § 831.1804(b)(4).

- the amount of the overpayment
- the reason(s) it occurred
- the right to request reconsideration, waiver and/or compromise, and
- the possibility of a right to a hearing

Government withholding

If you are denied a waiver of overpayment, or while you are still seeking a waiver, the government may attempt to collect its money from you by withholding up to:

- 15 percent of your net disposable pay after deductions, or
- 50 percent of your net annuity [7]

Disposable pay means the portion of your paycheck remaining after deductions of amounts required by law to be withheld (for example, tax, Social Security, Medicare, etc.). Voluntary withholdings (such as for a car loan repayment) would not be included.

There is no limit on the amount which can be offset from your annuity if the case involves fraud or misrepresentation or if the government is collecting an overpayment of an annuity. The government can also recover its money by deductions from any lump sum amount due to you, for example, for leave or retirement.[8]

If the government obtains a civil judgment for the amount of the debt, rather than validating the debt through the administrative process, the government can withhold up to 25 percent of your disposable pay! [9] Unlike private employees, you are not able to avoid repayment by filing bankruptcy even if financial hardship would make the approach advisable. This partly explains the availability of the government's waiver process.

How do I file against the government for money?

Two basic types of monetary claims against the government are addressed here:

- claims for pay or leave which are not covered by the Fair Labor Standards Act (FLSA), and
- claims relating to travel and relocation allowances and transportation rates

Wage-related claims covered by the FLSA are discussed in Chapter 11.

---

7 *See* 5 USC § 5514.

8 *See* 31 USC § 3711 and 3716; 5 CFR § 550.1101 *et seq.*

9 *See* Section 124 of Public Law 97-276.

Non-FLSA claims for pay or leave

If you believe that the government owes you money for pay or leave, you must first submit a written claim to your agency head. If turned down, you have a right to file an appeal with OPM.[10] Unfortunately, an appeal to the OPM usually results in little more than a rubber stamp of the agency decision. Claims which are either covered by the FLSA or which may be brought as a negotiated grievance under a collective bargaining agreement, are excluded from this OPM appeal process.

The OPM appeal must be in writing and include the following information:

- your name
- address
- telephone and fax number
- a description of your claim and all reasons supporting your claim
- the name, address, telephone, and fax number of the agency employee who denied your claim
- a copy of the agency's denial
- any other information which you believe OPM should consider
- precisely what relief, including a dollar amount, you are seeking, and
- your signature

TIP

Submit claims to:

Program Manager, Room 6484
Center for Merit Systems Accountability
Office of Personnel Management
1900 E Street NW
Washington, DC 20415

Inquiries may be made by telephone at 202/606-7948.

---

[10] Until June 30, 1996, the General Accounting Office heard such appeals, but Congress amended the relevant statute and required that the Office of Management and Budget (OMB) decide the appeal. OMB delegated the function to OPM. On December 31, 1997, OPM published final rules, found at 5 CFR § Part 178, which govern the procedure for settling claims for federal (including deceased) employees' compensation and leave, and for claims regarding the proceeds of canceled checks for veterans' benefits payable to deceased beneficiaries.

The claim must be filed within *6 years* of the date when the claim arose. OPM must actually *receive* your appeal within this six-year time frame. A timely postmark showing you mailed the appeal within six years will be insufficient.

When an agency initially denies your claim, it may sometimes forward your claim directly to OPM on your behalf. You are still responsible for ensuring that OPM receives all the essential information. OPM may request specific information from the agency or proceed without an agency report.

OPM will make its decision on your appeal based upon the written submissions only. No oral argument or hearing is available. OPM's regulations specify that the burden is on you to establish the timeliness of the appeal and your right to relief. The regulations further provide that OPM will accept the facts asserted by the agency unless you present clear and convincing evidence to the contrary.[11] There is no time limit set for OPM's review of an appeal. Once issued, the OPM decision is the final decision of the government.

If you are turned down by OPM in a dispute over pay, allowances, and/or leave matters, you may file a case in federal court. There is a 6-year statute of limitations, but there is no need to exhaust administrative remedies with OPM. For further information on filing claims in federal court, please see Chapter 11 – Overtime and Special Pay.

TIP

File claims by mail with the GSA at the following address:

Clerk, Civilian Board of Contract Appeals
General Services Administration
1800 F street, NW
Washington, DC 20405

Inquiries may be made by telephone at 202/606-8800, by facsimile at 202/606-009 or online at cbca.gsa.gov.

Claims relating to travel, relocation, and transportation rates

If you have a claim relating to travel and relocation allowances and transportation rates, you may appeal an agency's denial of your claim with the General Services Administration, Civilian Board of Contract Appeals (CBCA). Include any information which verifies your right to the amount

---

11 *See* 5 CFR § 178.105.

specified. For instance, include a copy of a receipt showing that you paid your credit card bills for a hotel expense, that your hotel expense was an approved expenditure related to agency business, and that you have not been reimbursed. Sign your appeal under the penalty of perjury, or have your signature notarized. You may research the decisions of the CBCA online at www.cbca.gsa.gov.

Final Thoughts

Some day or week, you may notice more money in your government check than you are supposed to have. The best thing to do is to check and see if the amount is correct. If it is not, notify the proper authorities and keep a record of it. If you are told it is correct, but it later turns out to be incorrect, you may be responsible for the overpayment made to you. It will greatly aid in your defense if you can establish that you were dealing in good faith and in reliance on what you were told, though it turned out to be incorrect. If, on the other hand, the government owes you money, you now have information as to how to get it back. But be patient. As a government employee, you, of all people, know that the wheels of government grind slowly. But they generally do grind.

28 Miscellaneous

The Stuff That Doesn't Fit Anywhere Else

In This Chapter You Will Learn:

- what the law says about nepotism in the federal government
- what your agency can do about your off-duty conduct
- whether you can file suit on behalf of the government for fraud
- whether you can rely on oral information from an agency official

?

Contents Chapter Twenty-Eight - Miscellaneous

Introduction

This chapter will address miscellaneous issues that do not neatly fit into any other chapter, including: off-duty misconduct, nepotism, *qui tam* (pronounced: "kwee tam") actions, and the question of whether you can rely on oral promises or information from any agency official.

Can my agency discipline me for my off-duty misconduct?

An agency will sometimes propose to discipline you for actions that took place while you were off duty. Examples of off-duty misconduct are limitless, but include:

- actions that lead to arrest
- drug offenses
- sexual misconduct
- fraud/theft
- illegal gambling
- failure to pay debts

To discipline you for off-duty misconduct, the agency must show that the disciplinary action will promote the "efficiency of the service."[1] Absent a "nexus"—or connection—between your misconduct and the disciplinary/adverse action taken by your agency, the discipline will not be upheld in a legal challenge to it.

Under MSPB case law, a nexus exists between your off-duty misconduct and the adverse action if:

- the off-duty misconduct is egregious, and substantially affects your ability to do your job, and
- you do not produce sufficient evidence rebutting the presumption that your retention as an employee would adversely affect the agency

To convince the MSPB that your misconduct substantially affects your ability to do your job, your agency will often contend that, based upon the

---

1 *See* 5 USC § 7513.

off-duty misconduct, you lack the trustworthiness necessary to adequately perform your job. Once the agency can establish that your ability to do the job is substantially affected, the burden shifts to you to rebut the presumption that your retention as an employee of the agency will not adversely affect the agency. The best way for you to do this is to gather witness support from supervisors and coworkers. You must establish that, the misconduct with which you have been charged notwithstanding, you can still be trusted to perform the duties of your job. Of course, as was addressed in the chapter on disciplinary and adverse actions, you also have the opportunity to argue that the agency's proposed penalty is excessive based on the *Douglas* factors.

TIP

Challenge disciplinary action for off-duty misconduct by showing that your ability to do your job is unaffected by off-duty behavior.

CAN MY SUPERVISOR HIRE HIS OWN FAMILY TO FILL POSITIONS?

The idea behind merit promotion plans and the issuance of vacancy announcements is that the most qualified individual for a particular position will be selected for that position. Of course, that is not always the case. This section will briefly discuss nepotism, which can affect an agency's decision-making process when filling a position, and prevent the most qualified individual from being selected.

Under the law,[2] an agency official who has the authority to take, recommend, or approve any personnel action is not permitted to employ, promote, or advance (or advocate for employment, promotion, or advancement) any individual who is a "relative" of that official. Of course, this anti-nepotism rule will only apply if the position at issue is in the agency in which the official works or exercises control. It is important to note that this official may not even advocate a relative for employment in a particular position. What does the term "advocate" mean here? In its regulations, OPM explains that a public official "advocates" someone for a position when that official

---

[2] *See* 5 USC § 2302(b)(7).

recommends or refers them for consideration for appointment, promotion, or advancement by another agency official lower in the chain of command. The anti-nepotism rule is meant to prevent high-ranking agency officials from pressuring other supervisors in the agency to select a relative of the high-ranking official for a position.

You might be wondering who qualifies as a "relative." According to the statutory definition,[3] a relative is a:

- father/mother
- son/daughter
- brother/sister
- aunt/uncle
- nephew/niece
- first cousin
- husband/wife
- father-in-law/mother-in-law
- son-in-law/daughter-in-law
- brother-in-law/sister-in-law
- stepfather/stepmother
- stepson/stepdaughter
- stepbrother/stepsister
- half brother/half sister

This list further includes "domestic partner," as used by the U.S. Office of Personnel Management in its decisions to extend certain federal entitlements, including health and tax benefits, to individuals deemed to be domestic partners of federal employees. If the supervisor and the individual whom the supervisor is recommending for a position are not related in one of these ways, then no valid allegation of nepotism under the statute exists.

As is the case with most rules, however, there is an exception to the general rule that nepotism will invalidate an appointment or promotion. An agency official may employ a relative in a position if the employment is necessary to meet urgent needs emanating from an emergency posing an immediate threat to life or property, or a national emergency. As you can imagine, this exception is applicable in very limited circumstances.

---

3 *See* 5 USC § 3110 (a)(3).

What in the world is a "*qui tam*" action?

Qui tam actions permit private individuals to file suit, on behalf of the United States government, against parties who attempt to defraud the federal government by filing false claims. Although the False Claims Act of 1863 provided private individuals with the opportunity to file a *qui tam* action, the procedures of this False Claims Act were complex. As a result, very few people filed actions under it. To make it easier for private citizens to file claims under the Act, Congress amended it and enacted the False Claims Act Amendments of 1986.

What claims are permissible in a *qui tam* action?

The most common type of false claim occurs when an individual or corporation knowingly presents a false or fraudulent claim for payment or approval to an officer of the federal government.[4] Overcharging or cheating the government and "padding" invoices are other examples of false claims.

TIP

If you have firsthand knowledge and written proof that someone is cheating or defrauding the government, you should first consult a private lawyer. You may have the right to file suit under the False Claims Act.

How do I bring a *qui tam* action?

You may file a civil action in federal district court in the name of the United States government. You need to serve a copy of the complaint, along with a written explanation of all important evidence which you relied upon to file this complaint, on the United States government, pursuant to Rule 4 of the Federal Rules of Civil Procedure.

To comply with Rule 4, you should send a copy of the complaint, by registered or certified mail, to:

- the United States Attorney for your district, and
- the Attorney General of the United States

[4] *For a complete list of other false claims, see* 31 USC § 3729.

A copy of the complaint is not issued to the defendant until the court so orders.

Within *60 days* of receiving the complaint and the description of the evidence it is based on from the individual filing the complaint, the government may elect to intervene and proceed with the action. If the government decides to proceed with the action, it will have the primary responsibility for prosecuting the action, although you still have the right to continue as a party to the action.

What happens if the action succeeds? (Show me the money!)

If the government proceeds with the action you filed, and it prevails, you are entitled to at least 15 percent, but not more than 25 percent, of the proceeds of the action or the settlement of the claim. Generally, the more significant and helpful the information is that you provided, the greater amount you will receive. If the government does not proceed with the action, and you proceed with the claim on your own, you are entitled to at least 25 percent, but no more than 30 percent, of the proceeds. In either case, the defendant will be responsible for paying a reasonable amount of costs, expenses, and attorney fees that you incur in pursuing the successful action.

Are there any *qui tam* type actions which are specifically barred?

Yes.[5] The most common type of barred action is the situation where a plaintiff obtains his/her information from another source, and then files a claim. According to the False Claims Act Amendments, no court will take jurisdiction over a claim based upon "the public disclosure of allegations or transactions in a criminal, civil, or administrative hearing, in a congressional, administrative, or Government Accountability Office report, hearing, audit, or investigation, or from the news media, unless the action is brought by the Attorney General or the person bringing the action is an original source of the information."[6] This provision prevents people from gaining a windfall when the information necessary to prevail in the suit was already available to the government.

Can I rely on oral promises/information from agency officials?

Sometimes you may be told one thing by someone in your agency, only later to discover that he/she provided you with the wrong information.

---

5 *For a complete listing of these actions, refer to* 31 USC § 3730(e).

6 *See* 31 USC § 3730(e)(4).

Most of us are used to this in the "office grapevine" context, and it may have little or no consequences here. The situation can be quite different, however, when the information comes from an agency official, and relates to an important matter such as key deadlines or rights we may have. Whether you can rely on oral information given to you by an agency official, without worrying about its accuracy, depends on the circumstances.

Oral promises

What legal recourse do you have if an agency official makes you an oral promise, but does not fulfill that promise? Unfortunately, not very much. An oral promise made to you by an agency official is unenforceable. Consider the following situation: You hear that a position in your agency is about to become vacant. You inform an agency official that you would like to be placed into that position. That agency official tells you that if you apply for that position, you will be selected for it. You submit your application in time, but you are not selected. In this situation, an agency official made you an oral promise to place you in that position if you applied for it. However, because oral promises are not enforceable, you have no legal right to be placed into the position for which you applied.

Oral information

Although an oral promise is unenforceable, if you rely on oral information provided to you by an agency official, this reliance can be a valid defense in certain situations. For example, suppose your agency is conducting a reduction-in-force, and, in a memorandum, the agency asks for all employees to update their SF-171s (job applications) by January 15 to ensure that they are accurate. You did not receive a copy of the memorandum, so you ask an agency official what the deadline is for submitting an updated SF-171. The official tells you that the deadline is January 30. When you try to submit an updated SF-171 on January 28, the agency refuses to accept it, and proceeds to separate you pursuant to the RIF procedures. Assume that, had you submitted your SF-171 by the January 15 deadline, you would not have been separated from your position.

In this hypothetical scenario, you will likely succeed in reversing the agency's decision to remove you because you relied on information regarding the submission deadline from a management official, and you suffered damage as a result of listening to his advice.

As another example, say that you ask your agency to compute the day on which you first become eligible for an immediate annuity. The agency computes the day and you retire on that day. Several months later, after not receiving an annuity, you learn from OPM that you were six months short of eligibility. In this scenario, you retired based on erroneous information provided by the agency. Therefore, your retirement is involuntary, and would most likely be reversed by the MSPB if you appealed it. (See Chapter 4 for more information on "constructive adverse actions.")

TIP

If an agency official makes an important oral promise to you, write down the conversation. Keep a record of the exact words, the date of the promise, and the date you made a record of the conversation.

Reliance on information from an agency official will not always preserve your legal rights, however. The Supreme Court has held that even if an agency official provides you with misinformation, and you are damaged by relying on this misinformation, you will not be able to "undo" the action if it is not otherwise permitted by law.[7]

For example, suppose that you are going to file an application for disability retirement. Pursuant to a statute passed by Congress, the deadline for filing this application is one year from the date you are separated from federal service. However, an agency official mistakenly tells you that the deadline for filing this application is two years from the date of separation. As a result, you do not file your application by the deadline, and are refused benefits. In this case, your appeal of the decision to deny benefits will not be successful because it is the law which mandates the filing deadline.

In all these hypothetical examples, an agency official provided the employee with false information. However, in the RIF example, the deadline for submitting the SF-171 was not established by a statute; the agency determined the deadline of January 15 on its own. Likewise in the immediate annuity example, the law did not mandate that the employee retire, nor prohibit him from returning to work. Therefore in both of these examples,

---

7 *See OPM v. Richmond*, 496 USC § 414 (1990).

you would have a valid legal defense to the agency's actions as a result of your reliance on the misinformation provided to you.

On the other hand, in the disability retirement example, a statute is in place which states that the federal government cannot issue an applicant disability benefits unless the applicant's application is submitted in a timely manner. Even if you rely on the misinformation of an agency official, a court cannot give you benefits in this case because the law prohibits the government from issuing benefits to an applicant who submits an untimely application.

As you can see, this area of the law is very confusing. Therefore, you should not rely on any oral information from an agency official. If possible, confirm the oral information in writing through an email. Always check the correctness of oral information or promises with someone else such as a lawyer with experience in civil service matters.

TIP

Be skeptical of oral information you receive from any agency official. Always ask for the information in writing and be sure to get the citation for any statute or regulation the agency is relying on for the information it provides to you.

Final Thoughts

While this was a catch-all chapter, don't let the informal nature of it fool you. There are important substantive rights covered by these legal principles. If you face any work-related issue that does not seem to fit within any of the other chapters of this book, and is not in this chapter, do not hesitate to consult with an experienced personnel official, union representative, or civil service lawyer for assistance.

29

Special Categories

What Rule Has No Exceptions?

In This Chapter You Will Learn:

- which groups of federal employees are not covered by the federal sector EEO process
- which groups of federal employees fall under special rules for adverse actions

Contents Chapter Twenty-Nine - Special Categories

Introduction

The federal civil service has existed in its modern form for over 130 years. Even the most recent global revision to the civil service system (the Civil Service Reform Act of 1978) is now more than 35 years old. That long timeframe has given Congress and the White House a huge opportunity to fiddle with the mechanics of the civil services system, creating carve-outs, exceptions and special categories of employees whose employment protections differ from other federal employees. Unfortunately, many federal employees only discover that they fall into one of these special categories when faced with possible dismissal of their case at the MSPB or EEOC, with alternate avenues for presenting their claims foreclosed by missed filing deadlines. Rather than risk wandering down the wrong path, it is important that federal employees become aware early on if they fall into a special category, so that they can effectively defend their rights.

Some of the largest of the special categories are discussed earlier in the Guide. Employees of the U.S. Postal Service are discussed in Chapter 25. Congressional employees and employees of the Executive Office of the President are discussed in Chapter 26. This Chapter looks at some of the other exceptions to the general rules concerning federal employee rights. Because of the great variety of exceptions applicable to federal employees, the list here is not exhaustive—and so employees with any questions about whether they fall into a special category would be well advised to consult an attorney for more information.

Intelligence Agency Employees

The Office of the Director of National Intelligence, the Central Intelligence Agency, and the various intelligence agencies under the umbrella of the Department of Defense constitute the Intelligence Community. Employees in the various intelligence agencies have normal federal sector EEO rights, and the EEOC has the capacity to adjudicate cases involving classified information. However, many intelligence agency employees do not have the right to appeal adverse actions to the Merit Systems Protection Board.[1] Similarly, intelligence agency employees cannot litigate whistleblower reprisal complaints under the Whistleblower Protection Act.[2] However, as discussed in greater detail in Chapter 7, intelligence agencies will be required to create a new mechanism for whistleblower reprisal claims for their employees, pursuant to Presidential Policy Directive 19 (PPD-19).

FAA and TSA Employees

Congress in 1996 passed several special statutes exempting many Federal Aviation Administration (FAA) employees from many civil service protections in Title 5 of the U.S. Code, and instead placing these employees under their own statutory framework. The 1996 legislation has been partially reversed in the intervening years; most recently, in 2012, Congress reinstated FAA employees' back pay eligibility for MSPB appeals. As a net result of these legislative modifications, FAA employees currently have most of the same MSPB appeal rights as other federal employees—both for adverse action appeals and for Independent Right of Action (IRA) claims—but are not covered by the same pre-adverse action procedures as other federal employees. Instead, pre-adverse action procedures for FAA employees are specified in FAA policies instead of OPM regulations, and so FAA employees should look to the current FAA adverse action policy when faced with an adverse action. The 1996 statute did not affect FAA employees' coverage by the federal-sector EEO complaints process, as the federal antidiscrimi-

---

1 *See, e.g.*, 5 USC § 7511(b)(7, 8).

2 *See, e.g.*, 5 USC § 2302(c)(i, ii).

nation statutes are not found in Title 5. FAA employees' Independent Right of Action appeals for whistleblower reprisal claims were reinstated by Congress in 2000.

At the time of the 1996 statute, employees of the predecessors to the Transportation Security Administration (TSA) were organizationally located within FAA. When TSA was created, Congress carried over the special FAA personnel authorities to TSA, although TSA has written its own pre-adverse action procedures rather than simply borrowing FAA's policies. TSA employees' IRA rights were only reinstated by Congress in the Whistleblower Protection Enhancement Act of 2012, a statute which also extended IRA appeal rights to TSA baggage screeners.[3] TSA screeners remain excluded from MSPB adverse action jurisdiction, and instead must appeal their adverse actions to a TSA grievance process.

FBI Employees

Federal Bureau of Investigation (FBI) employees are covered by the normal federal-sector EEO complaints process. However, FBI employees are excluded from MSPB jurisdiction for adverse actions and USERRA claims.[4] FBI employees are not covered by the normal Independent Right of Action whistleblower appeal mechanism, but instead are covered by a separate whistleblower reprisal complaints system administered by the Department of Justice, Office of Inspector General and Office of Professional Responsibility.[5]

Inspector General Employees

Employees of the various Inspector General (IG) offices ordinarily have the same appeal rights to the EEOC and MSPB as do other employees in their agencies. The IG's office is considered separate from the agency. Therefore, many IGs have promulgated their own adverse action policies solely applying to IG employees. These IG-specific policies may differ from generally applicable adverse action policies at a given agency (for example, by omitting or having a different table of penalties), and so it is important for IG employees facing adverse actions to be sure that they are looking at the IG-specific adverse action policy when dealing with a proposed adverse action.

---

3 *See, e.g.*, Pub.L. 112-199 § 109; 5 USC § 2304.

4 *See* 5 USC § 7511(b)(8); *Erlendson v. Dept. of Justice*, 2014 MSPB 61 (2014).

5 *See* 5 USC § 2302(a)(2)(C)(ii)(I), 2303; 28 CFR § 27.1 *et seq.*

Smithsonian Institution

Ordinary Smithsonian employees are covered by both the federal sector EEO complaints process and MSPB jurisdiction over adverse actions and whistleblower reprisal complaints.[6] However, the Smithsonian is not treated like a federal agency for purposes of the Privacy Act.[7] Smithsonian "trust fund" employees are not federal civil service employees and thus fall outside MSPB jurisdiction for adverse actions,[8] but are covered by the federal sector EEO complaints process.[9]

Government Corporations

No categorical rule exists for what rights apply to employees of government corporations. Treatment of employees of government corporations is highly inconsistent, with some government corporations treated fully like federal agencies, some like private employers and some like a mix of the two. For example, Amtrak and the Corporation for Public Broadcasting are not subject to MSPB jurisdiction nor the jurisdiction of the federal-sector EEO process, as they are not legally deemed federal agencies—although Amtrak is subject to FOIA (although not the Privacy Act).[10] The Federal Deposit Insurance Corporation (FDIC), the Millennium Challenge Corporation and the Pension Benefit Guarantee Corporation (PBGC) all fall within the jurisdiction of the federal-sector EEO process.[11] FDIC is within MSPB jurisdiction for Chapter 75 adverse actions, but not Chapter 43 performance-based adverse actions.[12] Most employees of government corporations can raise as an Independent Right of Action claim at the MSPB, but

---

6 *See, e.g., Seigla v. Smithsonian Institution,* 62 MSPR 55 (1994) at fn.1; *Pessa v. Smithsonian Institution,* 60 MSPR 421 (1994); *Goodman v. Smithsonian Institution,* EEOC Appeal No. 01900411 (February 2, 1990) at fn.3.

7 *See Dong v. Smithsonian Institution,* 125 F.3d 877 (D.C.Cir. 1997).

8 *See Bisson v. Office of Personnel Management,* 908 F.2d 947 (Fed.Cir. 1990); *Molina v. Smithsonian Institution,* MSPB Docket No. DC-0752-08-0567-I-1 (August 19, 2008).

9 *See Valenza v. Smithsonian Institution,* EEOC Petition No. 04A20020 (July 3, 2003); *Keeley v. Smithsonian Institution,* EEOC Appeal No. 01982447 (April 1, 1999) at fn.1; *Goodman v. Smithsonian Institution,* EEOC Appeal No. 01900411 (February 2, 1990) at fn.3.

10 *See* 47 USC § 396(b); 49 USC § 24301(a)(3), 24301(e); *Newman v. Presidio Trust,* EEOC Appeal No. 01A24736 (March 18, 2003) at fn.10; *Ehm v. National Railroad Passenger Corp.,* EEOC Appeal No. 01840571 (1984).

11 *See, e.g., Teixeira v. Dept. of State,* EEOC Appeal No. 0120100372 (April 9, 2010); *Vagle v. Federal Deposit Insurance Corp.,* EEOC Appeal No. 01986069 (June 15, 2000); *Leonardo v. Pension Benefit Guarantee Corp.,* EEOC Appeal No. 01981056 (January 5, 2000).

12 *See Compare Shelton v. Federal Deposit Insurance Corp.,* 38 MSPR 303 (1988) at fn.1 to *Dockery v. Federal Deposit Insurance Corp,* 64 MSPR 458 (1994).

cannot pursue other, non-IRA Prohibited Personnel Practice claims at OSC.[13] The appeal rights of Postal Service employees are discussed in Chapter 25. As a result, employees of government corporations cannot assume that their rights will (or will not) match those of other federal employees, and should look into the specifics of what rules apply to their specific employer.

Federal Reserve

Employees of the Federal Reserve receive different treatment based on whether they work for the central Board of Governors versus working for one of the regional federal reserve banks.[14] Employees at the 12 regional reserve banks are not treated as federal employees. Employees of the Board of Governors do have access to the federal sector EEO process (albeit under a different regulation specific to the Federal Reserve), but do not have access to whistleblower Independent Right of Action claims before the MSPB or to VEOA appeals. Only "preference eligible" veterans at the Federal Reserve Board of Governors have MSPB appeal rights for adverse actions.

Judicial Branch Employees

Judicial branch employees cannot appeal adverse actions to MSPB, nor do they fall within the MSPB's jurisdiction for Independent Right of Action whistleblower reprisal claims. EEOC jurisdiction over judicial branch employees depends on whether or not they are in the competitive service (a category which normally only applies to certain employees hired through the Administrative Office of the U.S. Courts, depending on when they were hired).[15] Competitive service employees have access to the federal sector EEO complaints process—except for disability discrimination claims under the Rehabilitation Act.[16] Other judicial branch employees with discrimination claims and competitive service employees who have disability discrimination claims can only take their claims to internal claims mecha-

---

13 *See* 5 USC § 2302(a)(2)(C)(i).

14 *See Donahue v. Federal Reserve System,* MSPB Appeal No. DC-4324-12-0692-I-1 (October 12, 2012), (Niedrick, AJ) at fn.6.

15 *See, e.g.,* 28 USC § 602 note (codifying Pub.L. 101-474, § 3.a.5); 29 CFR § 1614.103(b)(4); Administrative Office of the U.S. Courts *Guide to Judiciary Policies and Procedures,* Vol. 2, Ch. 1, §§ A, C.3, C.4.

16 *See, e.g.,* 28 USC § 602 note (codifying Pub.L. 101-474, § 3.a.5); 29 CFR § 1614.103(b)(4); Administrative Office of the U.S. Courts *Guide to Judiciary Policies and Procedures,* Vol. 2, Ch. 1, §§ A, C.3, C.4.

nisms such as the Administrative Office of the U.S. Courts' Fair Employment Practices System. Judicial branch employees denied reemployment rights under USERRA due to a lack of available reinstatement positions in the judicial branch are entitled to request placement in an executive branch position through the Office of Personnel Management.[17]

Non-Appropriated Fund Employees

A non-appropriated fund (NAF) entity is an agency (or portion of an agency) that does not directly fund its operations from money appropriated annually by Congress, but instead pays its bills from a revolving fund replenished from other sources such as commercial operations. Perhaps the best known examples of NAF entities are the base exchanges, commissaries and child-care centers found on many military bases. Employees who work for Department of Defense (DoD) NAF entities fall outside MSPB jurisdiction both for adverse actions and whistleblower reprisal claims. DoD-employed NAF employees are entitled to raise whistleblower reprisal claims through a separate, limited whistleblower reprisal complaint system administered by the Inspector General's Office. DoD NAF employees are covered by the federal-sector EEO complaints process.

Title 38 VA Employees

The Department of Veterans Affairs ("DVA") has special hiring authority, found in Title 38 of the United States Code, for hiring certain specific categories of medical personnel for positions in the Veterans Health Administration.[18] Some—but not all—individuals hired under this Title 38 authority are excluded from MSPB jurisdiction for ordinary adverse actions and appeals concerning their retirement pension issues, but not for whistleblower reprisal complaints under the Independent Right of Action mechanism; the rest have normal MSPB appeal rights similar to other federal employees. Direct appeal of adverse actions relating to those employees exempted from MSPB jurisdiction goes either to the DVA Disciplinary Appeals Board (DAB) or to other DVA grievance processes, depending on the nature of the charge involved.[19] The federal courts have split on whether DAB decisions/other grievances can then be appealed into federal court

---

17 *See* 38 USC § 4314(c).

18 *See* 38 USC § 7401, 7405, 7406.

19 *See* 38 USC § 7461 *et seq.*

under the Administrative Procedure Act.[20] Judicial review of DAB decisions is also available under 38 USC § 7462(f). Title 38 DVA employees are covered by the federal-sector EEO complaints process, and by USERRA.

Certain Title 38 DVA employees are excluded from the federal sector Family and Medical Leave Act (FMLA) provisions, and are covered instead by the provisions which apply to private-sector employers and state/local government employees—which means that they potentially have the ability to sue in court in the event of improper denial of FMLA leave or retaliation for requesting FMLA leave, or to have the complaint investigated and potentially prosecuted by the U.S. Department of Labor, with a statute of limitations of 2 years (3 years for a willful violation).[21]

A separate category of DVA employees who work for the Veterans Canteen Service are excluded from MSPB appeal rights unless they are preference eligible veterans.[22] Veterans Canteen Service employees are covered by the federal-sector EEO complaints process, and may raise whistleblower reprisal claims through the Independent Right of Action complaints mechanism.

Title 42 NIH Employees

The Department of Health and Human Services, National Institutes of Health ("NIH") has special hiring authority, found in Title 42 of the United States Code, for hiring certain specific categories of research scientists and research fellows;[23] a separate Title 42 provision allows NIH to hire individuals under personal service contracts.[24] These Title 42 employees not on personal services contracts have recourse to the federal-sector EEO complaints process and in some cases to raise whistleblower reprisal claims through the IRA process at OSC and the MSPB,[25] but are excluded from the MSPB's general adverse action jurisdiction.[26] Title 42 employees not on personal services contracts may administratively grieve adverse actions.

---

20 *See Compare Fligiel v. Sampson*, 440 F.3d 747 (6th Cir. 2006) to *Khan v. United States*, 201 F.3d 1375 (Fed. Cir. 2000); *Ward v. Brown*, 22 F.3d 516 (2nd Cir. 1994); *Berry v. Hollander*, 925 F.2d 311 (9th Cir. 1991).

21 *See, e.g.*, 5 USC §§ 6301(2)(b)(v), 6381(1)(A); 29 USC § 2611(2)(b)(i); 29 CFR § 825.109(c); *Bonzani v. Shinseki*, 895 F.Supp.2d 1003 (E.D.CA. 2012); *see generally* 29 USC § 2601 *et seq.*

22 *See* 38 USC § 7802(e).

23 *See* 42 USC § 209(f, g), 237.

24 *See* 42 USC §§ 282(d)(1), 285b-3(b)(1).

25 *See Usharauli v. Dept. of Health and Human Services*, 116 MSPR 383 (2011).

26 *See Fishbein v. Dept. of Health and Human Services*, 102 MSPR 4 (2009).

Title 42 employees—irrespective of which specific Title 42 authority was used to hire them—may alternatively seek assistance through the NIH Center for Conflict Resolution, Office of the Ombudsman.

DoDEA Employees

Certain employees of the Department of Defense Education Activity (DoDEA) are hired under a special statutory authority unique to DoDEA.[27] This category primarily applies to administrative, logistical and personnel office employees.[28] Under that statute, DoDEA employees can appeal adverse actions to the MSPB—except that claims regarding reassignments, demotions and modifications to salaries are excluded from MSPB jurisdiction.[29] DoDEA employees affected by such actions can still potentially raise such claims based on discrimination theories through the federal sector EEO process.[30]

Certain DoDEA teachers and teaching personnel are excluded from the federal sector Family and Medical Leave Act (FMLA) provisions, and are covered instead by the provisions which apply to private-sector employers and state/local government employees—which means that they potentially have the ability to sue in court in the event of improper denial of FMLA leave or retaliation for requesting FMLA leave, or to have the complaint investigated and potentially prosecuted by the U.S. Department of Labor, with a statute of limitations of 2 years (3 years for a willful violation).[31]

National Guard Technicians

Certain employees of the National Guard occupy hybrid positions involving both a part-time National Guard military position and civilian position which combine to create a full-time position.[32] Maintaining a qualifying military posting is a job prerequisite for the civilian position, and so loss of the military position can result in loss of the civilian position as well for failure to meet this prerequisite.[33] National Guard Technicians are excluded from MSPB jurisdiction, both for whistleblower reprisal claims and

---

27 *See* 10 USC § 2164.

28 *See* 10 USC § 2164 (e)(4)(B).

29 *See* 10 USC § 2164(e)(4)(A); *Stewart v. Department of Defense,* 82 MSPR 649 (1999).

30 *Cf. Hargrove v. Dept. of Defense,* 77 MSPR 266 (1998).

31 *See, e.g.,* 5 USC §§ 6301(2)(b)(ix), 6381(1)(A); 20 USC § 901; 29 USC § 2611(2)(b)(i); 29 CFR § 825.109(c); *see generally* 29 USC § 2601 *et seq.*

32 *See, e.g.,* 5 USC § 3101; 10 USC § 10216; 32 USC § 709.

33 *See, e.g.,* 10 USC § 10216(d); 32 USC § 709(b, f).

for appeals of civilian adverse actions, with appeals only to their adjutant general.[34] National Guard Technicians are covered by the federal sector EEO complaints process to the extent that the specific issues in the complaint fall on the civilian side or the military side of the employee's position—a fact-specific case-by-case determination, looking at factors such as whether the employee was on civilian or military duty at the time of the specific incident in the complaint, and whether the responsible management officials were on civilian or military duty at the time of the incidents in question, is required.[35]

Senior Executive Service

Senior Executive Service (SES) employees are subject to separate personnel statutes and regulations, including separate performance evaluation standards and adverse action procedures, including a probationary period when joining the SES. More specifically, SES employees cannot be suspended for 14 days or less or demoted as disciplinary adverse actions; they can only be disciplined by removal or suspensions longer than 14 days.[36] Disciplinary adverse actions can only be taken against SES employees on charges of misconduct, neglect of duty, malfeasance or failure to accept a directed reassignment or to accompany a position in a transfer of function.[37] SES employees are covered by the federal-sector EEO complaints process. SES employees who are removed from the SES and demoted to another civil service position as a performance-based action can appeal removal from the SES to an 'informal hearing' before the MSPB, but then have no right to appeal the MSPB's decision to the Federal Circuit.[38] SES employees who are suspended for 15 or more days or removed for disciplinary reasons can appeal to the MSPB. SES employees also are covered by the whistleblower reprisal protections under the Independent Right of Action appeal mechanism.[39]

---

34 *See, e.g.*, 32 USC § 709(f, g); *Ockerhausen v. New Jersey Department of Military and Veterans Affairs*, 52 MSPR 484 (1992).

35 *See, e.g.*, *Neville v. Dept. of the Air Force*, EEOC Appeal No. 0720110023 (August 1, 2013).

36 *See, e.g.*, 5 USC § 7543.

37 *See* 5 USC § 7543(a).

38 *See, e.g.*, 5 USC § 3592(a); 5 CFR § 1201.143 *et seq.*

39 A new statute for adverse actions against SES employees working for the Department of Veterans Affairs was just enacted when this Guide went to press (Section 707 of Pub. L. 113-146), and had not yet been implemented. If you are an SES employee covered by this statute, you should consider consulting with an attorney or representative to discuss your rights.

Administrative Law Judges

Due to the need to preserve their judicial independence from the agencies in which they work, Administrative Law Judges (ALJs) are not subject to the ordinary disciplinary procedures which apply to other federal employees. Instead, disciplinary actions against ALJs are covered by a separate statute and separate regulations.[40] Under these rules, ALJs can only be disciplined for "good cause," a different standard than the "efficiency of the service" standard used in discipline for other federal employees, and one which may or may not be stricter than the "efficiency of the service" standard.[41] ALJs are entitled to a hearing before another ALJ (not a regular MSPB administrative judge) conducted under procedures meeting heightened requirements specified in the Administrative Procedure Act. The MSPB, not the employing agency, selects the penalty to apply to an ALJ.[42] ALJs are covered by the normal federal-sector EEO process. ALJs are also may litigate whistleblower reprisal claims in Independent Right of Action appeals before the MSPB.[43]

Reemployed Annuitants

Reemployed annuitant status arises from the situation where an employee retires from federal civilian jobs and collects a FERS or CSRS annuity, and then later decides to reenter the federal civilian workforce. Those retirees have the option of seeking noncompetitive placement into a position. If they accept the noncompetitive appointment, then they are deemed to be continuing to work while still receiving their preexisting annuity payments (their work salary is reduced to reflect the annuity payment) and they are deemed a "reemployed annuitant."[44] Alternatively, these retirees can leave their retiree status, waive their annuity for the duration of their reemployment, compete for the position in the fashion of a normal applicant, and then reenter federal service as a normal employee with normal MSPB appeal rights and not as a "reemployed annuitant."[45] Not every retiree has the option of accepting reemployed annuitant status. For example, if an employee is on CSRS (but not FERS) discontinued service retirement and is rehired by any agency other than the Department of Defense, he can only

---

40 *See* 5 USC § 7521; 5 CFR § 1201.137 *et seq.*

41 *See Social Security Administration v. Goodman,* 19 MSPR 321 (1984) at fn.8.

42 *See* 5 USC § 7521; 5 CFR § 1201.137 *et seq.*

43 *See, e.g., Lawson v. Dept. of Health and Human Services,* 64 MSPR 673 (1994).

44 *See* 5 USC § 3323(b)(1); *Walsh v. General Services Administration,* 3 MSPR 558 (1980).

45 *See Vesser v. Office of Personnel Management,* 29 F.3d 600 (Fed.Cir. 1994).

reenter federal service as a normal employee and his annuity automatically terminates.[46] This election also only applies to those receiving annuities from OPM; annuitants receiving Office of Workers' Compensation Programs benefits do not become "reemployed annuitants" just by virtue of their reentering federal service.[47] Different forms of retirement are described in greater detail in Chapter 18.

A reemployed annuitant serves "at will," and can be removed by the agency at any time without MSPB appeal rights, and is not entitled to pre-adverse action procedures in the same fashion as ordinary federal employees.[48] However, the MSPB does have jurisdiction over whistleblower IRA appeals for reemployed annuitants.[49] Reemployed annuitants are also covered by the federal sector EEO complaints process.[50]

Foreign Service Officers and Foreign Service Nationals

Foreign Service Officers (FSOs) are a special category of State Department employees who work either domestically or overseas. Foreign Service Nationals (FSNs) are non-citizens hired to staff certain lower level positions in overseas embassies and consulates (for example, janitorial positions), working either for the State Department or for other federal agencies' overseas offices.

Both FSOs and FSNs, as members of the foreign service, lack the right to directly appeal adverse actions to the Merit Systems Protection Board, but the MSPB has jurisdiction over Foreign Service whistleblower reprisal claims through the Independent Right of Action appeal.[51] FSOs appeal their adverse actions to the Foreign Service Grievance Board.[52] FSOs can raise their EEO complaints through the EEOC federal sector process or through the Foreign Service Grievance Board.[53] FSNs have no recourse to the federal-sector EEO complaints process.[54] The MSPB also lacks juris-

---

46 *See* 5 USC § 8344(b), 8468, 9902(g); *Garza v. Department of the Navy,* 119 MSPR 90 (2012); *Colbert v. Department of the Army,* 54 MSPR 492 (1992).

47 *See, e.g., Hays v. Department of the Air Force,* 84 MSPR 443 (1999).

48 *See* 5 USC § 3323(b)(1); 7511(b)(4); 7701(j).

49 *See Acting Special Counsel v. U.S. Customs Service,* 31 MSPR 342 (1986).

50 *See generally Malone v. Dept. of the Treasury,* EEOC Appeal No. 01955425 (October 25, 1996); *Malone v. Dept. of the Treasury,* EEOC Appeal No. 01941056 (September 6, 1994); *Serpas v. Dept. of the Navy,* EEOC Appeal No. 01840853 (March 17, 1986).

51 *See, e.g.,* 5 USC § 7511(b)(6); *Ang v. Dept. of State,* 103 MSPR 324 (2006).

52 *See* 22 USC § 4131(a)(1)(A-C).

53 *See* 22 USC § 4131(a)(1)(H); *Smith v. Dept. of State,* EEOC Appeal No. 0120055349 (January 3, 2008).

54 *See, e.g.,* 5 USC § 7511(b)(6); *Ang v. Dept. of State,* 103 MSPR 324 (2006).

diction over FSN claims regarding reductions in force (RIFs), but has jurisdiction over some claims by FSNs concerning OPM determinations about their federal pensions.[55] FSNs who are non-U.S. citizens cannot take claims into the Foreign Service Grievance Board.[56]

USDA County Employees

Many employees of the Department of Agriculture's Farm Services Agency (USDA) at the county office level officially work for the county committee for their county and not USDA. These employees are excluded from the civil service, and so cannot appeal adverse actions to the MSPB; instead, they can appeal adverse actions in federal district court under the federal Administrative Procedure Act.[57] However, these county employees are covered by the federal-sector EEO process.[58]

BIA Schools Employees

Educators in the school system administered by the Department of the Interior, Bureau of Indian Affairs (BIA) are excluded from MSPB jurisdiction, with all appeal rights lying within a BIA grievance process.[59] However, these educators are covered by the federal-sector EEO complaints process.[60]

Volunteers, Peace Corps and Corporation for Public and Community Service

Generally, volunteers are not deemed "employees," and so do not normally have access to the MSPB or federal-sector EEOC processes. Even though Peace Corps volunteers are paid some living allowances and a readjustment allowance at the end of their tenure, they are also not treated as federal employees.[61] Instead, Peace Corps volunteers (and certain volunteers in programs under the Corporation for Public and Community Service, such

---

55 *See Ang v. Dept. of State,* 103 MSPR 324 (2006); *compare Monasteri v. Merit Systems Protection Board,* 232 F.3d 1376 (Fed.Cir. 2000)) *to DeLaet v. Office of Personnel Management,* 70 MSPR 390 (1996).

56 *See* 22 USC § 4131(a)(1).

57 *See United States v. Massey,* 380 F.3d 437 (8th Cir. 2004); *Moore v. Glickman,* 113 F.3d 988 (9th Cir. 1997).

58 *See Hall v. Department of Agriculture,* EEOC Appeal No. 01930309 (September 9, 1993); *Jones v. Department of Agriculture,* EEOC Appeal No. 01902704 (August 29, 1990); *Taylor v. U.S. Department of Agriculture,* EEOC Appeal No. 01902538 (August 6, 1990).

59 *See* 25 USC § 2012; 25 CFR § 38.9; *Wilhoite v. Merit Systems Protection Board,* Case No. 99-3032 (Fed.Cir. June 23, 1999).

60 *See, e.g., Pfulb v. Department of the Interior,* EEOC Appeal No. 01986180 (August 27, 2001).

61 *See* 22 USC § 2504; *Correri v. Peace Corps,* EEOC Request No. 05921050 (May 27, 1993).

as AmeriCorps) can raise claims through an internal grievance process administered by the Peace Corps itself, which allows for unspecified corrective remedies (and reimbursement of attorneys' fees and costs).[62] Very limited whistleblower protection policies also apply to Peace Corps volunteers.[63]

Public Health Service and NOAA Uniformed Corps

Although the Public Health Service is part of the Department of Health and Human Services, only civilian employees of the Public Health Service receive access to the full assortment of federal civil service protections. Members of the Commissioned Corps of the Public Health Service are treated as military, and must seek recourse for claims through military channels (for example, EEO protections for the Commissioned Corps are similar to the military EEO claims process).[64] Members of the National Oceanic and Atmospheric Administration (NOAA) Commissioned Corps are also treated as military employees who must seek recourse through military channels.[65]

Contractors, Consultants and Tribal Employees

Ordinarily, employees of government contractors don't fall within the scope of civil service protections. However, in some cases, a federal agency will be sufficiently active in directing the work of a contract employee to be deemed a 'co-employer' or 'joint employer' of the individual for purposes of discrimination law—in which case the contract employee then can bring a claim against the agency in the federal sector EEO complaints process, in addition to any private sector remedies against the employing government contractor. The test used by the EEOC to make this determination is highly fact-specific, and requires weighing 15 separate factors concerning the employment arrangement. A similar analysis applies to employees of tribal government who work in conjunction with federal agencies such as the Bureau of Indian Affairs.[66] A similar analysis applies for

---

62 *See* 22 CFR § 306; 45 CFR § 1225.1 *et seq.; Correri v. Peace Corps,* EEOC Request No. 05921050 (May 27, 1993).

63 *See* 22 USC § 2507; MS 271 HANDLING OF VOLUNTEER/TRAINEE ALLEGATIONS (January 14, 2011).

64 *See* 42 USC § 213(f); *Special Counsel ex rel. Hardy v. Dept. of Health and Human Services,* 117 MSPR 174 (2011).

65 *See McCaffrey v. Dept. of Commerce,* EEOC Appeal No. 01830964 (December 5, 1984); *cf. Special Counsel ex rel. Hardy v. Dept. of Health and Human Services,* 117 MSPR 174 (2011).

66 *See Smith v. Department of the Interior,* EEOC Appeal No. 01970503 (August 27, 1997).

USERRA claims.[67] However, contractors do not otherwise fall within MSPB jurisdiction, nor do they fall within the whistleblower reprisal complaints process administered by the MSPB and OSC.[68]

Final Thoughts

Federal personnel law, at times, can be a maze of exceptions within exceptions. It is vitally important that employees be aware of what specific protections they have, so that they can be prepared to effectively enforce their rights and to defend against actions taken against them by management. With many causes of action having short filing deadlines, any employee would be well advised to familiarize themselves in advance with the rights and procedural protections specific to their position and to their agency, rather than be caught unawares if they happen to fall into one of these special categories.

67 *See Silva v. Department of Homeland Security,* 112 MSPR 362 (2009).

68 *See Thompson v. Merit Systems Protection Board,* 421 F.3d 1336 (Fed.Cir. 2005); *Felts v. Merit System Protection Board,* 62 F.3d 1430 (Fed.Cir. 1995)(Table); *Watts v. Office of Personnel Management,* 814 F.2d 1576 (Fed.Cir. 1987)

30

Internet Research

Where in the World (Wide Web) Can I Find the Info I Need?

In This Chapter You Will Learn:

- the basics of internet research
- helpful websites for federal agencies that adjudicate employment disputes

Contents Chapter Thirty - Internet Research

Although the internet is an amazing source of information and a wonderful research tool, you have to be careful and understand a few basic points before jumping in. First, know where your information is coming from. There is no control over the internet, and anyone can post any information they wish. Accordingly, if you find a wonderful site that appears to have all the information regarding the topic you are interested in, keep in mind that it may be one person's individual site, a partisan organization's site, or a government agency's site. The trustworthiness of the information will depend on who is posting the information. For example, if you are looking for an authoritative statement of the law of discrimination and the rights of employees, the EEOC's website will be a better place than the website of a huge corporation. However, if you are looking for practical advice on how to litigate your case, the website of an individual who has filed a similar action may be just the source you are looking for.

Second, websites on the internet are constantly changing and evolving, and therefore the listed websites in this chapter, and listed throughout this book, may have changed between the publishing date and now. However, many main sites, such as OPM's "home page," have either a "site tree" or a "search function," or both, which will make your ability to find the information you are seeking easier. Also, many times, when sites move, they leave behind a page with a link to the new location.

In addition, keep in mind that a link may take you to "older" information that has (or has not) been updated. For example, if you use a link to the MSPB regulations page, you may be sent to an outdated page. When it comes to statutes, regulations, policies, etc., you must make a concerted effort to make sure you are reading the latest version. First, click on the "refresh" button of your browser, which will update the page. Or, if the information seems outdated, return to the website's "home page" and see if you can find a newer link.

With these caveats in mind, we are ready to explore the information the internet has to offer regarding the topics contained in this book.

Where to start

General search engines

If you know what topic you are interested in researching, but are just getting started, a general "search engine" may be the place to begin. At these sites, you enter certain key words, and your computer will then search the internet for web pages that contain your key words. Keep in mind that depending on the site, where on the internet the engine "searches," what order the key words are in, and the parameters the engine uses to order your results, you can get very different answers from each engine. The following are the most frequently used general search engines:

GOOGLE: www.google.com

BING: www.bing.com

ASK: www.ask.com

YAHOO: www.yahoo.com

Legal search engines

An excellent source of general legal information is located at (www.findlaw.com). This site is an incredible free resource containing statutes, regulations, policies, treatises on subject areas of the law, etc. This site is also a good place to go if you are looking for legal information outside the scope of this book as it also contains information regarding different states' laws. If you see a law or regulation cited somewhere and you need to read it, findlaw.com is the place to go.

The University of Cornell's law school also has an excellent site, with court cases, statutes and commentary at (www.law.cornell.edu/). At the Cornell site, you can also find pages dedicated to employment law, (www.law.cornell.edu/wex/employment), employment discrimination law, and (www.law.cornell.edu/wex/employment_discrimination.html), and an employment law discussion forum (www.elinfonet.com/phpBB2/ viewforum.php?f=18).

Another great site useful for researching Supreme Court decisions is located at (www.oyez.org). Not only does this site provide summaries of Supreme Court decisions, but it is a complete and authoritative source for all audio recorded in the Court since the installation of a recording system in October 1955. Google also has a dedicated legal research site, Google Scholar (www.scholar.google.com), which provides access to court opinions and law review articles, among other things.

Federal statutes and regulations

The Office of the Law Revision Counsel of the U.S. House of Representatives prepares and publishes the United States Code. The Code is a consolidation and codification by subject matter of the general and permanent laws of the United States. If you are interested in reading the text of a federal statute cited in this book, you can access the United States Code (Code) at (uscode.house.gov), at (findlaw.com), or at the Cornell website at (www.law.cornell.edu/uscode). These sites allow you to identify the statute you are looking for, will retrieve the statute, and allow you to download and print the statute. If you are unsure of the section of the Code, you can also search by topic or key words.

The Code does not include regulations issued by executive branch agencies, decisions of the Federal courts, treaties, or laws enacted by state or local governments. Regulations issued by executive branch agencies are available in the Code of Federal Regulations (CFR). You can find specific sections, search by topic, and print sections of the CFR at (www.gpoaccess.gov/cfr/index.html), at (findlaw.com), or at the Cornell website at (www.law.cornell.edu/cfr/). Proposed and recently adopted regulations may be found in the Federal Register (www.gpoaccess.gov/fr/index.html).

To find an agency's website, go to: (www.findlaw.com/10fedgov/exagencies/index.html) or go to www.google.com and search by the name of the agency.

Chapter 1 Appointment in the Federal Service

Chapter 1 of this book deals with appointment in the federal service. The primary source of information for this topic, as well as most topics related to employment with the federal government, would be the Office of Personnel Management's (OPM) website found at (www.opm.gov). The OPM home page has an excellent "site tree" as well as a "search" engine, so that you can find the information you are looking for.

As to specific topics mentioned in this Chapter, you can find OPM's explanation of the primary appointment authority for federal agencies at (http://www.opm.gov/policy-data-oversight/hiring-authorities/competitive-hiring/#url=Types-of-Appointments).

You can find the Code of Federal Regulations online at: (www.gpoaccess. gov/cfr/index.html) or at the Cornell website at (www4.law.cornell.edu/cfr/).

Applications for federal employment can be found at (www.opm.gov/forms/html/appn.htm). In addition, there are several internet sites where you can search for federal job vacancies. Some of these include:

www.usajobs.gov

www.americajobs.com

www.federaljobsearch.com/

www.fedjobs.com/

Chapter 2 Performance Appraisals; and
Chapter 3 Performance-Related Discipline

OPM's "Performance Management" information can be found at (http://www.opm.gov/perform/). The site contains information regarding planning, monitoring, developing, measuring, rating and rewarding performance. OPM's guidance to employers, can be found at (http://archive.opm.gov/er/poor/index.asp). While primarily offering advice to managers, the site contains interesting information for employees as well.

OPM's regulations governing agency performance appraisal systems, which are in Title 5 of the CFR, and OPM's regulations governing agency performance based reduction in grade or removal actions, can be found at (http://www.law.cornell.edu/cfr/text/5/part-430). Of course, as to all regulations, they can also be found at (www.gpoaccess.gov/cfr/index.html), at (www.findlaw.com), or at the Cornell website at (www.law.cornell.edu/cfr/).

If you are removed for poor performance, the MSPB's website is located at (www.mspb.gov). If you are interested in filing an appeal with the MSPB regarding a performance based action, go to (http://www.mspb.gov/appeals/forms.htm) to get started. If you are unsure in which regional or field office to file your appeal, go to (http://www.mspb.gov/contact/contact.htm) for a list of the regions, and what areas of the country are covered. The regulations governing proceedings before the MSPB as well as MSPB decisions are also found on (www.mspb.gov). An appeal may be filed electronically by using the Board's e-filing option available at the Board's website (https://e-appeal.mspb.gov/).

Chapter 4 Misconduct: Adverse Actions and Discipline

If you are removed for poor performance, the MSPB's website is located at (www.mspb.gov). If you are interested in filing an appeal with the MSPB regarding a performance based action, go to (http://www.mspb.gov/appeals/forms.htm) to get started. If you are unsure in which regional or field office to file your appeal, go to (http://www.mspb.gov/contact/contact.htm) for a list of the regions, and what areas of the country are covered. The regulations governing proceedings before the MSPB as well as MSPB decisions are also found on (www.mspb.gov). An appeal may be filed electronically by using the Board's Internet filing option available at the Board's website (www.mspb.gov/e-appeal.html).

Chapter 5 Discrimination: What It Is and How to Prove It; and Chapter 6 Discrimination: The Complaint Process

The EEOC website is located at (http://www.eeoc.gov). There is a separate section for federal employees at (http://www.eeoc.gov/federal/fed_employees/). This site contains the applicable laws, procedural regulations and EEOC decisions, as well as EEOC guidelines and policies on many topics. Cornell University also has assembled several resources regarding discrimination at (www. law. cornell.edu/wex/employment_discrimination.html). Information regarding the complaint process is also found at (http://www.eeoc.gov/publications/fedprocess.cfm).

Chapter 7 Whistleblowing and Prohibited Personnel Practices

The Office of Special Counsel website is located at (www.osc.gov). Whistleblower disclosures are discussed at (www.osc.gov/wbdisc.htm) and prohibited personnel practices at (www.osc.gov/ppp.htm). Some complaints to the OSC can be filed online at (www.osc.gov/oscefile/). If you are interested in filing an Individual Right of Action appeal with the MSPB, the MSPB's website is located at (www.mspb.gov). If you are interested in filing an appeal with the MSPB, go to (http://www.mspb.gov/appeals/forms.htm) to get started.

Chapter 8 Unions and Collective Bargaining

The website of the Federal Labor Relations Authority, the independent agency responsible for administering the labor-management relations program for Federal employees worldwide, is located at (www.flra.gov/). The site contains the applicable statutes, regulations, FLRA decisions, and information regarding filing with the FLRA. Decisions of the Federal Service Impasses Panel can be found at (www.flra.gov/20.html). The Federal Mediation and Conciliation Service, the agency which provides mediation and conflict resolution services to industry, government agencies and communities, has its website is at (http://www.fmcs.gov).

Chapter 9 Reductions-in-Force

OPM's regulations and guidance to federal agencies regarding reductions-in-force are located at (https://www.opm.gov/policy-data-oversight/workforce-restructuring/reductions-in-force/). Information regarding restructuring and downsizing is here: (https://www.opm.gov/policy-data-oversight/workforce-restructuring/). The MSPB's procedures for appeals can be found at (www.mspb.gov).

Chapter 10 Security Clearances

OPM's "Getting a Security Clearance...In a Nutshell" is located at (http://govcentral.monster.com/benefits/articles/8311-getting-a-security-clearance-in-a-nutshell).

Guidance regarding the DoD's implementation of restrictions on the granting or renewal of security clearances as mandated by the provisions of the Floyd D. Spence National Defense Authorization Act for fiscal year 2001 (the "Smith Amendment") is located at (www.fas.org/sgp/news/2001/08/dss_smith.htm). The Defense Office of Hearings and Appeals has a website containing links to various issues concerning appealing denials or revocation of security clearances, at (www.defenselink.mil/dodgc/doha).

Chapter 11 Overtime and Other Special Pay

Overtime pay provided under Title 5, United States Code, is pay for hours of work officially ordered or approved in excess of 8 hours in a day or 40 hours in an administrative workweek. OPM's guidance is found at (www.opm. gov/oca/pay/html/factot.htm). In addition, OPM's outline of how to compute FLSA overtime pay can be found at (www.opm.gov/oca/pay/HTML /computeflsa.htm). The Department of Labor's "e-advisor" on the Fair Labor Standards Act is at (www.dol.gov/elaws/flsa.htm).

Chapter 12 Classification Appeals

OPM's guidance on classification appeals is found at (http://www.opm.gov/policy-data-oversight/classification-qualifications/appeals-decisions/). The electronic "reading room" concerning position classification policy for work performed in the Federal Government in white collar occupations that are covered by the General Schedule and blue collar occupations that are covered by the Federal Wage System is located at (www.opm.gov/fedclass/index.htm).

Chapter 13 Promotions and Within-Grade Increases

A good starting point is OPM's document "Promotions within the General Schedule," found at OPM's website at (http://www.opm.gov/oca/pay/html/promotion.htm). This site also contains a link to OPM's "Questions and Answers" regarding promotions in the General Schedule: (http://www.opm.gov/oca/pay/html/promotQA.htm).

The Within-Grade Fact Sheet can be found at (www.opm.gov/oca/pay /html/wgifact.htm), and Questions and Answers on Within-Grade Increases can be found at (www.opm.gov/oca/pay/html/wgiQA.htm).

Chapter 14 Leave Issues

The Department of Labor's "e-advisor" regarding the Family Medical Leave Act is found at (http://www.dol.gov/elaws/fmla.htm). OPM's regulations can be found at (www.opm.gov/oca/fmla/). OPM's guidance on entitlement for FMLA leave for federal employees is found at (http://www.opm.gov /oca/leave/html/fmlafact.htm).

OPM's guide to "Leave Administration" in the federal government is found at (www.opm.gov/oca/leave/index.asp). This site contains all applicable laws, regulations and policies regarding leave for the federal employee, including OPM's Handbook on Alternate Work Schedules can be found at (www.opm.gov/oca/aws/index.htm).

Chapter 15 Workers' Compensation

The Department of Labor's "resources" page for information about claims under FECA is located at (http://www.dol.gov/compliance/laws/comp-feca.htm).

Chapter 16 Federal Employees Health Benefits

Information regarding the Federal Employees Health Benefit Program can be found at (www.opm.gov/insure/health/index.htm).

Chapter 17 Unemployment Compensation

An outline of the unemployment compensation for federal employees is located at (www.workforcesecurity.doleta.gov/unemploy/unemcomp.asp). The Department of Labor's "About Unemployment Insurance" is located at (www.workforcesecurity.doleta.gov/unemploy/aboutui.asp). The Cornell law school website has an overview of unemployment compensation, found at (www.law.cornell.edu/topics/unemployment_compensation.html).

Each state may also have unemployment compensation information on its own website. For example, for employees in the Washington, DC, metropolitan area, check out:

District of Columbia: http://does.dc.gov/service/unemployment-compensation-process
Maryland:
http://www.dllr.state.md.us/employment/claimfaq.shtml
Virginia:
http://www.vec.virginia.gov/unemployed

Chapter 18 Retirement

The OPM website, (http://www.opm.gov), has a wealth of information regarding many topics relevant to federal employees. If you have questions regarding your retirement, the place to start is (http://www.opm.gov/re-tire). For free publications regarding retirement, head to (http://www.opm.gov/retire/html/library/index.html). The Thrift Savings Plan Home Page is located at (http://www.tsp.gov/).

Chapter 19 Veterans' Rights

For OPM's "VetGuide," which explains the special rights and privileges that veterans enjoy in Federal civil service employment, go to (http://www.fedshirevets .gov/hire/hrp/vetguide/index.aspx).

The Department of Labor's "USERRA Advisor" is at (http://www.dol.gov /elaws/userra0.htm). Additional information can be found at (http://www.osc.gov/userra.htm). The MSPB's regulations regarding processing USERRA appeals are at (http://www.mspb.gov/netsearch/viewdocs.aspx? docnumber=274456&version=274762&application=HTML).

The DOL's Veterans' Employment and Training Service website is located at (http://www.dol.gov/vets/welcome.html), which has links to applicable laws, regulations, procedures, "Question and Answer" documents, and much more.

Chapter 20 Ethics

The U.S. Office of Government Ethic's homepage is located at (www.usoge.gov).

Chapter 21 Constitutional Rights

Research cases regarding constitutional rights is probably best left to seasoned legal researchers. However, legal research on constitutional issues can be done by going to (http://www.findlaw.com/casecode/constitution/).

Chapter 22 Privacy Act Rights/ Access to Information

The Privacy Act of 1974, as amended is found at (http://www.justice.gov/opcl/privstat.htm). The Department of Justice Overview of the Privacy Act is found at (http://www.justice.gov/opcl/1974privacyact-overview.htm). The Freedom of Information Act overview is found at (http://www.justice.gov/oip/).

Each federal agency home page may have a link to its "FOIA" site. For example:

Department of Agriculture: www.dm.usda.gov/foia/
Department of Health and Human Services: http://www.hhs.gov/foia
Department of Defense: http://www.defenselink.mil/pubs/foi
Department of Interior: http://www.doi.gov/foia
Department of State: http://foia.state.gov
Department of the Treasury: http://www.ustreas.gov/foia
Federal Bureau of Investigation: http://foia.fbi.gov
National Institutes of Health: http://www.nih.gov/icd/od/foia

Chapter 23 The Hatch Act: Prohibited Political Actives

The OSC's website discusses the Hatch Act at (www.osc.gov/hatchact.htm) and (https://www.osc.gov/haFederalfaq.htm).

Chapter 24 Federal Tort Claims Act

A good site that explains the mechanics of filing a claim under the "FTCA" is (http://www.bphc.hrsa.gov/ftca/about/index.html).

Chapter 26 Congressional and Presidential Employees' Rights

The Office of Compliance's website is at (http://www.compliance.gov). The procedural rules governing the processing of complaints are found at (http://www.compliance.gov/proful3.html), and recent decisions by the Office are at (http://www.compliance.gov/bddecis.html).

Chapter 27 Waivers of Overpayment and Financial Claims against the Government

The General Services Administration Board of Contract Appeals website is located at (http://www.gsbca.gsa.gov/).

Chapter 32 Resolving Disputes Through Settlement

As of January 1, 2000, all federal agencies were required to establish or make available an ADR program during the pre-complaint and formal complaint stages of the EEO process. Chapter 3 of the EEO Management Directive (MD)-110 provides a detailed description of the ADR techniques: http://www.eeoc.gov/federal/directives/mc110/chapter3.html. The EEOC's information regarding federal sector ADR can be found at http://www.eeoc.gov/ federal/adr/. The "ADR Questions and Answers" is located at (http://www .eeoc.gov/federal/qanda and the "Fact Sheet" at http://www.eeoc .gov/federal/adr/facts.cfm. Each agency may have information on its website regarding its own ADR program.

Final Thoughts

The internet has certainly made legal research much easier. With a little patience utilizing "search engines" or searching agency websites, you can probably locate a lot of information which will assist you in understanding and enforcing your employment rights. Remember, though, that the reliability of the information you find is related to the trustworthiness of the individual, organization or entity who posted the information. The information posted by government agencies is generally very reliable. If you are "computer challenged" or "internet illiterate," do not despair. If you have access to a child above the age of 12 (or maybe even younger), you mostly likely have a seasoned research assistant at your ready disposal! Happy surfing.

31

How to Find a Lawyer

Where's a Good One When You Need One?

In This Chapter You Will Learn:

- what you should consider when seeking legal counsel
- what sources are available to assist you in finding counsel
- how to maximize your legal assistance

Contents Chapter Thirty-One - How to Find a Lawyer

Introduction

This book describes the countless laws, rules, and regulations that apply to the federal workforce. Often, agencies violate more than one of these laws at a time, or several in a long series of actions. Making matters more difficult is the fact that federal employee's rights are often spelled out in hard-to-understand "legalese." Further compounding the challenge to federal employees trying to protect their rights is that deadlines for taking action are short, and sometimes overlapping between different forums.

This may result in a maze of procedural nightmares that, if not properly navigated, will leave you with rights that cannot be enforced or protected.

Sometimes cases involve numerous election of remedies issues, when employees must choose between different forums that offer relief. How are you to know whether it is best to file a grievance under the union contract or to go through the EEO procedures? How do you know that you *can* file a grievance or go through EEO? You can easily get lost in the labyrinth that is created by the confusing and overlapping laws and regulations that could apply to your case. Even lawyers can find these laws confusing and difficult to understand. Lawyers unfamiliar with federal sector employment law can, and do, get lost in these puzzles. If someone unfamiliar with the process is guiding your case, your case and your potential remedies could be seriously harmed. Because of this, we strongly recommend that you find an attorney who is familiar with federal sector employment law.

How do you find a qualified attorney? And once you find a lawyer, what does it mean to retain (engage) him or her? How can you prevent a lawyer from taking advantage of your situation? These are important questions that we try to answer in this chapter.

In our society, attorneys have a poor reputation and are often viewed as "sharks" or "sleazy." These inaccurate characterizations are the result of just a few "bad apples" in the legal profession. But there are, in fact, those apples among us, so we will also identify ways that you can help protect yourself from them. We will also identify resources that may help you select a good attorney.

What if I don't live near lawyers familiar with federal employment?

Finding a lawyer for your federal employment case may be difficult, especially if you are located in a geographical area that does not have a large number of federal employees or even lawyers. It may be easier to find an experienced attorney in large cities (such as Washington, D.C., Denver, New York, Chicago, Atlanta, Los Angeles and the like) that house large federal complexes, than in rural areas where only a small federal facility is located. Those of you not located in a major city might have to seek an out-of-town attorney.

Can I use my family lawyer?

Just as you would not want your family physician to perform open-heart surgery, and instead would want a heart surgeon or cardiologist, you probably do not want your general practice lawyer to litigate your federal employment case. Not all lawyers are well versed in the same areas. Employment law is a very complex area. Federal employment law, with all of its laws, rules and regulations, is even more complex. Experience is key.

How do I find a lawyer who knows federal employment law?

You can find attorneys with experience through a variety of resources. First, Workplace Fairness, the publisher of the first two editions of this book, is a national organization committed to providing resources for employees in employment-related matters. The National Employment Lawyers Association (NELA) is a bar association of attorneys whose primary practice involves representing employees rather than employers. NELA also has local affiliates in some major cities. For example, the Metropolitan Washington Employment Lawyers Association ("MWELA") is located in the Washington, DC area.

By contacting these organizations, you can get lists of attorneys who specialize in employment law and federal workplace issues. (See Appendix F for a list of organizations that can help you find an attorney.)

In addition, there are many other ways to find attorneys:

- Word of mouth is the best way—recommendations from satisfied clients with your type of case. (Be careful about on-line "reviews" of attorneys. A client who has a bad case can unfairly blame the lawyer. The one disgruntled client may be more likely to write a negative review than the hundreds of satisfied clients are to write positive ones.)

- Many of the federal agencies charged with overseeing federal employee laws, such as the EEOC and the MSPB, may have lawyer referral lists. You can call your local office and ask for a list of attorneys who practice the relevant type of law. (The phone numbers and addresses of the regional offices of these agencies can be found in Appendix H and L).

- Call your state, county, or local bar association, which will also have lawyer referral lists that often identify lawyers by the type of law they practice.

- Unions also often know which attorneys in the geographical area have experience with the agencies they deal with and the applicable federal laws.

- Ask another attorney. If you know any attorneys, even if they are unfamiliar with federal sector employment law, ask them if they know another lawyer who does have experience in the field.

- In some locales, local magazines do an annual or biannual review of "top" lawyers by area of specialty. (For example, in the Washington, DC area, *Washingtonian Magazine* publishes such a feature.) These lawyers are often peer reviewed to be accepted for the list. These same publications often have an on-line version that can be searched as well.

- The Yellow Pages is a less desirable method for finding an attorney in the employment field. If you have no other options, at least make sure that the attorney advertises as having experience in federal employees' rights.

- Lawyer referral sites have sprung up on the internet. Many of these sites allow you to search for lawyers by area of specialty and geographic area. Some sites allow you to give detailed information about your case for evaluation. Be careful in selecting an attorney through this method. Make a specific inquiry as to the attorney's experience in federal sector employment cases.

Here are a few internet search sites for lawyers:

- www.avvo.com
- www.findlaw.com
- www.lawyers.com
- www.martindale.com
- www.superlawyers.com

If you do a simple "google" search for employment lawyers, remember that the lawyers who appear at the top in the "pale yellow" box are simply those lawyers who paid to have those top spots. You should always do your own independent research to find out information about the lawyers who you find solely through an internet search.

What happens in the initial interview?

Rarely will an attorney or a firm agree to take your case over the telephone in your initial call to the office. Because employment cases are factually and procedurally complex, experienced federal employment attorneys usually want to talk with you first to find out what type of case you have and the specific facts. Most lawyers charge for this meeting, which is called an initial consultation. This consultation can take place by telephone if you do not live near the lawyer's office. Some attorneys even require you to fill out a detailed form (like an application or a questionnaire) before agreeing to meet with you. You should, of course, be truthful and detailed in answering the questions.

TIP

Finding the right lawyer usually takes time and sometimes money for consultation fees. Not all lawyers have the knowledge, expertise, and experience necessary to represent federal employees. You may have to make phone calls and schedule several appointments with different lawyers, before making the right selection. Do not be discouraged. The end result will be worth your effort.

The initial meeting, or consultation, is important. You will have to present to the lawyer the merits of your case. You should have all of your relevant documents with you. Be sure to bring (or send if your consultation is by telephone):

- the collective bargaining agreement, if there is one
- your recent performance evaluations
- any disciplinary actions against you
- any evidence you have about your case
- it is also helpful if you draft a time-line or chronology of events, a brief narrative explanation of the facts of your case, and a list of questions you would like answered for the attorney to review
- bring the originals of all your relevant documents with you, plus copies for the attorney

Use the initial consultation as an opportunity to get legal advice on your case. Find out what procedural avenues are available to you and what your deadlines are. Ask the lawyer to identify the strongest and weakest points of your case. Often people want to know if they will win, or the likelihood of winning. Lawyers are not fortune tellers. A good lawyer will not be able to say for certain that you will win, particularly not at an early stage of your case.

Also use the initial consultation to interview the lawyer. Ask:

- have you handled cases of this type before?
- how many years have you been practicing this type of law?
- are you familiar with the laws that apply to my case, and
- have you ever dealt with my agency before?

TIP

Use the initial consultation to interview the lawyer to find out if he or she has had experience with your kind of case, and with your federal agency.

The lawyer might already know the agency representatives and can comment on their strengths and weaknesses.

As the attorney talks about your case and the applicable law, listen for whether he or she talks about how the law affects your particular set of facts. If the lawyer talks about the legal aspects of the case, he/she probably is familiar with the relevant law. If he/she instead talks only about how terribly you were treated and how unfairly the agency has dealt with you, but does not talk very much about the law, this may be a sign he/she may not know very much about the law.

As you can tell from the complexities outlined in this book, there may not be a remedy for every unfair action that has been taken against you. A lawyer unfamiliar with the law may not know this, leading you to think that you have a stronger case than you do.

Many people want to know the lawyer's win/lose ratio. In many states, it is unethical for a lawyer to answer that question, because the answer would be misleading. For example, suppose the lawyer has handled only one discrimination case and won on the merits (that is, the judge found that there was discrimination), but lost on the damages (that is, the client did not win any money). This scenario is entirely possible. In response to the question of his success rate, the lawyer could say that he/she won the case and has a one hundred percent win record. In truth, though, this attorney probably does not have the experience you are looking for. "Win/lose" ratios will also not reveal success in settlements—and most cases settle.

Another factor to consider is the lawyer's ability to accomplish your most significant goals through settlement. With a settlement, the lawyer and his client are often sworn to secrecy after the settlement is signed. But the lawyer can talk with you generally about the settlements he/she has achieved. A settlement is neither a "victory" nor a "defeat" when looking at an attorney's win/lose record. But a settlement is considered a "win," because it almost certainly puts the employee in a better position.

When you talk with the lawyer, discuss his/her approach to the case, how he plans to pursue it, and what legal theory she believes is applicable. Each attorney is different. Some may have general philosophies or practices with which you may or may not be comfortable. You will be disclosing very personal and private information to this person. You may be investing a lot of time and money in him or her. If you do not feel comfortable with the attorney, find someone else.

TIP

Finding a lawyer is not like trying to find the best price for a certain brand of TV or computer. Whenever possible, meet the lawyer in person or have an extended telephone interview to get a sense of whether he or she has a command of the subject matter and a genuine interest in you and your problem. The most important question is not what the hourly rate is, but whether you have true confidence in this lawyer.

DOES MY AGREEMENT WITH MY ATTORNEY NEED TO BE IN WRITING?

When you hire an attorney, it is critical to understand all the terms and conditions of your relationship. You should always have the terms and conditions in writing. Most attorneys will require that you sign a written fee agreement. If the attorney says that you and he/she can act "on faith" and do not need an agreement, insist upon a written agreement or find another attorney. The agreement protects you. The attorney should also sign the agreement. That agreement is a personal service contract between you and the attorney or the law firm. Read the agreement carefully and make sure you understand all of the fine print. If you have any questions or concerns, raise them *before* you sign.

TIP

Most employees are not familiar with legal disputes, lawsuits, and lawyers. Don't be afraid to ask your lawyer questions about legal fees, about the fee agreement, and about what you can expect from the legal process and from the lawyer.

WHAT SHOULD THE AGREEMENT WITH MY LAWYER INCLUDE?

If you find a lawyer you feel satisfied with, you will enter into what might be called a "retainer" agreement, "engagement" agreement or letter, or simply a "fee" agreement. It is the contract between you and the lawyer regarding the services the lawyer is to provide for you. For your understanding, protection, and security, several points should be addressed in a retainer agreement:

1. What are the specific tasks the lawyer is to perform in representing you?

   For example, if you are retaining an attorney to represent you in response to a proposed removal, does the representation include an appeal to the MSPB, if necessary? If you are retaining the attorney to represent you in a union grievance, does the representation include a hearing before an arbitrator?

2. The estimated or exact dollar amount of the fee should be stated.

   If the attorney charges by the hour, the hourly rate should be clearly identified. If you are engaging a firm, the agreement should state the hourly rate for each attorney. If you are hiring an attorney based upon an hourly rate, ask whether there are any minimum or maximum fees that are involved. Ask whether any stated fee is merely an estimate subject to change.

   A few attorneys charge a flat rate, or one single amount for their representation, regardless of how long it takes. Accept these conditions with caution. Flat rates may not provide sufficient incentive for the attorney after he/she has spent considerable time on the case.

3. What are the anticipated expenses and are those expenses in addition to the fee advance/estimate or are they already included?

Expenses can be simple and small, like postage, or complex and significant, like deposition transcripts. Check the charge for copies. Some firms charge up to fifty cents per page for copying services, a sum which can add up quickly. The average rate seems to be about twenty cents.

TIP

The most important thing about a fee agreement is not what it is, but that you understand it!

4. What if the fees and costs are less than the attorney estimated? Will you be entitled to a refund?

5. What if the fees and costs are more than the attorney estimated?

6. What are the payment arrangements? Will the attorney accept a monthly payment plan, or is all the money to be paid "up front"? Will the attorney require an additional retainer or fee advance after a certain period of time has elapsed?

7. Does the attorney accept contingency fee cases?

Contingency cases are those in which the attorney agrees to take a percentage of the proceeds of your recovery (often one-third) instead of requiring you to pay a fixed amount or pay by the hour. If you lose and recover nothing, there is usually no fee except for any "up front" retainer and actual expenses. Lawyers usually only agree to contingency representation if it is probable that there will be a large cash settlement or cash award. This is often the case only where liability is clear and large sums of back pay and/or compensatory damages are likely. If the lawyer or the firm is willing to take your case on a contingency basis, make sure that the agreement clearly identifies the percentage to which the lawyer is entitled and what happens if you choose to terminate representation by the attorney before the case is completed. Frequently lawyers require a reasonable "up front" fee advance in addition to, or as an advance towards, the contingent fee payable at the end of the case. Normally you are still responsible for out-of-pocket expenses, even where there is a contingency fee arrangement.

8. What if you choose to end the representation? Will you be entitled to a refund of the funds not yet spent by the attorney?

9. Will the attorney send you statements identifying exactly what is being done on your case, and what fees have been incurred to date? Monthly statements are the ideal.

Some attorneys do not provide their clients with periodic statements identifying the actions the attorney is taking. In those situations, you do not know if the attorney is following up or is taking action at all. Make sure that under your written agreement the attorney is required to provide statements of all activities on your case. Also request that your attorney send you copies of all significant correspondence and other important papers concerning the case. Ask what the deadlines for action in your case are, if you don't know them, so you can make sure they are being met, if you have any doubts. If your attorney is not answering questions, appears incompetent or disinterested in your case, and is not doing all you think to be proper, you should not hesitate to get a second opinion on the progress of your case from another lawyer.

TIP

- *Keep your lawyer up to date on your case. This is your responsibility.*
- *If you feel that you should have heard something about your case from your lawyer, don't hesitate to call or e-mail and ask. The squeaky wheel still gets the grease.*
- *On the other hand, don't call an attorney too often, as you are usually billed for every minute of that time.*
- *If you are having trouble getting a busy lawyer on the phone, consider other means of communication, such as voice mail, fax, or e-mail.*

Final Thoughts

Making sure you look into the matters discussed in this chapter *before* you enter into an agreement with an attorney can save a great deal of aggravation afterwards. If your case is serious enough that you have engaged the services of an attorney, chances are the stakes are pretty high for you and so is the emotional price. What you don't want at this point is a fight with your attorney as well as your agency. Feeling that your attorney doesn't know enough to handle your case, nothing is being done on your case, your calls aren't being returned, or that your attorney is not working in your best interest, is not only frustrating, but it can be costly.

If you follow guidelines in this chapter, you should be able to find a competent attorney capable of handling your case, and build a trusting relationship with him or her.

32

Resolving Disputes Through Settlement

Can We Talk?

In This Chapter You Will Learn:

- the advantages of settlement over litigation
- how to know when it is best to settle
- how to reach a good settlement agreement
- what to do if settlement doesn't work

Contents Chapter Thirty-Two - Resolving Disputes Through Settlement

INTRODUCTION

All through this book we have apprised you of the rights available to you if you do not get what you think you are entitled to as a federal employee. Because your employer is the federal government and the federal government has many restrictions placed on it by the Constitution for your protection as a citizen, your employer has more of a duty than private employers to conduct its dealings with you in a manner which protects your rights. Many times, when you are not given something you think you are entitled to, you can appeal that decision, often up to, and including, the federal courts. That is your right.

But for most of us, engaging in the administrative appeal and litigation approach is more than we wish to do. Even though these rights are available to us, they still can cost a great deal of time, energy, goodwill, and money. This is your workplace and your source of income. It may even feel like your "home away from home." Most of the time, all you want is to get what you think you are entitled to with as little fuss as possible. You don't want to sue. You don't want to create ill will with your supervisor or coworkers. You don't want to cause a hassle that takes your mind way from your work. You just want to get what you think you deserve.

Often, the answer is to enter into a good settlement agreement. That doesn't mean settling for "just anything." A good settlement agreement should guarantee you a few things which are really important to you, and protect your rights in the case of a breach of the agreement. A settlement will not always give you everything you want or deserve. But a settlement will get results for you sooner and with less disruption to your life and work than if you fight a nasty battle and win (or lose!).

Before you make a decision as to how to proceed in getting what you think you deserve, weigh the following reasons to settle your claim against the option of going forward with your claim to a trial or hearing.

- By going as far as you have, you have already demonstrated that you are serious about your complaint.
- You are able to capitalize on the leverage you created by filing your complaint.
- You do not give up your conviction that you are right.
- You avoid the risk of losing.
- The other side gives you something that is important to you.
- You may receive a definite and certain sum of money.
- You receive a benefit far sooner than might have been possible through litigation.
- You will begin to mend your relationship with your agency.
- You can end the frustration caused by the dispute.
- Your family and friends will now get more of your attention.
- You can obtain types of relief in a voluntary settlement which you might not be entitled to even if you won your case.

The best practical tip on strategy is to not be too worried about it. Settling cases is an art, not a science. There are plenty of "artists" you can hire to pursue a settlement for you. You need to be concerned with identifying and prioritizing what you want—especially what you want *most*—so that you can make sure you do not settle for less.

No one gets what they want if they cannot identify what they want. If you simply want a lot of money, you are probably not going to be successful without first hiring a lawyer to build a strong case against your agency. So, try to identify all the items you want such as:

- training which would be helpful to your career
- job assignments you desire
- a promotion with or without back pay
- an increase to your pension
- a good (or even neutral) job recommendation
- the specific expenses you want reimbursed (such as medical costs and attorney fees)
- a reasonable sum to cover other economic and financial losses, past and future

---

TIP

If at all possible, retain a lawyer or other representative to negotiate on your behalf because the representative can establish a relationship with your agency's representative. Negotiating through a representative can circumvent the strong emotional barriers that are generally present between the parties, which can get in the way of effectively dealing with each other. A knowledgeable representative can also advise you on what may or may not be feasible in a given case, and can help you craft a settlement position that is most likely to be effective.

It is important when identifying settlement terms not to limit yourself to what you may be entitled to if you win your case. Settlements are creative instruments which can get parties relief that may not be otherwise available. For example, if you claim a wrongful denial of a promotion, maybe priority consideration for another position and a lateral transfer to a different office to work under a preferred supervisor may be a good settlement because your opportunities for career advancement may be much improved under a different supervisor.

When making a settlement demand, it is generally expected that, in a show of compromise, you will ask for less than what you would receive if you won your case. Otherwise, you are asking the agency to cave in completely, which is unlikely to occur. Sometimes, if your case is strong, you may be able to start negotiations with a demand for full relief, but such a position may cause the agency to refuse to negotiate further because of your perceived unwillingness to compromise.

Expect that the agency may be unwilling or unable to give you everything you ask for in your starting settlement offer. However, you should normally ask for more than you may be actually willing to settle for, in order to provide room for negotiations. "Splitting the difference" is not a rule, but it is generally seen as a fair negotiation and compromise strategy which can often resolve and close "the deal." Plan ahead for it.

Alternative dispute resolution ("ADR")

Direct settlement negotiations between an employee and the agency frequently do not occur, or break down after getting started, because of "macho" attitudes, "principle" disagreements, other emotional issues, politics, misunderstandings, or honest disagreements as to the facts or law. If your opportunities to engage in face-to-face settlement discussions are limited, alternative dispute resolution (ADR), which includes mediation, may provide an opening for settlement. ADR provides alternatives to litigation that the parties agree to engage in mainly to save the expense, aggravation, and delay of litigation.

ADR may also be mandated by a judge or governing regulations. In earlier years, the judiciary was fairly hostile to ADR. But as our society has become more litigious, court dockets have become more crowded. Sometimes it can take years just to get your case scheduled for trial! The cost of litigation has also skyrocketed. For these reasons, judges and lawyers have come to appreciate the availability of an alternative to litigation. Many court systems now have ADR programs administered under their auspices.

Mediation

ADR can take several forms. Mediation is the most common. The agency frequently has a procedure for selection and payment of the mediator, if required. The EEOC and MSPB provide mediators and settlement judges for cases under their jurisdiction, and the OSC also offers mediation in some cases. Mediation generally involves a meeting with you, your representative (if any), your agency, a representative for your agency (if any), and at least one mediator.

During mediation, you will generally have the first opportunity to speak and explain what you want and why. Your agency will have an opportunity to do the same in reply to your comments. A discussion about your request, led by the mediator, may then take place. The gathering will probably then break into two groups so that you can each discuss privately with the mediator the specifics of what you want or are willing to give to the other side in a settlement agreement.

Mediation is not a sure path to settlement. Sometimes mediation is a waste of time, especially when parties are not willing to discuss settlement positions or listen to the legitimate concerns of the other party. It is the mediator's role to see the positions of the parties and try to suggest ways to work things out. If the mediator doesn't take a leadership role, mediation may fail.

You need to be truthful about what you want and how you feel, but do not speak too much about the details of your claim and your supporting evidence. Mediation is not a fact-finding conference. You are not there to be convinced that you are wrong, and the agency is not there to be convinced that you are right. You each hold onto your convictions and see if there is middle ground. The mediator is not there to decide the case as a judge would. Instead, a mediator is there as a facilitator, to help move the parties' settlement negotiations along. The mediator may help define the middle ground and explore whether it is possible to get both of you to reach it.

In addition to the conversations with the agency and mediator, you may also speak confidentially to the mediator when you meet separately with him or her. You, as well as the agency, can authorize the mediator to reveal only certain things to the other side. The mediator needs enough information to verify the strengths of your case to the other side. A good mediator will also inform you and the agency what your respective weak points may be in hopes of convincing you each to reduce your settlement demand toward the middle ground.

If you and your agency agree in principle on settlement terms during a mediation session, they will not be enforceable unless they are set forth in a written settlement agreement. The mediator can assist you in drafting the agreement or take the lead in putting the key elements in writing so that you and the agency can later formalize the agreement in a more comprehensive written settlement agreement.

IMPORTANT SETTLEMENT PRINCIPLES AND PROVISIONS

If you go into negotiations without understanding some of the key principles, you will be at a disadvantage. It may also look as if you are not acting in good faith or in the spirit of compromise. So be aware of the principles below.

NO FAULT

When agencies enter into a settlement agreement they usually demand that you agree to a "non-liability," or no-fault clause. A non-liability clause states that the agency does not admit any wrongdoing or fault by virtue of entering into and signing the settlement agreement.

A non-liability clause is often the primary motivation for an agency to enter into a settlement agreement because an official finding of wrongdoing is precisely what the agency wishes to avoid. By including this term, you are not agreeing that the agency did nothing wrong. You are merely agreeing that settlement does not represent an admission of wrongdoing by the agency. Many agencies may be willing to also include parallel language stating that the settlement agreement does not represent your admission that the agency's actions were fair or legitimate, or that your allegations against the agency were without merit.

If an arbitrator or judge has already decided that the agency has wronged you, then in order to avoid appeals, the agency may be prepared to enter into an agreement which states that the agency violated a law, rule, or regulation and then settles any disputed amount of damages. Without a finding or admission of liability or otherwise clearly established "guilt" on their part, agencies have little incentive to agree that they have wronged you because it makes them look bad.

SATISFACTION/DISMISSAL/RELEASE OF CLAIMS

The essential element of a settlement agreement is that you promise to withdraw your claim in its entirety "as settled and fully resolved and satisfied." In a settlement, it would be common for you to agree to file a letter with the judge or arbitrator requesting dismissal of your claim due to a settlement agreement. Generally, you should attach a copy of the agreement to your withdrawal.

A "release of claims" (or waiver) is related to the withdrawal and dismissal clause, but it carries with it a much greater meaning. A simple "release" provides that you agree to release the agency from the claim being settled and agree not to file the claim again. Thus, the agency is released and forever discharged from dealing with such a claim from you in the future. Simple releases are to be expected as a typical part of a binding settlement agreement.

On the other hand, a "general release" provides that you agree to release and forever discharge the agency from any and all claims, known or unknown, which you may have or which could arise from the facts which form the basis of the claim presently being settled. Notice how much broader and more inclusive the language is, and thus, how much more you are giving up by entering into a general release.

TIP

General releases should be avoided if at all possible. Rarely do you know the full scope of claims that you compromise by signing a general release. It may be unlikely that you have other claims, or that you would consider bringing a new action against the agency after signing a settlement agreement for what has already happened, but for your own protection, attempt to narrow the language as much as possible anyway. Release only those claims which are bound up with the claims being settled. After all, the agency is not "giving" you anything for claims which you have not asserted.

For the most part, settlement agreements and releases of any type are valid as of the date of your signature.

As discussed below, in some cases (in particular, those involving age discrimination claims), the agreement may set the effective date at 7 days after signature in order to comply with certain statutes which give a waiver period after signature. In most cases, you cannot validly waive claims for future violations by the agency.

If you are aware of a potential or actual issue important to you which you do not want to risk releasing, simply add sentences which state that this issue is not settled or released as a part of the settlement agreement.

If you are resigning from the agency, you should also obtain the agency's agreement not to contest your subsequent claim for unemployment compensation benefits as a condition for you agreeing to a settlement and release.

Promotions and Reassignments

In many cases, an employee's chief goal will be to receive a promotion or a reassignment. While these goals can sometimes be accomplished through settlement, certain limitations do exist. Generally, it is not possible to get a full grade-level promotion in settlement unless the case directly involves some sort of denial of promotion issue (such as a nonselection or a denied career-ladder promotion). An agency can agree to award a step increase without a denied step increase claim pending. However, an agency can only provide a step increase in settlement if the employee is currently eligible for a step increase (either a Within Grade Increase or a Quality Step Increase), or if there is a 'gap' with a missed opportunity for a step increase somewhere in the employee's work history.

Lateral reassignments are not limited in the same fashion as grade and step increases, and agencies will sometimes agree to reassign employees even if a denied reassignment was not at issue in the case. The ability to get a reassignment increases greatly if the employee can identify a specific open, vacant and funded position to be reassigned into—especially if the position is one that the employee can perform without needing substantial extra training. However, an agency cannot agree in a settlement agreement to reassign an employee to a position in different agency; the receiving agency would also have to agree.

Retirement

For some employees, especially those close to retirement, the most useful benefit an employee can get in settlement is enhancement to their retirement benefits, either through enhancing their "high-3 salary" to increase their pension annuity payment or through changing their circumstances of departure from federal service to make them eligible for an early retirement category.[1]

The decision on granting retirement applications rests with the Office of Personnel Management (OPM), and no other agency can direct OPM how to decide a particular retirement application as part of a settlement.

1 See Chapter 18 for discussion on federal retirement issues.

However, a settlement agreement can 'stage manage' the circumstances surrounding retirement to maximize the chances that OPM will grant retirement. In cases where the settlement seeks to enhance the "high-3 salary," the settlement agreement must ensure—even if no other back pay is paid—that OPM is paid the necessary deposits to ensure full 'retirement service credit,' preferably with the agency paying all required deposits.

It is possible to structure a settlement agreement to place an employee in a category eligible for early retirement. These agreements have to be set up extremely carefully to ensure that OPM is likely to approve of the retirement application. Employees who desire this sort of a settlement agreement are strongly advised to consult with an attorney or representative before the start of negotiations.

Tax liability

If you receive money as a result of a settlement agreement, you will most likely have to pay taxes on the entire amount. The settlement agreement should clearly state who carries the burden of tax liability. Generally, the person receiving the money carries the tax liability. In order to calculate your after-tax proceeds, you may need to consult a tax advisor prior to agreeing on the gross settlement amount. Otherwise, you may find yourself with much less of a settlement than you anticipated.

TIP

If you have any questions regarding the tax consequences of your settlement, you should consult a tax advisor before agreeing to and signing the settlement agreement.

In some settlement agreements, the agency may agree to pay you one amount (a "lump sum") of money for all your alleged harm—back pay, interest, attorney fees and costs, pain and suffering compensatory damages, medical costs, etc. You will be required to report that lump sum as income on your tax return. If you split the lump sum into separate items, you may possibly be able to exclude some of the items from taxes. For example, reimbursing attorneys fees and costs separately might reduce your tax liability if those expenses are not subject to being taxed in your personal situation.[2] Compensatory damages are taxed differently than back pay.

Confidentiality

Confidentiality of the fact of settlement and/or the actual terms of settlement is not a part of the settlement unless it is specifically included in writing in the agreement. Agencies usually want to keep any settlement quiet. Parties frequently agree to keep the terms and amount confidential, and indeed confidentiality may be helpful for employees in some cases (such as where the settlement agreement sanitizes the employee's record). However, a confidentiality clause is not mandatory or automatic, and must be negotiated separately in each case. It is much more difficult and rare to agree to keep the fact of the settlement confidential. Avoid that type of clause if at all possible, because it is too easy to violate, even inadvertently.

If you must include a confidentiality clause in a settlement agreement be sure to include a provision that you are still free to share the agreement's terms with your immediate family, legal advisors, and tax or financial advisors. You should agree that you will inform those persons of their obligation to abide by the confidentiality terms of the agreement. Avoid agreeing to terms which force you to return your proceeds of settlement if you violate the confidentiality clause. Such a provision is very harsh and usually impossible to enforce.

Please note that certain statutes and federal regulations prohibit confidentiality clauses that bar some types of future whistleblowing and future disclosures of discrimination to the EEOC.[3] Further, certain agencies have decided by regulation to not seek confidentiality clauses in their settlement agreements.[4]

Implementation deadlines

Whenever possible, include a definite deadline for completion of any and all aspects of the settlement. For example, if money is to be paid, make sure you agree to a deadline for you to receive it, how it is to be delivered to you, and how you are to receive it. Direct deposit while harder to track, is now a common method agencies use to make payments due in settlements.

---

2 Reimbursement of attorneys' fees and costs in some discrimination and whistleblower reprisal claims may be deductible from "adjusted gross income." *See* 26 USC § 62(a)(20, 21). Talk to your tax advisor to see if this exception applies to you.

3 *See* 5 USC § 2302(b)(13); EEOC *Enforcement Guidance on Non-Waivable Employee Rights under Equal Employment Opportunity Commission (EEOC) Enforced Statutes* (April 10, 1997).

4 *See* 28 CFR § 50.23.

Time to review before signing

Do not agree to or sign a settlement agreement under duress or within a short time frame. Be sure there is time to consult an attorney and financial advisor about the agreement if at all possible. Make sure you understand exactly what you are signing. Never assume that something is included in your settlement unless you actually see it in the settlement agreement, because if it is not in writing, it will not be enforceable.

If an agreement waives rights that you may have under the Age Discrimination in Employment Act (ADEA), the settlement agreement must specifically state that this is the case. The ADEA requires that you have a *21-day* waiting period before you must sign, or forfeit your right to accept the settlement agreement. You may sign earlier than the expiration of the *21 days* if you want to, but you cannot be forced to sign it early.

Under ADEA, once you sign the settlement agreement, you have *7 days* to change your mind and revoke the agreement. Even if you sign the agreement and do not wish to revoke it, the settlement agreement cannot and will not become effective until the *7 days* pass from the date you signed the agreement. As with all other aspects of a settlement agreement and release, nothing in a settlement agreement waives your rights or claims under the ADEA (or other laws) that may arise after the date you sign the settlement agreement.

TIP

In age discrimination cases, to revoke a signed settlement agreement effectively, contact the agency in writing within 7 days after you signed the agreement and state "I hereby revoke the settlement agreement signed by me on [date]." Sign and date your revocation statement and keep proof of its delivery to the agency.

Breach of settlement agreements

The agreement should state clearly what the options are if the other party breaches the agreement. Retain the option of enforcing the specifics of the settlement agreement or refiling your complaint at the point when the breach occurs. Also retain the right to seek damages from the agency for damage you suffer by virtue of their breach. For the most part, the principles of contract law are used to determine if there has been a breach and what the remedy shall be. You will be able to enforce the terms of a settlement agreement as you would a contract.

It is your responsibility to monitor the agency's implementation of the settlement. If you believe the agency is in breach of a signed settlement agreement—because it failed to implement a term or did so incorrectly—immediately give the agency a written demand specifying the settlement agreement provision breached and stating what the agency must do to come into compliance with the settlement agreement. Depending on the forum you are in at the time your case is settled, there are different rules or procedures for enforcing correct compliance with a settlement agreement. For example, the procedures vary in the MSPB,[5] EEOC,[6] and arbitration.[7] The EEOC and the MSPB have specific regulations on how to enforce a settlement. Make sure the rules are followed so the agency does not get away with breaching the agreement. Be warned that some settlement enforcement procedures have extremely short deadlines for filing a breach claim, after which it may be too late to seek enforcement for a particular breach.

For some settlement agreements in federal personnel matters, there is more than one avenue to press a breach of settlement agreement claim. One possibility is to seek administrative enforcement of the settlement agreement from the administrative body governing the claims process for the case which led to the settlement. Another possibility is to sue for breach of contract under the Tucker Act at the U.S. Court of Federal Claims. It is important to consider the nature of the breach and how the breach needs to be fixed in order to assess which method for enforcement you use. If the breached provision is best fixed by an order directing the agency to do (or not do) something, or by voiding the settlement agreement and reinstating the old case, then these administrative breach mechanisms are the way forward.[8]

If the issue is seeking damages because of the harms caused by an agency's breach (for example, due to losing a new job when an agency breaches

---

5 *See* 5 CFR § 1201.182. Settlements entered into the record of an MSPB case are enforced like a Board order.

6 *See* 29 CFR § 1614.504.

7 Failure to comply with the settlement of a grievance or arbitration case is pursued as an unfair labor practice, filed with the FLRA, under 5 USC § 7116(a).

8 Be warned that the EEOC or MSPB may require you to repay any money you received under the original settlement agreement in order to have the old case reinstated. Also, the MSPB will only enforce settlement agreements if it has found jurisdiction over the case. If jurisdiction is in question at the time of settlement, the MSPB may not be able to later enforce the settlement agreement.

a clean-record provision in a settlement agreement and badmouths an employee to the new employer), then the best enforcement mechanism may be a breach of contract lawsuit under the Tucker Act.[9]

However, some settlement agreements have no effective administrative enforcement mechanism (for example, settlements of non-union administrative grievances, settlements, of proposed adverse actions at the agency level, settlements of MSPB appeals without a jurisdictional finding). In these cases, the Tucker Act procedure may be the only effective breach remedy. Finally, please note that sometimes a breach of settlement agreement can also be a new act of retaliation, and so it is important to consider if both a breach claim and a reprisal claim may be available.

Congressional assistance

Writing or calling your Congressional representative is always an option for you which may make you feel more active in your advocacy, and can be a useful tool for prodding agencies to take actions in undisputed situations such as implementing settlement agreements. A letter apprising your representative of your complaint, addressed to your local Congressional district office, will often result in a letter from your representative to your agency seeking information about what the agency is doing to address your situation.

Representatives and their staff rarely undertake an investigation or become personally involved in the matter. However, a letter from your representative to the agency will be treated with a high level of attention because of the possibility of publicity or adverse political ramifications. When your agency responds to your representative, you will generally receive a copy of the agency letter from the representative's office.

Keep in mind that your statements to a Congressional representative or staff person may become part of the agency file regarding your claim. If you do not want greater exposure in your agency about your complaint, and you prefer a low profile, then you should not enlist Congressional assistance. As with all communication, you will come across most strongly and effectively by being professional in any communication with Congressional

---

9 *See Cunningham v. U.S.*, 748 F.3d 1172, (Fed. Cir. 2014) *(citing VanDesande v. U.S.*, 673 F.3d 1342 (Fed. Cir. 2012), *Holmes v. U.S.*, 657 F.3d 1303 (Fed. Cir. 2011)). Please note that compensatory damages for emotional pain and suffering are not available in most proceedings at the Court of Federal Claims, and so this remedy only allows for other categories of money damages (such as back pay). *See Pratt v. U.S.*, 50 Fed. Cl. 469, 482 (2001).

staff and portraying your case in a fair manner, which will surely help you once you reach the settlement stage.

Final Thoughts

Litigation is not the only path to an ultimate solution of your problem with your agency. There are several other things you can do that will not take as long, be as expensive, or carry the emotional cost of obtaining a decision or legal judgment against the agency. Litigation should be your last resort, since there is nowhere to go from there. So before reaching that point, you should explore the other avenues for resolving your conflict, such as mediation, in an effort to achieve as quick, effective, honorable, and satisfying a resolution as possible.

33

How to Prepare for an Administrative Hearing

Tell it to the Judge!

IN THIS CHAPTER YOU WILL LEARN:

- how to prepare for a hearing
- how to get and stay organized for the hearing
- how to conduct yourself while testifying

Contents Chapter Thirty-Three - How to Prepare for an Administrative Hearing

Introduction

Many federal employees represent themselves in their administrative hearings at the EEOC or the MSPB. The hearing process begins when a judge is assigned to a case and ends with a decision by that judge. The hearing process breaks down into two parts: preparation and the hearing itself. This chapter discusses how to plan for your hearing, as well as tricks and tactics to help you make a persuasive presentation to the administrative judge before and during the hearing.

TIP

A good source on how to prepare for and conduct an administrative hearing is* LITIGATING FEDERAL SECTOR EMPLOYMENT AND LABOR LAW DISPUTES, *by Renn Fowler and Joseph V. Kaplan (Dewey Publications 2002). (See www.deweypub.com.)

What is a hearing?

A hearing is your "day in court". A hearing is different from a trial. We are all familiar with television trials that have a court, a judge, and, in many cases, a jury. A hearing is different. Hearings may be closed to the public, and there is no jury.[1] Administrative hearings are less formal than court trials. Court rules, such as the federal rules of evidence or procedures, are not strictly followed, but often are used for guidance. At the MSPB, your hearing may be at one of the Board's offices in a hearing room that is similar to a small court room, or may be in a conference room at a neutral site. At the EEOC, your hearing will more likely than not be in a conference room at your agency. More hearings are now being conducted by video teleconferencing, although it is strongly recommended that you be at the same location as your representative.

---

[1] MSPB hearings are public; EEOC hearings are not.

The purpose of a hearing is to give the administrative judge (AJ) evidence so that the judge can determine the facts to see if your claims have merit. The judge plays two roles: that of adjudicator and of fact-finder. Evidence takes many forms, including documents, reports, witness testimony, and deposition transcripts.

During the hearing, it's your job to show the AJ evidence which will prove your claim(s) that the agency's actions were wrongful in a particular way. The agency is represented by an agency representative or attorney. The agency attorney has the opposite job: to show evidence that will prove that the agency's actions were legal. In some instances, if your case has merit, you might be entitled to be compensated for damages you suffered. If this is the case, you are also allowed to present evidence of the damages you suffered because of the agency's illegal actions. The agency is allowed to respond to your evidence.

At the close of the hearing, both parties are usually given a chance to sum up the facts, and make legal arguments—sometimes orally and sometimes in writing. The AJ then issues a decision on whether the agency did anything wrong and, if so, what actions the agency must take to remedy the harm that you suffered as a result.

Good preparation and organization are the keys to making a persuasive presentation to the AJ. You must be an expert of the events relating to your situation, know what law applies, know the facts you need to prove your claims, know the documents, know the witnesses, and know the procedure that the judge will use. You should learn the judge's preferences for how the hearing will be conducted. Each of these is discussed in more detail, below.

Can you do your own hearing?

Yes, you can. There is no rule that you cannot represent yourself. Representatives are allowed. If they know the procedures and the law, representatives are encouraged. A representative can be anyone who you trust to promote your best interests. Hiring an attorney should be seriously considered. But, because attorneys can be expensive, not all cases warrant a large financial investment. If you choose to represent yourself, you should prepare for an intellectual and emotional challenge.

Hearing preparation

A hearing involves procedures that apply to how cases are processed and substantive law that applies to the facts of your case. To prepare for your hearing, you must learn both. This requires patience, diligence and research.

TIP

Preparing for an administrative hearing is challenging and time consuming. To make sure you don't lose any opportunities, begin preparing as soon as you start your case.

The acknowledgment order

At the MSPB and the EEOC, cases are assigned to administrative judges who preside over the case. The first step of a hearing is when the AJ issues an acknowledgment order to both parties. This order allows the parties to begin discovery. The acknowledgment order also identifies critical deadlines and rules that the parties must follow, such as when the parties must initiate discovery, the amount of time the parties will have to do discovery, deadlines for filing motions, the amount of discovery allowed, and more. At the MSPB, you may elect to become an "e-filer." If you do so, you will file all pleadings and motions electronically, and receive all orders electronically. At the EEOC, some offices have piloted programs which mandate the filing of pleadings and motions electronically.

Deadlines and motions

It is critical to comply with all deadlines and orders set by the AJ. If any deadline or order cannot be met, you should tell the AJ immediately and file a motion to request an extension. When you file any motion, first try to ask the agency representative if he objects. In your motion, state that you tried to consult with the agency and, if known, whether the agency objects to your motion. If your motion is about a discovery dispute (see discovery, below), try to resolve the disagreement with the agency first. File a motion only if you cannot resolve the problem without the judge's involvement.

Whenever you file anything with the judge, include a certificate of service, stating the date and method of service on the agency attorney. For example:

> Certificate of Service: I, Adam Smith, hereby certify that on September 1, 2014, I served, by fax, a copy of the attached witness list on Mr. Bob Jones, General Counsel, 1234 Avenue, Suite 567, City, State, Zip, Fax Number.[2]

Motions may be filed for any issue or problem that comes up in litigation. For example, if a party fails to timely respond to a request for discovery, a motion asking the judge to compel the other side to answer may be appropriate. If your personal information, such as medical documents, is exchanged during discovery, you may ask the judge for a protective order, which would protect against disclosure to others.

When a motion is filed, the other side can file a response or a reply, explaining whether they object and if so, why. Responses must be filed within set deadlines identified by the AJ or in the procedures.

Know the procedures that apply to your claims

The procedures are identified in the EEOC federal sector regulations (29 CFR 1614 et seq.) and in the MSPB regulations (5 CFR 1201 et seq.) and in the orders issued by the judges. The Commission's Management Directive 110 ("MD-110") and Administrative Judges' Handbook, both available at its website (www.eeoc.gov), identify the applicable procedures and standards used at the Commission and are useful references.[3]

As soon as you file your complaint or appeal, you should start learning the procedures that apply to your case. Knowing the applicable procedures is vital because you are responsible for meeting deadlines and knowing standard rules. Make a copy of the regulations and keep them with your paperwork for easy reference, as you will need to refer to them throughout the process.

---

2 See sample certificate of service, Appendix E-5.

3 While this chapter focuses on procedures before the MSPB and the EEOC, there are other agencies that hold hearings concerning various claims or defenses of federal employees. Make sure you look at the rules and regulations governing those proceedings. Most adjudicatory administrative agencies have a web site containing their procedures.

Know what happened

By mastering the facts, you can master the case. Your case will be persuasive only if you have a thorough understanding of what happened and how the substantive law will reflect on those events. Focusing on the facts that help your case is obviously critical. In addition, there are probably many facts you don't already know. In preparing for your hearing, you can learn these facts and use them to your advantage.

Your version of what really happened, and the agency's version, will probably conflict. During your hearing, one of your goals is to disprove the agency's version. To do this, you have to know in advance what the agency's version is and what evidence is helpful to disprove the agency's allegations. Ignoring any of the agency's contentions may be a grave or fatal mistake, as any one important fact could make the judge find that your case is not meritorious.

TIP

Try to put yourself in the agency's shoes, so you can anticipate how the agency will see the facts and argue the case.

Know the law that applies to your claims

Long before the hearing, you should start learning the law that applies to your case. It is critical to understand what substantive law your judge will use to analyze your claims. The MSPB and the EEOC publish decisions of their cases where they discuss claims, the applicable law, and how the law applies to certain circumstances.

MSPB law: Peter Broida's, *A Guide to Merit Systems Protection Board Law and Practice* (Dewey Publications), provides historical background and a summary of current law at the Board, including the law relating to the Whistleblower Protection Act and prohibited personnel practices. You can obtain MSPB caselaw and regulations at the MSPB website (www.mspb.gov) or at your local law library. Specific cases can be found in the Merit Systems Protection Reporter ("MSPR") published by West and available at most law libraries.

EEOC law: You can obtain EEOC case law and procedures at the EEOC website (www.eeoc.gov) or at your local law library. The EEOC's Office of Federal Operations (OFO) is the Commission's appellate office that issues decisions relating to federal employees. OFO decisions are reported through the Federal Equal Opportunity Reporter (FEOR) which is available at major law libraries. Ernest Hadley publishes a helpful summary of OFO law in *A Guide to Federal Sector Equal Employment Law and Practice* (Dewey Publications). If there is a particular case that you want but it is not published through FEOR, OFO sometimes faxes decisions upon request.

If you are successful in proving that the agency's action was wrongful, then you may be entitled to remedies. Knowing the appropriate legal remedies is important so that you have reasonable expectations of what you can obtain by winning your case, and so that you can anticipate what evidence you need to offer. If an agency wrongly suspends an employee, the judge may order the agency to rescind the suspension and to restore back pay with interest. If an agency discriminatorily denies an employee an accommodation for a disability, the judge might order the agency to provide an accommodation and to compensate the employee for emotional damages, pain and suffering she suffered as a result. Gary Gilbert publishes a book titled *Compensatory Damages and Other Remedies in Federal Sector Employment Discrimination Cases* (Dewey Publications), which provides an exhaustive review of the damages available to victims of employment discrimination and the evidence needed to prove damages.

When you start your legal research, it is usually best to begin by reading a summary of the law, such as you will find in the Broida, Hadley and Gilbert books identified above. After you have learned the basic points of law, you will know the names of some of the cases that are relevant to your own. Through legal research, you can use these cases to find more cases that may be helpful to you.

Know what facts you need to prove to win your legal arguments

To be successful, each claim requires that certain facts be proven. For example, in a discrimination case where you are claiming you were treated differently than others (disparate treatment), you, as the "complainant," have to first prove a *prima facie* case. There are certain elements to a *prima facie* case and if those elements are not present, the judge may dismiss your complaint. Similarly, in conduct-related claims at the MSPB, the agency must prove that you (the "appellant") engaged in the activities specified, must prove each element of each charge, and must prove that the penalty was appropriate. You can prove the legal requirements of your case only if you know what they are.

After researching your legal issues, identify the key elements of the claim. As you prepare your case for hearing, you want to find the facts that will support your claims, that the agency thinks are important, and finally, the facts that you will use to disprove the agency's allegations.

Develop the record

The "record" is the evidence and legal arguments that make up the case. The facts are submitted as evidence, and the legal arguments are developed throughout the litigation, and submitted in your prehearing statement and your closing argument. In an EEO case, the Report of Investigation (ROI) provides many helpful facts and documents. In an MSPB case, the agency is required to produce its file (the "Agency File") shortly after the case is assigned to a judge. This file contains most of the facts the agency relies upon to justify its actions. These documents are given to the AJ, and the appellant, at the beginning of the process, and are part of the "record" of the case.

The record develops during the course of the pre-hearing phase and the hearing when parties submit evidence, generally in the form of documents and testimony. The ROI or the Agency File do not generally provide the whole picture, but they help you identify what evidence is missing. You can attempt to get this missing information through the use of discovery. After discovering this missing evidence, you can try to admit it during the hearing so that the record is complete.

Discovery

Both the EEOC and the MSPB generally allow the parties to conduct "discovery". Don't miss your chance to serve discovery on the other side. Discovery is a process where each party can make the other side answer written questions ("interrogatories"), produce documents, make certain admissions, and make witnesses available for recorded interviews under oath ("depositions"). If used properly, through discovery you can learn critical evidence. To be discoverable, the information sought must be relevant, likely to lead to the discovery of admissible evidence, and not unduly burdensome. If you don't use discovery, you may be "surprised" by evidence admitted at the hearing.

Comparative evidence is used to show that a personnel action was wrong and that other people were treated differently. During discovery, you can ask for statistics, information and documents showing how other employees were treated when facing the same circumstances. You can then try to submit this evidence to the AJ at the hearing. For example, if you received a 30-day suspension for leave abuse, what type of discipline did other employees receive for leave abuse?

TIP

Avoid surprises at the hearing by getting the agency's evidence beforehand in discovery.

Parties can also conduct depositions, which are taped or transcribed witness interviews. When you depose any witnesses, the interview is "on the record," and the witness should be under oath. By being deposed, witnesses are locked into their testimony. If they change their testimony at hearing, you can use their deposition transcript to correct or impeach their testimony, thus bringing their credibility into question. When a witness is unavailable for the hearing, the transcript can be submitted into evidence to show what the witness would have said if the witness was available. You are responsible for hiring a court reporter to attend and record the deposition. Shop around, because prices vary. If you depose witnesses, it's worthwhile to pay the court reporter a small fee to provide the transcript on computer disk and in a mini-script format (minimized pages, allowing 4 full transcript pages on a single 8½ x11 sheet).

Discovery is most helpful when it gives information that is missing from the record or when it shows that missing information doesn't exist. For example, in an affidavit, a manager may mention an agency policy that she relied on when she made the personnel decisions at issue. That policy should be in the record and if it is not, you should ask for it in discovery. You can also ask for evidence showing whether the agency followed the policy correctly.

For example, an agency may allege that it took a certain action because the employee violated leave procedures. Under this example, the following might be appropriate discovery requests:

INTERROGATORIES

1. Identify all rules, regulations, policies, and procedures which Complainant allegedly violated or disregarded.
2. Identify all instances when Complainant allegedly violated her leave procedures. For each, identify the date, the circumstances, and exactly how Complainant violated the leave restrictions.

REQUEST FOR DOCUMENTS

1. Please produce a copy of all regulations, policies and procedures relating to the use of leave and leave restrictions.
2. Please produce all documents that reference Complainant's attendance for each date when she was allegedly late.
3. Please produce all documents which show the attendance of all Division employees from 2013-2014.
4. Please produce all leave restrictions issued to Division employees from 2013-2014.
5. For all Division employees placed on leave restrictions in 2013 and 2014, produce all documents reflecting the employee's compliance and/or violation of those procedures.

These requests will let you see if other employees were late as frequently, if they were also put on leave restrictions, if they were put on the same types of leave restrictions, and if they were penalized for violating the procedures.

REQUEST FOR ADMISSIONS

Please admit or deny:

On June 1, 2014, Complainant left a message for her supervisor at 8:11 a.m. explaining that she was in the emergency room with an asthma attack.

Imagine that Complainant allegedly violated the leave restrictions on June 1, but also that the leave restrictions allow tardiness if the employee faces a medical emergency and calls in before her 8:30 duty time. If so, then this is helpful evidence.

As another example, the following might be appropriate requests for admissions:

REQUESTS FOR ADMISSIONS

Please admit or deny the following:

1. In June 2013, Manager D issued to Complainant a year-end performance evaluation with a rating of "outstanding."
2. On June 1, 2014, the EEO counselor contacted Manager D about Complainant's claims of race discrimination.
3. On June 12, 2014, Manager D issued to Complainant a year-end performance evaluation with a rating of "meets expectations."

Because you did your legal research before filing your discovery requests, you learned that you can prove a retaliation claim by showing that you engaged in protected activity, that the agency knew about your protected activity, and that the retaliatory action took place shortly thereafter, implying that there is a connection between your EEO action and the agency's action. If the agency admits to these facts, then you have a prima facie case that the 2014 evaluation was retaliatory. Of course, the agency can try to show other, legitimate reasons for its action. To make your discovery requests more thorough, you may also serve an interrogatory asking the agency to "identify all reasons that the agency issued a 'meets expectations' evaluation to Complainant in June 2014 and not an 'outstanding'." As these examples demonstrate, discovery requests are unique to each situation and each case.

TIP

Preparing discovery requests does not require a detailed knowledge of the law, but it demands preparing and planning.

Sample MSPB and EEOC discovery requests are at Appendices P and Q.

There are other ways to get evidence. One includes filing Freedom of Information Act requests or requests for information under the Privacy Act, although agencies often delay responding to such requests. For more on these avenues, see Chapter 22 (FOIA and Privacy Act). In addition, when litigating a case before the MSPB, a party may ask the AJ for a subpoena ordering another (non-party) agency to produce specified documents or information.

Know and maintain your documents

It is critical that you know and safely retain the documents that are important to your case. Organization is key, and you should use an organizational method that is simple and easy. All the evidence and correspondence should be kept so that you can quickly access it and easily identify the source of each document or piece of evidence. Binders or clasped files are usually best. Create an index of your documents.

Keeping documents in chronological order is often a good way to manage them. Keeping all of the agency's discovery responses in one folder may be helpful. Evidence that you already had or that you found through witnesses or FOIA requests should be kept separately and maintained in a way that you know how you found the evidence.

Read all of the documents thoroughly and keep a chronological outline of events. It's important to keep your events in proper order, because that will help you understand and develop the evidence. Often the importance of a document may not be clear until you know the events that surrounded it. For example, in a non-selection claim, a document showing that Mr. Jones was selected on April 1 may not seem important, until you learn that the certificate of eligibles was issued on April 7.

Always keep original documents in a separate place, and do not write on them or allow anyone else to write on them. Notations, highlights and comments can be written on copies, but originals should always be preserved.

Know your witnesses/keep them informed

A witness is generally someone with first-hand knowledge of events: testimony should focus on the witnesses' knowledge. If a witness did not actually see, hear or read something personally, the witness probably does not have much helpful information. (Hired expert witnesses, who usually have no first-hand knowledge of the events, are an exception).

There are two basic types of witnesses: "favorable" and "adverse/hostile." Favorable witnesses are those who you expect will support your case and who will cooperate. Generally, these witnesses do not need to be deposed, as they are willing to talk to you without the cost or difficulties of a deposition. Almost exclusively, witnesses who will testify in support of your damages will be "favorable."

"Adverse" or "hostile" witnesses probably made or approved the decision that led to your complaint, and are unlikely to cooperate with you. Adverse witnesses may have information that can help you prove the elements of your claim or disprove the agency's allegations. Such witnesses are called "adverse" or "hostile" not because they are likely to scream or yell (we try to avoid such behavior), but because they likely support the other side. Adverse or hostile witnesses might not want to help you, but you can depose them.

It is important to maintain all of your witnesses' information. Ask witnesses to notify you of a change of address or phone number, keep notes of your discussions and interviews, keep deposition transcripts (if any), and keep a list and a copy of the documents about which they have specific knowledge.

It is also important to keep in mind that you have an obligation to disclose to the agency the names and contact information of any potential witnesses if requested by the agency in discovery. Moreover, you will be required to disclose your witnesses in your prehearing report (EEOC) or prehearing submission (MSPB) that you file with the Administrative Judge before the hearing. Finally, always keep witnesses informed of important dates, such as the hearing date(s) and location of the hearing, to avoid conflicts with their schedules.

KNOW YOUR JUDGE'S PREFERENCES FOR HOW THE HEARING WILL BE CONDUCTED

Prior to the hearing, the AJ will order you to prepare a prehearing report. Each AJ has his or her own style, but your prehearing submission can require the following: an outline of the claims, your evidence, the applicable law, your witnesses, the length of time for each witness, your exhibits, anticipated objections to the agency's witnesses or exhibits, and the relief you are seeking.

TIP

It's okay to ask the AJ assigned to your case how she normally does routine things, such as who initiates a conference call or whether she accepts emails. It's usually NOT okay to talk to the AJ without the agency attorney present during the conversation.

The AJ will have a prehearing conference during which the parties may discuss these matters, as well as settlement.. After the close of discovery, but prior to the hearing, you should ask the AJ assigned to your case how she prefers to deal with certain issues, such as:

- Does the judge want the witnesses in a particular order?
- Does the judge want you to give him/her all your exhibits in advance, or does the judge prefer to get exhibits as they come up during the course of the testimony?
- How many copies of each exhibit will the judge want you to bring? Usually, there are four: one for the judge, one for the witness, one for the agency representative and one for you. Some judges may prefer more or less.
- Does the judge prefer that you have an extra copy of the exhibit for the court reporter?
- Does the judge allow opening statements?
- Does the judge want closing arguments presented orally at the end of the hearing or in writing (usually after the hearing transcript has been provided)?
- Does the judge anticipate that he/she will issue a bench decision (i.e., rule orally at the close of the hearing, on the record, with the court reporter present) or that the judge will issue a written decision (issued usually several weeks or months after the close of the hearing and after the judge receives the hearing transcript)?
- If you anticipate that you or your witnesses will need any special accommodations at the hearing (e.g., wheelchair access, frequent breaks), let the AJ know in advance.

There may be other issues that arise as well, and you should ask your judge how he/she prefers to address those issues.

The hearing

The hearing is usually scheduled several weeks or months in advance. Hearings may last one or more days. If all witness testimony cannot be completed during the initially-scheduled hearing dates, additional hearing dates may be scheduled. The following outlines the basic things you need to know if you choose to represent yourself at an administrative hearing.

Professional conduct

Conduct during the hearing is very important. Oftentimes, the hearing is the AJ's first opportunity to meet you, and first impressions are critical. The hearing can be long, exhausting, and tedious. Also, information and evidence may come out during the hearing which you did not expect. The mix of these factors can make anyone angry, bitter, short-tempered, and unprofessional. There are important rules that you should follow to make sure that you remain professional at all times:

- Wear professional, but comfortable, clothes.
- Never interrupt the judge or the other side.
- Never raise your voice or argue.
- Always show respect and deference to the judge and the process.
- Refer to the judge as "Judge —" or "Your Honor."
- Refer to the agency representative respectfully, using "Ms." or "Mr."
- Do not "hedge" or argue with the other attorney or the judge.
- Do not lose your temper—*ever*.
- Ask the judge for a break if you need one.
- Stop speaking instantly when the judge interrupts you or when the agency representative makes an objection.
- It is not customary to stand when speaking to an administrative judge (unlike in a courtroom).
- Don't be "smart alecky," "cocky," condescending, rude, accusatory, or sarcastic.
- At all times, act with dignity and treat others with dignity and respect, including the managers against whom you filed the complaint.
- Avoid laughing and talking about the case in the halls, restrooms, or any place in the courthouse or hearing building.
- Be polite to everyone involved.
- Do not engage in any type of expressive body language, such as rolling your eyes, hitting or banging the table, making noises, throwing documents, flipping through papers in a frantic or disruptive manner, or any other behavior designed to show your disapproval or disagreement with what someone is saying.
- In other words, at all times, behave yourself.

TIP

You will be judged on how you behave. Drama may be good in Hollywood, but not in an administrative hearing.

Employment issues can be very personal and emotional. If you think that these rules will be difficult to follow, or if you think that you may not be able to maintain dignity and respect for all the people involved at all times, you should reconsider whether it is in your interest to represent yourself. Adversarial or quarrelsome conduct at the hearing will hurt your case.

The room

Arrive early. Survey the location, know where you will sit, where the restrooms are, where the witness room is, and where you can get a snack or drink during a break.

The AJ will have preferences for where the parties and the witnesses sit, and much of this will depend on the size of the conference room and how the court reporter sets up the recording equipment. Do not presume where you will sit; ask the AJ what he or she prefers.

After you have found your place in the room, set up your documents and notebooks around you, so that you can easily access them without causing a distraction.

Supplies

Bring water for yourself and your witnesses. Water is often not provided, and witnesses become parched during their testimony.

Bring snacks for yourself and your witnesses. You will tire and food will keep you energized. Do not eat during the hearing or in the hearing room, unless you ask the AJ for permission because of a medical condition or because the AJ asked the parties to skip or have a very brief lunch. If you need a lunch break, ask the AJ for one.

You also need to bring office supplies and all the evidence.

Hearing Checklist

- 4 copies of each of your hearing exhibits
- All of the agency's hearing exhibits
- The ROI or agency file
- All documents and pleadings exchanged in discovery (in case there is a question as to whether a document was produced in discovery)
- Your Hearing Notebook (see below)
- Extra dividers for your Hearing Notebook
- Several pads of paper
- Pens, highlighters and pencils in various colors
- Paperclips
- Travel-size stapler, staples and staple remover
- Post-its and colored flags
- Quarters and small bills for parking meters, soda machine, etc.
- Cell phone (turned off during the proceedings) and charger
- Ruler
- File label stickers
- Binder clips
- Exhibit stickers
- Clear tape
- Rubber bands
- File folders
- Telephone numbers for everyone you may need to reach in case the hearing runs into the evening
- Travel hole-punch

Please note that many of the above items, particularly the hearing exhibits, ROI, and agency file, come in electronic format. However, for purposes of the hearing, it is always advisable to bring at least 4 copies of all of your exhibits, as well as at least one copy of the agency's exhibits, agency file, and the ROI.

Preliminary matters

At the beginning of the hearing and before going "on the record", the AJ will address outstanding motions or issues, recite the issues accepted for the hearing, and often discuss settlement. During this time, the parties may discuss matters with the judge and any last-minute concerns. After initial issues are resolved, the AJ will direct the court report to go on the record and will officially begin the hearing with a recitation of the case and the issues presented. Then, if already agreed to, the AJ will allow opening statements.

Opening statement

If the AJ has allowed one, you may prepare and give an opening statement. Administrative hearings are different from jury trials. Unlike a jury that knows little about the case, AJs are well-versed in the facts and issues of the case before the hearing begins. Therefore, it is important to keep your opening statement brief and understated, not dramatic or theatrical.

Opening statements are different from closing arguments (see below). Unlike a closing argument, an opening is not designed to make a legal argument. Instead, an opening statement is a concise road map of what the testimony and evidence will show. Draft your opening statement in writing a day or two before the hearing. Practice it out loud a few times and time yourself. Keep your opening short, less than five minutes. Point out the key pieces of evidence which you are certain will come to light during the hearing and briefly explain why these pieces of evidence are so important. Try to project your voice so that it is audible, do not rush through your presentation, and keep eye contact with the AJ throughout.

Testimony

After opening statements, the AJ will allow witness testimony. In MSPB adverse actions cases, the agency brings its witnesses forward first because the agency bears the burden of proof. In EEOC hearings, the complainant usually brings his witnesses forward because the complainant bears the burden of proof.

When asking witnesses questions, certain rules apply. If examining a favorable witness, it is generally inappropriate to ask leading questions, such as "Isn't it true that you saw Mr. Smith write a note that said...." This type of examination is often less persuasive because the witness is not telling the story, but you are. Testimony is most helpful if the witness can describe persuasively and consistently what he or she personally observed. By interviewing your witnesses prior to the hearing, you already know what the witness knows and doesn't know. It's important to ask your favorable witnesses open-ended questions, which will allow them to tell the story themselves. As the story progresses, you ask more narrow questions until the key points of the events have been divulged.

When asking an adverse witness questions, you can use a different technique. You can ask questions that are direct and pointed, such as, "You've testified this morning about the many counselings you issued to me in 2014. However, you don't have any documents reflecting those counselings, do you?" When asking a question like this, you should already know the answer because you should have covered this ground in discovery. However, the AJ may not know the answer, and the lack of supporting documents may be important evidence that helps to discredit the agency's version of the events.

Other general rules apply:

- Listen to the answer. It may not be what you were expecting.
- Ask follow-up questions, as appropriate.
- Do not ask multiple or compound questions.
- Always allow the witness to finish the question asked.
- If the witness strays off the topic, gently direct them back to the question or the topic.
- If the agency attorney objects to the question, ask him or her to explain the objection so that you can understand it and how to overcome it. After the other attorney has finished speaking, ask the judge for an opportunity to respond.
- Do not use pronouns ("he," "she," "they," "it").
- Use precise language.
- Speak clearly so that the judge, the witness and the agency attorney can hear you.

For adverse or hostile witnesses:

- If the witness refuses to answer a question or avoids an answer, calmly ask again. If he continues, ask the judge to direct him to answer.
- Try to ask questions to which you already know the answers. This will avoid surprises. This may not be possible if you did not have a chance to do thorough discovery and/or depositions.
- If a witness changes his or her testimony from the deposition, have the deposition transcript ready and have the pages of the testimony marked. Tell the agency attorney and the AJ what page in the deposition you are looking at and give the attorney time to find their copy and the correct page. Read the witness's conflicting deposition testimony. Ask the witness if they recall giving that testimony at the deposition. Move on to the next question. Allow the witness to read the transcript if they ask.

For your own testimony:

- If required to stand upon taking the oath, stand upright when taking the oath. Pay attention and say "I do" clearly.
- Tell the truth.
- Speak in your own words and sound natural.
- Talk to the AJ, not to the attorney. Make eye contact with the judge and speak to the judge openly.
- Speak clearly and loudly. Do not cover your mouth with your hand.
- Tell the AJ what you personally observed in chronological order. Prepare an outline of the events and use it to keep you on track. Although you may try to read from a prepared statement, the AJ may ask you not to. A prepared statement is less natural and may appear less credible.
- Give direct, specific, definite information when possible. Avoid qualifiers such as "I guess," "I think," and "In my opinion" or comments that impinge credibility like "to tell you the truth."
- While it is normal to be nervous, try not to act too nervous. Avoid mannerisms such as looking down when speaking or fidgeting with clothing.
- Do not exaggerate.
- Do not speculate or make assumptions. It is best to discuss only what you actually saw, did, or read. During testimony, your job is to describe the events which you personally observed. Do not comment on events you did not observe.
- Be prepared to be interrupted by the AJ with questions during your testimony.
- Stop instantly when the judge interrupts you.
- Be prepared for questions from the agency attorney at the end of your statement.
- Listen carefully to the questions asked of you.
- Make sure you understand the question. Have it repeated if necessary.
- If a question can be fully and truthfully answered "yes" or "no," then do so.
- If a question is asked as a "yes" or "no" question, but can't be truthfully answered with a "yes" or "no," tell the judge. You can say "yes" or "no" but "with an explanation." You have a right to explain the answer.

- Give direct and simple answers to the question asked. Do not answer a question you think was asked, should be asked, or want to be asked.
- Do not volunteer information not asked for. A question that asks where a meeting took place does not call for an explanation of why the meeting took place, who initiated the meeting, who was present, or what was discussed.
- Do not be afraid of silence. After you've answered the question, be quiet and wait for the next one, even if it takes some time. Don't add to your answer.
- If your answer was wrong or incorrect, correct it immediately. If your answer was not clear, clarify it immediately.
- When asked "is that all" type questions, a "yes" response will mean that you cannot credibly add to or clarify your answer later. Maybe after more thought or another question, you remember something important. By leaving the door open, you can enhance your testimony with your refreshed memory, rather than diminish your testimony by making it look like you gave a false answer or were trying to hide information. Instead of answering "yes", say "that's all I can recall right now."
- If you do not know the answer to a question, say so.
- Do not argue with anyone.
- Do not lose your temper.
- If you do not want to answer a question or you think it is objectionable, tell the judge that you object, and give the reasons for your objection. If the judge then says to answer it, do so.

Ask your witnesses to follow these same rules when they testify.

TIP

To make sure that you hear and understand everything that's going on during the hearing, do not rush through any part. Take your time when asking and answering questions.

When questioning witnesses, several questions are not appropriate and are objectionable. The Federal Rules of Evidence do not strictly apply in administrative hearings, but they provide guidance on the types of evidence that may not be allowed because it is unreliable or otherwise suspect.

Asking a witness to guess or speculate about something may be objectionable, but you may be able to ask for their beliefs or conclusions based upon their observations. Asking a witness to give an opinion on a topic that generally requires expert or specialized knowledge is objectionable if the witness doesn't have that knowledge. Asking about rumors or hearsay may be objectionable. An objection may result if you ask for irrelevant or highly prejudicial information. Also, when asking a question, you need to make sure that the witness has enough specific, first-hand knowledge to give a knowing answer.

When posing an objection, you should first clearly state "objection," followed by a very brief explanation of the reason for your objection, such as "speculation." In an administrative hearing (unlike in court), it is not customary to stand when you make an objection. A short discussion may follow with the agency attorney, you and the judge, and the judge will either "sustain" and allow the objection or "overrule" the objection. Generally, in administrative proceedings, because the judge plays the role of judge and fact-finder, objections should be very limited and most will be overruled.

Documents

Managing documents during the hearing can be challenging, but it is very important. The record contains many documents before the hearing begins, such as the agency file or the ROI. Documents can be any tangible piece of evidence, such as a tape recording, an email, a letter, or a computer file. In discovery you may find many useful documents, and you may have your own set of documents that are important. The judge probably has not seen those documents, and if you want her to consider them, you have to "admit them into evidence" so that they become a part of the record.

Before the hearing, you should choose which documents you will want to admit into evidence at the hearing. Bring at least four copies of each of those documents to the hearing with you: one for the judge; one for the witness to review while testifying; one for the agency attorney to keep and one for yourself. All copies should be clean and free of any notations, highlights or other marks. You may write on or highlight your own copy, but only if you have a spare copy with you, in case you need to make another copy.

When dealing with documents at the hearing, refer to them explicitly by date and type (e.g., "an August 23, 2014 email from Smith to Jones"). If you wish to have documents admitted into evidence, tell the judge what the document is and why it's important to the case. The agency may object to documents, in which case you need to explain to the judge why the document is important. Similarly, you can object to documents that the agency tries to admit into evidence. The judge will decide whether the document becomes a part of the record and will give it the weight she thinks is appropriate, in light of all the evidence. When documents are admitted into evidence, they will be marked as exhibits (e.g., Complainant's Hearing Exhibit 1, or Agency Exhibit A). Try to refer to the document by its exhibit identification. During the hearing, you should keep an exhibit log (see below). If the judge does not admit a document into the record, you should note on your log why.

TIP

Don't forget to include documents and testimony on your remedies. For example, if you are asking for reimbursement for medical bills or prescription medications, you have to submit the bills into evidence.

You can try to get documents admitted at the beginning of the hearing, or while you are examining witnesses, or while you testify. Under the rules of evidence, witnesses with firsthand knowledge about the document should "authenticate" the document, that is, confirm that it existed at the time indicated and that the witness received, sent or otherwise saw it at that time. In an administrative hearing, the rules of evidence are not strictly followed, so this requirement may not be strictly followed either. But, if there is any question about a document's "authenticity," this information is helpful.

Rebuttal evidence

If you had to present your case first, after the agency presents its evidence, you generally have an opportunity to present rebuttal evidence. Rebuttal evidence is presented near the end of the hearing. Your presentation of rebuttal evidence should be brief. Limit your rebuttal evidence exclusively to things that the agency brought up which you need to disprove and which you did not address earlier in the hearing. Rebuttal evidence can be presented in the form of testimony or documents.

Closing arguments

At the end of the hearing, the AJ will "close the record." After the record is closed, no additional evidence may be submitted. After this, the parties usually can present closing arguments. These may be orally at the hearing or in writing. In EEOC hearings, you will have to give your closing argument first as you have the burden of proof. You should ask the AJ for a short rebuttal to the agency's closing argument before you begin your closing.

In closings, you can make a legal argument by merging the facts that were presented at the hearing with the applicable law. Effective closings usually focus on the facts that are most helpful to you, a brief synopsis of the law, and an analysis showing that the law commands an outcome in your favor. This is often done by finding cases that have addressed a situation similar to yours and applying the same analysis to your case.

Often, oral closing arguments have time limits. Ask the judge in advance how much time you will have. Written closing arguments are used in complex cases or cases where there are attorneys on both sides. If your judge asks for written closing arguments, you need to know the following parameters: is there a page limitation (based on double-spaced, 12 pt. font); when are the statements due; and will you have an opportunity to use the hearing transcript.

The hearing notebook

The hearing notebook is an invaluable tool that attorneys use to keep organized. Sometimes multiple notebooks may be necessary, but for an average hearing, one notebook, plus hearing exhibits, should be enough.

A hearing notebook is a blueprint to the case. The notebook is usually a 3-ring binder with dividers. Each divider is labeled, similar to the sections of this Chapter. While under the stress and pressure of litigation, it is easy to forget things. The notebook preserves the many essentials that you need to remember. The notebook should be organized so that you can flip through it easily to find the information that you need at any time. It should also be organized in the same order that you expect things to come up during the hearing.

The following sections and tabs may be useful. Behind each tab, you should place all the documents you will need for that part of the hearing.

- Unresolved prehearing issues (outstanding motions, questions about witness orders, etc.).
- Agency's Prehearing Statement and Witness Proffers: It is useful to have these documents accessible. They provide the agency's blueprint of the case and what the agency expects the witnesses to testify about.
- Your Prehearing Statement and Witness Proffers.
- Opening Statement: attach your written statement.
- Exhibit Log: A prepared list of all your and the agency's expected hearing exhibits. If you have more than a few exhibits, this is extremely helpful. The list should identify each exhibit and have a place where you can make notations, such as exhibit number and if it was admitted into evidence. Review this list before you finish each witness examination, to make sure that you are addressing the exhibits when necessary. Before the AJ closes the record, review the list again to make sure that all your exhibits were admitted into evidence.

Exh. #	Date	Title	Witness	Admitted	Denied
C1	3/27/02	Email re: meeting	Me	√	
C2	4/06/02	Memo re: hiring	S. Jones (HR spec.)		√: try again w/Smith (Div. Dir.)

- Witness Tabs: Prepare a tab for each witness, in the order you expect the witnesses to appear. Behind the tab, put the following: notes from your witness interviews, questions for that witness with references to relevant documents, and a list of the documents that you want the witness to review and discuss. Your document list should show where they are in the record, such as "ROI tab 2, p. 5" or "Agency File, tab A4, p. 2." Documents not already in the record should be easily found in your files containing hearing exhibits and listed on your Exhibit Log. If you took depositions of any witnesses, put the mini-script in the witness tab. Include witness tabs for the agency's witnesses as well.

- Closing Arguments: Attach draft closing argument. This will only be a draft that will be modified during the course of the hearing as you learn more facts. Use post-its and wide margins so that you can easily add or change points during the hearing and as the evidence develops. Also attach key legal research.

The above suggestions are a good start for any employee facing an upcoming administrative hearing. For a more in-depth look at how to prepare for and litigate an administrative hearing, Litigating Federal Sector Employment and Labor Law Disputes: A Practitioner's Handbook, Dewey Publications, Inc., by Renn C. Fowler and Joseph V. Kaplan, is an excellent resource.

Organization means that you can quickly, quietly and easily find something during the hearing without interrupting, asking for a break, or disturbing the flow of the hearing. A "hearing notebook" may not be the right tool for you, but make sure you develop some device that lets you be organized at all times. Many attorneys prefer to use a laptop or other software to organize the exhibits and other elements of their case. The most important thing is that you are comfortable with whatever system of organization you choose!

Final Thoughts

Preparing for and conducting an administrative hearing can take months of preparation, hard work and diligence. The culmination is the hearing itself, a brief and intense experience where you have a small window of opportunity to present your most compelling evidence and arguments. The stakes are high and you should be prepared for an exhausting and emotional experience. Good luck!

Epilogue

For better or worse, federal employees are the most regulated in our nation. As a federal worker, you have more job security and more Constitutional rights than most of your friends in the private sector. Your fringe benefits, including health and retirement benefits, are generally better. If you are improperly denied promotions or unfairly disciplined, you have many rights and options for obtaining justice. Thirty percent of the federal workforce is unionized. Those covered by labor agreements have special options and grievance remedies.

One thing is clear—you will probably, at some point in your career, need to consult this book to find out about your rights and remedies. Ideally, you will not need to consult or hire a lawyer. However, if you are in trouble, the best course is to obtain legal counsel.

We hope this book will help you stand up for your rights.

We are grateful for your work in making our government the best in the world.

The lawyers of Passman & Kaplan, PC, wish you every bit of good luck and success in the days and years ahead.

Appendices

Contents: Appendices

Appendix A Filing Deadlines/Statutes of Limitations

MSPB Appeals of Adverse Actions

Appeals of adverse actions to the Merit Systems Protection Board (MSPB) must be filed with the Board no later than *30 calendar days* from the effective date of the adverse personnel action. Appeals of adverse actions which also involve claims of discrimination or EEO reprisal may be subject to a choice of procedural avenues under the "mixed case" procedures which are discussed in greater detail in Chapter 6. Appeals of adverse actions which also involve claims of whistleblower reprisal may be subject to a choice of procedural avenues which are discussed in greater detail in Chapter 7.

Petitions to enforce breached MSPB settlements agreements must be filed with the MSPB no later than *30 calendar days* from the date of the agency's statement of compliance, or within a reasonable time of the breach, absent good cause shown. See Chapter 32 for further details.

EEO Complaints and Requests for Hearings

An EEO counselor must be contacted within *45 calendar days* of the date of the alleged discriminatory event. A few limited exceptions apply, as discussed in greater detail in Chapter 6.

Formal EEO complaints must be filed with the discriminating agency within *15 calendar days* of the date you receive the Notice of Final Interview from the EEO counselor.

Requests for hearings before an administrative judge of the Equal Employment Opportunity Commission (EEOC) must be filed with the EEOC and your agency within *30 calendar days* of the date you receive the report of investigation concerning your complaint.

Complaints of breach of EEO settlement agreement must be filed with the Agency's EEO office within *30 calendar days* of when the employee knew or should have known of the breach. See Chapter 32 for further details.

For most legislative branch employees, a counselor from the Office of Compliance must be contacted within *180 calendar days* of the date of the alleged discriminatory event. For Library of Congress employees, the deadline is *20 business days.*[1] See Chapter 26 for further details concerning employees of the legislative branch and of the Executive Office of the President.

---

[1] *See Terveer v. Billington*___F. Supp. 2d___, 2014 WL 1280301 (DDC March 31, 2014)(citing Section 4(A) of Library of Congress Regulation 2010-3.1).

Unfair Labor Practice Charges

Unfair labor practice charges must be filed with the Federal Labor Relations Authority (FLRA) within *6 months* of the date of the violation.

Whistleblower Protection Act/Prohibited Personnel Practice Complaints

Technically, there is no deadline for filing a complaint with the Office of Special Counsel alleging that you have been retaliated against for whistle-blowing. However, you should file as soon as possible.

If the whistleblower reprisal claim is being raised as part of an MSPB Appeal of an adverse action, the *30 calendar day* deadline for filing an appeal with the MSPB applies and the appeal then can be filed directly with the MSPB. The consequences of each of these procedural avenues are discussed in greater detail in Chapter 7.

For whistleblowers at intelligence agencies covered by Presidential Policy Directive 19 (PPD-19), and for whistleblowers claiming whistleblower reprisal in the denial of their security clearance under PPD-19, see your agency's particular policy implementing PPD-19 for applicable deadlines.

Veterans Claims

Claims under the Veterans Employment Opportunities Act (VEOA) must be filed with the Department of Labor, Veterans' Employment & Training Service (DOL-VETS) within *60 calendar days* of the violation. Technically, there is no deadline for filing claims under the Uniformed Services Employment and Reemployment Rights Act (USERRA) with the MSPB or with DOL-VETS. However, you should file as soon as possible. These USERRA procedural avenues are discussed in greater detail in Chapter 19.

Workers' Compensation Claims

Workers' Compensation claims must be filed with the Office of Workers' Compensation Programs, which is part of the Department of Labor, within *30 calendar days* of the date of the workplace injury.

Federal Tort Claims Act Claims

Claims under the Federal Tort Claims Act must follow certain procedures. First, you must file your claim with the agency which allegedly injured you within *2 years* of the date of the injury. Second, if and when an agency finally denies a claim, you have *6 months* from that date to file your claim with an appropriate U.S. district court.

Privacy Act Violations

Claims under the Privacy Act must be brought within *2 years* of the date of the violation of the law.

Back Pay Act Claims

Claims under the Back Pay Act must be brought to the U.S. Court of Federal Claims or U.S. district court within *6 years* of the date the claim arises.

Union Contract Grievances	The deadlines for filing grievances under union contracts (or collective bargaining agreements) differ. You must look at the provision in your union contract that concerns "grievances" to determine what the deadline is. Deadlines for filing a grievance under a union contract can be very short—for example, *5 to 10 calendar days.*
Agency Administrative Grievances	The deadlines for filing grievances under administrative grievance procedures differ from agency to agency. You must look at the provision in your agency's administrative procedures to determine what the deadline is. Deadlines are often very short.
Disability Retirement Requests	Employees may apply for disability retirement with the Office of Personnel Management (OPM) at any time before they leave their employment with the government, or within *1 year* after their separation from employment with the government.
Security Clearance Denials and Revocations	The deadline for initiating a challenge to a denial or revocation of a security clearance can be very short—as short as *10 calendar days*. See Chapter 10 for discussion in greater detail.
Family and Medical Leave Act Leave Denials and Retaliation	For those employees who have a private right of action for FMLA violations, the filing deadline for filing a complaint at the U.S. Department of Labor or filing a lawsuit in court is *2 years* (or *3 years*, if it is deemed a willful violation). See Chapters 14, 25 and 29 for details on which employees have this private right of action.
Tucker Act Claims	Claims under the Tucker Act must be brought to the Court of Federal Claims within *6 years* of the date the claim arises.

Appendix B Names of Some Laws Covering Federal Employees

Age Discrimination in Employment Act
29 USC § 633a

Americans with Disabilities Act
42 USC § 12111

Back Pay Act
5 USC § 5596

Civil Rights Act of 1964, as amended (Title VII)
42 USC § 2000e-2

Civil Service Reform Act of 1978
See generally 5 USC Chapters 11, 12, 21, 23, 43, 71, 75, and 77

Congressional Accountability Act
2 USC § 1301

Fair Labor Standards Act
29 USC § 201

Family and Medical Leave Act
5 USC § 6381

Federal Employees Compensation Act
5 USC § 8101

Federal Service Labor-Management Relations Statute
5 USC Chapter 71

Federal Tort Claims Act
28 USC § 2671

Freedom of Information Act
5 USC § 552

Hatch Act
5 USC § 7321

Homeland Security Act
5 USC § 9701

National Labor Relations Act (Postal Employees Only)
29 USC § 151

Presidential and Executive Office Accountability Act
3 USC § 401

Privacy Act
5 USC § 552a

Rehabilitation Act
29 USC § 791

Uniformed Services Employment and Reemployment Rights Act
38 USC § 4301

Veterans Employment Opportunities Act
5 USC § 3330a

Whistleblower Protection Act
5 USC §§ 1201, 1211, and 1221;
5 USC § 2302(b)(8)

CODE SECTIONS	SUBJECT MATTER
5 CFR §§ 293, 294, 297; 29 CFR §§ 1610-1611	Privacy Act/Freedom of Information Act
5 CFR §§ 330, 332	Recruitment, selection, and placement of employees
5 CFR § 339	Medical qualifications
5 CFR § 351	Reductions-in-force
5 CFR § 530	Pay rates and systems
5 CFR § 752	Adverse/disciplinary actions
5 CFR §§ 841-846	Federal Employees Retirement System
5 CFR §§ 1200-1210	Merit Systems Protection Board
5 CFR §§ 1201.121-1201.129	Actions brought by the Office of Special Counsel
5 CFR §§ 2401-2430	Federal Labor Relations Authority
29 CFR § 1604	Guidelines on discrimination because of sex
29 CFR § 1605	Guidelines on discrimination because of religion
29 CFR § 1606	Guidelines on discrimination because of national origin
29 CFR § 1608	Affirmative Action under Title VII
29 CFR § 1614	Federal Sector Equal Employment Opportunity
29 CFR §§ 1620-1621	Equal Pay Act
29 CFR §§ 1625-1626	Age Discrimination in Employment Act

Appendix D Election of Remedies for Employees Covered by Union-Negotiated Grievance Procedures

If Grievable Under Union Contract	Appeal Avenues
Failure to be promoted	Negotiated grievance procedure
Failure to be promoted where discrimination is alleged	Negotiated grievance procedure or EEO process, *but not both*
Disciplinary action (suspension of 14 days or less)	Negotiated grievance procedure
Disciplinary action (suspension of 14 days or less) in which discrimination is alleged	Negotiated grievance procedure or EEO process, *but not both*
Adverse action (removal, demotion, suspension of more than 14 days)	Negotiated grievance procedure or MSPB, *but not both*
Adverse action (removal, demotion, suspension of more than 14 days) in which discrimination is alleged	Negotiated grievance procedure or MSPB (either directly or through the EEO process), *but not both*
Reduction-in-force	Negotiated grievance procedure (MSPB appeal available only if a RIF is not grievable under the negotiated grievance procedure)
Denial of within-grade (WIGI) (step) increase	Negotiated grievance procedure (MSPB appeal available only if a WIGI is not grievable under the negotiated grievance procedure)
Reprisal for whistleblowing where MSPB has jurisdiction (for example, adverse actions)	MSPB or complaint to the Office of Special Counsel followed by appeal to the MSPB, or negotiated grievance procedure, *but only one*
Reprisal for whistleblowing where MSPB does not already have jurisdiction (for example, minor suspension)	Negotiated grievance procedure or complaint to the Office of Special Counsel followed by appeal to the MSPB, *but not both*

Appendix E-1 Sample Medical Request Form—Letter to Doctor Requesting Information

[Date]

Dear Dr. :

My employer, the [your agency], has asked for medical documentation of my medical condition. [if applicable: Attached is a copy of the agency's request for medical documents and a copy of my position description]. The agency's request is very important, and if I do not provide this information, it could affect my job. The agency wants this information within [time frame requested by agency]. Therefore, please give me the written report by [date]. If there is any charge for this report, please contact me in advance.

Please address the report "to whom it may concern" and describe my medical condition in detail. Specifically, the report should include the following:

1. The diagnosis, including current clinical status;
2. The prognosis, including plans for future treatment and an estimated date of full or partial recovery;
3. A history of my medical condition, including references to examinations, treatments, and responses to treatments;
4. Clinical findings from the most recent medical evaluation, including, if applicable, findings from physical examinations, results of laboratory tests, x-rays, EKGs, or other diagnostic procedures;
5. In the event of a psychiatric or psychological evaluation, the findings of mental status examinations and psychological test results;
6. An explanation of the impact of the medical condition on my overall health and activities;
7. If the condition affects any major life activity (for example, sleeping, walking, lifting, working, traveling, breathing, etc.), the basis for any conclusion that work restrictions or accommodations are or are not warranted and, if warranted, an explanation of the therapeutic or risk-avoiding value of such restrictions or accommodations;
8. What accommodations, if any, are recommended so that I can successfully perform all of the duties of my position [if applicable: attach a copy of your position description];
9. An explanation of any possibility of a sudden or subtle incapacitation that would be the result of conducting, with or without accommodation, the duties and responsibilities of my position [if applicable: attach a copy of the position description];
10. A statement of whether my medical condition is likely to change and if so, under what conditions and in what way;
11. Overall, how does my medical condition currently affect my ability to perform my job, and how is it likely to affect my ability to perform my job in the future.

If, for any reason, you cannot complete the report by the deadline, please let me know immediately. If you have any questions, please call me. My telephone numbers and fax are: and my address is: . Thank you very much for your help.

Sincerely,

Jane Doe

APPENDIX E-2 SAMPLE REQUEST FOR INFORMATION FROM AGENCY IN SUSPENSION OR OTHER ADVERSE ACTION PROCEEDING AND REQUEST FOR AN EXTENSION OF TIME TO REPLY TO A PROPOSED ADVERSE ACTION

Via Fax and
Regular Mail [Date]

[Agency Deciding Official's Name and Address]

Re: [Employee's Name, Title, Grade]
Request for information; and Request
for Extension of Time to Reply

Dear [agency deciding official]:

This letter concerns my reply to the proposal of [agency proposing official's name, title], to suspend me from my position as [employee's title, grade] for forty-five (45) days. As stated in [proposing official's name]'s proposal letter, you have been designated the deciding official (DDO) for this proposed suspension, and thus are the proper person to receive this request.

Pursuant to 5 USC § 7513(b) and 5 CFR § 752.404, I plan to respond orally and in writing to the allegations set forth in the proposal and will also be raising affirmative defenses, including, but not limited to the following: [Examples: sex discrimination; reprisal for engaging in activity protected under 5 USC § 2302(b)(8)(engaging in protected activity under the Whistleblower Protection Act, including complaints of ongoing prohibited personnel practices); harmful procedural error, including intentional or willful violations of the Privacy Act, 5 USC § 552a; disparate, unduly harsh, and severe penalty; and mitigating circumstances].

In order to be in a position to present an adequate reply to this proposed suspension, it is necessary that the agency provide me with the following information:

1. For the time period [three years prior to the date of the proposed action], through the present, copies of any proposed disciplinary or adverse actions issued to agency employees for the offenses of [quote charges listed in proposed action notice] and/or like offenses/charges. The documents requested in requests #1, #2 and #3 will be accepted in sanitized form (with the names deleted) in order to protect the privacy of the individuals involved;
2. For the documents disclosed in response to the request immediately above, the final agency decision;
3. For the documents disclosed in response to the requests immediately above, the decision after appeal, whether through the agency grievance process, a negotiated grievance process, the Merit Systems Protection Board, the Federal Labor Relations Authority, the Equal Employment Opportunity Commission, or any other administrative or judicial forum;
4. Copies of all documents applicable to the [agency's name] concerning disciplinary and adverse actions, including regulations, handbooks, procedures, bulletins, and supplements;
5. Copies of any Table of Penalties applicable to [the agency's name]'s employees;

6. Copies of any and all files, documents, memoranda, drafts, or notes maintained by the proposing official, yourself, the Management Employee Relations Division (MERD) and/or the Civilian Personnel Office (CPO), or any other office in the agency which mention or pertain to the following: me and my affirmative defenses; the proposed action against me; and any favorable information, including witness statements and any consideration of seeking a lesser penalty;
7. Copies of all proposed and final disciplinary and adverse actions taken against agency employees in which [the proposing official's name] and/or [the deciding official's name] have served as proposing or deciding officials;
8. A copy of the agency's official case file relating to this matter;
9. A copy of my Official Personnel File;
10. Copies of my performance appraisals/awards for the last three years;
11. Copies of all drafts of the proposed letter and of any documents, records of advice, or notes, including notes made by, for, or regarding [the proposing official's name]'s decision to propose the adverse action at issue;
12. Copies of all communications from/to any official regarding the proposed suspension or [employee's name]'s affirmative defenses thereto;
13. Any other documents relating to this proposed adverse action or regarding my past employment record that have not yet been furnished to me.

If you refuse to disclose this information, and only upon such refusal, you are then to consider this request for information to be made pursuant to the Freedom of Information Act, 5 USC § 552, and the Privacy Act, 5 USC § 552a. If you refuse to disclose any of the information under either of those statutes, then please state your specific reasons for such refusal. I believe that this request is in the public interest. Therefore, I ask that you waive any search and/or copying fees. As provided for in the Freedom of Information Act, I will expect to receive a reply within 10 working days.

Because it is not possible to present an adequate reply to this proposed action without the requested information, I hereby request that the deadline for the reply to this proposed suspension be delayed until at least two weeks after my receipt of the requested information. In the absence of a specific denial of this requested extension of time, I will assume that this requested extension has been granted. When you know when I can expect to receive this information, please call me so that we may schedule the date, time, and place of the reply.

If you have any questions concerning this matter, please do not hesitate to contact me.

Very truly yours,

[Your Name]

Enclosure
cc: Designated Personnel Representative

Appendix E-3 Affidavit for Absent Witnesses

I, [full name], hereby make the following statement under oath:

1. I am over the age of eighteen and competent to testify as a witness.
2. My address is [mailing address] and my telephone number is [number].
3. I personally witnessed or heard the following:

[State your testimony in full sentences - use as many pages as necessary]

OATH

I affirm under penalty of perjury that the above statement is true and accurate to the best of my personal knowledge, information, and belief.

____

Date Affiant's Signature

APPENDIX E-4 REQUEST FOR REASONABLE ACCOMMODATION BY DISABLED EMPLOYEE

Dear Supervisor or Disability Coordinator::

I, [insert name], am employed as a [insert position title] in the [insert name of division, organization]. I suffer from [insert diagnosis or description of symptoms that result in a functional limitation]. Due to my disability, I am unable to perform the essential functions of my job with reasonable accommodation. Therefore, I am hereby requesting, under the Rehabilitation Act, that the Agency reasonably accommodate my disability. Specifically, I request the following accommodations [insert your suggestions].

Thank you for your cooperation in this matter. Time is of the essence in granting my accommodation request. If there are any questions concerning this, please do not hesitate to contact me.

Sincerely,

APPENDIX E-5 SAMPLE REQUEST FOR INFORMATION FROM PRIVACY ACT/FOIA OFFICER

[Your Name]
[Your Address]
[Daytime Phone Number]   [Date]

[Privacy Act/FOIA Officer]
[Agency]
[Agency Address]

Re: Privacy Act/FOIA Request

Dear [FOIA Officer]:

Pursuant to the Freedom of Information Act (FOIA), 5 USC 552, and the Privacy Act, 5 USC 552a, please provide me with a copy of the following items:

[List documents or records]

If you determine that portions of these documents are exempt under either of these statutes, I will expect you to release the non-exempt portions to me as the law requires. I, of course, reserve the right to appeal any decision to withhold information.

I promise to pay reasonable fees incurred in the copying of these documents up to the amount of $_____. If the estimated fees will be greater than that amount, please contact me by telephone before such expenses are incurred.

If you have any questions concerning this request, please contact me by telephone. Thank you for your assistance. I will look forward to receiving your prompt reply.

Very truly yours,

[Your Name]

Appendix E-6 Sample Certificate of Service

I, [full name], hereby certify that a copy of the foregoing [name of document] was served this date, [month, day, year] by [method of service, e.g., first-class mail, postage prepaid; certified mail; facsimile transmission] upon the following:

Name of Agency Representative
Title
Name of Agency
Street Address
City, State, Zip code
Fax# [if you served by fax]

____
Your Name
Street Address
City, State, Zip code

Appendix F Organizations Which can Provide Information for Federal Employees

American Federation of Government Employees, AFL-CIO (AFGE)
80 F Street, NW
Washington, DC 20001
202/737-8700
web: www.afge.org

National Federation of Federal Employees (NFFE)
805 15th Street, NW, Suite 500
Washington, DC 20005
202/216-4420
web: www.nffe.org

National Association of Government Employees
159 Burgin Parkway
Quincy, MA 02169
617/376-0220
web: www.nage.org

FPMI Solutions
66 Canal Center Plaza, Suite 305
Alexandria, VA 22314
web: www.fpmi.com

Federal News Websites

- **Federal News Radio**
  www.federalnewsradio.com
- **Federal Soup**
  www.federalsoup.com
- **Federal Times**
  www.federaltimes.com
- **FedScoop**
  http://fedscoop.com
- **FedWeek**
  www.fedweek.com
- **Government Executive**
  www.govexec.com
- **Washington Post**
  http://www.washingtonpost.com/politics/federal-government/

National Treasury Employees Union (NTEU)
1750 H Street, NW
Washington, DC 20006
202/572-5500
web: www.nteu.org

Dewey Publications, Inc.
1840 Wilson Boulevard, Suite 203
Arlington, VA 22201
703/524-1355
fax: 703/524-1463
web: deweypub.com

National Employment Lawyers Association (NELA)
2201 Broadway, Suite 402
Oakland, CA 94612
415/296-7629
fax: 415/677-9445
web: www.nela.org

Government Accountability Project (GAP)
1612 K Street, NW, Suite 1100
Washington, DC 20006
202/408-0034
fax: 202/408-9855
web: www.whistleblower.org

LRP Publications
360 Hiatt Drive
Palm Beach Gardens, FL 33418
800/341-7874
web: www.lrp.com

Project on Government Oversight (POGO)
1100 G Street NW, Suite 500
Washington, DC 20005-3806
202/347-1122
fax: 202/347-1116
email: info@pogo.org
web: http://www.pogo.org

Workplace Fairness
920 U Street NW
Washington, DC 20001
202/683-6114
fax: 240/282-8801
web: www.workplacefairness.org

American Foreign Service Association
2101 E Street NW
Washington, DC 20037
202/338-4045
fax: 202/338-6820
web: www.afsa.org

Federal Law Enforcement Officers Association (FLEOA)
1100 Connecticut Avenue NW, Suite 900
Washington, DC 20036
202/293-1550
web: www.fleoa.org

Fraternal Order of Police (FOP)
701 Marriott Drive
Nashville, TN 37214
615/399-0900
fax: 615/399-0400
web: www.fop.net

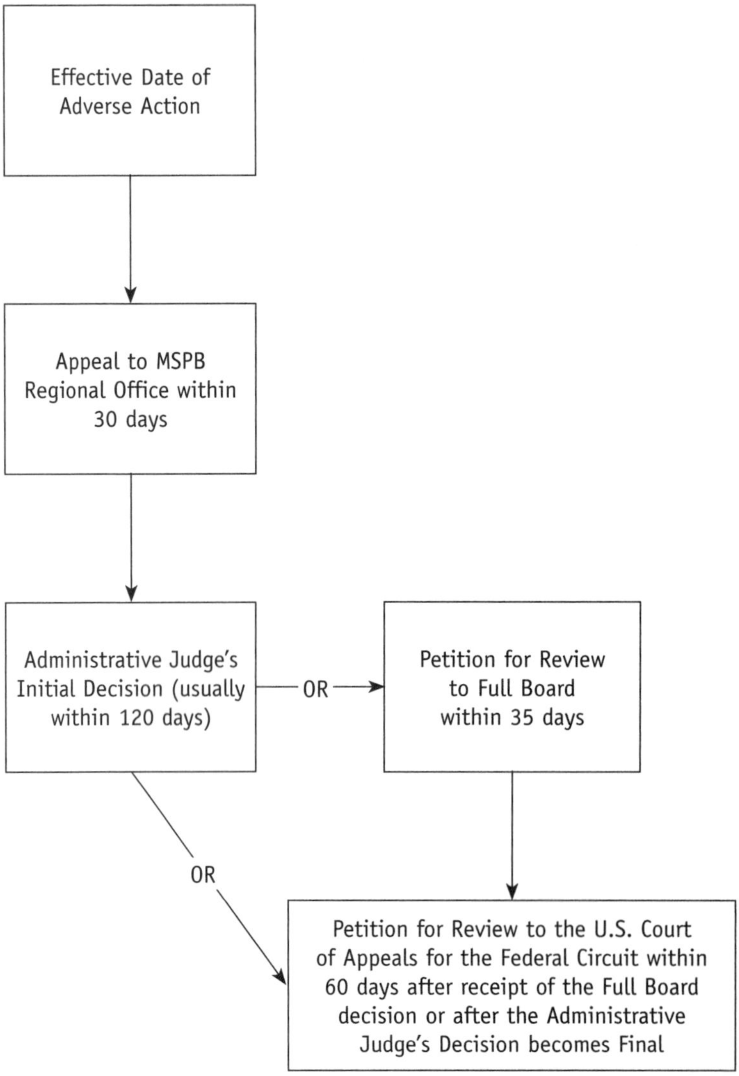
Effective Date of Adverse Action
Appeal to MSPB Regional Office within 30 days
Administrative Judge's Initial Decision (usually within 120 days)
OR
Petition for Review to Full Board within 35 days
OR
Petition for Review to the U.S. Court of Appeals for the Federal Circuit within 60 days after receipt of the Full Board decision or after the Administrative Judge's Decision becomes Final

APPENDIX G-2 "MIXED CASE" ADVERSE ACTION FILED THROUGH THE EEO PROCESS

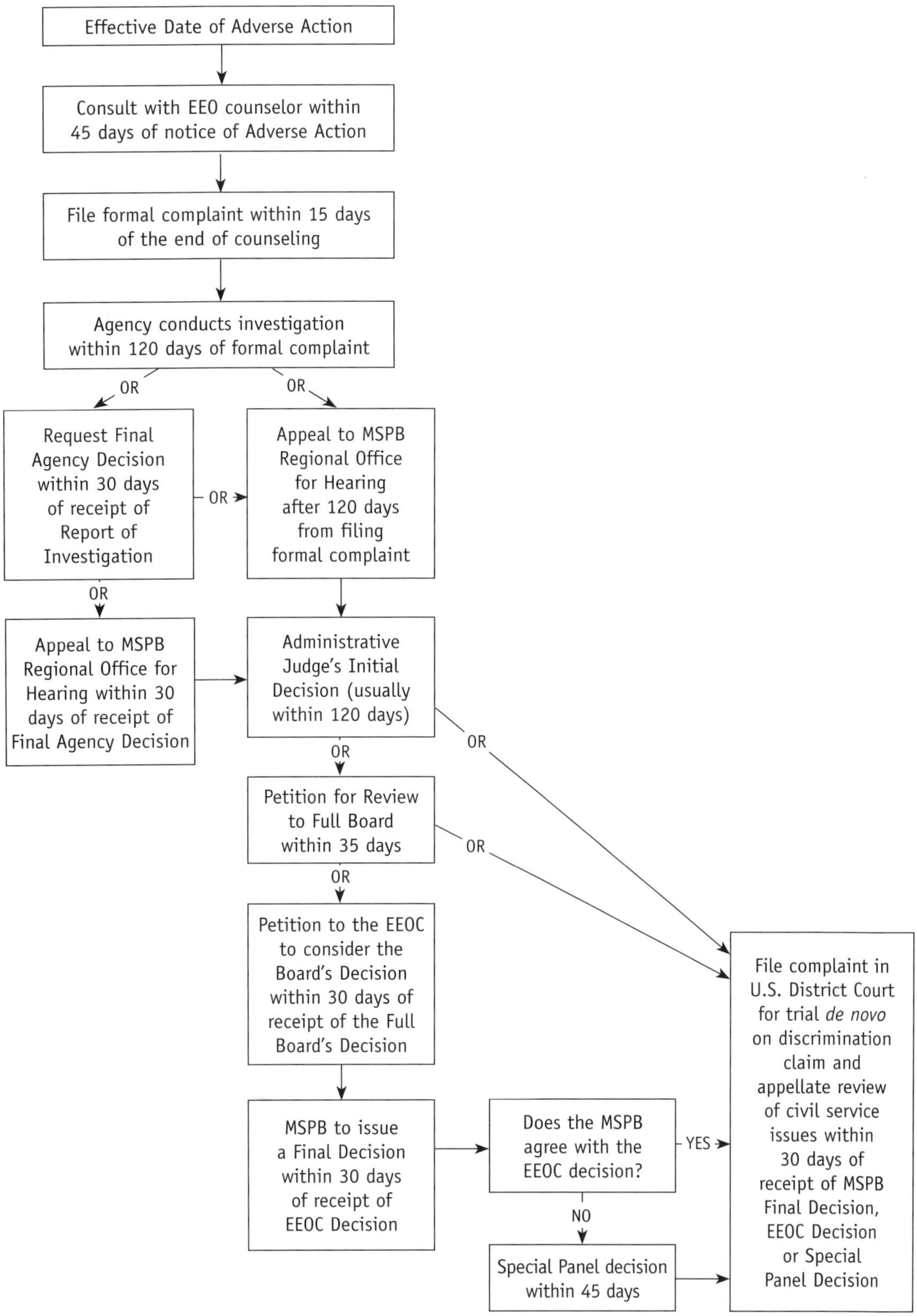

APPENDIX G-3 "MIXED CASE" ADVERSE ACTION FILED DIRECTLY WITH THE MSPB

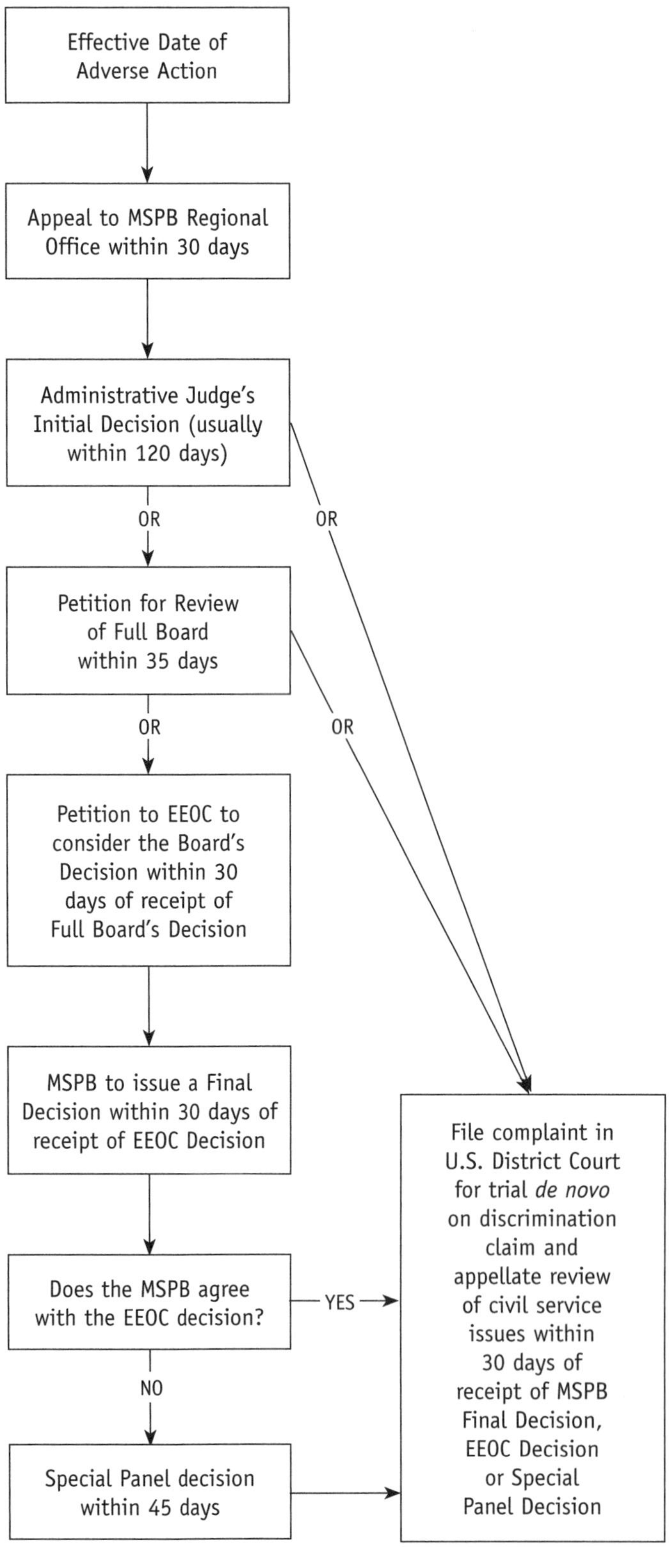

Appendix G-4 Whistleblower Reprisal Case Adverse Action (removal, demotion, or suspension of 15 days or more)

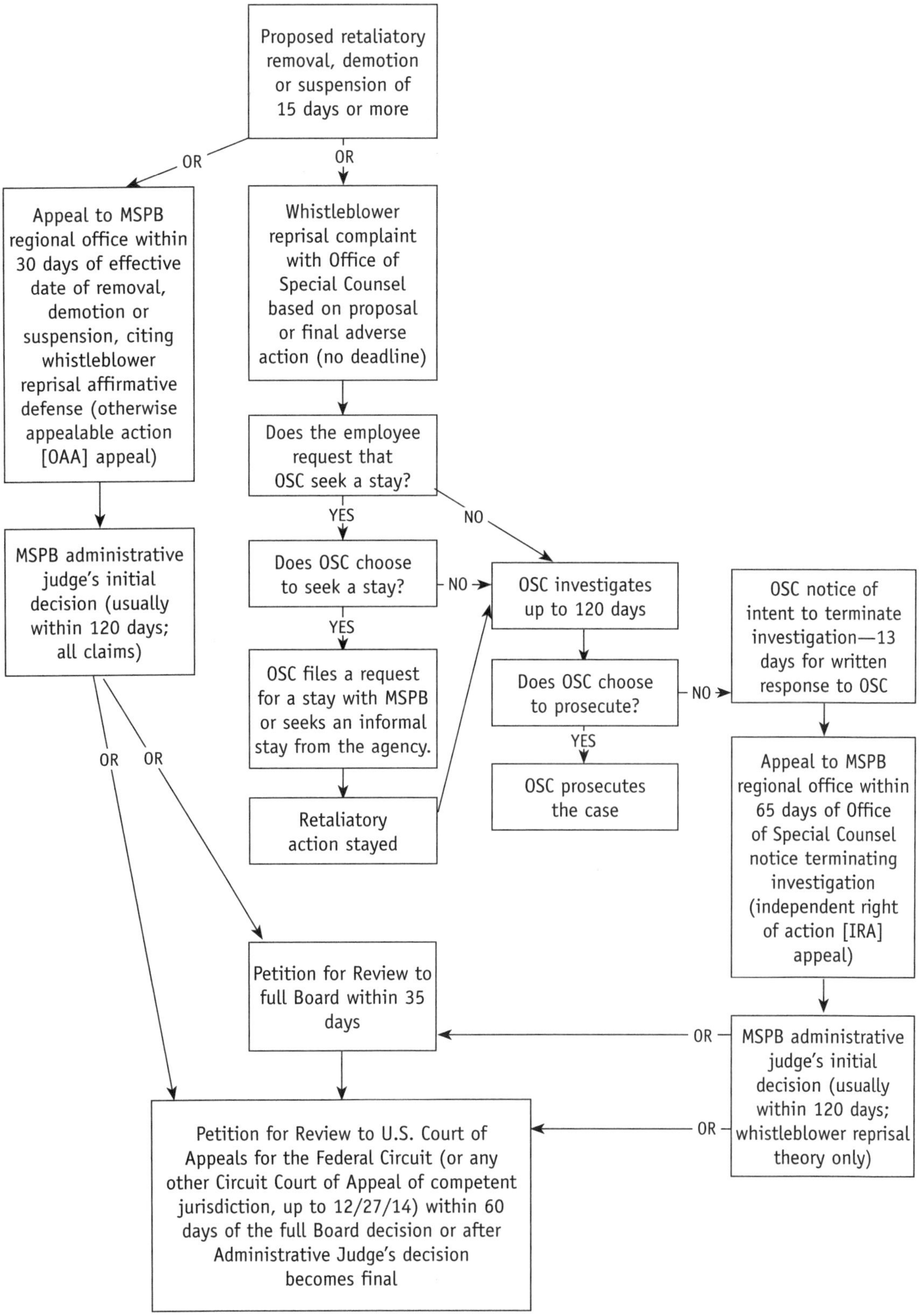

Appendix G-5 Whistleblower Reprisal Case Non-Adverse Action

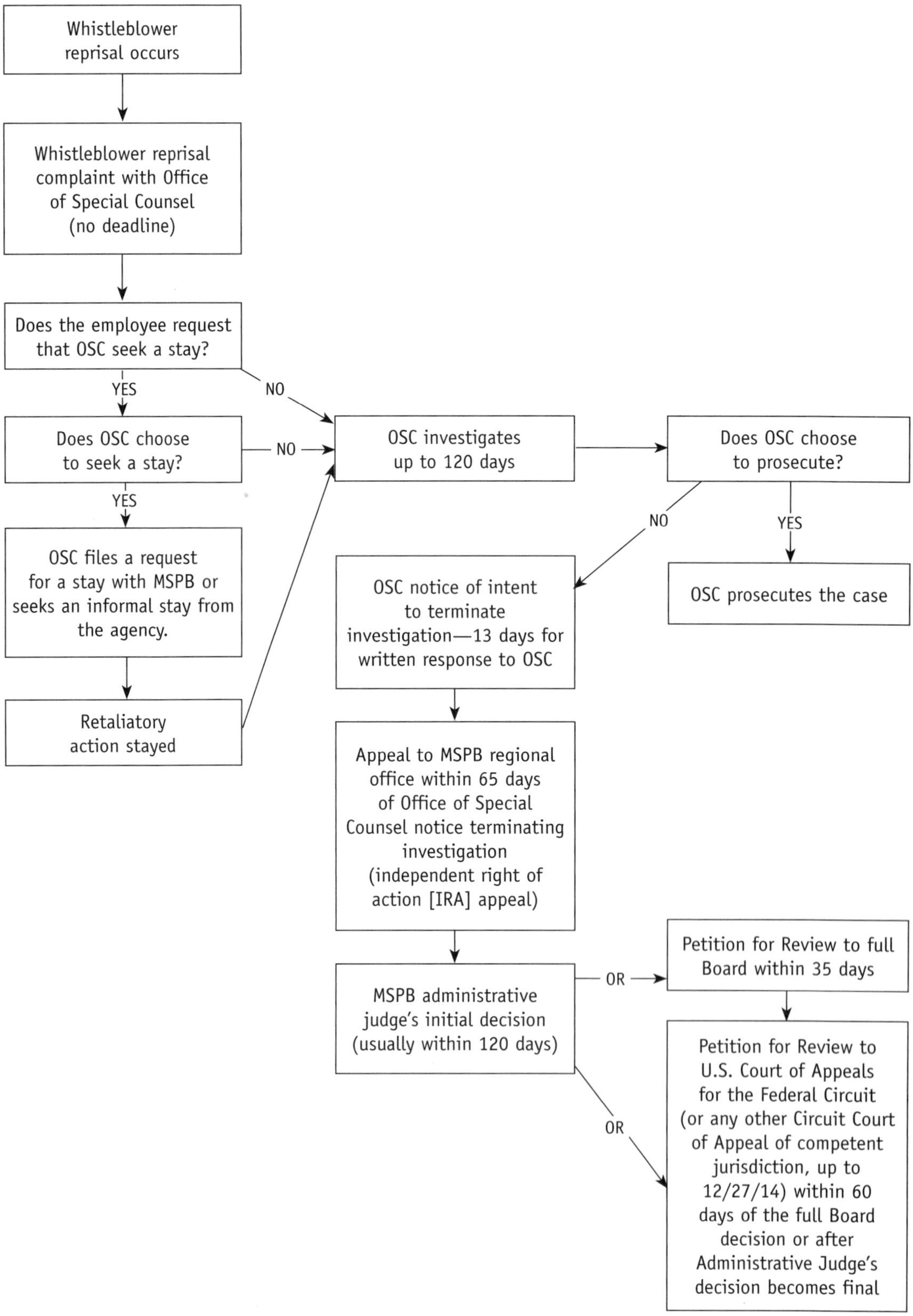

Appendix H Contacting the Equal Employment Opportunity Commission—Addresses and Telephone Numbers of EEOC Headquarters and Field Offices

Headquarters
U.S. Equal Employment
Opportunity Commission
131 M Street, NE
4th Floor, Ste. 4NWO2F
Washington, DC 20507
202/663-4900
TDD: 202/663-4494
web: www.eeoc.gov

Field Offices
To be automatically connected with the nearest EEOC field office, call: 1 800/669-4000
TDD: 1 800/669-6820

Atlanta District Office
100 Alabama Street, SW Ste. 4R30
Atlanta, GA 30303
404/562-6800
TDD: 404/562-6801
(Georgia, South Caroline-southern)

Savannah Local Office
7391 Hodgson Memorial Drive, Ste. 200
Savannah, GA 31406-2579
912/652-4234
TDD: 912/652-4439

Birmingham District Office
Ridge Park Place
1130 22nd Street South, Suite 2000
Birmingham, AL 35205
205/212-2100
TDD: 205/212-2112
(Alabama, Mississippi, Florida-western)

Jackson Area Office
Dr. A. H. McCoy Federal Bldg.
100 West Capitol Street, Ste. 338
Jackson, MS 39269
601/965-4537
TDD: 601/965-4915

Mobile Local Off ice
63 South Royal St., Ste. 504
Mobile, AL 36602
1 800/669-4000
TDD: 1 800/669-6820

Charlotte District Office
129 West Trade Street, Suite 400
Charlotte, NC 28202
704/344-6682
TDD: 704/344-6684
(North Carolina, South Carolina)

Raleigh Area Office
434 Fayetteville St., Ste. 700
Raleigh, NC 27601-1701
919/856-4064
TDD: 919/856-4296

Greensboro Local Office
2303 W. Meadowview Road, Suite 201
Greensboro, NC 27407
336/547-4188
TDD: 336/547-4035

Greenville Local Office
301 N. Main Street, Suite 1402
Greenville, SC 29601-9916
864/241-4400
TDD: 864/241-4103

Norfolk District Office
Federal Building
200 Granby Street, Ste. 739
Norfolk, VA 23510
1 800/669-4000
TDD: 1 800/669-6820

Richmond Area Office
400 North Eight Street, Ste. 350
Richmond, VA 23219
1800/669-4000
TDD: 1 800/669-6820

Chicago District Office
500 West Madison St., Ste. 2000
Chicago, IL 60661
312/353-2713
TDD: 312/353-2421
(Illinois-northern)

Milwaukee Area Office
Reuss Federal Plaza
310 West Wisconsin Avenue
Ste. 500
Cincinnati, OH 45202
1 800/669-4000
TDD: 1 800/669-6820

Minneapolis Area Office
Towle Building
330 South Second Ave., Ste. 720
Minneapolis, MN 55401-2224
1 800/669-4000
TDD: 1 800/669-6820

Dallas District Office
207 S. Houston Street, 3rd Floor
Dallas, TX 75202-4726
214/253-2700
TDD: 214/253-2710
(Texas-western, New Mexico-southern)

San Antonio Field Office
Legacy Oaks, Building A
5410 Fredericksburg Road
Ste. 200
San Antonio, TX 78229
1 800/669-4000
TDD: 1 800/669-6820

El Paso Area Office
300 E. Main Drive, Ste. 500
El Paso, TX 79901
1 800/669-4000
TDD: 1 800/669-6820

Houston District Office
Total Plaza
1201 Louisiana Street, 6th Floor
Houston, TX 77002
713/209-3320
TDD: 713/209-3439
(Texas-eastern)

New Orleans Field Office
1555 Poydras Street, Ste. 1900
New Orleans, LA 70112
1 800/669-4000
TDD: 1 800/669-6820

Indianapolis District Office
101 W. Ohio Street, Ste. 1900
Indianapolis, IN 46204-4203
317/226-7212
TDD: 317/226-5162
(Indiana, Kentucky, Michigan, Ohio-western)

Detroit Field Office
Patrick V. McNamara Building
477 Michigan Ave., Room 865
Detroit, MI 48226-9704
313/226-4600
TDD: 313/226-7599
(Michigan)

Cincinnati Area Office
John W. Peck Federal Office Bldg.
550 Main Street, 10th Floor
Cincinnati, OH 45202
1 800/669-4000
TDD: 1 800/669-6820

Louisville Area Office
600 Dr. Martin Luther King, Jr. Place, Ste. 268
Louisville, KY 40202
1 800/669-4000
TDD: 1 800/669-6820

Los Angeles District Office
Roybal Federal Building
255 East Temple Street, 4th Floor
Los Angeles, CA 90012
213/894-1000
TDD: 213/894-1121
(California-southern, Hawaii, Nevada-southern)

Fresno Local Office
2300 Tulare Street, Ste. 215
Fresno, CA 93721
1 800/669-4000
TDD: 1 800/669-6820

Honolulu Local Office
300 Ala Moana Boulevard, Room 7-127
P.O. Box 50082
Honolulu, HI 96850
1 800/669-4000
TDD: 1 800/669-6820

Las Vegas Local Office
333 Las Vegas Blvd. South
Ste. 8112
Las Vegas, NV 89101
1 800/669-4000
TDD: 1 800/669-6820

San Diego Area Office
555 West Beech Street, Ste. 504
San Diego, CA 92101
619/557-7253
TDD: 619/557-7234

Memphis District Office
1407 Union Avenue, 9th Floor
Memphis, TN 38104
901/544-0115
TDD: 901/544-0112
(Arkansas, Mississippi-northern, Tennessee)

Little Rock Area Office
820 Louisiana Street, Ste. 200
Little Rock, AR 72201
501/324-5060
TDD: 501/324-5481

Nashville Area office
220 Athens Way, Ste. 350
Nashville, TN 37228
1 800/669-4000
TDD: 1 800/669-6820

Miami District Office
Miami Tower
100 SE 2nd Street, Ste. 1500
Miami, FL 33131
305/536-4491
TDD: 305/536-5721
(Florida, Puerto Rico, US Virgin Islands)

Tampa Field Office
501 East Polk Street, Ste. 1000
Tampa, FL 33602
813/228-2310
TDD: 813/228-2003

San Juan Local Office
525 F. D. Roosevelt Avenue
Plaza Las Americas, Ste. 1202
San Juan, Puerto Rico
00918-8001
787/771-1464
TDD: 787/771-1484

New York District Office
33 Whitehead Street, 5th Floor
New York, NY 10004
1 800/669-4000
TDD: 800/669-6820
(Connecticut, Massachusetts, New Hampshire, New Jersey-northern, New York, Rhode Island, Vermont)

Boston Area Office
John F. Kennedy Federal Bldg.
475 Government Center
Boston, MA 02203
1 800/669-4000
TDD: 800/669-6820

Newark Area Office
1 Newark Center, 21st Floor
Newark, NJ 07102-5223
973/645-6383
TDD:201/645-3004

Buffalo Area Office
6 Fountain Plaza, Ste. 350
Buffalo, NY 14202
973/645-6383
TDD:201/645-3004

Philadelphia District Office
21 South Fifth Street, Suite 400
Philadelphia, PA 19106
215/440-2600
TDD: 215/440-2610
(Delaware, New Jersey, Pennsylvania, West Virginia)

Baltimore Field Office
City Crescent Building
10 South Howard St., 3rd Floor
Baltimore, MD 21201
410/209-2237
TDD: 510/637-3234

Cleveland Field Office
Anthony J. Celebrezze
Federal Building
1240 East 9th Street, Ste. 3001
Cleveland, OH 44199
1 800/669-4000
TDD: 800/669-6820

Pittsburgh Area Office
William S. Moorhead
Federal Building
1000 Liberty Avenue, Ste. 1112
Pittsburgh, PA 15222-4187
412/644-3444
TDD: 412-644-2720

Phoenix District Office
3300 N. Central Avenue, Ste. 690
Phoenix, AZ 85012-2504
602/340-5000
TDD: 602/640-5072
(Arizona, Colorado, New Mexico-northern, Utah, Wyoming)

Denver Field Office
303 E. 17th Avenue, Ste. 400
Denver, CO 80203
1 800/669-4000
TDD: 800/669-6820

Albuquerque Area Office
505 Marquette Avenue, NW
Ste. 900 - 9th Floor
Albuquerque, NM 87102
1 800/669-4000
TDD: 800/669-6820

San Francisco District Office
450 Golden Gate Avenue
5 West, P.O. Box 36025
San Francisco, CA 94102
1 800/669-4000
TDD: 800/669-6820
(Alaska, California-northern, Idaho, Montana, Nevadanorthern, Washington)

Seattle Field Office
Federal Office Building
909 First Avenue, Ste. 400
Seattle WA 98104-1061
206/220-6883
TDD: 206/220-6882

Oakland Local Office
1301 Clay Street, Ste. 1170-N
Oakland, CA 94612-5217
510/637-3230
TDD: 510/637-3234

San Jose Local Office
96 North Third St., Ste. 250
San Jose, CA 95112
408/291-7352
TDD: 408/291-7374

St. Louis District Office
Robert A. Young Building
1222 Spruce Street, Room 8100
St. Louis, MO 63103
314/539-7800
TDD: 314/539-7803
(Kansas, Missouri, Illinois-various counties)

Kansas City Area Office
Gateway Tower II
400 State Avenue, Ste. 905
Kansas City, KS 66101
913/551-5655
TDD: 913/551-5657

Oklahoma Area Office
215 Dean A. McGee Ave.,
Ste. 524
Oklahoma City, OK 73102
1 800/669-4000
TDD: 800/669-6820

Washington Field Office
131 M Street, NE, 4th Floor,
Ste. 4NWO2F
Washington, DC 20507
202/663-4900
TDD: 202/663-4494

Note:
Contact information current as of date of printing and may have changed.

APPENDIX I EEOC DISCRIMINATION COMPLAINT FORM

COMPLAINT OF DISCRIMINATION IN THE FEDERAL GOVERNMENT *(This form is subject to the Privacy Act of 1974)* *(See Page 3 for Privacy Act Statement and Iinstructions - Please type or print)*	FOR AGENCY USE
1. FULL NAME OF COMPLAINANT *(Last, First, Middle Initial)*	**2. TELEPHONE NUMBER** *(Include Area Code)*
3. ADDRESS *(Street, City, State, and ZIP Code)*	a. HOME ( ) b. OFFICE ( )

4. FEDERAL OFFICE YOU BELIEVE DISCRIMINATED AGAINST YOU *(Prepare a separate complaint form for each office which you believe discriminated against you.)*	**5. ARE YOU NOW WORKING FOR THE FEDERAL GOVERNMENT?** *(If answer is "Yes" complete a, b, and c below.)* ☐ YES ☐ NO
a. NAME OF OFFICE THAT YOU BELIEVE DISCRIMINATED AGAINST YOU	a. NAME OF AGENCY WHERE YOU WORK
b. ADDRESS OF OFFICE *(Street, City, State, and ZIP Code)*	b. ADDRESS OF YOUR AGENCY *(Street, City, State, and ZIP Code)*
c. NAME AND TITLE OF PERSON(S) YOU BELIEVE DISCRIMINATED AGAINST YOU *(If you know)*	c. TITLE AND GRADE OF YOUR JOB

6. ELECTION OF REPRESENTATION ☐ ATTORNEY ☐ NON-ATTORNEY ☐ NO REPRESENTATION			**7. DATE ON WHICH MOST RECENT ALLEGED DISCRIMINATION TOOK PLACE** *(YYYYMMDD)*
a. NAME OF REPRESENTATIVE *(If applicable)*			
b. ADDRESS *(Include ZIP Code)*			
c. TELEPHONE NUMBER *(Incl. area code)*	d. FAX NUMBER *(Incl. area code)*	e. E-MAIL ADDRESS	

8. CHECK BELOW WHY YOU BELIEVE YOU WERE DISCRIMINATED AGAINST

☐	a. RACE *(If so, state your race)*
☐	b. COLOR *(If so, state your color)*
☐	c. RELIGION *(If so, state your religion)*
☐	d. NATIONAL ORIGIN *(If so, state your national origin)*
☐	e. SEX *(If so, state your sex)*
☐	f. AGE *(If so, state your age) (See Note 1)*
☐	g. DISABILITY *(If so, state whether mental or physical)*
☐	h. SEXUAL HARASSMENT *(If so, state your sex and the sex of the person you believe harassed you)*
☐	i. REPRISAL FOR PREVIOUS EEO ACTIVITY *(If so, when)*
☐	j. GENETIC INFORMATION
☐	k. PREGNANCY

Note 1: Complaints of discrimination because of age apply only to employees or applicants who were at least 40 years of age at the time the discriminatory action is alleged to have occurred.

9. EXPLAIN IN SPECIFICS HOW YOU BELIEVE YOU WERE DISCRIMINATED AGAINST *(treated differently from other employees or applicants)* **DUE TO YOUR RACE, COLOR, RELIGION, NATIONAL ORIGIN, SEX, AGE, PREGNANCY, GENETIC INFORMATION, DISABILITY, OR REPRISAL** *(For each allegation, please state to the best of your knowledge, information and belief what incident occurred and when the incident occurred. If you need more space, continue on another sheet of paper.)*

PREVIOUS EDITION IS OBSOLETE.

10. I HAVE DISCUSSED MY COMPLAINT WITH AN EQUAL EMPLOYMENT OPPORTUNITY COUNSELOR *(See instructions)* ☐ YES ☐ NO		11. NAME OF COUNSELOR *(If applicable)*
12. HAVE THE ISSUES IDENTIFIED IN BLOCK 9 BEEN APPEALED TO THE MERIT SYSTEMS PROTECTION BOARD (MSPB) OR FILED UNDER A UNION NEGOTIATED GRIEVANCE PROCEDURE? ☐ NO ☐ YES *(If Yes, complete 12.a., b., and c. below)*		
a. *(X one)* ☐ MSPB ☐ UNION NEGOTIATED GRIEVANCE	b. DATE FILED *(YYYYMMDD)*	c. MSPB OR UNION DOCKET NUMBER *(If known)*
13. WHAT RELIEF ARE YOU SEEKING TO RESOLVE THIS COMPLAINT? *(State specific corrective action desired for each allegation.)*		
14. LIST NAME(S) OF WITNESS(ES) AND BRIEFLY STATE WHAT INFORMATION WITNESS MAY CONTRIBUTE TO THE INVESTIGATION OF YOUR COMPLAINT.		
15. SIGNATURE OF COMPLAINANT		16. DATE OF THIS COMPLAINT *(YYYYMMDD)*

DESIGNATION OF REPRESENTATIVE

Complainant: ____________________ **Agency:** ____________________

EEOC Case No. ________________ **Agency Case No.** ______________

Presiding Administrative Judge: ______________________

I, ____________________, hereby designate the following individual as the representative for the [check one: ___ COMPLAINANT ___ AGENCY] in the above-referenced EEOC case:

____________________ ______________ ______________

Name of Representative **Telephone No.** **FAX No.**

Address: ____________________________________

____

____

____

E-mail Address: __________________________

______________________________ ____________

Signature of Complainant/Agency Official Authorizing the Foregoing Designation **Date**

Complainant, please also provide your current address, telephone number, fax number, and E-mail address:

____

____

____

____

Appendix K How to Contact the Federal Labor Relations Authority (FLRA)—Telephone Numbers and Addresses of FLRA Headquarters and Regional Offices

FLRA Headquarters Offices

Federal Labor Relations Authority

1400 K Street, NW, 2nd Floor
Washington, DC 20424-0001

Carol W. Pope - Chair
Ernest DuBester - Member
Patrick Pizzella - Member
Julia Akins Clark - General Counsel

Office of Chair Pope
202/218-7900

Office of Member DuBester
202/218-7930

Office of Member Pizzella
202/218-7920

General Counsel of the FLRA
202/218-7743

Administrative Law Judges
202/218-7910

Federal Service Impasses Panel

1400 K Street, NW, Ste. 200
Washington, DC 20424-0001

Mary Jacksteit - Chair

General Information
202/218-7790

FLRA Regional Offices

Mr. Philip Roberts
Regional Director
Federal Labor Relations Authority
10 Causeway Street, Ste. 472
Boston, MA 02222
617/565-5100 FTS or Commercial
fax: 617/565-6262

Ms. Richard Jones
Regional Director
Federal Labor Relations Authority
225 Peachtree Street, Ste. 1950
Atlanta, GA 30303-1730
404/331-5212 FTS or Commercial
fax: 404/331-5280

Mr. James E. Petrucci
Regional Director
Federal Labor Relations Authority
Suite 926, LB107
Federal Office Building
525 South Griffin Street
Dallas, TX 75202-1906
214/767-6266 FTS or Commercial
fax: 214/767-0156

Ms. Jean Perata
Regional Director
Federal Labor Relations Authority
901 Market Street, Ste. 470
San Francisco, CA 94103-1791
415/356-5002 FTS or Commercial
fax: 415/356-5017

Ms. Barbara Kraft
Regional Director
Federal Labor Relations Authority
1400 K Street, NW, 2nd Floor
Washington, DC 20424-0001
202/357-3029
fax: 202/482-6724

Mr. Peter Sutton
Regional Director
Federal Labor Relations Authority
224 S. Michigan Ave., Ste. 445
Chicago, IL 60604-2505
312/886-3465 FTS or Commercial
fax: 312/886-5977
Federal Labor Relations Authority
Suite 446
1244 Speer Boulevard
Denver, CO 80204-3581
303/844-5226 FTS or Commercial
fax: 303/844-2774

Note:
Contact information current as of date of printing and may have changed.

APPENDIX L CONTACTING THE MSPB—ADDRESSES AND FAX NUMBERS OF REGIONAL AND FIELD OFFICES

All submissions shall be addressed to the Regional Director, if submitted to a regional office, or the Chief Administrative Judge, if submitted to a field office, Merit Systems Protection Board, at the addresses listed below, according to the geographic region of the employing agency or as required by 5 CFR 1201.4(d). The facsimile numbers listed below are TDD-capable; however, calls will be answered by voice before being connected to the TDD.

ATLANTA REGIONAL OFFICE

401 West Peachtree NW, Suite 1050
Atlanta, Georgia 30308-3519
404/730-2751
fax: 404/730-2767
(Alabama, Florida, Georgia, Mississippi, South Carolina, Tennessee)

CENTRAL REGIONAL OFFICE

230 South Dearborn Street
31st Floor
Chicago, IL 60604-1669
312/353-2923
fax: 312/886-4231
(Illinois, Indiana, Ohio, Iowa, Kansas City, Kansas, Kentucky, Missouri, Michigan, Minnesota, and Wisconsin)

DALLAS REGIONAL OFFICE

1100 Commerce Street, Room 620
Dallas, TX 75242-9979
214/767-0555
fax: 214/767-0102
(Arkansas, Louisiana, Oklahoma, and Texas)

DENVER FIELD OFFICE

165 South Union Boulevard, Suite 318
Lakewood, CO 80228-2211
303/969-5101
fax: 303/969-5109
(Arizona, Colorado, Kansas except for Kansas City, Montana, Nebraska, New Mexico, North Dakota, South Dakota, Utah, and Wyoming)

NEW YORK FIELD OFFICE

26 Federal Plaza, Room 3137-A
New York, NY 10278-0022
212/264-9372
fax: 212/264-1417
(New Jersey-counties of Bergen, Essex, Hudson, and Union, New York, Puerto Rico, and Virgin Islands)

NORTHEASTERN REGIONAL OFFICE

1601 Market Street, Ste. 1700
Philadelphia, PA 19103
215/597-9960
fax: 215/597-3456
(Connecticut, Delaware, Maine, Maryland (except for Montgomery and Prince George's counties), Massachusetts, New Hampshire, New Jersey (except for Bergen, Essex, Hudson, and Union counties), Pennsylvania, Rhode Island, Vermont, and West Virginia)

WASHINGTON REGIONAL OFFICE

1901 South Bell Street, Ste. 950
Arlington, VA 22202
703/756-6250
Fax: 703/756-7112
(Maryland-counties of Montgomery and Prince Georges, North Carolina, Virginia, Washington, DC, and all overseas areas not otherwise covered)

WESTERN REGIONAL OFFICE

201 Mission Street, Ste. 2310
San Francisco, CA 94105-1831
415/705-2935
fax: 415/705-2945
(Alaska, California, Hawaii, Idaho, Nevada, Oregon, Washington and Pacific overseas)

WEBSITE

www.mspb.gov

NOTE:

Contact information current as of date of printing and may have changed.

OMB No. 3124-0009

MERIT SYSTEMS PROTECTION BOARD APPEAL FORM (MSPB FORM 185)

INSTRUCTIONS FOR COMPLETING YOUR APPEAL

MSPB's Authority to Review Employment Related Actions or Decisions

The MSPB (the Board)'s legal authority (jurisdiction) to review employment-related actions or decisions is limited to those matters specifically entrusted to it by law, rule, or regulation. A listing of matters over which the Board has jurisdiction can be found in the Board's regulations at **5 C.F.R. § 1201.3**. The administrative judge assigned to your case will determine whether the Board has jurisdiction over the particular circumstances of your appeal.

Where to Obtain Additional Information

Much more information about the adjudication of appeals before the MSPB, including the Board's regulations, may be found at the Board's website: **www.mspb.gov**. The Board's regulations are also published in the Code of Federal Regulations, 5 C.F.R. Part 1200 et seq., available in many libraries.

Time Limits for Filing an Appeal

You must file your appeal within **30 calendar days** of the effective date, if any, of the action or decision you are appealing, or the date you received the agency's decision, whichever is later. (Please note that Individual Right of Action (IRA), Uniformed Services Employment and Reemployment Rights (USERRA), and Veterans Employment Opportunities Act (VEOA) appeals have different time limits, as described in **Appendix A**). In limited circumstances, the 30-day filing time limit may be extended if you and the agency mutually agree in writing to try to resolve your dispute through an alternative dispute resolution process before you file an appeal. *See* **5 C.F.R. § 1201.22(b)-(c)**. The 30-day time limit may also be extended if you have previously filed a formal equal employment opportunity (EEO) complaint regarding the same matter, as described in **Appendix A**. The date of filing is the date your appeal is postmarked, the date of the facsimile (fax) transmission, the date it is delivered to a commercial overnight delivery service, the date of receipt in the regional or field office if you personally deliver it, or the date of submission if you file your appeal electronically. **Do not delay filing your appeal merely because you do not currently have the documents requested in this form.**

Where to File an Appeal

You must file your appeal of the agency's action or decision with the Board's regional or field office responsible for your actual or potential duty station. If you are appealing a retirement or suitability decision by the Office of Personnel Management (OPM), you must file your appeal with the Board's regional or field office responsible for where you live. *See* **5 C.F.R. § 1201.4(d)** and **1201.22(a)**. For a list of regional and field offices, see **Appendix B**.

Attachments

Please submit only the attachments requested in this form. The filing of an appeal is just the beginning of the adjudication process, and you will have additional opportunities to submit evidence and argument before a decision is issued. Further, the agency will submit all the documents contained in its record of the action. **5 C.F.R. § 1201.25(c)**.

If you prefer to file your appeal electronically, please visit MSPB e-Appeal Online — https://e-appeal.mspb.gov

MSPB Form 185, Page 1 (5/13)
5 C.F.R. Parts 1201, 1208 and 1209

PART 1 - Appellant and Agency Information

Everyone must complete Part 1.

Please type or print legibly.

1. Name *(last, first, middle)*

Last ☐ First ☐ M. Initial ☐

Please list your first name as it appears in your official personnel records. For example, if your first name is "William" on your official personnel records, please list it that way on the appeal form, not "Bill" or "Willy."

2. Present address *(number and street, city, State, and Zip code)*

You must promptly notify the Board in writing of any change in your mailing address while your appeal is pending.

Address:

City: State: Zip Code:

3. Telephone Numbers *(include area code) and E-Mail Address*

You must promptly notify the Board in writing of any change in your telephone number(s) or e-mail address while your appeal is pending.

Home: Work: Fax: Cell:

e-Mail Address:

4. Name and address of the agency that took the action or made the decision you are appealing *(include bureau or division, street address, city, State and Zip code)*

Agency Name:

Bureau:

Address:

City: State: Zip Code: Phone Number:

5. Your Federal employment status at the time of the action or decision you are appealing:

☐ Permanent ☐ Temporary ☐ Term

☐ Seasonal ☐ Applicant ☐ Retired

☐ None

6. Type of appointment (if applicable):

☐ Competitive ☐ Excepted

☐ Postal Service ☐ SES

☐ Other (*describe*):

7. Your position, title, grade, and duty station at the time of the action or decision you are appealing (if applicable):

Occupational Series or Cluster: Position Title:

Grade or Pay Band: Duty Station:

8. Are you entitled to veteran's preference? See 5 U.S.C. § 2108.

☐ Yes ☐ No

9. Length of Federal service (if applicable):

☐ Years ☐ Months

10. Were you serving a probationary, trial, or initial service period at the time of the action or decision you are appealing?

☐ Yes ☐ No

11. **HEARING:** You may have a right to a hearing before an administrative judge. If you elect not to have a hearing, the administrative judge will make a decision on the basis of the submissions of the parties. Do you want a hearing?

☐ Yes ☐ No

MSPB Form 185, Page 2 (5/13)
5 C.F.R. Parts 1201, 1208, and 1209

PART 2 - Agency Personnel Action or Decision (non-retirement)

Complete this part if you are appealing a Federal agency personnel action or decision other than a decision directly addressing your retirement rights or benefits. This includes certain actions that might not otherwise be appealable to the Board: individual right of action (IRA) appeals under the Whistleblower Protection Act (WPA); appeals under the Uniformed Services Employment and Reemployment Rights Act (USERRA); or appeals under the Veterans Employment Opportunities Act (VEOA). An explanation of these three types of appeals is provided in **Appendix A**.

12. Check the box that best describes the agency **personnel action or decision** you are appealing. (If you are appealing more than one action or decision, check each box that applies.)

- ☐ Removal (termination after completion of probationary or initial service period)
- ☐ Termination during probationary or initial service period
- ☐ Reduction in grade, pay, or band
- ☐ Suspension for more than 14 days
- ☐ Failure to restore/reemploy/reinstate or improper restoration/reemployment/reinstatement
- ☐ Negative suitability determination
- ☐ Involuntary resignation
- ☐ Involuntary retirement
- ☐ Denial of within-grade increase
- ☐ Furlough of 30 days or less
- ☐ Separation, demotion or furlough for more than 30 days by reduction in force (RIF)
- ☐ Other action (describe):

13. Date you received the agency's final decision letter (if any) *(MM/DD/YYYY)*:

14. Effective date (if any) of the agency action or decision *(MM/DD/YYYY)*:

15. Prior to filing this appeal, did you and the agency mutually agree in writing to try to resolve the matter through an alternative dispute resolution (ADR) process?

☐ Yes ***(attach a copy of the agreement)*** ☐ No

16. Explain briefly why you think the agency was wrong in taking this action, including whether you believe the agency engaged in harmful procedural error, committed a prohibited personnel practice, or engaged in one of the other claims listed in **Appendix A**. **Attach the agency's proposal letter, decision letter, and SF-50, if available**. Attach additional sheets if necessary (bearing in mind that there will be later opportunities to supplement your filings).

MSPB Form 185, Page 3 (5/13)
5 C.F.R. Parts 1201, 1208, and 1209

PART 2 - Agency Personnel Action or Decision (non-retirement) (continued)

17. With respect to the agency personnel action or decision you are appealing, have you, or has anyone on your behalf, filed a grievance under a negotiated grievance procedure provided by a collective bargaining agreement?

☐ Yes ☐ No

If "Yes," **attach a copy of the grievance**, enter the date it was filed, and enter the place where it was filed if different from your answer to question 4 in Part 1.

Agency Name: ______ Date Filed (*MM/DD/YYYY*): ______

Bureau: ______

Address: ______

City: ______ State: ______ Zip Code: ______

If a decision on the grievance has been issued, **attach a copy of the decision** and enter the date it was issued *(MM/DD/YYYY):*

Date Issued (*MM/DD/YYYY*): ______

Answer Question 18 ONLY if you are filing an IRA appeal.

18. If you filed a whistleblowing complaint with the Office of Special Counsel (OSC), provide the date on which you did so and the date on which OSC made a decision or terminated its investigation, if applicable. **Attach copies of your complaint and OSC's termination of investigation letter**, notifying you of your right to seek corrective action from the Board.

Date Filed (*MM/DD/YYYY*): ______

Date of OSC decision or termination of investigation (*MM/DD/YYYY*): ______

Answer Question 19 ONLY if you are filing a USERRA or VEOA appeal.

19. If you filed a complaint with the Department of Labor (DOL), list the date on which you did so, and **attach a copy of your complaint**. If DOL has made a decision on your complaint, list the date of this decision, and **attach a copy of it**. If DOL has not made a decision on your complaint within 60 days from the date you filed it, state whether you have notified DOL of your intent to file an appeal with the Board, and **attach a copy of such notification**.

Date Filed (*MM/DD/YYYY*): ______

Has DOL made a decision on your complaint?

☐ Yes ☐ No

If "Yes," enter the date it was made. If "No", state whether you have notified DOL of your intent to file an appeal with the Board, and **attach a copy of such notification**.

Date of DOL decision (*MM/DD/YYYY*): ______ ☐ Notified DOL of your intent to file an appeal with the Board?

MSPB Form 185, Page 4 (5/13)
5 C.F.R. Parts 1201, 1208, and 1209

PART 3 - OPM or Agency Retirement Decision

Complete this part if you are appealing a decision of the Office of Personnel Management (OPM) or other Federal agency directly addressing your retirement rights or benefits.

20. In which retirement system are you enrolled?

☐ CSRS ☐ CSRS Offset ☐ FERS

☐ Other, *describe:*

21. Are you a:

☐ Current Employee ☐ Annuitant

☐ Surviving Spouse

☐ Other, *describe:*

22. If retired, date of retirement, or if unknown, approximate date:

Date Retired (*MM/DD/YYYY*):

23. Describe the retirement decision you are appealing.

24. Have you received a final or reconsideration decision from OPM or another Federal agency?

☐ Yes ***(attach a copy)*** ☐ No

If "Yes," on what date did you receive the decision?

Date Received (*MM/DD/YYYY*):

Provide the OPM processing (CSA or CSF) number in your appeal:

OPM Claim Number:

25. Explain briefly why you think OPM or another Federal agency was wrong in making this decision.

MSPB Form 185, Page 5 (5/13)
5 C.F.R. Parts 1201, 1208, and 1209

PART 4 — Designation of Representative

26. Has an individual or organization agreed to represent you in this proceeding before the Board? (You may designate a representative at any time. However, it is unlikely that the appeals process will be delayed for reasons related to obtaining or maintaining representation. Moreover, you must promptly notify the Board in writing of any change in representation.)

☐ Yes *(Complete the information below and sign)* ☐ No

DESIGNATION:

"I hereby designate ______________________ to serve as my representative during the course of this appeal. I understand that my representative is authorized to act on my behalf. In addition, I specifically delegate to my representative the authority to settle this appeal on my behalf. **I understand that any limitation on this settlement authority must be filed in writing with the Board.**"

Representative's address *(number and street, city, State and Zip code)*	Representative's telephone numbers *(include area code) and e-mail address*
Address:	Office:
City:	Fax: Other:
State: Zip Code:	e-Mail Address:

SIGN BELOW TO MAKE YOUR DESIGNATION OF REPRESENTATIVE EFFECTIVE

Appellant's Signature

Date *(MM/DD/YYYY)*

MSPB Form 185, Page 6 (5/13)
5 C.F.R. Parts 1201, 1208, and 1209

PART 5 - Certification

27. I certify that all of the statements made in this form and any attachments are true, complete, and correct to the best of my knowledge and belief.

Signature of Appellant or Representative

Date *(MM/DD/YYYY)*

Privacy Act Statement

This form requests personal information that is relevant and necessary to reach a decision in your appeal. The Merit Systems Protection Board collects this information in order to process appeals under its statutory and regulatory authority. Because your appeal is a voluntary action, you are not required to provide any personal information to the Merit Systems Protection Board in connection with your appeal. Conceivably, failure to provide all information essential to reaching a decision in your case could result in the dismissal or denial of your appeal.

Decisions of the Merit Systems Protection Board are available to the public under the provisions of the Freedom of Information Act and are posted to the Merit Systems Protection Board's public website. Some information about the appeal also is used in depersonalized form for statistical purposes. Finally, information from your appeal file may be disclosed as required by law under the provisions of the Freedom of Information Act and the Privacy Act. See 5 U.S.C. §§ 552, 552a.

Public Reporting Burden

The public reporting burden for this collection of information is estimated to vary from 20 minutes to 4 hours, with an average of 60 minutes per response, including time for reviewing the form, searching existing data sources, gathering the data necessary, and completing and reviewing the collection of information. Send comments regarding the burden estimate or any other aspect of the collection of information, including suggestions for reducing this burden, to Office of the Clerk of the Board, Merit Systems Protection Board, 1615 M Street, N.W., Washington, DC 20419 or by e-mail to mspb@mspb.gov.

MSPB Form 185, Page 7 (5/13)
5 C.F.R. Parts 1201, 1208, and 1209

U.S. OFFICE OF SPECIAL COUNSEL
Form OSC-11 (2/28/14)

(202) 254-3600 / (202)254-3670 / (800) 872-9855
OMB Control No. 3255-0002

COMPLAINT OF POSSIBLE PROHIBITED PERSONNEL PRACTICE OR OTHER PROHIBITED ACTIVITY

IMPORTANT

Before filling out this Office of Special Counsel (OSC) form, please read the following information about:(1) the required complaint format; (2) the scope of OSC's jurisdiction; and (3) certain OSC policies. OSC cannot investigate a complaint if it lacks jurisdiction over the subject matter. Further, filing a complaint with OSC will not extend any time limits that may exist under any other complaint procedures that may be available. It is important, therefore, that you consider whether OSC may lack jurisdiction over your complaint.

If you plan to file a complaint alleging reprisal for whistleblowing, important information about the elements required by law to establish such a violation is provided in Part 2 of this form (at page 4).

INFORMATION ABOUT FILING A COMPLAINT WITH OSC

Required Complaint Form. Complaints alleging a prohibited personnel practice, or a prohibited activity other than a Hatch Act violation, must be submitted on this form. OSC will not process complaints (except a complaint alleging only a Hatch Act violation) that are not submitted on this form. OSC will return the material received, with a blank complaint form to complete and return to OSC. The complaint will be considered to be filed on the date on which OSC receives the completed form. 5 C.F.R. § 1800.1, as amended.

No OSC Jurisdiction. OSC has no jurisdiction over complaints filed by employees of –

- the Central Intelligence Agency, Defense Intelligence Agency, National Security Agency, or other intelligence agency excluded from coverage by the President;
- the armed forces of the United States (*i.e.,* uniformed military employees);
- the General Accounting Office;
- the Postal Rate Commission; and
- the Federal Bureau of Investigation.

Limited OSC Jurisdiction. OSC has jurisdiction over certain types of complaints filed by employees of some agencies, as follows –

- Federal Aviation Administration employees alleging reprisal for whistleblowing;
- employees of government corporations listed at 31 U.S.C. § 9101 alleging reprisal for whistleblowing; U.S.
- Postal Service employees alleging nepotism; and
- Transportation Security Administration (TSA) employees alleging reprisal for whistleblowing: TSA non-screener employees may file complaints alleging retaliation for protected whistleblowing under 5 U.S.C. § 2302(b)(8). OSC will process these complaints under its regular procedures, including filing petitions with the Merit Systems Protection Board, if warranted. TSA security screeners may also file complaints alleging retaliation for protected whistleblowing under 5 U.S.C. § 2302(b)(8) pursuant to a Memorandum of Understanding (MOU) between OSC and TSA executed on May 28, 2002. The MOU and TSA Directive HRM Letter No. 1800-01 provide OSC with authority to investigate whistleblower retaliation complaints from screeners and recommend that TSA take corrective and/or disciplinary action when warranted. Additional information on OSC procedures for reviewing security screener whistleblower complaints under the MOU is available at http://www.osc.gov/tsa-info.htm.

(over)

VISIT WWW.OSC.GOV
FOR MORE INFORMATION ABOUT OSC JURISDICTION AND COMPLAINT PROCEDURES

INFORMATION ABOUT FILING A COMPLAINT WITH OSC *(cont'd)*

Election of Remedies for Employees Covered By a Collective Bargaining Agreement. Pursuant to 5 U.S.C. § 7121(g), if you are covered by a collective bargaining agreement, you must choose one of three possible avenues to pursue your prohibited personnel practice complaint: (a) a complaint to OSC; (b) an appeal to the Merit Systems Protection Board (MSPB) (if the action is appealable under law or regulation), or (c) a grievance under the collective bargaining agreement. If you have already filed an appeal about your prohibited personnel practice allegations with the MSPB, or a grievance about those allegations under the collective bargaining agreement, OSC lacks jurisdiction over your complaint and cannot investigate it.

Deferral of Certain Complaints Involving Discrimination. Although OSC is authorized to investigate discrimination based upon race, color, religion, sex, national origin, age, or handicapping condition, as well as reprisal for filing an EEO complaint, OSC generally defers such allegations to agency procedures established under regulations issued by the Equal Employment Opportunity Commission (EEOC). 5 C.F.R. § 1810.1. If you wish to report allegations of discrimination based upon race, color, religion, sex, national origin, age, or handicapping condition, or reprisal for filing an EEO complaint, you should contact your agency's EEO office immediately. There are specific time limits for filing such complaints. Filing a complaint with OSC will not relieve you of the obligation to file a complaint with the agency's EEO office within the time prescribed by EEOC regulations (at 29 C.F.R. Part 1614).

> ***Note***: This deferral policy does not apply to discrimination claims outside the jurisdiction of the EEOC, such as complaints alleging discrimination based upon marital status or political affiliation.

Complaints Involving Veterans Rights. By law, complaints alleging denial of veterans' preference requirements must be filed with the Veterans Employment and Training Service (VETS) at the Department of Labor. 38 U.S.C. § 4301, *et seq.*, and 5 U.S.C. § 3330a(a). Certain allegations of discrimination based on the past, current, or future performance of military service (*e.g.*, discrimination based on veteran or reservist status) may be filed with OSC. Thus, you are encouraged to contact OSC's Uniformed Services Employment and Reemployment Rights Act (USERRA) Unit by e-mail at userra@osc.gov or by telephone at 202-254-3600.

SEND COMPLETED COMPLAINT FORMS TO OSC -

By Mail:	**Complaints Examining Unit Office of Special Counsel 1730 M Street, N.W. (Suite 218) Washington, DC 20036-4505**
By Fax:	**(202)254-3711**
Electronically:	WWW.OSC.GOV (AT "FILE COMPLAINTS ONLINE")

PLEASE KEEP A COPY OF YOUR COMPLAINT, ANY SUPPORTING DOCUMENTION, AND ANY ADDITIONAL ALLEGATIONS SENT IN WRITING TO OSC NOW, OR AT ANY TIME WHILE YOUR COMPLAINT IS PENDING
REPRODUCTION CHARGES UNDER THE FREEDOM OF INFORMATION ACT MAY APPLY TO ANY REQUEST YOU MAKE FOR COPIES OF MATERIALS THAT YOU PROVIDED TO OSC.

IF YOU ARE FILING AN ALLEGATION OF REPRISAL FOR WHISTLEBLOWING,
PLEASE SEE PART 2 OF THE COMPLAINT FROM, AT PAGES 4-5, FOR OTHER RECORDKEEPING CONSIDERATIONS.

U.S. OFFICE OF SPECIAL COUNSEL (202) 254-3600 / (202) 254-3670 / (800) 872-9855

COMPLAINT OF POSSIBLE PROHIBITED PERSONNEL PRACTICE
OR
OTHER PROHIBITED ACTIVITY

(Please print legibly or type and complete all pertinent items. Enter "N/A" (Not Applicable) or "Unknown" where appropriate. (If more space is needed, use Continuation Sheet at page 12.)

PART 1: PROHIBITED PERSONNEL PRACTICES PROHIBITED ACTIVITY (GENERAL)

1. Name of person seeking OSC action ("Complainant"): Mr. (●) Ms. ( ) Mrs. ( ) Miss ( )

   For USERRA complaints only - please provide the last digit only of your Social Security Number (SSN):
   (needed to determine jurisdiction under § 204(c)(2) of Public Law No. 108-454.)
2. Position, title, series, and grade:
3. Agency name:
4. Agency Address:
5. Home or mailing address:
6. Contact information: Telephone number(s): ( ) (Home)
   ( ) (Office) Ext.
   Fax number: ( )
   E-mail address:
7. If you are filing this complaint as a legal or other representative of the Complainant, please supply the following information:

   Name and title of filer: Mr.( ) Ms.( ) Mrs.( ) Miss( )

   Address:

   Telephone number(s): ( ) (Home)
   ( ) (Office) Ext.
   Fax number: ( )
   E-mail address:
8. Are you (or is the Complainant, if you are filing as a representative) covered by a collective bargaining agreement? (Check one.)

   ( )Yes ( ) No ( ) I don'tknow
9. How did you first become aware that you could file a complaint with OSC?

   ( ) OSC Web site ( ) OSC Speaker ( ) OSC Brochure ( ) OSC Poster
   ( ) NewsStory ( ) AgencyPersonnel Office ( ) Union ( ) Co-worker
   ( ) Other (*please describe*):

   Date (approximate):

10. What is the employment status of the person affected by the suspected prohibited personnel practice or other prohibited activity? (Check all applicable items - more than one item may apply.)

a. ( ) Applicant for Federal employment

b. ( ) Competitive Service

- ( ) temporary appointment
- ( ) term appointment
- ( ) career or career-conditional appointment
- ( ) probationary employee

c. ( ) Excepted Service

- ( ) Schedule A
- ( ) Schedule B
- ( ) Schedule C
- ( ) National Guard Technician
- ( ) Non-appropriated Fund
- ( ) Postal Service
- ( ) Tennessee Valley Authority
- ( ) VA Dept. of Medicine and Surgery
- ( ) Veterans Readjustment Act (VRA)
- ( ) Other (Specify) ____________________

d. ( ) Senior Executive Service (SES), Supergrade, or Executive Level

- ( ) career SES
- ( ) noncareer SES
- ( ) career GS-16, 17, or 18
- ( ) noncareer GS-16, 17, or 18
- ( ) Executive Level V or above (career) fund
- ( ) Executive Level V or above (noncareer)
- ( ) Presidential appointee (Senate-confirmed)

e. ( ) Other

- ( ) civil service annuitant
- ( ) former civil service employee
- ( ) competitive service
- ( ) excepted service
- ( ) military officer or enlisted person
- ( ) contract employee
- ( ) other(*specify*): ____________________
- ( ) unknown

11. What other action(s), if any, have you taken to appeal, grieve, or report this matter under any other procedure?(*Check all that apply.*)

( ) None, or not applicable — Date: ____________
( ) Appeal filed with Merit Systems Protection Board (MSPB) — Date: ____________
( ) Petition for reconsideration of initial decision filed with MSPB — Date: ____________
Initial Decision No. ____________
( ) USERRA claim filed with VETS (Department of Labor) (Form VETS/USERRA/VP-1010) — Date: ____________
( ) Grievance filed under agency grievance procedure — Date: ____________
( ) Grievance filed under negotiated grievance procedure — Date: ____________
( ) Matter heard by arbitrator under grievance procedure — Date: ____________
( ) Matter is pending in arbitration — Date: ____________
( ) Discrimination complaint filed with agency — Date: ____________
( ) Agency or Administrative Judge (AJ) decision on discrimination complaint appealed to Equal Employment Opportunity Commission — Date: ____________
( ) Appeal filed with Office of Personnel Management — Date: ____________
( ) Unfair labor practice (ULP) complaint filed with Federal Labor Relations Authority General Counsel — Date: ____________
( ) Lawsuit filed in Federal Court — Date: ____________
Court name: ____________
( ) Reported matter to agency Inspector General — Date: ____________
( ) Reported matter to member of Congress — Date: ____________
Name of Senator or Representative: ____________
( ) Other (*specify*): ____________

12. What official is responsible for the violation(s) that you are reporting, and what is his/her employment status? (*See question 10 for appropriate description of employment status. If space is needed to identify more than one official, use Continuation Sheet at page 12.*)

    Name: ______________________________

    Position/Title: ______________________________

    Employment Status: ______________________________

13. What are the actions or events that you are reporting to OSC? (*To the extent known, specifically list: (a) any suspected prohibited personnel practices or other prohibited activity, other than reprisal for whistleblowing; and (b) any personnel actions involved.* ***(IF YOU ARE ALLEGING REPRISAL FOR WHISTLEBLOWING, SKIP TO PART 2 ON THE NEXT PAGE.***)

14. Provide details of the actions or events shown in your response to question 13. (*Be as specific as possible about dates, locations, and the identities and positions of all persons mentioned. In particular, identify actual and potential witnesses, giving work locations and telephone numbers when possible. Also, attach any pertinent documents that you may have. Please provide, if possible, a copy of the notification of the agency's proposal and/or decision about the personnel action(s) covered by your request for OSC action. If more space is needed, use Continuation Sheet at page 12.*)

15. What action would you like OSC to take in this matter (that is, what remedy are you asking for?)

PART 2: REPRISAL FOR WHISTLEBLOWING

***This part of the form is solely for use by persons alleging reprisal for whistleblowing* (that is, persons who believe that personnel actions were taken, not taken, or threatened because of a whistleblower disclosure). Please read the introductory material before answering the questions that follow. If more space is needed, use the continuation sheet at page 12.**

Complainants not alleging reprisal for whistleblowing should proceed to Part 3 ("Consent to Certain Disclosures of Information"), at page 9.

Reprisal for Whistleblowing Allegations

As a general rule, it is a prohibited personnel practice to take or fail to take, or threaten to take or fail to take, a personnel action because of a protected disclosure of certain types of information by a Federal employee, former employee, or applicant for Federal employment. 5 U.S.C. § 2302(b)(8).

Legal Elements of a Violation

By law, certain elements must be present before OSC can establish that a legal violation of law has occurred. Two of the required elements that must be established are: (1) that a whistleblower disclosure was made; and (2) that an agency took, failed to take, or threatened to take or fail to take a personnel action because of the whistleblower disclosure. Your description of these elements will help OSC's investigation of your allegation(s).

Protected Disclosures

A disclosure of information is a protected whistleblower disclosure if a Federal employee, former employee, or applicant for Federal employment discloses information which he or she reasonably believes evidences: (a) a violation of any law, rule, or regulation; (b) gross mismanagement; (c) a gross waste of funds; (d) abuse of authority; or (e) a substantial and specific danger to public health or safety.

Covered Personnel Actions

The law prohibiting reprisal for whistleblowing requires proof that one or more of the following personnel actions occurred, or failed to occur, because of a protected disclosure:

(1) an appointment;
(2) a promotion;
(3) an action under 5 U.S.C. chapter 75 or other disciplinary or corrective action;

(4) a detail, transfer, or reassignment;
(5) a reinstatement;
(6) a restoration;
(7) a reemployment;
(8) a decision about pay, benefits, or awards, concerning education or training if the education or training may reasonably be expected to lead to an appointment, promotion, performance evaluation, or other action described in 5 U.S.C. § 2302(a)(2);
(9) a performance evaluation under 5 U.S.C. chapter 43;
(10) a decision to order psychiatric testing or examination; or
(11) any other significant change in duties, responsibilities, or working conditions.

Reporting Your Allegation(s)

In the section that starts below (pages 6-8), provide the information requested about all disclosures that you believe led to reprisal by the agency involved. If more space is needed, use extra copies of page 6-8, or the Continuation Sheet at page 12. **If any of the disclosures were in writing, please provide a copy of the disclosure with your complaint.**

IT IS IMPORTANT THAT YOU LIST ALL DISCLOSURES AND PERSONNEL ACTIONS INVOLVED IN YOUR COMPLAINT. This is because: (1) failure to list any disclosure or personnel action may delay the processing of your complaint by OSC; and (2) a comprehensive listing will avoid disputes in any later Individual Right of Action (IRA) appeal that you may file with the Merit Systems Protection Board (MSPB) about its jurisdiction to hear case.

Additional allegations of reprisal for whistleblowing may be added to this complaint while it is pending at OSC. Submission of any such additional allegations to OSC **in writing** will help you if you decide to file any later IRA appeal with the MSPB. Form OSC-11a is available for that purpose at OSC's web site, under "Forms."

Appeal to the Merit Systems Protection Board (MSPB)

If OSC fails to complete its review of your whistleblower reprisal allegation within 120 days after it receives your complaint, or if it closes your complaint at any time without seeking corrective action on your behalf, you have the right to file IRA appeal with the MSPB. 5 U.S.C. § 1214(a)(3).

Recordkeeping

To establish its jurisdiction over any later IRA appeal that you may file, the MSPB will require you to show that the appeal relates to the same whistleblower disclosure(s) and personnel action(s) involved in your complaint to OSC. A copy of the whistleblower reprisal allegations in your complaint, any supporting documentation about those allegations that you sent with the complaint, and any additional allegation of reprisal that you submitted in writing to OSC while the complaint was pending, will serve as proof in any IRA of the disclosure(s) and personnel action(s) involved in your OSC complaint. **IT IS IMPORTANT, THEREFORE, THAT YOU MAKE AND KEEP COPIES OF ALL THESE DOCUMENT FOR YOUR RECORDS.**

MUST BE COMPLETED FOR ALL DISCLOSURES REPORTED IN THIS COMPLAINT

A. WHAT INFORMATION WAS DISCLOSED? *(DESCRIBE WHISTLEBLOWER DISCLOSURE).*	
	1. WHEN WAS THE DISCLOSURE MADE? (MO/DA/YR)
	2. TO WHOM (NAME AND TITLE) WAS THE DISCLOSURE MADE?
	3. DISCLOSURE OF INFORMATION EVIDENCED ***(check all that apply):*** ( ) VIOLATION OF LAW, RULE, OR REGULATION ( ) GROSS MISMANAGEMENT ( ) GROSS WASTE OF FUNDS ( ) ABUSE OF AUTHORITY ( ) SUBSTANTIAL AND SPECIFIC DANGER TO PUBLICHEALTH OR SAFETY ( ) NONE OF THE ABOVE
	4. WHAT PERSONNEL ACTION(S) OCCURRED, FAILED TO OCCUR, OR WAS THREATENED BECAUSE OF THE DISCLOSURE? *(List all applicable personnel action numbers from pages 4-5).*
	5. WHEN DID PERSONNEL ACTION(S) OR THREAT(S) OCCUR? (MO/DA/YR)

B. WHAT INFORMATION WAS DISCLOSED? *(DESCRIBE NEXT WHISTLEBLOWER DISCLOSURE).*	
	1. WHEN WAS THE DISCLOSURE MADE? (MO/DA/YR)
	2. TO WHOM (NAME AND TITLE) WAS THE DISCLOSURE MADE?
	3. DISCLOSURE OF INFORMATION EVIDENCED (***check all that apply):*** ( ) VIOLATION OF LAW, RULE, OR REGULATION ( ) GROSS MISMANAGEMENT ( ) GROSS WASTE OF FUNDS ( ) ABUSE OF AUTHORITY ( ) SUBSTANTIAL AND SPECIFIC DANGER TO PUBLICHEALTH OR SAFETY ( ) NONE OF THE ABOVE
	4. WHAT PERSONNEL ACTION(S) OCCURRED, FAILED TO OCCUR, OR WAS THREATENED BECAUSE OF THE DISCLOSURE? (*List all applicable personnel action numbers from pages 4-5).*
	5. WHEN DID PERSONNEL ACTION(S) OR THREAT(S) OCCUR? (MO/DA/YR)

KEEP A COPY OF THIS PAGE FOR YOUR RECORDS

MUST BE COMPLETEDFOR ALL DISCLOSURES REPORTEDIN THIS COMPLAINT

C. WHAT INFORMATION WAS DISCLOSED?
(DESCRIBE NEXT WHISTLEBLOWER DISCLOSURE).

1. WHEN WAS THE DISCLOSURE MADE? (MO/DA/YR)

2. TO WHOM (NAME AND TITLE) WAS THE DISCLOSURE MADE?

3. DISCLOSURE OF INFORMATION EVIDENCED *(check all that apply):*

( ) VIOLATION OF LAW, RULE, OR REGULATION
( ) GROSS MISMANAGEMENT
( ) GROSS WASTE OF FUNDS
( ) ABUSE OF AUTHORITY
( ) SUBSTANTIAL AND SPECIFIC DANGER TO PUBLICHEALTH OR SAFETY
( ) NONE OF THE ABOVE

4. WHAT PERSONNEL ACTION(S) OCCURRED, FAILED TO OCCUR, OR WAS THREATENED BECAUSE OF THE DISCLOSURE?

5. WHEN DID PERSONNEL ACTION(S) OR THREAT(S) OCCUR? (MO/DA/YR)

D. WHAT INFORMATION WAS DISCLOSED?
(DESCRIBE NEXT WHISTLEBLOWER DISCLOSURE).

1. WHEN WAS THE DISCLOSURE MADE? (MO/DA/YR)

2. TO WHOM (NAME AND TITLE) WAS THE DISCLOSURE MADE?

3. DISCLOSURE OF INFORMATION EVIDENCED *(check all that apply):*

( ) VIOLATION OF LAW, RULE, OR REGULATION
( ) GROSS MISMANAGEMENT
( ) GROSS WASTE OF FUNDS
( ) ABUSE OF AUTHORITY
( ) SUBSTANTIAL AND SPECIFIC DANGER TO PUBLICHEALTH OR SAFETY
( ) NONE OF THE ABOVE

4. WHAT PERSONNEL ACTION(S) OCCURRED, FAILED TO OCCUR, OR WAS THREATENED BECAUSE OF THE DISCLOSURE? *(List all applicable personnel action numbers from pages 4-5).*

5. WHEN DID PERSONNEL ACTION(S) OR THREAT(S) OCCUR?

KEEP A COPYOF THIS PAGE FOR YOURRECORDS

MUST BE COMPLETED FOR ALL DISCLOSURES INCLUDED IN THIS COMPLAINT

3. If you are **not** the person who actually made a disclosure described in boxes A, B, C, D above, please check below to specify the disclosure involved, and provide the name, address, and telephone number of the person who made the disclosure, if known. (*If space is needed to identify more than one person, use Continuation Sheet at page 12.)*

   Disclosure: A ( ) B ( ) C ( ) D ( )

   Name: ______________________________

   Address: ______________________________

   Telephone number: ( ) ____________ Ext. ______

4. Explain why you believe that the personnel action(s) listed above occurred because of the disclosure(s) that you described. *(Be as specific as possible about any dates, locations, names, and positions of all persons mentioned in your explanation. In particular, identify actual and potential witnesses, giving work locations and telephone numbers, if known. Attach a copy of any documents that support your statements. Please provide, if possible, a copy of the notification of the agency's proposal and/or decision about the personnel action(s) covered by your complaint. If more space is needed, continue on page 12.)*

5. What action would you like OSC to take in this matter (that is, what remedy are you asking for)?

KEEP A COPY OF THIS PAGE FOR YOUR RECORDS

PART 3: CONSENT TO CERTAIN DISCLOSURES OF INFORMATION

OSC asks everyone who files a complaint alleging a possible prohibited personnel practice or other prohibited activity to select one of three Consent Statements shown below. ***IF YOU DO NOT SELECT ONE OF THE THREE CONSENT STATEMENTS BELOW, OSC WILL ASSUME THAT YOU HAVE SELECTED CONSENT STATEMENT 1.*** Please: (a) select and sign (or check, if filing electronically) one of the Consent Statements below; and (b) keep a copy of the Consent Statement you select (as well as a copy of all documents that you send to OSC) for your own records.

If you initially select a Consent Statement that restricts OSC's use of information, you may later select a less restrictive Consent Statement. If your selection of Consent Statement 2 or 3 prevents OSC from being able to conduct an investigation, an OSC representative will contact you, explain the circumstances, and provide you with an opportunity to select a less restrictive Consent Statement.

You should be aware that the Privacy Act allows information in OSC case files to be used or disclosed for certain purposes, regardless of which Consent Statement you sign. See 5 U.S.C. § 552a(b). Information about certain circumstances under which OSC can use or disclose information under the Privacy Act appears on the next page.

(Please sign one)

Consent Statement 1

I *consent* to OSC's communication with the agency involved in my complaint. I agree to allow OSC to disclose my identity as the complainant, and information from or about me, to the agency if OSC decides that such disclosure is needed to investigate the allegation(s) in my complaint (for example, to request information from the agency, or seek a possible resolution through mediation or corrective action). I understand that regardless of the Consent Statement I choose, OSC may disclose information from my complaint file when permitted by the Privacy Act (including circumstances summarized in Part 5, below).

Complainant's Signature for Consent Statement 1 ____________ Date Signed ____________

Consent Statement 2

I *consent* to OSC's communication with the agency involved in my complaint, but I do not agree to allow OSC to disclose my identity as the complainant to that agency. I agree to allow OSC to disclose only information from or about me, without disclosing my name or other identifying information, if OSC decides that such disclosure is needed to investigate the allegation(s) in my complaint (for example, to request information from the agency, or seek a possible resolution through mediation or corrective action). I understand that in some circumstances (for example, if I am complaining about my failure to receive a promotion), OSC could not maintain my anonymity while communicating with the agency involved about a specific personnel action. In such cases, I understand that this request for confidentiality might prevent OSC from taking further action on my complaint. I also understand that regardless of the Consent Statement I choose, OSC may disclose information from my complaint file when permitted by the Privacy Act (including circumstances summarized in Part 5, below).

Complainant's Signature for Consent Statement 2 ____________ Date Signed ____________

Consent Statement 3

I *do not consent* to OSC's communication with the agency involved in my complaint. I understand that if OSC decides that it cannot investigate the allegation(s) in my complaint without communicating with that agency, my lack of consent will probably prevent OSC from taking further action on the complaint. I understand that regardless of the Consent Statement I choose, OSC may disclose information from my complaint file when permitted by the Privacy Act (including circumstances summarized in Part 5, below).

Complainant's Signature for Consent Statement 3 ____________ Date Signed ____________

PART 4: CERTIFICATION AND SIGNATURE

I certify that all of the statements made in this complaint (including any continuation pages) are true, complete, and correct to the best of my knowledge and belief. I understand that a false statement or concealment of a material fact is a criminal offense punishable by a fine of up to $250,000, imprisonment for up to five years, or both. 18 U.S.C. § 1001.

Signature

Date Signed

PART 5: PRIVACY ACT / PAPERWORK REDUCTION ACT STATEMENTS

Routine Uses. Limited disclosure of information from OSC files is needed to fulfill OSC's investigative, prosecutorial, and related responsibilities. OSC has described 18 routine uses for information in its files in the *Federal Register* (F.R.), at 66 F.R. 36611 (July 12, 2001), and 66 F.R. 51095 (October 5, 2001). A copy of the routine uses is available from OSC upon request. A summary of the routine uses appears below.
OSC may disclose informatiofrom its files in the following circumstances:

1. to disclose that an allegation of prohibited personnel practices or other prohibited activity has been filed;
2. to disclose information to the Office of Personnel Management (OPM) as needed for inquiries involving civil service laws, rules or regulations, or to obtain an advisory opinion;
3. to disclose information about allegations or complaints of discrimination to entities concerned with enforcement of antidiscrimination laws;
4. to the MSPB or the President, when seeking disciplinary action;
5. to the involved agency, MSPB, OPM, or the President when OSC has reason to believe that a prohibited personnel practice has occurred, exists, or is to be taken;
6. to disclose information to Congress in OSC's annual report;
7. to disclose information to third parties as needed to conduct an investigation; obtain an agency investigation and report on information disclosed to OSC's whistleblower disclosure channel; or to give notice of the status or outcome of an investigation;
8. to disclose information as needed to obtain information about hiring or retention of an employee; issuance of a security clearance; conduct of a security or suitability investigation; award of a contract; or issuance of a license, grant, or other benefit;
9. to the Office of Management and Budget (OMB) for certain legislative coordination and clearance purposes;

10. to provide information from an individual's record to a congressional office acting pursuant to the individual's request;
11. to furnish information to the National Archives and Records Administration for records management purposes;
12. to produce summary statistics and work force or other studies;
13. to provide information to the Department of Justice as needed for certain litigation purposes;
14. to provide information to courts or adjudicative bodies as needed for certain litigation purposes;
15. to disclose information to the MSPB as needed in special studies authorized by law;
16. for coordination with an agency's Office of Inspector General or comparable entity, to facilitate the coordination and conduct of investigations and review of allegations;
17. to news media or the public in certain circumstances (except when the Special Counsel determines that disclosure in a particular case would be an unwarranted invasion of personal privacy); and
18. to the Department of Labor and others as needed to implement the Uniformed Services Employment and Reemployment Rights Act of 1994, and the Veterans' Employment Opportunities Act of 1998.

If OSC officials believe that disclosure may be appropriate in a situation not covered by one of OSC's routine uses, or one of the 11 other exceptions to the Privacy Act's general prohibition on disclosure, OSC will seek written authorization from the complainant permitting the disclosure.

Purposes, Burdens, and Other Information. An agency may not conduct or sponsor a collection of information, and persons may not be required to respond to a collection of information, unless it: (a) has been approved by OMB, and (b) displays a currently valid OMB control number. The information in this form is collected pursuant to OSC's legal responsibility to investigate: (a) allegations of prohibited personnel practices, to the extent necessary to determine whether there are reasonable grounds to believe that a prohibited personnel practice has occurred, exists, or is to be taken (5 U.S.C. § 1214); and (b) other allegations of prohibited activity (5 U.S.C. § 1216). The information will be reviewed by OSC to determine whether the facts establish its jurisdiction over the subject of the complaint, and whether further investigation and corrective or disciplinary action is warranted. The reporting burden for this collection of information is estimated to be an average of one hour and 15 minutes per response, including the time for reviewing instructions, searching existing data sources, gathering the data needed, and completing and reviewing the form. Please send any comments about this burden estimate, and suggestions for reducing the burden, to the Office of Special Counsel, Legal Counsel and Policy Division, 1730 M Street, N.W. (Suite 218), Washington, DC 20036-4505. Use of this form to file a complaint alleging a prohibited personnel practice or other prohibited activity is required; use of this to file a complaint alleging only a Hatch Act violation is not required. 5 C.F.R. § 1800.1(d), as amended. As stated in Part 3 of this form, complainants may request that OSC maintain their name, and information provided by them, in confidence.

CONTINUATION SHEET

Part No.	Item/Question No.	Response Continuation

KEEP A COPY OF THIS PAGE FOR YOUR RECORDS IF YOU ARE ALLEGING REPRISAL FOR WHISTLEBLOWING

CLAIM FOR DAMAGE, INJURY, OR DEATH	**INSTRUCTIONS:** Please read carefully the instructions on the reverse side and supply information requested on both sides of this form. Use additional sheet(s) if necessary. See reverse side for additional instructions.	FORM APPROVED OMB NO. 1105-0008 EXPIRES 4-30-88

1. Submit To Appropriate Federal Agency:	2. Name, Address of claimant and claimant's personal representative, if any. *(See instructions on reverse.) (Number, street, city, State and Zip Code)*

3. TYPE OF EMPLOYMENT ☐ MILITARY ☐ CIVILIAN	4. DATE OF BIRTH	5. MARITAL STATUS	6. DATE AND DAY OF ACCIDENT	7. TIME *(A.M. OR P.M.)*

8. Basis of Claim *(State in detail the known facts and circumstances attending the damage, injury, or death, identifying persons and property involved, the place of occurence and the cause thereof) (Use additional pages if necessary.)*

9. **PROPERTY DAMAGE**

NAME AND ADDRESS OF OWNER, IF OTHER THAN CLAIMANT *(Number, street, city, State, and Zip Code)*

BRIEFLY DESCRIBE THE PROPERTY, NATURE AND EXTENT OF DAMAGE AND THE LOCATION WHERE PROPERTY MAY BE INSPECTED. *(See instructions on reverse side.)*

10. **PERSONAL INJURY/WRONGFUL DEATH**

STATE NATURE AND EXTENT OF EACH INJURY OR CAUSE OF DEATH, WHICH FORMS THE BASIS OF THE CLAIM. IF OTHER THAN CLAIMANT, STATE NAME OF INJURED PERSON OR DECEDENT.

11. **WITNESSES**

NAME	ADDRESS *(Number, street, city, State, and Zip Code)*

12. *(See instructions on reverse)* **AMOUNT OF CLAIM** *(in dollars)*

12a. PROPERTY DAMAGE	12b. PERSONAL INJURY	12c. WRONGFUL DEATH	12d. TOTAL *(Failure to specify may cause forfeiture of your rights.)*

I CERTIFY THAT THE AMOUNT OF CLAIM COVERS ONLY DAMAGES AND INJURIES CAUSED BY THE ACCIDENT ABOVE AND AGREE TO ACCEPT SAID AMOUNT IN FULL SATISFACTION AND FINAL SETTLEMENT OF THIS CLAIM

13a. SIGNATURE OF CLAIMANT *(See instructions on reverse side.)*	13b. Phone number of signatory	14. DATE OF CLAIM

CIVIL PENALTY FOR PRESENTING FRAUDULENT CLAIM

The claimant shall forfeit and pay to the United States the sum of $2,000. plus double the amount of damages sustained by the United States. *(See 31 U.S.C. 3729.)*

CRIMINAL PENALTY FOR PRESENTING FRAUDULENT CLAIM OR MAKING FALSE STATEMENTS

Fine of not more than $10,000 or imprisonment for not more than 5 years or both. *(See 18 U.S.C. 287, 1001.)*

95-107
Previous editions not usable.

NSN 7540-00-634-4046

STANDARD FORM 95 (Rev. 7-85)
PRESCRIBED BY DEPT. OF JUSTICE
28 CFR 14.2

PRIVACY ACT NOTICE

This Notice is provided in accordance with the Privacy Act, 5 U.S.C. 552a(e)(3), and concerns the information requested in the letter to which this Notice is attached.

A. *Authority:* The requested information is solicited pursuant to one or more of the following: 5 U.S.C. 301, 28 U.S.C. 501 et seq., 28 U.S.C. 2671 et seq., 28 C.F.R. Part 14.

B. *Principal Purpose:* The information requested is to be used in evaluating claims.

C. *Routine Use:* See the Notices of Systems of Records for the agency to whom you are submitting this form for this information.

D. *Effect of Failure to Respond:* Disclosure is voluntary. However, failure to supply the requested information or to execute the form may render your claim "invalid".

INSTRUCTIONS

Complete all items - Insert the word NONE where applicable

A CLAIM SHALL BE DEEMED TO HAVE BEEN PRESENTED WHEN A FEDERAL AGENCY RECEIVES FROM A CLAIMANT, HIS DULY AUTHORIZED AGENT, OR LEGAL REPRESENTATIVE AN EXECUTED STANDARD FORM 95 OR OTHER WRITTEN NOTIFICATION OF AN INCIDENT, ACCOMPANIED BY A CLAIM FOR MONEY DAMAGES IN A **SUM CERTAIN** FOR INJURY TO OR LOSS OF PROPERTY, PERSONAL INJURY, OR DEATH ALLEGED TO HAVE OCCURRED BY REASON OF THE INCIDENT. THE CLAIM MUST BE PRESENTED TO THE APPROPRIATE FEDERAL AGENCY WITHIN **TWO YEARS** AFTER THE CLAIM ACCRUES.

Any instructions or information necessary in the preparation of your claim will be furnished, upon request, by the office indicated in item #1 on the reverse side. Complete regulations pertaining to claims asserted under the Federal Tort Claims Act can be found in Title 28, Code of Federal Regulations, Part 14. Many agencies have published supplemental regulations also. If more than one agency is involved, please state each agency.

The claim may be filed by a duly authorized agent or other legal representative, provided evidence satisfactory to the Government is submitted with said claim establishing express authority to act for the claimant. A claim presented by an agent or legal representative must be presented in the name of the claimant. If the claim is signed by the agent or legal representative, it must show the title or legal capacity of the person signing and be accompanied by evidence of his/her authority to present a claim on behalf of the claimant as agent, executor, administrator, parent, guardian or other representative.

If claimant intends to file claim for both personal injury and property damage, claim for both must be shown in item 12 of this form.

The amount claimed should be substantiated by competent evidence as follows:

(a) In support of the claim for personal injury or death, the claimant should submit a written report by the attending physician, showing the nature and extent of injury, the nature and extent of treatment, the degree of permanent disability, if any, the prognosis, and the period of hospitalization, or incapacitation, attaching itemized bills for medical, hospital, or burial expenses actually incurred.

(b) In support of claims for damage to property which has been or can be economically repaired, the claimant should submit at least two itemized signed statements or estimates by reliable, disinterested concerns, or, if payment has been made, the itemized signed receipts evidencing payment.

(c) In support of claims for damage to property which is not economically repairable, or if the property is lost or destroyed, the claimant should submit statements as to the original cost of the property, the date of purchase, and the value of the property, both before and after the accident. Such statements should be by disinterested competent persons, preferably reputable dealers or officials familiar with the type of property damaged, or by two or more competitive bidders, and should be certified as being just and correct.

(d) Failure to completely execute this form or to supply the requested material within two years from the date the allegations accrued may render your claim "invalid". A claim is deemed presented when it is received by the appropriate agency, not when it is mailed.

Failure to specify a sum certain will result in invalid presentation of your claim and may result in forfeiture of your rights.

INSURANCE COVERAGE

In order that subrogation claims may be adjudicated, it is essential that the claimant provide the following information regarding the insurance coverage of his vehicle or property.

15. Do you carry accident insurance? ☐ Yes, If yes, give name and address of insurance company *(Number, street, city, State, and Zip Code)* and policy number. ☐ No

16. Have you filed claim on your insurance carrier in this instance, and if so, is it full coverage or deductible?	17. If deductible, state amount

18. If claim has been filed with your carrier, what action has your insurer taken or proposes to take with reference to your claim? *(It is necessary that you ascertain these facts)*

19. Do you carry public liability and property damage insurance? ☐ Yes, If yes, give name and address of insurance carrier *(Number, street, city, State, and Zip Code)* ☐ No

☆ U.S.G.P.O.: 1986 -491-003/50508

SF 95 (Rev. 7-85) BACK

Before the Merit Systems Protection Board
[name] Field Office

[Your Name],	
Appellant,	
v.	Docket No.________________
[Agency Name],	
Agency.	

Appellant's First Request for Discovery

Pursuant to 5 § CFR 1201.73, the Appellant, [Your Name], hereby serves his first request for discovery and requests that the Agency respond to said discovery request within twenty (20) calendar days. Each interrogatory and document request should be fully responded to on the basis of information which is reasonably available or subsequently becomes available. Each request for admission should be responded to on the basis of information which is reasonably available and should be amended if appropriate, if or when other information subsequently becomes available. This is a continuing request, and the Agency should continue to supplement its responses up to and at the hearing requested by the Appellant.

All documents are to be produced at [Your Address or Representative's Address].

Definitions

a) The words "you" and "your(s)" refer to the Agency.

b) The word "Agency" refers to the [Name of Agency].

c) The word "Appellant" refers to [Your Name].

d) The word "person(s)" means any natural person, private or public corporation, partnership (limited or general), agent, principal, group, firm, association, or any other type of entity or organization.

e) The word "date" means the month, day and year, if ascertainable, or if not, the best approximation thereof.

f) The word "communication" means any statement by a person that is either written or oral.

g) The word "document" means any tangible thing, which constitutes or contains matter within the scope of Fed. R. Civ. P. 34(a); and means the original (or duplicate, identical copies when originals are not available), and any non-identical copies (whether different from the originals because of notes made on such copies or otherwise) of writings of every kind and description whether inscribed by hand or by mechanical, facsimile, electronic, magnetic, microfilm, photographic or other means, as well as phonic or visual reproductions of oral statements, conversations or events, and including, but not limited to, any manual, book, pamphlet, periodical, letter, report, memorandum, notation, message, telegram, cable, facsimile, record, study, working paper, accounting paper, computer disk, computer tape, telephone log, computer mail, computer printout, teletype message, chart, graph, index, tape, minutes, contract, lease, invoice, record of purchase or sale correspondence, electronic or other transcription of taping of telephone or personal conversations or conferences, or any and all written, printed, typed, punched, taped, filmed or graphic matter however produced or reproduced. The word "document" also includes the file, folder Exhibits and/or containers and labels appended thereto associated with each such aforesaid original and/or copy.

h) Where an interrogatory calls for you to "identify" an oral communication, please include the following information as to each oral communication:

    (1) the means of communication (e.g., telephone, personal conversation, or otherwise);

    (2) where the communication took place;

    (3) actual date, or if unknown, approximate date;

    (4) identify each person who was a party to, overheard, or may have overheard the communication;

    (5) the substance of what was said, who said it, and to whom;

    (6) whether the communication or any part thereof is recorded, described or referred to in any document, and if so identify such document according to the above definition of "identify."

i) Where an interrogatory calls for you to "identify" or "state the identity" of a document or written communication, your answer should include the date of the document, its title (if any) and the subject matter, its author(s), addressees, recipients, parties, the nature of the document (e.g., memorandum, letter), the individual or other source from whom or which you obtained it, and if it is not in your possession, the identity of its last known custodian and location. "Identify," when used in reference to any data, means to state the software and/or operating system under which the data was created, title and author, the type of data (e.g., word processing document, spreadsheet, database, application program, etc.), and all other means of identifying it with sufficient particularity to meet the requirements for its inclusion in a Request for Production pursuant to the Federal Rules of Civil Procedure, and its present or last known location or custodian. If any such data was, or no longer is, in the possession or subject to your control, state what disposition was made of it and the reason for such disposition.

j) Where an interrogatory calls for you to "identify" or "state the identity" of a person, please include that person's full and legal name, business title or position, grade, series, dates of employment in that position, and most recent business address and telephone numbers.

k) Where an interrogatory calls for you to "state the legal basis" of a particular claim, assertion, or legal contention please:

    (1) identify each document and where pertinent, the section, article, and/or subparagraph thereof which forms, constitutes, evidences, relates or refers to, directly or indirectly, any part of the source of your information regarding the alleged facts and/or claims and/or legal contentions referred to by the interrogatory;

    (2) identify each oral communication which forms any part of the source of your information regarding the alleged facts and/or legal contentions and/or earlier answer referred to by the interrogatory;

    (3) state separately the acts and/or omissions to act on the part of any person which, directly or indirectly, constitutes, forms the basis of, evidences, relates or refers to your information regarding the alleged facts and/or claims and/or earlier answers referred to in the interrogatory;

        aa) For each interrogatory, identify each person, who furnished information in preparing the answer thereto and indicate which interrogatories, or section thereof, each person is providing information towards.

        bb) For each document, identify each person who provided it to you.

Instructions

A. Each interrogatory and document request should be fully responded to on the basis of information which is reasonably available or subsequently becomes available.

B. This discovery request shall be continuing in nature. Therefore, you are required to supplement your responses if and when new or supplemental information is obtained. All documents are to be produced at [Your Address or Representative's Address].

C. Any objection or claim of privilege or confidentiality asserted in response to any discovery should be stated with sufficient specificity so as to permit an informed ruling by the Administrative Judge, if necessary. It should be noted that OPM has issued regulations under which information about specific persons contained in Federal agency personnel records, such as Official Personnel Files (OPF), may be disclosed by Federal agencies: 1) to another "party in . . . an administrative proceeding being conducted by a Federal agency, when the Government is a party to the . . administrative proceeding;" and/or 2) "in response to a request for discovery" when the information requested "is relevant to the subject matter involved in a pending administrative proceeding," as routine use exceptions to the Privacy Act, 5 USC § 552a. See 61 Fed. Reg. 3,6919, 3,6921-22 (Jul. 15, 1996)(final regulations as of Sept. 13, 1996).

D. In any instance where you deny knowledge or information sufficient to answer an interrogatory or any part thereof, identify each person, if any, known, who should know, is believed to know, may know or possess such knowledge and/or information.

F. If any document responsive to this discovery request is no longer in your possession or subject to your control or no longer exists, please identify whether such document is: a) missing or lost; b) destroyed (by any means); c) transferred to others; and/or d) otherwise disposed of. In any of the above instances, please describe in detail the circumstances surrounding and any reason, authorization, and/or approval of such disposition, and state the actual and/or approximate date of such disposition.

INTERROGATORIES

1. Identify each person who the Agency believes has, or may have, relevant information regarding the claims and allegation in the Appellant's appeal. For each such person, identify the following: (a) name; (b) cur rent business and home address and work and home telephone numbers; (c) current (or last known) title and grade; and (d) a detailed description of the information the person possesses concerning the appeal.
2. Explain in detail the reasons for removing [Name of Appellant] from his employment with the Agency.
3. Identify each action by [Name of Appellant] considered by the Agency to be neglect of duty and/or insubordination on January 1, January 5 and January 6, 2004, stating for each: a) the nature of the action; b) the date the action occurred; c) whether the action constituted neglect of duty, insubordination or both; d) how the action constituted neglect of duty and/or insubordination per any established Agency guideline/definition of such. [Substitute with the misconduct charged against you.]
4. Identify all persons who had any input whatsoever into the decision to remove [Name of Appellant] from his position with the Agency. Your response should describe when such discussions or consultations took place and the input provided by each participant to the discussion or consultation.
5. For any admission that was not unequivocally admitted, please explain in detail the reason for the denial (partial or full).
6. For each individual identified in response to Interrogatory Nos. 1 and 3, identify when and how each such individual learned of [Name of Appellant]'s EEO activity. [If you are alleging discrimination as an affirmative defense.]
7. Identify all the evidence relied upon by the Deciding Official to support the charge of [Misconduct Charged].
8. Identify all the evidence relied upon by the Deciding Official to justify the penalty of removal.
9. Explain why the Deciding Official relied upon the reprimand issued to [Name of Appellant] on January 1, 2003, in "deciding what action to take." [If a prior discipline is involved.]
10. Explain how the reprimand issued to [Name of Appellant] on January 1, 2003, factored into the Deciding Official's decision-making process.

11. Explain in detail why each defense to the misconduct charged that [Name of Appellant] raised at his oral reply of [Date] was rejected by the Deciding Official.

12. Explain specifically how each of the *Douglas* factors were analyzed by the Deciding Official when making the penalty determination.

13. Identify the duties of [Name of Appellant]'s position.

14. Identify all reasons why the Agency assigned [Name of Appellant] the duties he allegedly refused to perform.

15. Identify all employees in [Name of Appellant]'s division who were assigned duties similar to the duties [Name of Appellant] allegedly refused to perform. Your answer should include the following information:

    a) The work order number for each such assignment;

    b) Whether each such individual completed the work order;

    c) The date the work order was completed;

    d) Whether those who did not were charged with misconduct or otherwise reprimanded in *any* formal or informal fashion;

    e) What the specific charges were;

    f) What penalty the Agency proposed;

    g) Whether the charges were sustained;

    h) What penalty was imposed, if any; and

    i) Whether each such individual had engaged in EEO activity.

16. Identify all other [Name of Agency Unit/Division/location] employees charged with [Type of Misconduct] in the last five (5) years. Your answer should include the following information:

    a) What the specific charges were;

    b) What penalty the Agency proposed;

    c) Whether the charges were sustained;

    d) What penalty was imposed, if any;

    e) Whether the decision was the subject of grievance or appeal;

    f) The disposition of any such grievance or appeal; and

    g) Whether each such individual had engaged in prior EEO activity.

17. Identify *all* formal complaints of discrimination filed on or after January 1, 2000, with the Agency wherein any person in the [Name of Agency Unit/Division/location] is alleged to have committed discriminatory acts, including:

    a) the bases;

    b) the issues;

    c) responsible management officials;

    d) a copy of the report of investigation; and

    e) the disposition or current status of each complaint.

18. Identify any complaints or allegations of any kind known to the Agency wherein [Names of Supervisors, Proposing and Deciding Officials Involved] are alleged to have discriminated against another employee. Your answer should include the following information:

    a) the individual who allegedly suffered the discrimination or retaliation;

    b) the individual who was alleged to have committed the discriminatory or retaliatory behavior;

    c) what the behavior was;

    d) when the behavior happened;

e) who reported the behavior, to whom, and when;
f) what actions were taken in response to the allegation(s);
g) whether an investigation was conducted and if so, by whom, and when;
h) any known witnesses (including names, addresses and telephone numbers); and
i) whether any relief or accommodations were given to the individual who allegedly suffered the discrimination.

Document Requests

1. Copies of all documents relied upon or referenced in responding to the interrogatories above.
2. Copies of all documents which support the Agency's contention that Appellant engaged in [Misconduct Alleged].
3. All evidence and material relied upon in removing the Appellant.
4. Copies of any written communication by, between and/or among the Proposing and/or Deciding Officials and any other individual in which [Name of Appellant] was discussed.
5. Copies of any notes, minutes of meetings, memoranda for file, supervisors' "drop files" and/or any other recordation regarding [Name of Appellant].
6. Copies of all drafts of the Proposed Removal issued to [Name of Appellant].
7. Copies of all drafts of the Notice of Removal issued to [Name of Appellant].
8. Copies of all prior discipline issued to [Name of Appellant].
9. Copies of all documents reviewed by the Deciding Official.
10. Copies of all documents relied upon by the Deciding Official to sustain the charges.
11. Copies of all documents relied upon by the Deciding Official to justify the penalty of removal.
12. Copies of all documents which reflect how each of the *Douglas* factors were analyzed by the Deciding Official when making the penalty determination.
13. Copies of all work orders issued to [Names of Appellant's co-workers] for the last two (2) years.
14. Copies of all discipline proposed or issued identified in the response to Interrogatory No. 14.
15. Copies of all discipline proposed or issued in the response to Interrogatory No. 15.
16. Copies of all versions of the Agency's Table of Penalties for the last five (5) years.
17. Copies of any and all administrative guidance or any other documents regarding the application and/or interpretation of the Table of Penalties.
18. Copies of any written analysis of the *Douglas* factors regarding [Name of Appellant]'s penalty determination.
19. Copies of any and all notes taken during [Name of Appellant]'s oral reply.
20. A copy of [Name of Appellant]'s official position description.
21. Copies of *all* formal complaints of discrimination filed on or after January 1, 2000, with the Agency where in any person in the [Agency Unit/Division/location] is alleged to have committed discriminatory acts.
22. Copies of *any* complaints or allegations of any kind known to the Agency wherein [Names of Supervisors, Proposing and Deciding Officials] are alleged to have discriminated against another employee.
23. Copies of any documents, including but not limited to decisions, judgments, and/or settlement agreements, reflecting the final disposition of any complaints and/or allegations produced in response to Document Request Nos. 20 and 21.
24. A copy of [Name of Appellant]'s Official Personnel File.

Request for Admissions

If the agency denies any request for admission, the reason for the denial should be explained with particularity.

1. The January 1, 2003, reprimand cited by the Deciding Official was not identified in the January 1, 2004, proposal to remove [Name of Appellant].
2. Prior to January 1, 2004, no other [Position Title] was tasked with [the assignment [Name of Appellant] allegedly refused to perform].
3. No other [Agency Unit/Division/location] employee has been removed for first-time discipline related to neglect of duty.
4. No other [Agency Unit/Division/location] employee has been removed for first-time discipline related to insubordination.
5. [Name of Appellant's Supervisor] was aware of the Appellant's prior EEO activity at the time of Appellant's proposed discharge.
6. [Name of Proposing Official] was aware of the Appellant's prior EEO activity at the time of Appellant's proposed discharge.
7. [Name of Deciding Official] was aware of the Appellant's prior EEO activity at the time of Appellant's proposed discharge.
8. The removal penalty imposed on the Appellant is inconsistent with those imposed on other employees charged with neglect of duty.
9. The removal penalty imposed on the Appellant is inconsistent with those imposed on other employees charged with insubordination.
10. The first offense for neglect of duty can result in a penalty of reprimand and/or other penalties less than removal.
11. The first offense for insubordination can result in a penalty of reprimand and/or other penalties less than removal.
12. The disorderly conduct charge originally proposed against Appellant was withdrawn by the Agency be cause it was unsubstantiated.
13. None of the facts related to the proposed disorderly conduct charge against Appellant contributed to Appellant's removal for neglect of duty/insubordination.

[Date]

Respectfully submitted,

____

[Your Name]

Address

Telephone Number

Before the Equal Employment Opportunity Commission
[name] District Office

[Your Name],	)	
Complainant,	)	
v.	)	EEOC No.________________
[Agency Name],	)	Agency No.________________
Agency.	)	

Complainant's First Request for Discovery

Pursuant to 29 CFR § 1614.109 and the Administrative Judge's Order dated February 20, 2004, in the above-captioned matter, the Agency is hereby requested to serve verified answers to the interrogatories and requests for admissions which follow, and to produce the documents requested within thirty (30) days from service hereof. The definitions and instructions below apply throughout these discovery requests. All documents produced should be labeled as to which request or interrogatory they are responsive. Finally, these requests are continuing in nature, and should be supplemented up to and at the time of hearing as additional information becomes available to the Agency.

Definitions and Instructions

A. "Your" and "you" refer to the party to whom these interrogatories are addressed, as well as the party's agents, employees, servants, or representatives, and, unless privileged, the party's attorneys.

B. Unless otherwise indicated, these requests pertain to information in the possession or control of the [Name of Agency], its agents, employees, lawyers, investigators or other representatives of the Agency and its attorney.

C. The term "person" includes a human, corporation, partnership, or other entity.

D. Where the name or identity of an organization is requested, please state the last known address of its offices, its name(s) and identify its leader.

E. When you are requested to identify a person, "**identify**" means to state the full name, code names or aliases known or ascertainable by you, home, permanent and other known work addresses and telephone numbers. If the person works for the Agency, also provide his or her job title and grade level. In addition, provide the person's race, color, sex and whether he or she engaged in EEO activity.

F. When you are requested to identify or produce a document, "**identify**" means to state the date, the author (or, if different, the signer or signers), the address, type of document (e.g., letter, memorandum, telegram, chart, etc.) and any other means of identifying it with sufficient particularity to meet the requirements for its inclusion in a motion for production. If any such document was, but is no longer in your possession or subject to your control, state what disposition was made of it and the reason for such disposition. In lieu of identifying any document, a true and correct copy thereof may be annexed to and incorporated in the answers to these interrogatories.

G. When you are requested to identify or produce a document, "**document**" means, but is not limited to, all written, printed, typed, microfilmed, electronic (e-mail) and recorded memoranda, transcribed communications, correspondence, pamphlets, books, notes, digests, logs, diaries, calendars, voice-mail, phone messages, computer printouts, and/or any machine-readable documents from which these are or may be produced, photographs, tape recordings and all non-identical copies thereof, including output of computerized records, if available. Any and all draft copies of all requested documents must also be produced as responsive to the request.

H. For each document, identify the person who provided it to you.

I. Unless otherwise indicated, the time period of these interrogatories and requests pertain to the period from January 2000, to the present.

J. For any objection based on privilege, a complete privilege log in conformity with FED. R. CIV. P. 26(b)(5) is necessary.

K. Any objection or claim of privilege or confidentiality asserted in response to any discovery request should be stated with sufficient specificity so as to permit an informed ruling by the Administrative Judge, if necessary. Because of the routine use exceptions that apply to EEO complaint files and employee personnel records, information that is maintained by an agency in any of its EEO complaint files or in employees' official personnel folders cannot be withheld on the basis of the Privacy Act. Records retained under EEOC/GOVT-1 System of Records may be used to disclose, in response to a request for discovery or for appearance of a witness, information that is relevant to the subject matter involved in a pending judicial or administrative proceeding. *See*, 59 Fed. Reg. 11,068 (1994) (routine use e.). Under OPM/GOVT-1 System of Records, general personnel records of federal employees may be used to disclose information to another federal agency, to a court, or a party in litigation before a court or in an administrative proceeding being conducted by a federal agency, when the government is a party to the judicial or administrative proceeding. *See* 65 Fed. Reg. 24,734 (2000) (routine uses b., p., and w.).

L. These interrogatories and requests for production are continuing in character, similar to that provided by FED. R. CIV. P. 26(e), which requires you to supplement your answers, setting forth any information within the scope of the interrogatories and requests as may be acquired by you, your agents, attorneys or representatives following your original answers.

M. The terms "Complainant" and "Mr. ______" refer to [Your Name].

N. The term "Agency" refers to the [Name of Agency, and sub-division (if applicable)].

O. The term "ROI" refers to the Report of Investigation in this matter.

P. For each interrogatory, identify each person who furnished information in preparing the answer thereto.

Q. For each document, identify each person who provided it to you. If any document is no longer in your possession or subject to your control or no longer exists, please identify whether such document is: (i) missing or lost; (ii) destroyed (by any means); (iii) transferred to others; and/or (iv) otherwise disposed of. Also, please describe in detail the circumstances surrounding and any reason, authorization, and/or approval of such disposition, and state the actual and/or approximate date of such disposition.

R. Please restate the interrogatory in full and then follow it with your response.

S. For each document produced, please identify which Interrogatory(ies) and/or Document Request(s) that are associated with that document.

T. Please have all responses provided under oath declared by the individual(s) providing the response.

U. For each and every Admission that the Agency does not unequivocally admit, provide all facts which support and/or explain the denial.

INTERROGATORIES

1. Identify each and every person, including expert witnesses, the Agency believes has or may have information relating in any respect to the allegations contained in [Your Name]'s Complaint and provide a summary of the information each person possesses.

2. Identify all formal complaints of discrimination filed on or after January 1, 1998, with the Agency wherein any person in the Office of ________ is alleged to have committed discriminatory acts, including:
   a) the bases;
   b) issues;
   c) responsible management officials;
   d) a copy of the report of investigation;
   e) and the disposition or current status of each complaint.
3. Identify any complaints or allegations of any kind known to the Agency wherein [Names of Supervisors or Responsible Management Officials] are alleged to have discriminated against another employee.
4. Identify any and all training concerning workplace discrimination provided to any of the following individuals: [Names of Supervisors or Responsible Management Officials], and provide the following:
   a) dates of training;
   b) who provided the training;
   c) certificates of completion; and
   d) the subject matter of the training.
5. Identify when and how [Names of Supervisors or Responsible Management Officials] first learned of the Complainant's EEO allegations.
6. For each and every admission that the Agency does not unequivocally admit, provide all facts which support the Agency's denial.
7. Identify all reasons why [Your Name] was transferred from his detail to the position of [Title of Position and Location].
8. Identify all individuals who had input into the decision to transfer [Your Name] from his detail to the position of [Title of Position and Location,] including the input provided by each such individual.
9. Provide all reasons which support [Names of Supervisors or Responsible Management Officials]'s statement that [Your Name] was transferred from the position of [Title of Position and Location], "to promote the efficiency of the government service."
10. Provide all reasons why Mr.________ made the decision to transfer [Your Name] from his detail to the position of [Title of Position and Location].
11. Explain why [Name of Comparator] is qualified for the position of [Title of Position and Location].
12. Identify all incidents known to the Agency where either [Names of Supervisors or Responsible Management Officials] is known to have made comments to [Your Name] regarding his age, and/or race .
13. Identify all complaints (both verbal and written) received by the Agency from [Your Name] regarding harassment, a hostile work environment, his treatment by [Names of Supervisors or Responsible Management Officials].
14. For each complaint identified in response to Interrogatory No. 13, identify all steps taken by the Agency to investigate or otherwise respond to the complaint.
15. Identify whether [Names of Supervisors or Responsible Management Officials; Name of Comparator] have ever been disciplined, subject to an adverse action, counseled, or warned regarding conduct and/or performance.

Requests for Documents

1. Provide all documents relied upon or referenced by the Agency in responding to this discovery request.
2. Provide a copy of [Your Name]'s Official Personnel File, medical file, performance file, and any supervisory files.
3. Provide copies of any formal complaints of discrimination filed since January 1, 1998, with the Agency wherein any person in the Office of ________ is alleged to have committed discriminatory acts, including copies of any reports of investigation.

4. Provide copies any complaints or allegations of any kind known to the Agency wherein [Names of Supervisors or Responsible Management Officials] is alleged to have discriminated against another employee, including copies of any reports of investigation or documents related to the complaints/allegations.
5. Provide copies of any documents relating to any complaints or allegations of any kind known to the Agency wherein the Complainant is alleged to have discriminated another employee.
6. Provide copies of all documents in the control and/or possession of [Names of Supervisors or Responsible Management Officials] which reference, mention, or discuss the Complainant in any fashion.
7. Provide copies of all written feedback collected by [Names of Supervisors or Responsible Management Officials] regarding [Your Name]'s performance while detailed to the position of [Title of Position and Location].
8. Provide copies of all notes from any occasion [Names of Supervisors or Responsible Management Officials] discussed [Your Name]'s performance while detailed to the position of [Title of Position and Location], with any other individual.
9. Provide all documents which relate to or reference in any fashion any of the allegations in [Your Name]'s complaint.

Requests for Admissions

1. Mr.________ first learned of how [Your Name] was being treated by [Names of Supervisors or Responsible Management Officials] in 2000.
2. Mr.________ commented to [Your Name] "You know you are the wrong color for the [Name of] Office," or words to that effect. ROI, Exhibit __, pg.__.
3. Mr.________ commented to [Your Name] "This staff is old enough to be your parents," or words to that effect. ROI, Exhibit __, pg. __.
4. The Complainant notified the Agency of how he was being treated by Mr.________ and Mr.________ in 2000. ROI, Exhibit __, pg. __.
5. [Name of Witness] stated that "He [Your Name] was facing animosity because he was a minority and he was not getting any support from management." ROI, Exhibit __, pg. __.
6. [Name of Witness] stated that he heard jokes made toward [Your Name] regarding his race by other employees. ROI, Exhibit __, pg. __.

[Date]

Respectfully submitted,

____

[Your name]
Address
Telephone Number

Certificate of Service

By my signature below, I, [Your Name], hereby certify that on [Date], a copy of the foregoing discovery request was served by first-class mail and by facsimile on the following individual:

[Agency Representative]
Address
Fax Number

____

[Your name]
Address

INDEX

My Notes

My Notes

My Notes

My Notes

My Notes

My Notes